THE NORMANS IN EUROPE

edited and translated by Elisabeth van Houts

Manchester University Press
Manchester and New York

distributed exclusively in the USA by St. Martin's Press

Copyright © Elisabeth van Houts 2000

While copyright as a whole and of all editorial matter is vested in Elisabeth van Houts, copyright of all other material belongs to the respective authors, translators and institutions as acknowledged, and no editorial or documentary material may be reproduced wholly or in part without the express permission in writing of both author and publisher.

Published by Manchester University Press
Oxford Road, Manchester M13 9NR, UK
and Room 400, 175 Fifth Avenue, New York, NY 10010, USA
http://www.man.ac.uk/mup

Distributed exclusively in the USA by
St. Martin's Press, Inc., 175 Fifth Avenue, New York, NY 10010, USA

Distributed exclusively in Canada by
UBC Press, University of British Columbia, 2029 West Mall,
Vancouver, BC, Canada V6T 1Z2

British Library Cataloguing-in-Publication Data
A catalogue record for this book is available from the British Library

Library of Congress Cataloging-in-Publication Data applied for

ISBN 0 7190 4750 1 *hardback*
     0 7190 4751 X *paperback*

First published 2000

07   06   05   04   03   02   01   00   10 9 8 7 6 5 4 3 2 1

THE NORMANS IN EUROPE

MANCHESTER
UNIVERSITY PRESS

Manchester Medieval Sources Series

series advisers Rosemary Horrox and Janet L. Nelson

This series aims to meet a growing need amongst students and teachers of medieval history for translations of key sources that are directly usable in students' own work. It provides texts central to medieval studies courses and focuses upon the diverse cultural and social as well as political conditions that affected the functioning of all levels of medieval society. The basic premise of the series is that translations must be accompanied by sufficient introductory and explanatory material, and each volume, therefore, includes a comprehensive guide to the sources' interpretation, including discussion of critical linguistic problems and an assessment of the most recent research on the topics being covered.

CONTENTS

III: The Normans and Britain: the Norman Conquest

ACKNOWLEDGEMENTS

When in 1994 Rosemary Horrox, one of the general editors of Manchester Medieval Sources Series, approached me with the suggestion that I might compile a volume on the Normans in Europe, I happily agreed, optimistically thinking that such a compilation would only take me two years. Now six years later the book has grown much larger and has a wider scope than I originally intended. Nevertheless, here for the first time are brought together the famous and less well-known texts illustrating the extraordinary history of the Normans.

I have incurred debts to many friends, colleagues and pupils. First of all I am indebted to Laura Napran, Caroline Vout and Robert Shorrock for having provided me with drafts for some of the translations included here. My graduate student Laura Napran drafted the translation of Marsilia's letter [23], while Caroline Vout and Robert Shorrock cooperated on draft versions for nos [4, 7, 26, 62, 68 and 82]. It goes without saying that the responsibility for the final text and any remaining mistakes lies with me. My colleague at Emmanuel College, Cambridge, Andy Orchard kindly offered his expertise and advice on several tricky Latin passages, for which I am deeply indebted to him. He also allowed me to use his translation of the poem *Jephthah* by Fulcoius of Beauvais [39]. Eric Christiansen generously made his translation of Dudo of Saint-Quentin available to me in advance of its publication, a gesture for which I am most grateful [4, 26 and 81]. Peter Llewellyn kindly allowed me to use abstracts from his (unpublished) translation of Amatus of Montecassino's History.

I owe immense gratitude to Graham Loud for his unstinting help and advice on the chapter on the Normans in Italy. Not only has he generously made available his own (unpublished) translations of several Italian chronicles on the Normans, but he also patiently answered my many queries on the history of the Norman emigration. Jonathan Shepard kindly commented on the section on the Normans and Byzantium. His advice has been invaluable.

David Bates read the whole text and spent many hours with me discussing the debates on the Normans. I should like to acknowledge with particular gratitude his help with shaping the introduction even though I know that he does not share all my thoughts. Talking about the Normans with my graduate student Ewan Johnson has also been a great pleasure. The final shape of the selected sources and the commentary on the viking history of Normandy owe a great deal to the lectures and classes on 'The vikings in Europe 700-1100' given by Rosamond McKitterick and myself. The lively discussions with the students are noted here with pleasure.

But my greatest debt is to the general editor Rosemary Horrox, whose common sense, perceptiveness and meticulous care have saved me from writing an unreadable book.

I am most grateful to the following publishers who have given permission for sections from their publications to be used here:

Nos **4, 16, 26, 34, 50, 66** and **81** Dr Richard Barber from Boydell and Brewer Ltd (Woodbridge).

No. **58** The Catholic University of America Press (Washington DC).

Nos. **40-2** Routledge for Eyre and Spottiswoode (London).

No. **47** Garland Publishing Ltd (New York).

Nos **13** and **51** Llanerch Publishing (Lampeter).

No. **27** is reprinted from Warner of Rouen, *Moriuht*, ed. and trsl. Christopher J. McDonough, pp. 73–107, by permission of the publisher. Copyright the Pontifical Institute of Mediaeval Studies, Toronto.

No. **63** is reprinted by permission of the publisher from *The Book of Sainte Foy*, translated with an introduction and notes by Pamela Sheingorn. Copyright 1995 University of Pennsylvania Press.

No. **85** is republished with permission of Columbia University Press, 562 W. 113th St., New York, NY 10025. *The Conquest of Lisbon* (Extracts), ed. and trsl. C. W. David, 1936. Reproduced by permission of the publisher via Copyright Clearance Centre, Inc.

Nos. **6** and **53** Copyright Elisabeth M. C. van Houts 1992. Reprinted from *The Gesta Normannorum Ducum of William of Jumièges, Orderic Vitalis and Robert of Torigni*, vol. I, ed. and trsl. Elisabeth M. C. van Houts (1992) by permission of Oxford University Press.

Nos **15, 28-9, 32, 53, 74, 76** Copyright Elisabeth M. C. van Houts 1995. Reprinted from *The Gesta Normannorum Ducum of William of Jumièges, Orderic Vitalis and Robert of Torigni*, vol. II, ed. and trsl. Elisabeth M. C. van Houts (1995) by permission of Oxford University Press.

Nos. **17, 33** and **60** Copyright Marjorie Chibnall 1998. Reprinted from *The Gesta Guillelmi of William of Poitiers*, ed. and trsl. R. H. C. Davis and Marjorie Chibnall (1998) by permission of Oxford University Press.

No. **75** Copyright Oxford University Press 1969. Reprinted from *The Ecclesiastical History of Orderic Vitalis*, vol. II, ed. and trsl. Marjorie Chibnall (1969) by permission of Oxford University Press.

No. **84** Copyright Oxford University Press 1978. Reprinted from *The Ecclesiastical History of Orderic Vitalis*, vol. VI, ed. and trsl. Marjorie Chibnall (1978) by permission of Oxford University Press.

No. **86** Copyright Oxford University Press 1975. Reprinted from *The Ecclesiastical History of Orderic Vitalis*, vol. V, ed. and trsl. Marjorie Chibnall (1975) by permission of Oxford University Press.

No. **35** Copyright Catherine Morton and Hope Muntz 1972. Reprinted from *The Carmen de Hastingae Proelio of Guy, Bishop of Amiens*, ed. and trsl. Catherine Morton and Hope Muntz (1972) by permission of Oxford University Press.

No. **36** Copyright Oxford University Press 1979. Reprinted from *The Letters of Lanfranc, Archbishop of Canterbury*, ed. and trsl. the late Helen Clover and Margaret Gibson (1979) by permission of Oxford University Press.

No. **43** Copyright Patrick McGurk 1995. Reprinted from *The Chronicle of John of Worcester*, vol. II, ed. R. R. Darlington and P. McGurk, trsl. Jennifer Bray and P. McGurk (1995) by permission of Oxford University Press.

No. **45** Copyright Diana Greenway 1996. Reprinted from *Henry, Archdeacon of Huntingdon, Historia Anglorum*, ed. and trsl. D. Greenway (1996) by permission of Oxford University Press.

No. **46** Copyright Leslie Watkiss and Marjorie Chibnall 1994. Reprinted from *The Waltham Chronicle*, ed. and trsl. Leslie Watkiss and Marjorie Chibnall (1994) by permission of Oxford University Press.

No. **55** Copyright Oxford University Press 1976. Reprinted from *The Letters and Poems of Fulbert of Chartres*, ed. and trsl. Frederick Behrends (1976) by permission of Oxford University Press.

Nos **64, 65** and **69** Copyright John France 1989. Translation of *Life* Copyright John France and Paul Reynolds 1989. Reprinted from Rodulfus Glaber, *The Five Books of the Histories*, ed. and trsl. John France; Rodulfus Glaber, *The Life of St William*, ed. Neithard Bulst, trsl. John France and Paul Reynolds (1989) by permission of Oxford University Press.

Nos **77** and **78** Penguin UK Publishers for excerpts from *The Alexiad of Anna Comnena*, trsl. E. R. A. Sewter (Penguin Classics, 1969) copyright E. R. A. Sewter, 1969.

No. **79** Penguin UK Publishers for excerpts from *Michael Psellus, Fourteen Byzantine Rulers*, trsl. E. R. A. Sewter (Penguin Classics, 1966).

To anyone whose permission I have inadvertently failed to obtain, I offer my apologies; full acknowledgement will be made in any future edition if the omission is drawn to my attention.

LIST OF ABBREVIATIONS

AA.SS	*Acta Sanctorum quotquot tot orbe coluntur* (Antwerp 1643–1940), 67 vols
AN	*Annales de Normandie*
ANS	*Anglo-Norman Studies: The Proceedings of the Battle Conference* (Ipswich-Woodbridge, 1978 onwards)
Bates	*Regesta regum Anglo-Normannorum: The Acta of William I (1066–1087)*, ed. D. Bates (Oxford, 1998)
Dudo	*De moribus et actis primorum Normanniae ducum auctore Dudone sancti Quintini decano*, ed. J. Lair (Caen, 1865)
EHD	*English Historical Documents*, ed. D. C. Douglas (London, 1953–77), 12 vols
EHR	*English Historical Review*
Fauroux	*Recueil des actes des ducs de Normandie de 911 à 1066*, ed. M. Fauroux, Mémoires de la Société des Antiquaires de Normandie, 36 (Caen, 1961)
Gallia Christiana	*Gallia Christiana in provincias ecclesiasticas distributa* (Paris, 1715–1865), 16 vols
GND	*The Gesta Normannorum Ducum of William of Jumièges, Orderic Vitalis and Robert of Torigni*, ed. and trsl. E. M. C. van Houts, Oxford Medieval Texts (Oxford, 1992–95), 2 vols
Ménager	*Recueil des actes des ducs normands d'Italie (1046–1127)*, vol 1: *Les Premiers Ducs (1046–1087)*, ed. L. R. Ménager, Società di storia patria per la Puglia: Documenti e monografie, 45 (Bari, 1980)
MGH SS	*Monumenta Germaniae Historica* (Hanover, 1826 onwards)
Migne, *PL*	*Patrologia latina*, ed. J. P. Migne (Paris, 1844–64), 221 vols
Orderic	*The Ecclesiastical History of Orderic Vitalis*, ed. and trsl. M. Chibnall, Oxford Medieval Texts (Oxford, 1969–80), 6 vols
Porée	A. Porée, *Histoire de l'abbaye du Bec* (Evreux, 1901), 2 vols

INTRODUCTION

The Normans were the people of Normandy, the north-western province of France that came into existence at the beginning of the tenth
century. The frontiers of Normandy fluctuated, but the region in
which Norman customs prevailed during the duchy's lifetime (from *c.*
911 to 1204) stretched from north to south and from east to west as
follows (see Map 2 on p. 000). From Eu near the mouth of the River
Bresle in the north, to the Rivers Epte and Eure in the east, towards
Dreux where the Rivers Avre and Sarthe formed the south-eastern
borderline. From Saint-Céneri in the south-east corner, the frontier
went westwards following the River Mayenne as far as a point half-
way between Domfront and Ambrières, from where the line continued
westwards to pick up the River Couesnon at Pontorson.[1] This region
roughly corresponded to the ecclesiastical province of the arch-
bishopric of Rouen, which itself was based on the Roman administrative unit centred on that city.

The inhabitants were for the most part Frankish but included a
significant minority of Scandinavian settlers from Norway, Denmark
and from Scandinavian settlements in Britain, who formed the ruling
elite. The immigrants assimilated so rapidly with the Frankish people,
however, that within three generations they ceased to use their own
language and lost most of their customs. What they retained were
personal names, some legal practices, stories which reminded them of
their homeland in Norway and Denmark, and above all their
collective name. That name derives from 'north men', which means
'men who came from the north', an etymology that was well understood by the Normans themselves [**12, 20, 70**]. From Normandy
they set out later to conquer southern Italy and the greater part of
Britain and some established themselves elsewhere in Europe. They
were at the height of their power in the eleventh and early twelfth
centuries.

---

1 For the early Norman frontier see Lewis, 1992, 147–56 and for the twelfth century
  Power, 1994, 181–202 with map on p. 182. For the view that the customs of
  Normandy crystallised during the reign of William the Conqueror, see Tabuteau,
  1988, 223–9. An interesting description of the Norman frontier can be found in
  no. **12**.

The purpose of this book, divided into five chapters, is to give readers a selection of the abundant (narrative) source material generated by the Normans and the peoples they conquered. Chapter I, 'From vikings to Normans', covers the process of assimilation and amalgamation between Scandinavians and Franks and the emergence of Normandy. Once firmly established in and around Rouen, the ruling dynasty of the Norse Rollo (d. *c.* 928), his son William Longsword (*c.* 928–43) and his grandson Richard I (943–96), enlarged the territory over which they held sway. They issued laws, kept order and through a network of kinship extended their influence to the furthest corners of the province. In particular, the dukes established pockets of political authority through their patronage of monasteries and churches. Their maintenance of law and order, their support for the Christian religion, and their exploitation of the remnants of Carolingian government structures enabled them to become one of the strongest of the territorial princes of France. Chapter II, 'The Normans in Normandy', illustrates the internal organisation of the principality with a variety of source material from chronicles, miracle stories and charters. It is in this chapter that evidence appears of the women and children who formed, as in every country, such an essential part of society.

The Normans had a turbulent relationship with the English kingdom. This country had been regularly attacked by vikings, who had settled in the east in an area known as the Danelaw. Afterwards in the early eleventh century the whole of England had been conquered by King Svein of Denmark (*c.* 988–1014) and his son Cnut (1016–35). But in 1002, fourteen years before the Danish occupation of England, King Aethelred II of England (978–1016) married Emma, the sister of the Norman duke Richard II (996–1026). The marriage negotiations formed part of the English king's strategy to prevent the vikings from seeking refuge in Norman harbours. This marriage established the family connection which set in motion the train of events that ultimately led to the Norman conquest of England in 1066. Chapter III, 'The Normans and Britain', presents material from the main chronicle sources for the history of the Norman invasion and settlement, supplemented with some poetry. It is roughly divided into Norman and English sections with a few texts about the Normans in Scotland and Wales.

Once Duke William had become king of England, the relationship with the kings of France, often strained anyway, became fraught with difficulties. As duke of Normandy William owed allegiance to the king of France, and in that position he was obliged to do service to him, but as king of England he was the French king's equal and in that role had no such obligations. Rollo's descendants maintained a fair degree of independence from the kings of France by acknowledging their overlordship but meanwhile going very much their own way. After 1066 the elevation of the duke to the status of king, albeit of another country, changed that relationship. With regard to the other territorial princes in France, especially those of Maine, Brittany, Anjou, Poitou/Aquitaine, Blois-Chartres, Burgundy and Flanders, the dukes followed the normal medieval pattern of warfare alternating with peace negotiations sealed by marriage alliances. Such contacts are highlighted in Chapter IV, 'The Normans and their neighbours'.

From the early eleventh century onwards we find Normans outnumbering the other west-European men who travelled around Europe looking for opportunities to earn a living, usually by fighting, and hoping to settle somewhere. Land awarded in return for military service and (or) as the result of marriage to a well-to-do heiress outside Normandy became the goal for these young émigrés. We find Normans among the first settlers in southern Italy and elsewhere in the Mediterranean. In Chapter V, 'The Normans in the Mediterranean', we can follow their careers particularly well in Italy, and to a lesser extent in Byzantium, Spain and the Holy Land.

The sources presented in those five chapters consist mostly of histories and chronicles written by the Normans themselves, or written by those whom they conquered, or written by contemporaries elsewhere in Europe who observed their actions from afar. The sheer volume of narratives written by or about them is exceptional. Few other medieval peoples generated historical writing of such quantity and quality or matched the pride and self-awareness of the Normans, as expressed not only in their own historiography but also in the reports of others. Around the first millennium the Normans became the first people in western Europe to produce a serial biography of their secular rulers, a type of chronicle previously used only for bishops and abbots. It was written c. 995–1015 by Dudo of Saint-Quentin, a Frank who had become friendly with the new rulers of Normandy and offered his services as their historian. Fifty years later his chronicle was extended and updated by a Norman monk, William of Jumièges, who after 1066 (the year of the conquest of England) had an extra reason to celebrate the deeds of the Norman dukes.

Dudo and William of Jumièges shaped the narrative framework for
the history of the Normans by sketching their metamorphosis from
pagan viking conquerors to Christian conquerors. Both of them
concentrated on dynastic history, however, that is on the deeds of
Rollo and the Norman dukes who descended from him. But William
of Jumièges revised and extended the framework established by Dudo
to allow more scope for the expression of the historical truth that
other vikings besides Rollo had had a hand in the colonisation of
Normandy. For example, he introduced Björn Ironside (a legendary
shadow of the viking Björn who is known to have been in France in
the 850s), and he attributed all viking activity in western France to
Danes in general until their arrival in Rouen, where Rollo was, as
William tells it, selected as leader by lot.[2] Dudo and William say very
little about the 'ordinary' Scandinavian settlers or indeed about the
process of colonisation and settlement. Surprisingly, more information on this process surfaces in the work of William of Jumièges's
successors Orderic Vitalis (d. c. 1142) and Robert of Torigni (d. 1189),
who updated William's chronicle in the twelfth century but inserted
information preserved orally which pertained to earlier events. For
example, Orderic Vitalis, writing c. 1113, mentions an ancestor of the
Tosny family named Malahulc, apparently an uncle of Rollo, but
unknown from any other source.[3] And Robert of Torigni, writing
about thirty years after Orderic, reveals much more than Dudo about
William Longsword's mother Sprota, her second Frankish husband
Esperleng of Pîtres and their children, even though Dudo was Sprota's
younger contemporary; Robert also gives the names of Countess
Gunnor's sisters and nieces as ancestors of many Norman families.
Such information was no doubt passed from mouth to mouth within
the family, until it was recorded in writing out of fear that it would
otherwise disappear into oblivion. The reliability of these written
sources remains, however, very difficult to establish.

Dudo of Saint-Quentin and William of Jumièges set out to fit the
story of Rollo's dynasty into the literary and classical tradition of the
so-called *origo* (origin) histories, chronicles about the origin of a
people. Erroneously equating Danes with Dacians, Dudo began his
account of the viking settlement of Normandy with remarks on the
Balkans, the home territory of the Dacians as described by Roman
authors like Jordanes; in this way he extended Rollo's historical

2 Van Houts, 1983, 112–17; for the historical Björn, see Coupland, 1998, 103–4.
3 *GND*, ii, 94–5; Musset, 1977, 48–9.

background by several centuries and matched it to the norm of classical historiography. In doing so he did not include the family traditions concerning individual immigrants which were still preserved in his day and those are the stories we would now prefer to know. Carolingian education, as represented in the person of Dudo,[4] with its emphasis on the authority of the written word in north-western France, is to blame; though Dudo's predilection for using Latin sources full of '*auctoritas*' (authority) was also a product of the Christian tradition. Fitting the vikings into a Romano-Christian tradition enabled Dudo and William of Jumièges to link the Roman period with the Norman period and to consider the pagan viking years as merely an interlude.[5] Nevertheless, in spite of their limitations, the Norman chronicles are unique in the historiography of viking settlement. By way of contrast the Norwegian settlement of Iceland from the late ninth century onwards was not recorded until 150 years after the initial settlement when it was based on oral, and predominantly pagan, tradition.[6]

Dudo's and William of Jumièges's preoccupation with the ducal dynasty meant that they had virtually nothing to say about the exploits of the Normans in southern Italy, even though the Norman emigration to the south began in the early decades of the eleventh century, during Dudo's lifetime. For the Norman exodus to the Mediterranean we are dependent on brief contemporary references in non-Norman chronicles from France and Germany. Otherwise, there are the late eleventh-century chronicles written in Italy as part of a new dynastic history tradition that emerged there centred on the Norman families of de Hauteville and the counts of Capua and Aversa. Robert Guiscard, duke of Calabria and Apulia (d. 1085) and his brother Roger I, count of Sicily (d. 1101) were scions of the de Hauteville dynasty which sprang from humble origins in the Norman Cotentin. Their deeds were described by Geoffrey Malaterra, probably a monk of Norman origin, who wrote his history *c.* 1090, and William of Apulia, a cleric whose first name likewise suggests a non-Italian origin, who wrote an epic poem on the deeds of Robert Guiscard in the late 1090s. A decade earlier their older contemporary Amatus, monk of Montecassino, had already

4 Shopkow, 1989, 19–37 and Shopkow, 1997, 68–79.
5 Lifshitz, 1995 has focused on the tenth-century Latin hagiography written in late Carolingian Neustria or early Normandy; her book fills an important gap in our knowledge about late Carolingian education and writing in the area.
6 Sawyer and Sawyer, 1993, 16–26; Benediktsson, 1993, 332–3.

completed his record of the history of the arrival of the Normans. Like their historian colleagues in Normandy the Italian historians are less forthcoming about the Norman settlers of lower rank.[7] The work of the Italian historians can be complemented by that of Orderic Vitalis and Robert of Torigni, using oral reports brought back by visitors from Italy, and the histories of Geoffrey Malaterra and William of Apulia.

With regard to the Norman conquest of England, the contemporary narrative texts are mostly of Norman origin. William of Jumièges, writing from the late 1050s until 1070, has already been mentioned. His contemporary William of Poitiers, at one time a ducal chaplain, wrote in the mid-1070s a biography of William the Conqueror, while in 1067 Guy of Amiens wrote a poem in praise of King William and his wife Matilda. The monumental embroidery known as 'the Bayeux Tapestry' was produced probably around 1080. All four sources defend the conquest of England by the Normans and the legitimacy of William the Conqueror's succession to the Anglo-Saxon king Edward the Confessor. Of the few contemporary English sources the Anglo-Saxon Chronicle in its different versions is the most important. For substantial narrative accounts of the Conquest in England we depend on works written by later English monks and clerics, some of whom were of mixed English and Norman parentage. The monk Orderic Vitalis, already mentioned, and Henry, archdeacon of Huntingdon (d. after 1154), had an English mother and a French father, while William, monk of Malmesbury (d. *c.* 1144), had one English and one Norman parent. Their writings were presumably influenced by their mixed nationality: they identified with the Norman cause because of their fathers, but they may have depended on their maternal family background for their pro-English sympathies. This applies most strongly to Orderic who was born in England but left the country at the age of ten to enter the Norman monastery of Saint-Evroult where he spent the rest of his life. Like Orderic, William was a monk and spent most of his life in a monastery, while Henry was an educated secular clerk. The other important historians of the period, like the monks Eadmer of Canterbury and John of Worcester, were, as far as we know, of English origin.[8] Their education and access to libraries

---

7 Wolf, 1995, 143–71, 123–42 and 87–122.

8 Simeon of Durham (d. *c.* 1130), whose work has not been incorporated in the present volume, was the most important chronicler for northern England. Although a monk at Durham from the 1090s onwards he came from north-western France (*Symeon of Durham, Historian of Durham and the North*, ed. D. Rollason (Stamford, 1998)).

enabled them to use a wide variety of written sources which combined with oral information provided them with the essential tools to write about the history of the English (and after 1066 the Normans). Their chronicles too are concerned with the military leaders and the aristocracy and contain only incidental references to the common soldiers and colonists.[9]

The narrative excerpts collected for this book, whether on Normandy, England or southern Italy, provide an incomplete picture of the material available to modern historians. Documentary sources such as charters, lawcodes and a variety of other administrative records (such as Domesday Book for England) provide supplementary information that is of crucial importance where questions to do with ethnicity, colonisation, settlement, language, legal custom, taxation and justice are under discussion. Consider, for example, what one can learn from the many records in which 'vicomtes' are referred to and named. The office of vicomte, which involved responsibility for such tasks as collecting taxes, acting as judge in court cases, and organising military operations on a regional scale, was of Carolingian origin.[10] It is possible that the position disappeared during the Scandinavian settlement of Normandy and that new arrangements emerged. No tenth-century records have survived to confirm or deny this. From Richard II's charters we may infer that Scandinavians took over senior posts in the existing structure. The appearance of Scandinavian names such as Thurstan, vicomte of the Avranchin, and Ansketil, vicomte of the Bessin, the earliest known vicomtes, suggest that the main positions were taken over by the new elite.[11] We are much better informed about what happened in England after the Norman Conquest. The Anglo-Saxon office of sheriff, closely equivalent to that of 'vicomte', was not abolished; although usually rendered in Latin as *vicecomes*, it remained essentially unchanged after 1066, but the holders of it were then mostly Normans or other continental newcomers.[12] In Italy the situation was somewhat different because no equivalent posts existed under Lombard or Byzantine rule.[13] Byzantine

9 Van Houts, 1996a, 167–80; 1996b, 9–15.

10 Haskins, 1918, 45–7 and Bouvris, 1985, 148–51.

11 Bouvris, 1985, 151–74.

12 Haskins, 1918, 46; Green, 1982, 129–45 and 1986, 194–214.

13 Jahn, 1989, 165–70. His conclusions are based on the pioneering work by Von Valkenhausen, 1977, 337–8 (Norman *vicecomites* or *viceprincipes* in Capua) and 343–5 (*stratagetes* and *vicecomites* in Apulia and Calabria).

stratagetes were of much higher rank and their responsibilities were wider. In this case the documentary evidence suggests that the Normans imposed the office of vicomte while initially suppressing that of the *stratagete*, though the latter was resurrected after about 1100. It also shows that until 1100 all vicomtes were Normans, and that after that date some *stratagetes* were Norman too.[14]

Those conclusions are obviously significant, illustrating as they do the adaptability which the Norman rulers displayed, and many other examples could be given of equally significant conclusions derived from documentary sources. Unfortunately, such sources do not lend themselves to quotation; they tend to be meaningful only when studied alongside other similar documents. Seven charters [1–3, 18, 19, 61], one administrative record [37], one pledge [73] and one treaty [66] are included in this book. In terms of their importance, however, documentary sources are underrepresented.[15]

Over the years the abundance of source material has inspired several historiographical debates. Perhaps the most intriguing questions about the Normans concern their homogeneity and their success. Did they form one people, *gens*, regardless of where they lived in Europe, drawing their identity from their common origin? Did they display characteristics uniquely associated with the land of their birth? Did they derive from their viking ancestors a conqueror's gene? Can we isolate the reasons for their apparent success? These and other questions crop up in the debates about the Normans, four of which need consideration here.[16]

First there is the on-going debate about the precise extent to which Carolingian and Frankish characteristics on the one hand and viking characteristics on the other, survived in Normandy. The late Eleanor Searle saw the Normans as distinctly Scandinavian, whose invasion of France altered the structure of society there in an essentially discon-

14 Jahn, 1989, 170–2.

15 The most important among them, Domesday Book (*Domesday Book seu Liber Censualis Willelmi Primi Regis Angliae*, ed. A. Farley, 2 vols (London, 1783)) can be conveniently consulted in English translation in the Philimore edition, ed. J. Morris, 40 vols (Chichester, 1974–86). For collections of Norman ducal charters, see Fauroux and Bates; for Norman ducal charters from Italy, see Ménager. The regesta of the royal charters from England under its Norman kings from 1087 can be consulted in *Regesta Regum Anglo-Normannorum*, ed. H. W. C. Davis *et al.*, 4 vols (Oxford, 1913–69).

16 What follows is of necessity a rather sketchy and at times simplified account of a series of important but complicated historiography.

tinuous fashion. She believed that they imposed Scandinavian customs based on kinship upon an alien society and that these customs survived until, and can be said to have caused, the Norman conquest of England.[17] David Bates, following in the footsteps of Jean Yver and Lucien Musset, discerned a powerful short-term Scandinavian impact lasting into the early eleventh century, arguing in favour of long-term continuity of Frankish institutions and practices.[18] These views are on the whole also espoused by Emily Tabuteau, who in her exhaustive study of Norman customs regulating the transfers of land found no evidence for Scandinavian influence.[19] Studies of historiography, literature, art and architecture by Maylis Baylé and myself supplemented the main thesis. While, on the whole, accepting the continuity model, we point to the Normans' profound awareness of their Scandinavian heritage and their willingness to use Scandinavian motifs in literary texts and sculpture as late as the second half of the eleventh century.[20] As a contribution to the same debate we also discussed the possibility that instead of such motifs having survived in Normandy uninterruptedly, they may have been reintroduced into Normandy from other areas of Scandinavian occupation (e.g. the English Danelaw) at the time of the third or fourth generation of settlers. Such reintroduction of Scandinavian narrative detail and art-historical motifs would only have been acceptable in a climate that still appreciated such northern material as recognisably Scandinavian and as part of a living Scandinavian heritage and a sense of 'belonging to our northmen's past'. The reintroduction of Scandinavian customs is a point also suggested by Lucien Musset with regard to one extremely important aspect of Norman law, namely the Scandinavian right of exile, *ullac*, which will be discussed below in Chapter II. Here it is important to underline Musset's suggestion that this custom may have been (re)introduced from Danelaw England into Normandy, suggesting a late tenth- or early eleventh-century date.[21]

Secondly, there is the debate about the *Normannitas* ('Normanness') which centres on the Normans' perception of themselves in Normandy

17 Searle, 1988, 1–11, 61–78, 237–49.

18 Bates, 1982, 15–25; Yver, 1969, 299–366 and Musset, 1970, 96–129.

19 Tabuteau, 1988, 4–5.

20 Baylé, 1982, 1–20 and 1990, 35–48; Van Houts, 1983, 120–1.

21 Musset, 1985, 45–59 at 58–9. Note also Fellows-Jensen, 1990, 149–59 who on the basis of personal names' distribution suggests pre–1066 migration to and fro between Normandy and the English Danelaw.

and elsewhere. In her analysis of the European-wide historiography of the Normans (Norman, English and Italian), the German historian Laetitia Boehm distinguishes four characteristics: its apologetical character (defence of conquests), expressions of ethnic consciousness (pride in the Norman fatherland), evidence of imperialistic planning (pan-Norman expansion throughout Europe) and a peculiarly Norman idea of leadership based on horsemanship. All four characteristics of *Normannitas*, so her argument goes, can be distinguished not only in historical narratives but also in documentary sources (though Boehm herself does not cite the latter).[22] R. H. C. Davis, on the other hand, argued that in the tenth and eleventh centuries the Normans displayed no particular self-awareness; he suggests that a myth of what it meant to be a Norman was invented in the twelfth century by Orderic Vitalis among others and projected backwards by him to a time when the Normans were in reality still striving to be as Frankish as the Franks.[23] Graham Loud differs from Davis by discerning self-awareness among the Normans (as being different from Franks) in the eleventh century and he stresses the influence of classical antiquity on the way in which Norman chroniclers chose to express it. All nations derive their sense of identity from their past and Dudo of Saint-Quentin gave the Normans a respectable past by linking Danes with Dacians as noted above; he created a myth thereby, but a myth different in kind from that discerned by Davis.[24] More recently, Cassandra Potts has emphasised the stress placed by Dudo on Rollo, to whom Dudo attributes the laws and customs under which the different peoples who inhabited Normandy had (by implication) united, as under an umbrella. The evidence, she argues, comes from *The Discovery and Miracles of St Vulfran* written *c.* 1053–54, which eloquently uses the phrase 'and he [Rollo] made one people out of many different ones'. Making one people out of many, so argues Potts, is not what Rollo did but what Dudo *c.* 1000 did when he created the Normans as a people.[25] It is important to note, however, that Dudo himself never used such a phrase nor expressed such an opinion and that therefore the St Vulfran text cannot be used as evidence for Dudo's thoughts.

22 Boehm, 1969, 623–704. A similar approach can be found in Neveux, 1994, 51–62 (on Norman imperialism) and in Bouet, 1994, 239–52 (on the Normans as 'a chosen people').

23 Davis, 1976, 15–17.

24 Loud, 1981b, 104–16.

25 Potts 1995, 139–52 and 1997, 1–13.

The third point concerns the debate about to what extent the Norman expansion into the Mediterranean was part of an exclusively Norman experience. Most historians would agree that the movement of young aristocratic men across Europe, fighting as mercenaries, was a northern French phenomenon.[26] A consensus is also emerging that among identifiable fighters the Normans did indeed stand out, both in their numbers and in the quality of their military skills. Graham Loud and Jonathan Shepard stress that medieval Italian and Greek chronicles and charters distinguish between Normans and other Franks, and single out what seem to have been peculiarly Norman characteristics.[27] They mention the Normans' exceptional familiarity with horses for military purposes: the Normans were said to be good at selecting and breeding horses, at fighting on horseback themselves, and at teaching others to do so. They also point to the Normans' willingness to fight and teach fighting in small fighting units called '*conrois*', and to their willingness to hire themselves out to foreign lords in return for cash and moveable goods or land. The Italian sources indeed single out the Normans as men who took ruthless advantage of local warfare to grab land for themselves. In Chapter V we will look more closely at this material. For the moment it suffices to note that non-Norman observers were commenting on the usefulness of Normans as mercenaries from the middle of the eleventh century onwards. That was one way, perhaps the principal way, in which their fame spread, and how they came to be perceived by themselves as well as others, as distinct from the Franks.

In the fourth and last place there is a debate which logically follows from the previous one: to what extent comparisons between the activities of the Normans in different corners of Europe help to understand the Normans as an identifiable group of people with a distinct culture. As the present book shows, the Normans themselves in the eleventh and twelfth centuries drew attention to their actions all over Europe. In chronicles, poems, battle speeches and inscriptions on weapons, a Norman in Normandy, say, might compare himself to his compatriots in England, Italy (Apulia, Calabria and Sicily), Byzantium and, even, Africa.[28] Thus there is plenty of room for argument on the differences and similarities between groups of Normans and between them and their neighbours.

---

26 Bartlett, 1993, 24–60 provides a good introduction.
27 Loud, 1981a, 13–34 and Shepard, 1992, 275–305.
28 Abulafia, 1984, 26–49.

The process by which viking and Norman newcomers adapted to and assimilated with other indigenous cultures can be traced in early Normandy, in England, in Italy and to a lesser extent elsewhere in southern Europe. Intermarriage and language as evidence for assimilation constitute tools for modern research which can illuminate how the Normans operated abroad. They married indigenous women so as to legitimise their claims to land won by conquest thus ensuring that their children and grandchildren would not be disinherited. Language illustrates how in a bilingual society the Normans would converse among themselves in French but talk to their wives in English, Italian, Spanish or Greek. The second generation would be bilingual but the third would probably be monolingual and have only memories of a mixed background transmitted to them.[29]

This book is meant to stimulate readers to reflect on the above observations and to reach conclusions of their own. Any selection of source material naturally imposes a limitation on the choices of texts on offer (and the vicomte example set out above illustrated the limitation of primarily narrative sources). Fairly tough restrictions on the word limit have forced me to leave out texts I might otherwise have included. I have deliberatedly devoted a good deal of my space to items concerning women and children, though I could easily have used twice as much. The result is a balancing act which I trust will enrich and, occasionally, amuse the reader. If the texts seem to repeat themselves in places this is evidence in itself that the Normans were proud of their Norman (viking?) ancestry, as the words of one eleventh-century Norman magnate, expressed in a charter of the early 1080s, illustrate:

I, Roger of Montgomery,
Norman [born] from Normans
(*ex northmannis, northmannus*).[30]

29 Searle, 1980, 159–70; Loud, 1996, 325–32; Short, 1995, 153–76.

30 R. N. Sauvage, *L'Abbaye de Saint-Martin de Troarn au diocèse de Bayeux des origines au seizième siècle* (Caen, 1911), no. 3, pp. 352–3 and Bates, no. 281 (dated to 1080 x 1082).

I: FROM VIKINGS TO NORMANS

Introduction

The inhabitants of Neustria, the area of western France which stretched from the River Seine to the River Loire, were the Franks.[1] From the late tenth century, as we have seen, part of the region that was roughly equivalent to the archdiocese of Rouen became known as Normandy as a result of the settlement of Scandinavian people and the grant of authority by the Carolingian king to the viking leader Rollo. However, most of the inhabitants of this land – the peasants who worked on it, those engaged in trade or industry, or those who lived as monks in monasteries – were Franks. When and how the government of the Franks and Scandinavians shifted from a predominantly Frankish elite to a predominantly Scandinavian elite is extremely difficult to establish. Due to a lack of late ninth- and tenth-century documentary and narrative sources, it is extraordinarily difficult to identify the individuals who wielded power and how they did so. The few surviving Carolingian documents [1–2] are charters from King Charles the Simple (898–922, d. 929), which show that the basic structures of royal administration were still in place: there is talk of bishops, the mechanism by which a change of ownership of serfs is effected seems valid, and the fisc (a royal estate at which taxes were collected) of Pîtres is still in operation. There is no evidence in these documents for large-scale disruption as a result of the viking invasions, even though the production of two of them [2–3] was inspired by viking activity.[2] The first hint of a viking take-over comes from 918, when another charter of Charles the Simple [3] refers retrospectively to his treaty with Rollo and his companions which gave them control of an area on the Seine (Rouen) which they defended on his behalf, presumably against other vikings. In order to understand

---

1 For general introductions to the early history of Normandy, see Musset, 1970, 96–129; Bates, 1982, 2–44; Searle, 1985, 198–213 and 1988, 61–78; Potts, 1997, 1–12. For the rivalries between groups of Franks and Scandinavians, see Searle, 1985, 198–213 and 1988, 15–26.

2 Though Searle, 1985, 198–213 and 1988, 42–3, 69–71 interprets the documents as showing disruption.

Rollo's emergence in Rouen we have to go back in time and consider the Carolingian royal policy of negotiations with the vikings.[3]

After Charlemagne (d. 814) nearly every Carolingian king negotiated with viking leaders, paid them off with tribute or offered them land. In return the kings received from the vikings pledges to go away, or to stay to defend the land given to them. The treaties also usually involved an additional promise by the viking leader to accept the Christian faith. The area of the Carolingian realm that features most prominently among the treaties that concern gifts of land is Frisia, stretching from Rüstingen in the north to Antwerp in the south. There many grants were given, most of which comprised the harbour of Dorestad on the River Waal, a tributary of the Rhine: in 807–12 to Hemming, in 829 to Harald I, in 855–73 to Rorik and in 882 to Godfrid. In contrast to what happened later in Normandy, Frisia never experienced any large-scale viking settlement and thus never showed signs of indigenous assimilation with Scandinavian settlers. Nor do we find signs of survival of Scandinavian names, laws or language. In Frisia prosperous harbours on rivers offered the vikings trading depots, while the kings received political and military support in locations vulnerable to attacks from the sea. Other places in France where short-lived viking settlements can be traced are around Nantes on the River Loire, and (in what became Normandy) on the isle of Oissel in the River Seine. Carolingian kings negotiated with the viking leaders there but none of the settlements on the River Seine lasted longer than a few winters before c. 911. In 852 and 856–8 we find in those areas vikings called Björn and Sidroc, and one called Hundi in 896. The arrival of Rollo in France probably followed the same pattern initially of a sizeable group of viking soldiers/sailors arriving by ship, raiding extensively inland and settling in the river valley as well as on the nearby coasts. The exact date of Rollo's arrival is unknown. The Norman eleventh-century historians are unanimous in offering the year 876 as the date, but modern historians are sceptical and prefer a date nearer to 900. In order for Rollo to have been offered the task of defending Rouen (which of course he may have held under his control anyway) one imagines him to have been around long enough to earn the confidence of the Frankish population, to receive a wife (Popa of Bayeux), to organise his army in such a way that it could effectively undertake a defensive task, and to be prepared to accept the Christian faith. King Charles the Simple's treaty with Rollo c. 911 was probably

3 For what follows, see Lot, 1908, 5–62; Nelson, 1997, 19–47 and Coupland, 1998, 85–114.

meant to be a temporary arrangement like the treaties made by his predecessors with viking leaders further north in Frisia. Interestingly, Dudo may have reminded his readers of the Frisia precedent by claiming that Rollo rejected an offer of Flanders when accepting Rouen [4]. That the treaty with Rollo would prove in the long term to constitute the longest lasting alienation of Carolingian land to a viking cannot have been foreseen by either Charles or Rollo or by any of their contemporaries. Rollo's dynasty survived at Rouen, against all odds, due to a combination of ruthless military action by the vikings and disastrous infighting among the Frankish aristocracy, which left them severely weakened and unable to resist the Rouen vikings' growing determination to stay put.

Before we can look at the extent and nature of Rollo's power it is important to establish who he was. The Norman historians Dudo of Saint-Quentin and William of Jumièges say that the pagan viking Rollo came from Dacia (Denmark) and thus they imply a Danish origin. Dudo doesn't name his father but calls his brother Gurim. The Scandinavian version of Rollo's ancestry, consisting of early thirteenth-century sagas written down by Snorri Sturluson, on the other hand, records a Norse origin. Snorri identifies Rollo as Hrolf or Rolf, son of Ragnvald, earl of Möre, in western Norway [14], and Hild, daughter of Rolf Nevja. Snorri, importantly, quotes a skaldic poem by Rollo's mother Hild, who, presumably addressing the king (Harold (c. 872–930)), laments the fact that her son was outlawed after a quarrel with his lord, who cannot be anyone but the king himself.[4] The saga tradition as recorded by Snorri then explains that as an exile Hrolf/Rollo settled for a while in the Orkneys and from there travelled further south via Scotland, where he is said to have had a child. This daughter, Kathleen, is mentioned in Icelandic tradition, a fact which prompted David Douglas to speculate no doubt correctly that her mother was Celtic and thus presumably a Christian. That conclusion matches the evidence from the *Plaintsong* on William Longsword that William had a Christian mother of overseas origin (see below).[5]

4 Skaldic poetry is named after its authors who were (court) poets known as skalds. Whereas modern historians are justified in their scepticism about the reliability of sagas, they are more inclined to put faith in the reliability of the skaldic poetry quoted by the saga writers on the grounds that the skalds were contemporaries of the events they described.

5 Douglas, 1977, 124–5. Dudo of Saint-Quentin claims that William's mother was Popa of Bayeux, evidence that is difficult to reconcile with the *Plaintsong* information. Keats-Rohan accepts Popa as William's mother and suggests that she was a daughter of Berengar, marquis of Neustria; she does not discuss the *Plaintsong* evidence (Keats-Rohan, 1997a, 187–204).

Thus Rollo (d. *c.* 928) and his men settled in Rouen after having received a grant of land from the Carolingian king which probably consisted of the *pagi* (the old Roman provinces) of Talou, Caux, Roumois and parts of the Evrecin.[6] He and his son William Longsword (*c.* 928–43) gradually acquired more territory to the west: in 924 Bayeux and Maine, and in 933 'the land of the Bretons situated on the sea-coast', an area that is usually identified as being the Cotentin and the Avranchin [10]. The 933 grant extended the province to more or less the boundaries that existed at the time of the Norman conquest of England.[7] The extent to which Rollo and William were given some form of authority over Brittany, or part of it, remains a subject of great debate among modern historians.[8] If the above identification of the land given in 933 is correct we have to remember that exactly that area had been given in 867 by King Charles the Bald to Salomon of Brittany. Rivalry between indigenous and viking rulers in these frontier areas gave rise to claim and counter claim. The lack of contemporary sources makes it very difficult to verify Dudo of Saint-Quentin's story that the royal grant of land to Rollo included the land of the Bretons. William's son Richard I (943–96) had to defend his hold over Normandy against frequent attempts by the Franks of central France to take back what Charles the Simple and his successors had granted. Piecing together the chronology of Rollonid expansion and exercise of authority is difficult because of the patchy nature of the source material.

The Frankish annals of Flodoard are the fullest record we have [10]. Flodoard (d. *c.* 966) was based in Reims, many miles away from the Atlantic coast, and relied for his information on those who fought against the vikings and were engaged in missionary activity. His entries are often short and were written for a contemporary public that already knew what he was talking about.[9] Although the geographical distance and the annalistic brevity of his notes make his work difficult to interpret, many precious details concerning viking activity along the west coast of France are known only from his work.[10] For example, under the year 943 Flodoard provides tantalising information on mysterious individuals called Turmod and Setric, both pagan viking leaders operating in the area of Rouen, nominally under the control of

---

6 Bates, 1982, 8–9.

7 Musset and Chanteux, 1973, 54–5.

8 For a useful summary, see Smith, 1992, 200–2 and *GND*, i, 64–5.

9 For Flodoard as historian, see Sot, 1993, 83–7.

10 Guillot, 1981, 101–16 and 181–219.

William Longsword. Flodoard's annals were continued by the historian Richer *c.* 998, who records the death in 996 of Richard I and describes him in scathing terms as 'Richard, leader of the pirates'.[11] Richer's contempt for one of Rollo's descendants, which presumably reflected the views of most of the clergy in Reims, could scarcely have been expressed more strongly. The only other strictly contemporary source is a literary 'plaint' song bewailing the murder of William Longsword in 943 at the hands of Count Arnulf I of Flanders (918–65) **[9]**. Its origin is unknown but is to be sought either in Normandy (where it may have been written at Jumièges, the monastery on the Seine to which William had planned to retire as a monk), or more likely in Aquitaine (where William's sister Gerloc, also known as Adela, was countess).[12] The song is so important because it clearly speaks of William and his son Richard I as counts of Rouen. Their position as 'dukes of Normandy' was attributed to them retrospectively by the Norman court apologist Dudo of Saint-Quentin **[4]** in the years *c.* 995–1015, followed by William of Jumièges in the mid-eleventh century **[6]**.[13]

We know very little about the Scandinavian settlers. Most of our information comes from place-name evidence and personal names found in written sources like charters and chronicles. Any discussion of this type of evidence is compounded by the difficulty that Scandinavian names and Frankish names ultimately derive from common Germanic roots. Unless extra information is provided, for example specific identification of someone as a Dane or a Norwegian, one cannot automatically equate a Germanic name with a Scandinavian one. Having said this, the work of Adigard des Gautries and Fellows-Jensen has dramatically advanced our knowledge of the Scandinavian settlement of Normandy.[14] The toponyms of Scandinavian origin, like Brametot (Seine-Mar.), Herquetot (Manche) or Colletot (Eure) indicate that they were once occupied by men called Brami, Helgi and Koli. Other place names contain Scandinavian words in them, like Carbec (*bec* = stream) or Oudalle (*dalle* = valley), illustrating that Scandin-

11 *Richer, Histoire de France (888–995)*, ed. R. Latouche, 2 vols (Paris, 1930), ii, p. 328.

12 For the state of research, see *GND*, i, xxviii–xxix.

13 For the use of titles, see Werner, 1976, 691–709; for the early medieval history of Rouen, see Gauthiez, 1991, 61–76 and Le Maho, 1994, 1–51. A useful map of Rouen *c.* 1000 can be found in *Dudo of St Quentin, History of the Normans*, trsl. E. Christiansen (Woodbridge, 1998), p. 231.

14 Adigard des Gautries, 1954, 264–70 and Fellows-Jensen, 1990, 149–59; see also Bates, 1982, 16–19.

avian people once lived there and named the sites in their own language. Toponymic evidence further suggests large-scale early settlement by Danes in the Pays-de-Caux (the land north of the Seine) and the north of the Cotentin (the peninsula) with some Irish/Scandinavian settlement in the tip of the peninsula as a result of immigration by Irish/Anglo/Scandinavian people from Britain, especially from the northern isles of Scotland. It is of course interesting that, if we can believe the skaldic poetry and sagas, the ruling clan came from Norway (via the Orkneys and Scotland) while the names of the 'ordinary' Scandinavians indicate immigration from Denmark. Recently Fellows-Jensen has called attention to the evidence suggesting late tenth- and eleventh-century migration of people bearing Scandinavian names between Normandy and the English Danelaw. Of the eighty Scandinavian names identified by Adigard des Gautries in Norman sources, most are male and Danish, with only three names belonging to women. From this it appears to follow that the Scandinavian (Danish) men settled down with, or married, Frankish women. Their offspring would have been brought up by their mothers, who no doubt taught them French as their first language. With language come customs, and we can perhaps assume that the children of mixed marriages were brought up to accept the prevailing manners and customs of France, even though they would not forget their Scandinavian origin and pass on Scandinavian folklore to future generations. The rarity of archaeological finds of unambiguously Scandinavian artefacts or remains reinforces the theory that a relatively speedy assimilation of Scandinavians and Franks took place. The most interesting of the rare finds is without doubt that of the two *fibulae* (brooches) from a female grave at Pîtres. They probably date from the second half of the ninth century, when similar ones are known to have been produced in Norway. Otherwise, the viking provenance of some swords and other weapons found in rivers in Normandy is beyond dispute, but their date is very difficult to establish. No conclusions can be drawn about whether such arms were imported from Scandinavia or were produced, according to Scandinavian models, in Normandy after the viking settlement of the early tenth century.[15]

Foreign contacts can be established thanks to the finds of coin hoards both in Normandy, where the hoard of Fécamp (980–85) discovered in 1963 and comprising over 9000 coins is the best known, and in England, Scandinavia, Ireland and the European continent as far

15 Perin, 1990, 161–88 at 161–3.

away as Russia.[16] The spread of coins minted in tenth-century Rouen suggests Norman contacts with the British Isles and Scandinavia (Denmark in particular) as well as Russia, Poland, Germany and Switzerland and therefore presents a Norman focus to the west, north and north-east of Europe. This is of course precisely the area where the viking traders and raiders were active. The eleventh-century coin evidence suggests that a marked shift from north to south, that is, to the rest of France and Italy, occurred c. 1030–40 onwards. The increase of coinage from finds in Rome and southern Italy is especially illustrative of the emigration of Normans to Apulia and Calabria. As far as the coinage itself is concerned, as opposed to the use and spread of coins, a paradox of continuity and discontinuity with the Carolingian past emerges. The main mints remained those of Carolingian Rouen: the count and the comital palace chapel, the cathedral and the abbey of Saint-Ouen all continued to mint coins as they had done before the vikings arrived. As Françoise Dumas has noted, there is no perceptible halt in production nor in the use of Rouen coinage at any time in the tenth century. Yet this picture of continuity of minting along the lines of Carolingian practice is deceptive, because the coins were different from those of pre-viking Rouen. William Longsword (no coins of Rollo survive) was the first territorial prince in Carolingian France to use his own name on his coins while at the same time omitting any reference to the Carolingian king. Richard I continued his father's practice after an hiatus c. 943, the year that William Longsword died, during which Rouen was briefly under the control of King Louis IV. The cunning use of coins by the counts of Rouen to display that they were independent of the very kings who had granted them Rouen provides a striking illustration of their power in Rouen and of the weakness of the kings of France. However, the survival in the hoard of Fécamp of a coin minted in the name of a Hugh the Dane, datable to the 980s, is evidence that other semi-independent viking leaders coexisted with the Rollonid family elsewhere in Normandy. A stray coin with the name William on it followed by the letters DV (for *dux* = duke or leader?), datable to the early tenth century and found near Mont-Saint-Michel, adds weight to Dudo's claim, mentioned above, that William Longsword controlled western Normandy and Brittany.[17]

16 What follows is based on Bates, 1982, 36 and Dumas, 1979, 84–140 at 87–96 and 101–2.

17 Dolley and Yvon, 1971, 7–11 and Searle, 1985, 209.

Thus archaeological evidence suggests a picture of continuity and to a
lesser extent discontinuity with the Carolingian past. Similar evidence
emerges from the study of legal practices, which remained predominantly Frankish. Nevertheless, in law some significant Scandinavian
traditions were retained. Among them were several rights belonging
to the dukes which derived from Scandinavian precedent.[18] Crimes of
murder in secret (*murdrum*) or assault on someone inside a house
(*hamfara*) were crimes subject to ducal jurisdiction, and penalties were
paid to him. The right of exile (*ullac*) and the right of shipwreck (*varech*)
also belonged exclusively to the duke originally. The tradition
whereby the duke provided protection for agricultural implements left
out in the fields, with thefts of agricultural tools punished by death
rather than fines as in Carolingian times, probably went back to
Rollo's time. It can be interpreted as the legacy of measures adopted
by an army of occupation determined to apply its own (Scandinavian)
rules rather than accept indigenous customs. Interestingly, the
documents which record those Scandinavian practices all come from
William the Conqueror's period and concern monasteries located on
rivers or in coastal areas, precisely those areas where the vikings
settled in the first place. *Ullac* and *hamfara* are uniquely mentioned in
the Conqueror's 1050 charter for Saint-Pierre at Préaux as rights
attached to the land at Vascoeuil, which were sold to the abbot,[19]
whereas the two examples of *varech* appear in charters for Coutances
and Cherbourg.[20] The late date of the documents recording those
Scandinavian customs prompted Lucien Musset to suggest that the
customs were the result of reimportation from Danelaw England,
rather than relics from Rollo's time.[21]

Contacts with Scandinavia persisted till the first quarter of the
eleventh century, that is, more or less till the end of the time of
Richard II (996–1026).[22] He was instrumental in negotiating the
release of Emma, viscountess of Limoges, who had been captured by
the vikings [**62**]. In *c.* 1003 or 1013 he concluded a treaty of alliance
with King Svein when the latter was *en route* to England. He employed

18 Bates, 1982, 22; Musset, 1971, 263; Yver, 1969, 319–21.

19 Fauroux, no. 121.

20 Fauroux, no. 224, p. 431 and no. 214, p. 406.

21 Musset, 1985, 58–9; very little is known about the right of shipwreck in Anglo-
    Saxon times and its possible Scandinavian origins, see F. E. Harmer, *Anglo-Saxon
    Writs*, 2nd edn (Stamford, 1989), p. 426.

22 Van Houts, 1983, 110–11.

viking troops under the leadership of Olaf and Lacman, who were called kings, in a border dispute with the French. Presumably they were the sort of viking leaders known as (sea) kings on account of the fact that they were in charge of one or more ships with which they roamed the oceans in search of booty, trade or mercenary employ-ment. After the successful conclusion of the border dispute with France c. 1013 Duke Richard II allowed Olaf to be baptised at Rouen by his uncle Archbishop Robert [53]. According to Snorri Sturluson, on this occasion Olaf sent his old guardian and teacher Hrani, who presumably accompanied him, from Rouen to England. Two years later, according to another saga, the Icelander Kari travelled through Normandy on his return journey from Rome to Scotland. And in 1025 Richard II welcomed Sigvatr and his friend Berg at Rouen, Sigvatr being an Icelandic skald who had come south on a diplomatic mission.[23] Shortly after the death of Richard II in 1026, during the reign of his son Richard III, his mother Gunnor and his uncle the archbishop of Rouen were given a poem in which the protagonist, Moriuht, was a viking captive from Ireland [27]. The poet Warner of Rouen implies that at that time Rouen was still a centre for the slave trade, which depended heavily on Scandinavian traders and raiders.

From the first quarter of the eleventh century comes another piece of intriguing evidence for Norman–Scandinavian contact. An inscription on a tombstone, reused as building material for the abbey of Troarn, identifies the deceased as 'Hugh, soldier of Richard, king of the Normans [HVGO MILES RICARDI REGIS NORDMANDORVM]', who died on 7 February in an unstated year.[24] The tombstone is decorated with motifs which can be dated to the early eleventh century because of the Anglo-Saxon/Scandinavian/Norman details of acanthus leaves and other stylised vegetation, and the inscription appears to date from that period too. However, the text is puzzling because there is no other evidence for a King Richard of the Normans at that time. As Maylis Baylé has suggested, we may have here a unique reference to Duke Richard II who could have been known to some as (sea) king in the viking sense; Olaf and Lacman, the (sea) kings mentioned above, are known to have supported Richard II. Alternatively, the inscription refers to an otherwise unknown Richard, king of Normans/vikings, like 'King' Harold, the viking leader of Bayeux c. 960, or Hugh the Dane of the 980s coin.

23 Adigard des Gautries, 1954, 70.
24 Baylé, 1985, 136–7.

Finally we should look at the role of the Church in early Normandy. Until recently the scholarly consensus, expressed by David Bates, saw the tenth-century history of the Norman Church as a period of severe disruption. Now, as a result of new research into tenth-century hagiography produced in Normandy, and especially at Rouen, a different picture emerges.[25] For tenth-century manuscripts to have been produced and copied a viable environment for writing must have existed in the cathedral and monastic scriptoria (writing workshops). Against such a background the eleventh-century stories that Rollo himself was responsible for restitutions of land to Rouen cathedral and the abbey of Saint-Ouen are perhaps less untrustworthy than has been hitherto thought. William Longsword, for example, was actively involved in the restoration of the abbey of Jumièges on the River Seine. By the time of Richard I we are on securer ground due to a greater variety of source material. His principal ally in ecclesiastical matters was his son, Archbishop Robert of Rouen, whose lengthy reign from 989 to 1037 guaranteed firm control over the secular and regular clergy. Increasingly, Robert's position as the senior male within the ducal kin enabled him to intervene in ducal affairs whenever necessary.[26] His interventions occasionally backfired, as in the early 1030s when he was banned from Normandy by his nephew Duke Robert the Magnificent, though he was restored to power after an intervention by Bishop Fulbert of Chartres [55]. During Richard I's reign many monasteries were restored and land that had been alienated during the time of the viking invasions was given back: the first short-lived restoration of Saint-Wandrille (also on the Seine) dates from his reign, while Fécamp in the Pays-de-Caux was his most famous restoration [64–5]. The foundation or re-foundation of monasteries and churches dotted around the country, some as far away as the western region of the modern *département* Manche adjacent to Brittany, was one aspect of Richard I's policy of using the Church as a means to acquire authority in the regions far away from Rouen.[27] His wife Gunnor, for example, is said to have laid the first stone for the rebuilding of the church of Coutances [8]. The increasing ducal interest in the south-west of Normandy had interesting consequences for the monastery of Mont-Saint-Michel. Richard II crowned his work

---

25 Lifshitz, 1995; for the conventional opinion, see Bates, 1982, 11–12 who emphasises the unique situation of less destruction in Rouen.

26 *GND*, ii, 78; *Moriuht*, line 21, p. 72, cf. Van Houts, 1998a, 622.

27 Potts, 1997, 62–81.

by taking Mont-Saint-Michel more firmly under Norman control,[28] at the same time as he strove to achieve a closer relationship with the counts of Rennes, who were also dukes of Brittany. The double marriage of his sister to Duke Geoffrey of Brittany and of Duke Geoffrey's daughter Judith to Richard II himself cemented a pact and thereby paved the way for firm control by Rouen in western Normandy. In the context of a growing Norman control over Mont-Saint-Michel a remark on the south-western frontier of Normandy by the Aquitainian chronicler Adémar of Chabannes, writing before 1034, is worth highlighting. Contrasting Normandy in his own time with what had gone before, he describes the area as 'that part of Normandy which used to be known as the "March" of France and Brittany' [62], implying that the frontier was considered French or Breton and not Norman or controlled from Rouen.

1 Charter of King Charles the Simple, 17 December 905

The last charter of Carolingian government in Normandy is dated 17 December 905 and still survives as an original. King Charles III the Simple grants to his chancellor Ernustus (who actually produced this charter) eleven serfs of the royal domaine at Pîtres (Eure). The charter is evidence that at this date the royal fisc (taxation collection point) was still in operation.

Recueil des actes de Charles III le Simple roi de France 893–923, ed. P. Lauer (Paris, 1949), no. 51, pp. 112–13.

In the name of the holy and indivisible Trinity, Charles by the favour of divine clemency, king to the faithful people who observe with magnanimity the laws of the king and who deserve to be honoured by his gifts. May the community of the faithful of the holy church of God and ours, present and future, know that the venerable Bishop Ralph and Count Odilard having come to the presence of our highness, have asked us to grant to a deacon, our chancellor Ernustus, several serfs of our serfs to own in perpetuity.[29] We have voluntarily given our assent to their wishes and we give to him in the fisc of Pîtres on the River Seine in the *pagus* of Rouen, the serfs to be owned as property and named as follows: Ingelram ... Dominicus. We hand them over, transfer them and grant them in full right and authority to the right

---

28 Potts, 1989, 135–56 and Potts, 1997, 81–104.

29 Ralph, bishop of Laon (897–921); Odilard is otherwise unknown, he may have been count of Rouen.

and authority of the deacon and chancellor Ernustus so that henceforth and from now on he shall have them without anybody's
objection to keep and possess them in perpetuity and everything he
wishes to do he may do freely in accordance with this act of our
government. And in order that this decision of our highness has
more force ... we have it confirmed below with our hand and sealed
with our ring.

Monogram of Charles the very glorious king.

The notary Ernustus, dealing instead of Bishop Askericus, has
witnessed and subscribed.[30]

Given on the 16 kalends of January, the 10th year of the
indiction, the 13th year of the reign of Charles, the very glorious
king, and the 8th year of his restoration.

Given at Laon happily in the name of the Lord. Amen.

2   Charter of King Charles the Simple, 22 February 906

This text is a charter, dated 22 February 906, from King Charles III the
Simple. It concerns the transfer of the body of St Marcouf together with the
monks from the monastery of Saint-Marcouf (Manche, c. Montebourg) to the
fisc of Corbény (Aisne, c. Craonne) out of fear for the attacks of vikings. The
charter shows that as late as 906 King Charles and Bishop Erleboldus (of
Coutances?) still exercised some authority in the western area of what would
become Normandy and that the viking attacks and invasions had not (yet)
prevented them from issuing royal commands.

ed. P. Lauer, no. 53, pp. 114–16.

Charles, by the clemency of God, king ... Let the faithful people know
that on account of the excessive and prolonged attacks of the pagans
[i.e. vikings] ... because of our sins in the whole of the church, the
very holy and happy Marcouf with his fleeing clerks has been driven
away from his own place by this pestilence. For the love of God, we
have as the circumstances commanded us received him in our fisc at
Corbény. As it remains uncertain whether divine providence wishes
that such treasure stays with us or whether he will have it brought
[back] to his monastery, we have received from our faithful people,
bishops as well as lay people, the advice that the precious body cannot
be kept [at Corbény] without the permission of the bishop under
whose authority he falls. Following wise counsel, we have asked
Bishop Erleboldus permission to keep him with us because his return

---

30 Askericus, bishop of Paris (886–910), and titular chancellor from 892.

remains difficult.[31] We have received a letter written by the bishop and witnessed by Archbishop Guy and by other bishops of the province concerning this case.[32] That is why, inspired by the love of God and full of desire to imitate our predecessors in human and spiritual affairs for the salvation of our soul, we have founded a monastery in our aforementioned fisc of Corbény in honour of St Peter prince of the apostles, because it is in the church that is dedicated to him that the precious body [of St Marcouf] has been placed.

3   Charter of King Charles the Simple, 14 March 918

An allusion to a treaty between King Charles III the Simple and Rollo can be found in a royal charter, which still survives as an original, of 14 March 918 for the abbey of Saint-Germain-des-Prés. The king grants to the monastery what was left of the patrimony of the old abbey of La Croix-Saint-Leufroi (Eure, c. Gaillon) which has been cut into two parts due to the treaty.

ed. P. Lauer, no. 92, pp. 209–12.

... we give and grant this abbey of which the main part lies in the area [pagus] of Méresais on the River Eure to Saint-Germain and to his monks for their upkeep, except that part of the abbey ['s lands] which we have granted to the Normans of the Seine, namely to Rollo and his companions [comitibus], for the defence of the kingdom [pro tutela regni] ...

4   Dudo of Saint-Quentin, History of the Dukes of the Normans

Dudo of Saint-Quentin wrote his History of the Dukes of the Normans over a period of several years. He was commissioned to write it before 996 while his patron Duke Richard I (943–96), was still alive and he had probably finished it by 1015 when the next duke, Richard II (996–1026), rewarded him with estates in Normandy. Dudo was from the Vermandois and had come as an ambassador of Count Albert to negotiate with Duke Richard I in the late 980s or early 990s. Dudo's history is the earliest Norman narrative of the viking settlement in Normandy.

---

31 Bishop Erleboldus, presumably of Coutances, is otherwise unknown. Note that he is not mentioned in no. **8**.

32 Guy, archbishop of Reims (c. 900–15).

Dudo, 119–20, 129–30, 168–9, 173–4, 179, 187–8, 191. The excerpts from the dedicatory letter, Books I and II have been translated with some indebtness to E. Christiansen. The excerpts from Book III are from *Dudo of St Quentin, History of the Normans*, trsl. E. Christiansen (Woodbridge, 1998), pp. 57, 64–5, 68.

[Dedicatory letter to Bishop Adalbero of Laon]

... But I want to assure you, so that you do not think that I stuck to this task voluntarily, or that I began it of my own volition. Two years before he died, I was never away from the court of Duke Richard,[33] son of William the marquis, desiring to return to him the courtesy of my service, on account of innumerable benefits, which he had seen fit to share with me, irrespective of my merits. On one particular day, Richard came up to me and began to enfold me in his arms of pious love, to influence me with the sweetest of his speeches, to persuade me with charming entreaties; he even began to denounce me and called in charity to witness, saying that if it was at all possible for me, I should relieve the long suffering of his soul: namely that I should describe the customs and deeds of the Norman Land, even of his forebear Rollo, who established law in the land.

I was dumbfounded – it was as though I had lost my mind, and for several days I denied his requests and refused. But then, moved by the number of prayers, worn out by the sheer weight of the entreaties, with great difficulty I turned my heart to the task of laying down the weight of such a great load from my shoulders. And although I reckoned that the task in question lay beyond the extent of my ability, I nevertheless placed the yoke of such a great task around my neck; for I was made obedient to that request which tells us: 'stand fast ... quit you like men', be strong and besides 'let all your things be done with charity'.

The pen of my inexperience had not yet touched the earliest part of my work when alas! – tearful rumour brought the announcement that Richard, prince of the whole world, was dead. I would have delayed everything, in grief for this prince, because of an excess of tears and an unbearable grief, which not only tortured my heart but also the limbs of my whole body, as I shook, if the most excellent of his sons the noble Richard had not brought back to me the same request. The same qualities were displayed by his distinguished Count Rodolf.[34]

---

33 Richard I of Normandy (943–96).

34 Richard II of Normandy (996–1026) and Rodolf, count of Ivry, half-brother of Richard I.

They both crowded round with entreaties that I should complete the task which Duke Richard had begun with his entreaty of his memorable life ...

So I gave in to their biddings and entreaties, and I finished the work which, although it is adorned with neither clever figures of speech, nor rhetorical arguments, I have arranged to be sent to your majesty, so that falsehoods may be cut out, and if there is anything of truth therein, it shall be confirmed by your authority. And as God is the marvellous requiter of mercies, who placed the excellent Duke Richard in paradise for his own glory, just as he raised you up as the pillar of his holy church, may he appoint you as a senator of the celestial hall, decorated with an eternal ornament amidst choirs of all the saints.

[Book I, c. 1] ... Europe, which is nourished by a profusion of river beds, is named after various provinces and is bordered at its boundary by several separate countries. The largest of all these and the one most richly provided with a diverse population of countless people is called Germany ... Dacia stands in the centre.[35] It resembles a crown and is like a city-state, protected by the massive Alps. Wild people, fighters, warlike from the threat of war live in these winding wastes; namely the Getae or Goths, Sarmatians, Amacsobii, Tragoditae, Alans and thousands of other tribes by careful cultivation, manage to stay on the Meotidian marshes. These peoples are inflamed by excessively wanton behaviour and through revelling in extraordinary shamefulness, mate with as many women as they can. As a result, they have fathered countless children from sexual intercourse of an immoral illicitness. After these have grown up, they fight with their fathers or grandfathers for property, or what is more cruel, fight fiercely among themselves. When they grow too many in number and become too numerous for the land which they cultivate, a crowd of adolescents is gathered together by lot – this most ancient of customs – and is expelled into other realms of the world to acquire by force their own kingdoms in which they can live in everlasting peace. They therefore do just as the Getae, or Goths, did and laid waste to almost all of Europe right up to the point where they now live.

[Book I, c. 2] But while carrying out their expulsions and dismissals, they used to offer sacrifices in worship of their god Thor. They did

35 Dacia is the Latin name for the Roman province which comprised modern Romania and Transylvania.

not make him an offering of sheep, nor cattle, nor wine, nor grain, but honoured him with human blood, considering it the most precious of all sacrifices. For this, a prophetic priest chose victims beforehand. They were cruelly struck on the head with one strike from an ox-yoke and then one of the battered heads was singled out by lot for one extreme and final blow. That man was then dashed to the ground and they would search for 'the tube of the heart' on the left-hand side, that is the aorta. Once the blood had been drained from it, as was the custom, they smeared their own heads and the heads of their men and quickly set the sails of their ships according to the direction of the winds. And believing that those men were appeasing the god with such an action, they fast put their weight behind the oars of the boats. But if, however, the lot determined that they go out on horseback, they would raise the martial standards of battle and slip away from their home territory with the intention to crush other people with great force. They do indeed live in exile from their fathers to tussle courageously with kings. They are sent away without resources from their own people to buy food from strangers. They are deprived of the farms of their ancestors in order to settle quietly on foreign ones. They are exiled and banished so that they can fight and despoil. They are urged out by their own people so that they can share territory with foreigners. They are segregated from their nation so that they might give thanks for the property of foreign folk. They are abandoned by their fathers and, perhaps – it is not impossible – by their mothers. The young men's harshness is encouraged, with the aim of overthrowing nations. Their fatherland is set free, cleared of its inhabitants. The other provinces suffer, badly poisoned by the enemy host. In this way they ravage everything, which does not oppose them. They sail near to the sea-shore so that they might claim for themselves the territories' plunder. The booty which they snatch from one kingdom, they bring to another. They make for havens where peace reigns in order to exchange their loot for profit.

[Book I, c. 3] The Dacians then are called 'Danai' or Danes by their own people and boast that they are descended from Antenor, who once upon a time, when the Trojan territory was being pillaged, escaped from the midst of the Greeks and penetrated Illyrican defences with his men. Those Dacians were once driven out by their own people, in a repeat of the above rite. As a result they migrated into France's expansive territory with Hasting as their leader. ...

[Here follows Dudo's account of the treaty between King Charles and Rollo]

[Book II, c. 28] Once the time had been set for this, they came to the appointed place which is called Saint-Clair.[36] Now Rollo's army camped on this side of the River Epte and the king's and Robert's army on the other.[37] Rollo immediately sent the archbishop to the king of the Franks to tell him these words:[38] 'Rollo cannot make peace with you, because the land which you want to give him is uncultivated by the ploughshare, entirely deprived of herds of cattle and flocks of sheep and lacking in human life. He does not consider it to be a place from which he can live, unless by plundering and pillage. Give him a kingdom from where he can get food and clothes for himself, until the land which you offer him is filled with a mass of riches and returns the fruits of food, people and animals. He will not be reconciled with you or with the land which you are about to give him, unless on oath of the Christian religion you swear, that is you and your archbishops, bishops, counts and abbots of the whole kingdom, that he and his successors may hold the land from the River Epte right up to the sea, as if it were a property and allodial possession [quasi fundum et allodum] for ever.'[39] Then Robert, the duke of the Franks, and the counts and bishops who were present with the abbots, said to the king: 'You will not have such an honourable duke as this one, if you do not do what he desires. If you will not grant this on account of the service which he demands from you, at least give it to him on account of the Christian religion so that a large number of people embraces Christ, people who have been caught up in satanic sin; and so that the future of your whole kingdom and of the Church are not brought to nothing by the onset of an attacking army, when you hold office as its advocate and protection in God's place and ought to be the most constant king and adviser.' The king then wanted to give him the territory of Flanders to live on – but he refused it because of the difficulty of its marshes. And so the king promised to give him Brittany which lies on the edge of the land he had pledged. Robert and Bishop Franco related everything to Rollo: once hostages had been given in the uprightness of the Christian faith, they took him to King Charles. The Franks gazed at Rollo, invader of France, and said to each other: 'Great is the power of this leader, great is his virtue,

---

36 Saint-Clair-sur-Epte (Seine-Mar.).

37 Charles III the Simple, king of the Franks (898–922); Robert, duke and later king of the Franks (922–23).

38 Franco, archbishop of Rouen, can be found in the sources after 909 and before c. 942.

39 Allodial properties were normally hereditary.

great is his counsel and judgement and even his effort for having fought so many battles against the counts of this kingdom' ...

[Book II, c. 29] The bishops said to Rollo, who was unwilling to kiss King Charles's foot: 'You who receive such a gift ought to kiss the king's foot.' And he said: 'I shall never bend my knees to the knees of another, nor shall I kiss anyone's foot.' Compelled, however, by the prayers of the Franks, he ordered a certain soldier to kiss the king's foot. This man immediately seized the king's foot, put it to his mouth and kissed it whilst the king was still standing. The king fell flat on his back. This raised a great laugh and greatly stirred up the crowd. However, King Charles and Duke Robert, counts and leading men, patrons and abbots swore an oath on the catholic faith upon their life and limbs to the patrician Rollo[40] and to the honour of the whole realm, that over and above he should hand down to his heirs the appointed country, as he held and possessed it, and that through the course of the time of his grandsons, from generation and to generation [nepotum in progenies progenierum] they should hold and cultivate it. When, as has been reported, these things were finished, King Charles went back home. Robert and Franco stayed with Rollo ...

[Book II, c. 34] When Robert [= Rollo], patrician of the Normans, was worn out by old age and the overtaxing toil of battles, the leaders of the Dacians and the Britons were called together, and Robert transferred all his land under his dominion to William, the son of Popa.[41] And placing his own hands between the hands of young William, he bound together the leaders by a sacred oath. He lived on for another five years after this, worn out by his age, with no strength left in his body and not strong enough to ride horseback, but holding on to a pacified, cohesive and quiet realm. He suffered the cost of woeful misfortune, and endured the inevitable misfortune of death. And so, full of days, he migrated to Christ, to whom is the honour and the glory for ever and ever. Amen ...

[Book III, c. 36] And so, as was declared in the preceding book, the most glorious duke and pre-potent William, who was also an athlete most highly beloved of the eternal king, was born of noble stock with a Dacian father, (Rollo that is) and a Frankish mother, namely Popa,

---

40 The word 'patrician' (*patricius*), used as synonym for 'leader', may imply Dudo's notion of Rollo as 'father of the new fatherland'.

41 Popa, daughter of Berengar 'of Bayeux', who may be the same as Berengar marquis of Neustria (Keats-Rohan, 1997a, 187–204).

and he began his life in the city of Rouen.[42] After he had been sprink-
led with holy baptism, his begetter, rich with an abundance of all
manner of goods, and adorned with every material possession,
entrusted him for his education to a very affluent count called Botho,
and handed him over to be instructed as was fitting. Eventually, the
lovely boy, living in a household alongside good orthodox men highly
honourable in their lives, and beginning to be memorably holy and to
promise well, consecrated to Jesus Christ the youthful years in which
he willingly inclined to the blessed exercise of the fourfold virtues and
strove to submit himself entirely to things divine ...

[Book III, c. 43] However, there was one Riulf, fiercely filled with
infamous perfidy,[43] and when he saw that Duke William, namely his
lord, was growing mightily strong and powerful with the assistance
of his friends, he gathered together several of the chiefs of the
Northmen and spoke these treacherous words: 'Our lord William,
who was begotten on the noble stock of the Frankish race, has
procured Frankish friends for himself and is deprived of our counsel
and has been inaccessible to the violence of our grief. For he is trying
to shut us out from the kingdom altogether, so as to press down hard
with the yoke of slavery on the necks of those who remain. And more:
he wants to give the land which we own to his kinsmen to be
possessed by their heirs, and he will enrich them generously with the
offices that are ours. Therefore let us try to find a shrewd plan which
will save us against that intended measure, and let us make a pact of
perpetual association between ourselves, and let us keep it unbroken
by the anchor of steadfast determination' ...

[Book III, c. 44] Having made this plan of deception they sent to
William men who would say to him the infamous words they had
devised. Having carried out the office he had been delegated, the
emissary stood before William and was himself amazed at the wonderful presumption of his words. Therefore when William had summoned
his own chief men to consult with him over such demands he sent the
legate back to Riulf with words of peace, to say as follows: 'I cannot
grant you the land you ask of me. However, I will freely concede to
you all the gear I own: armlets, that is, belts, hauberks and helmets;
and coursers, horses, axes and outstanding swords wonderfully
chased in gold. If you are ready and willing to serve me, you will

42 William Longsword, count of Rouen (c. 928–43).
43 Riulf has not been identified.

enjoy within my household my constant favour, and the rewards of active service ...' When the announcer of this abasement had reached Riulf the all presumptuous, and related to him the message of such humility and gentleness that he brought him, Riulf was infatuated by his own conceited audacity and slighted Duke William's most humble and deprecatory message. Having called together his chiefs, the followers of his own presumptuous will, he reported what he had heard from the envoy's mouth in words of cunning falsehood ... : 'He is expecting that we will be pacified by such humble words as you have heard, and grow drowsy: and thus while a long delay stretches out, he labours to unite against us the Frankish-born relations of his noble family and the chiefs who join him in conspiracy. Therefore let us take heed lest we be tricked and ground down by the French peoples. Let him not trample over us any longer by means of his cunning arguments, but let us form into an army, and go quickly to meet him at the city of Rouen, so that he himself and his advisers may be thrown out of Rouen' ...

Bernard made the inquiry and three hundred men were found ready to fight and die with William.[44] They came before him with one mind, and made their act of association, fealty and support in the manner of the Danes, by clashing their weapons together as a way of showing unanimity. But the rest of the people were frigid in war and made a rapid retreat to the protection of the city ...

[Book III, c. 46] Then with his three hundred mail-clad men did William suddenly charge the hostile camp of the reckless multitude, crushing them and slashing them with swords and spears. He broke up the tents of the leaders, and burned the bivouacs of their knights. Those whom he found he felled with the sword and he himself dispatched to Orcus those who resisted. And so William gained a triumph over his enemies, and Riulf disappeared in flight. Part of the army pursued him but was unable to catch him because he concealed himself in the depths of a wood. But the Seine swallowed up very many of them, and the wood hid many who were wounded. When William inspected the corpse-strewn field and found none of his own men among the dead, he and his men glorified God who comes to the aid of those who trust in themselves. And the place where the wonderful battle was fought is called Pré-de-la-Bataille [Field of Battle] today ...[45]

44 Bernard the Dane, and adviser of William Longsword.
45 North-west of Rouen.

5 Norman annals, 842–915

All Norman annalistic writing goes back to the now lost Annals of Rouen dating from the eleventh or early twelfth century which can be reconstructed on the basis of the Annals of Jumièges, Saint-Wandrille, Saint-Evroult, Mont-Saint-Michel and Saint-Etienne at Caen. The entries were written probably on the basis of Dudo's and William of Jumièges's texts. What follows here are the dates referring to the viking invasions. For the date and relationship between these annals, see ed. Laporte (see below), pp. 7–10.

Annales de l'abbaye Saint-Pierre de Jumièges, ed. J. Laporte (Rouen, 1954), pp. 49, 51.

842 The translation of St Ouen, the archbishop, when the Normans [*Normanni*] destroyed Rouen, and put his [St Ouen's] monastery to flames on 15 May ...

851 The Normans arrived at the Seine. And again other Normans came ...

865 The Normans came to Mantes ...

875 Archbishop Witto died. Franco succeeded him ...

876 Rollo arrived in Normandy [*in Normannia*] with his men on 17 November ...

908 The Hungarians devastated Saxony and Thuringia. At this time Rollo and his army besieged the town of Chartres. But the bishop of the town called Wlatelmus, a religious man, called to his support Duke Robert of Burgundy and Ebalus of Poitou and carrying the tunic of the Holy Virgin in his hands with the help of God put Rollo to flight and liberated the town ...

912 Franco, archbishop of Rouen, christened Rollo; and gave him the lordship of the city of Rouen and granted him the duchy of Neustria. Peace was established between Rollo and Charles, king of the Franks and Charles gave him his daughter Gisla and the whole of Neustria and little Britain. Robert duke of Burgundy received him from the holy font and gave him his own name [Robert]. After Gisla's death by whom he had no issue, Rollo married Popa, daughter of Wido count of Senlis, sister of Bernard, by whom he had William.[46]

915 The body of St Ouen was returned from France to Normandy on 1 February in the forty-second year of King Charles's reign.

46 Dudo tells that Rollo married Gisla, daughter of Charles III the Simple. She has not been identified.

6   William of Jumièges, Deeds of the Dukes of the Normans

William of Jumièges wrote his Deeds of the Dukes of the Normans from the
late 1050s to *c.* 1070 adapting and revising Dudo's story of the settlement of
the vikings. The most important point of difference is William's unique
reference to Björn Ironside, son of Lothbroc, and his relationship with Hasting,
as well as his specific point that Rollo was chosen as leader of the viking
army upon their arrival at Rouen. William is also our sole authority for the
information that Hasting (who may or may not have been a viking) changed
sides, having first harassed the Carolingian king Charles and then supported
him, in return for which he is said to have received the city of Chartres.

GND, i, 17–19, 27, 51–3, 57.

[Book I, c. 4] For many years this law [of exile] remained unchal-
lenged until Lothbroc, whom we have mentioned above, succeeded his
father as king.[47] Prompted by the laws of his ancestors Lothbroc drove
into exile his son Björn Ironside, together with a large group of young
men compelled by a similar lot, and his tutor Hasting, in every
respect a very deceitful man, in order that he might explore foreign
countries and win by force new lands to settle. He was called Ironside
because, when his shield did not protect him and he stood unarmed in
the battlefield, he was invulnerable and scorned all force of arms
whatever for his mother had imbued him in very strong magic.
Hasting as an exile, banished from the country with his pupil, sent out
messengers inviting soldiers of nearby provinces, who were impulsive
and eager to fight, to join the expedition and so gathered an army of
innumerable warlike recruits ... On the appointed day the ships were
pushed into the sea and the soldiers hastened to go aboard. They
raised the standards, spread the sails before the wind and like agile
wolves set out to rend the Lord's sheep, pouring out human blood to
their god Thor ...

[Book I, c. 10] After the destruction of this city [Luna] the heathens
discovered that they had by no means captured Rome.[48] Fearing that
they would enjoy no further profit – for speedily the fame of their
profane deeds had reached the ears of the Romans – they took counsel
and decided to return. On his way back to his native country, Björn,
standard bearer of the destruction and king of the armies, suffered

---

47 William of Jumièges is the first historian to mention him and his son Björn. For
     possible identifications with Ragnarr Lodbrok, see Van Houts, 1983, 107–21 at
     113–17.

48 Luna is the ancient Roman town near La Spezia on the north Italian coast.

shipwreck and barely reached the coast of England while a number of his ships were lost. From England he went to Frisia where he died. Hasting, however, went to King Charles of the Franks requesting peace, which was granted to him alone along with the city of Chartres as tribute. Thereafter France began to breathe again after the tumult and disaster; sentence of punishment was suspended, owing to the fearful nature of these crimes ...

[Book II, c. 3] When these matters had been settled the Danes set their sails to the wind, left the River Schelde, and crossed the sea. In the year 876, they entered the mouth of the Seine and with favourable wind arrived at Jumièges, where they deposited the relics of a holy virgin called Ameltrudis which they had brought from 'Britannia' on the altar of the chapel of St Vedast, which is situated on the other side of the river.[49] The chapel is still called after that virgin to the present day. When Franco, archbishop of Rouen, was told about their arrival he wisely decided, realising that the walls of the city had been broken down by the ferocity of the enemy and despairing of any support to resist them, to make peace with them instead of challenging them in any way to his own destruction. He went to see them immediately with a request for peace, and after he obtained it, he established a firm pact with them. Thereafter, in haste, the Danes sailed their ships as quickly as possible to the city walls. appreciating wisely the strategic position on land and near the sea, which could easily be provided with food, they unanimously decided to make it the capital of the whole province. By lot they chose one of their number, named Rollo, and appointed him to be lord of the army, promising fealty to him ...

[Book II, c. 5] [After Rollo and Hasting met] When Count Theobald reckoned that he had a suitable opportunity to deceive Hasting, he addressed him deceitfully with these words:[50] 'Why distinguished man are you inactive and idle? Do you not know that King Charles desired your death on account of the Christian blood you have shed in the past? For he remembers the enormous crimes you then inflicted upon him and has therefore determined to expel you from his country. Your army, as he says, together with the heathen Rollo intends to destroy the Franks; therefore the next time you will really be destroyed by them. Take care not to be punished unexpectedly.' Terrified by these

49 This saint is otherwise unknown.

50 Either Theobald, vicomte of Tours (908–43), or his son Theobald I the Trickster, count of Chartres, Blois and Tours (943–77).

words Hasting promptly sold the town of Chartres to Theobald and, having collected all his possessions, wandered off and disappeared.

7 The Discovery and Miracles of St Vulfran

This hagiographical collection was written in the years 1053–54 at Saint-Wandrille. It covers the history of the re-foundation of the monastery after the viking invasions and relates the discovery and miracles of its patron saint St Vulfran. Chapters 4 to 7 contain a brief account of the arrival of the vikings in Normandy and the disruption it caused at the site of the Carolingian monastery of Saint-Wandrille, also called Fontenelle.

Inventio et miracula sancti Vulfranni, ed. Dom J. Laporte, Mélanges publiés par la Société de l'Histoire de Normandie, 14e s. (Rouen, 1938), pp. 18–19, 20–1.

[C. 4] Some time passed under the rule of twenty-four abbots, who followed each other in uninterrupted succession for 281 years when with God's permission and as the outrageous result of human perversity, the Danish people were dislodged from their distant homes and wandered across the whole of the sea and the ocean's shore with the cruelty of pirates and laid everything waste with sword and flame. In particular, they attacked those regions and places on either side of the big river Seine and its banks. They subdued them in a wretched defeat, and by fire and pillage took possession of the most prosperous city all, called Paris by its founder Ysio. And they established the most famous metropolis Rouen, so called since antiquity, as their main head-quarters, having done away with its bishop, and laid low the people and the soldiers. They set fire to the fortifications and demolished its walls; engaged in dreadful cruelty they even set fire to the monastery of Jumièges with devouring flames.

[C. 5] Since there was nowhere for anyone to hide with no safe place anywhere for those who were running away, the monks in the monastery of Fontenelle, mentioned above, were at this point in time very frightened and terribly distressed. They seemed to be paralysed by uncertainty, rather than getting away with their lives. For they themselves had purchased the site of the monastery from the pagans at a good price.[51] But when their funds had dried up and their immunity from attack was waning, they made up their minds, at the last moment, to embrace the safeguard of flight. Therefore the tombs of

---

51 Payment of ransom is mentioned in the Annals of Saint-Wandrille under the year 841.

the saints Wandrille and Ansbert were dug up. They removed the most sacred bones, such as they were, with great reverence and honour around 862 after the birth of Christ. The bones were then placed in portable caskets, along with all the grave goods found with them. They made a speedy escape, in case they were suddenly besieged by an enemy attack and departed, leaving behind on the same spot where it was later discovered unharmed the most sacred body of St Vulfran ...[52]

[c. 6] Not long after the violent army of barbarians had left the sea, they approached this place and, seeing it empty of men and bare of all resources, with all its buildings destroyed by fire, exactly 280 years after the first building had been erected, they burned the remains, along with the sanctuary itself, destroyed the place and left. Then the army, wandering far and wide through the whole area, occupied it and laid everywhere waste with pillage and fire. They destroyed cities, they pulled down fortifications, churches and noble monasteries in the most beautiful and visited region among all principalities, which, like Egypt once, flourished and was then razed to the ground. Meanwhile, there arose the indiscriminate murder of men, and the slaughter of numerous sorts of animals. Chosen young men were driven towards depravity. Maidens and girls fell victim to the libidinous pagans; the rest of the people were led away as captives to foreign realms to be handed over [? sold] to the local population [distrahenda ethnicis]. And since for eighteen successive years this great misfortune did not abate due to continuous attacks from several leaders [ducibus], the district of western Gaul, along the length of the coast of the English Channel, was reduced to a desert but at length returned to peace.

[C. 7] Meanwhile Rollo, the latest leader [dux] of the Normans, was militarily more powerful than others, more even-handed, and more prudent in council. Having been driven away from his home, he put ashore on the banks of the Seine. He attacked individual manors and cities which stood on their own. Few of the people whom he came up against fled, instead they were put under the auspicious yoke of his authority [lacuna in manuscript: probably 'and the land'] he distributed by lot among his companions and fellow soldiers. First Rollo ordered that boundaries between himself and the marcher principalities on the fringes [finitimas nationes] be firmly settled, so that he

---

52 For the alleged discovery of St Vulfran, whose relics in fact had been taken to Ghent, see Van Houts 1989b, 233–51.

would not be forced to push them back in frequent border skirmishes. He then established excellent rights and judicious laws for his house [?hold] and soldiers [*domi militiaeque*]; thus in a short time he won over people of different origin and of various skills and so made one people out of a mixture of different ones. In this way he quickly grew so strong, that his [people] became more numerous and stronger than the neighbouring realms and kingdoms. And when after some time he had been christened, he died with his realm in excellent order, which he left to his son and successor, named William, then in the flower of his youth.

8   The Miracles of Coutances

The history of the church of Coutances was written in the first quarter of the twelfth century by Canon John, whose father Peter had been chamberlain in the time of Bishop Geoffrey of Coutances (1048–93). For the early post-viking period of the diocese this biography of Bishop Geoffrey of Coutances is our only narrative source. No manuscript of the Latin text has survived, the only known one having been lost after the eighteenth-century edition was published by the Maurists.

De statu hujus ecclesiae ab anno 836 ad 1093, in *Gallia Christiana*, xi, Instrumenta, cols 217–18.

After the first most serious attack of the Normans [*Normanni*], the most wicked and sacrilegious Hasting and his Danes, which lasted for more than thirty years, that is from the year of the incarnation of the Lord in 836, there followed a second attack led by Rollo, the most illustrious duke [*dux*] of the Normans in the year of the incarnation of the sacrosanct 875, when ... Walcheren, Frisia, Flanders, Burgundy, Brittany and the whole of Neustria, which is now called Normandy, and parts of France were destroyed in an indescribable manner: many cities were captured and burned, towns were laid waste, churches destroyed, estates [*praedia*] of saints and churches robbed of their rights and privileges, the clergy and people fled from the sword and were annihilated. The relics and bodies of the saints were taken from their hiding places or by fugitives transported to various regions. While this misery took place, the holy church of Coutances, which for a long time had flourished and had faithfully put up a fight for God under thirty-three bishops, was completely razed to the ground, robbed of its lands and privileges, separated from the relics and bodies of its saints and during the next 74 years, as can be read in the chronicles, fouled by idolatry and trampled upon by the fury of the pagans. After such a long time of desolation many who had taken away the relics and bodies of saints had long since died in exile and consequently many bodies of saints deprived of their custodians remained spread out over many regions. After Rollo, the most powerful duke, was reborn through the fountain of healthy regeneration and sacred faith [i.e. he had been christened] in the year 911, the fourteenth indiction, and two years after he had made peace with King Charles, the bodies of the holy bishops of Coutances, Laudus and Rumpharius, which had been taken away, were brought to Rouen and with the agreement of Rollo received in the church of Saint-Sauveur.[53]

Rollo, who after his christening was called Robert, gave to the church where the bodies of the aforesaid saints had been received, to Saint-Laudus and to Dom Theodoric, who at that time was bishop of Coutances, and to all his successors in perpetual right, the land pertaining to the aforesaid church, where the bishop lived together with the clergy who served in the church.[54] Because the region of Coutances was deprived of Christians and open to paganism, the aforesaid bishop of Coutances served Saint-Laudus and his church at Rouen and there he worked as if he were in his own see. The same church, which for a long time had been called Saint-Sauveur, was renamed Saint-Laudus in honour and merit of its holy and glorious guest. In order to revive by the grace of God the Christian religion at Coutances and its neighbourhood, after deliberation and [forced by] the necessity of time and circumstances, the aforesaid bishop came hither and having done business concerning the church property he returned to Rouen, where he wished to stay as if in his own see while freely exercising the office of bishop in the church of Saint-Laudus as if he were in Coutances. This surely is the true reason why until this very day the bishop of Coutances is called bishop of Saint-Laudus.

At Rouen, as if at Coutances, five bishops held the see: the aforesaid Theodoric, Herbert, Algerund, Gilbert and Hugh. After them for one year Herbert and Robert, who became bishop of Lisieux, held the see at Saint-Laudus on the River Vire. After the reigns of the invincible Rollo, and of his son count [*marchio*] William, who similarly was duke and who, as can be read, was a martyr of Christ, Richard, son of William, most famous count [*marchio*], belligerent duke, invincible,

---

53 In the early tenth century Coutances was probably situated outside the territory ruled by the counts of Rouen (Bates, 1982, 12, 30).

54 For what follows this text is the only source of information.

fearless, with devout and catholic faith ... established canons and gave and confirmed land and income for their living ... the aforesaid bishop Hugh transferred seven canons of those who had looked after the church of Coutances to the aforesaid church of Saint-Laudus which was at Rouen. After the death of Bishop Hugh, Herbert became bishop. He threw the canons who seemed to him the least civil and the least educated out of the church of Coutances, expelling them as illiterate and useless and retained their lands and ample possessions under his authority in order to hand them to the more educated and gifted canons. But the following year Herbert himself was transferred to Lisieux. In those days Blainville, Courcy and the land of Soulles with its large forest formed the canons' prebends as is shown up to this day by the charter of Count [*marchio*] Richard and Bishop Herbert.[55] Bishop Robert, however, who succeeded Herbert and became bishop of Lisieux not only did not return the prebends of the said canons to the service of the church, but he even distributed them and others in fief and as inheritance [*in feodum et haereditatem*] to his nephews, relatives and sisters, not generously but prodigiously.

At that time a beginning was made of the construction of the church of Coutances, founded and supported by Countess Gunnor, with the help of the canons, who made available half the returns of the altar for the duration of the work, and of the barons and faithful parishioners, some of whose names carved into the stones of the church's arches can be seen up to this day.[56] In that time the church was an unstable, careless and rough construction which housed five canons and contained hardly any bibles or other authentic or canonical books; those they had had no illumination. The merciful and compassionate Lord, patient and most pitiful, lamenting this holy and poor church, because the time had come to take mercy on her as he had raised the lame from the ground and the poor from the dung, so that he could sit with princes and hold the throne of glory, due to his liberality he showered the church with various signs of virtue and miracles and put it under the love of princes and the authority of Bishop Geoffrey.

---

55 Fauroux, nos 6 and 28.

56 Gunnor, countess of Normandy, wife of Richard I, was probably born *c.* 950 and died in 1031. She laid the first stone for Coutances cathedral (Fauroux, no. 214, p. 406).

9 The *Plaintsong* of William Longsword

The *Plaintsong* (*Planctus*) of William Longsword was composed shortly after his murder in 943 instigated by Count Arnulf I of Flanders. The poem, which survives in two manuscripts, has never been properly edited and presents many linguistic and historical problems. It was composed either at Jumièges in Normandy or, more likely, considering the southern French provenance of the manuscripts, under the patronage of William's sister Gerloc/Adela, countess of Aquitaine and Poitou. As a contemporary text it is one of the most important sources for information about Rollo's dynasty.

What follows is a translation of five strophes of which the Latin can be reconstructed, MSS Clermont Ferrand BM MS 240 fo. 45r (10th century) and Florence Biblioteca Laurenziana MS Ashburnham 83 fos 21r–22v (11th century).

[2] Born overseas from a father who stuck to the pagan error/ and from a mother who was devoted to the sweet religion,/ he [William] was blessed with the holy chrism/

Shed tears for William/ who died innocently

[3] After the death of his father,/ the pagans rose in war against him;/ firmly trusting in God/ he subdued them with a strong force/

Shed tears for William/ who died innocently

[15] [only in Florence MS] There were two great men on earth,/ who like you [?] bore the name of William/ of whom one [was] count [?] of Rouen/ and the other still lives in Poitou/ let us pray for them[57]

Shed tears for William/ who died innocently

[16] O, William, defender of peace and lover and/ consoler of the poor and defender of orphans/ and protector of widows who is now joined to heavenly joy/

Shed tears for William/ who died innocently

[17] Greetings, Richard, count of Rouen/ greetings, prince and father of the county/ may Christ the child commend you to live/ so that you can be with him indefinitely/ Amen[58]

---

57 This strophe is addressed to Richard I and his uncle William III, duke of Aquitaine (= I of Poitou), d. 963 and mentions as dead his Richard's father William Longsword.

58 The reference to Richard I as count (*comes*) of Rouen in this strophe of a poem written shortly after 943 is one of the earliest references we have. Normally one might expect information on titles to be found in charters, but there are no charters available for mid-tenth-century Normandy.

10   Flodoard of Reims, Annals

Flodoard, priest and canon of Reims (893/4–c. 966), wrote the Annals over a period of forty years from c. 925 to 966. In his work he gives a contemporary view from north-eastern France of the arrival and settlement of the vikings in Normandy. As a contemporary witness his opinions are almost unique and difficult to verify. For the evaluation of his story it is important to bear in mind the fact that he lived at a great distance from the North Sea coast. All references to lands 'across the Seine' have to be interpreted from Flodoard's point of view, and thus refer to lands beyond the left or west bank of the Seine.

Les Annales de Flodoard, ed. P. Lauer (Paris, 1906), pp. 15–17, 24, 29–32, 39–40, 41, 55, 68, 73–6, 82, 84, 86, 88, 91, 94–99, 148.

[923] Meanwhile, Rognvald, the leader of the Normans, who were encamped on the River Loire, had been long since stirred up by Charles's constant charges, and joining very many men from Rouen to him, plundered France across the River Oise. But at Rognvald's camp, there arrived the followers of Herbert, who had remained in more than one of the fortresses and had joined Count Ralph, the stepson of Roger, and Count Ingobrannus to them.[59] They snatched a vast amount of booty and at the same time set one thousand captives free. When Rognvald had heard the news, he was ablaze with anger and set out to plunder the district [*pagus*] of Arras. There to meet him was Count Adelelm.[60] He killed six hundred of Rognvald's men, while the others slipped away in flight. Together with these, Rognvald hurried to the refuge of his own defences and from there, did not stop carrying off as much booty and carrying out as many robberies as he was able. With the situation pressing, King Rodulf was summoned by Hugo, son of Robert, and came from Burgundy to Compiègne beyond the River Oise.[61] And when he heard that the Normans were plundering the district [*pagus*] of Beauvais,[62] he went across, accompanied by Archbishop

---

59 Rognvald (*Ragenoldus*) a viking chief in the Loire area. Herbert II, count of Vermandois (d. after 979); Count Ralph of Laon, prototype of the hero of the *chanson de geste Raoul de Cambrai*, and Ingobrannus are only known from this reference.

60 Adelelm, count of Arras (d. 932).

61 Ralph, king of the Franks (923–36) and Hugh the Great (d. 956), son of Robert, king of the Franks (922–23).

62 The Latin word *pagus* denotes an (originally Roman) administrative area in France. The Merovingian and Carolingian kings kept most of these units intact and the Church's ecclesiastical organisation in (arch)dioceses usually corresponded with the *pagi*. There is no satisfactory English equivalent for the word and 'district' is a fairly arbitrary translation.

Seulf, Count Herbert and several other chosen brave men.[63] Having crossed the River Epte, he entered the territory which had some time ago been given to the Normans on their conversion to the Christian faith so that they might honour this faith and live in peace. Part of this very land, the king devastated with slaughters and with fire since the Normans had broken the peace which they had held with the Franks on account of the pledges of Charles who had promised them the breadth of the country. But envoys from the Lotharingians approached him as he was intent on this plundering, promising to subjugate themselves and their property. Recalled from this destruction by the delegation of these people, he discharged those who were with him and then proceeded to meet the Lotharingians to discuss matters. Count Hugo and Count Herbert were left to guard their country across the River Oise ... Meanwhile after the Normans had plundered some of our districts across the River Oise and our men had plundered some of the Normans' lands and both sides had exchanged messengers, the Normans promised peace to Count Herbert and to Archbishop Seulf and to the other Franks, who with them had rebelled against the Normans, and requested more extensive land across the Seine than they had been given. Meanwhile after, as has been said, King Rodulf had returned to Laon the Normans sent hostages and agreed a truce with him until the middle of May.

[924] The Normans entered upon peace with solemn promises in the presence of Count Hugo, Count Herbert and also Archbishop Seulf. King Rodulf was not there, but with his consent, their [the Normans'] land increased with Maine and the Bessin [Cinomannis et Baiocae], which in a pact of peace was conceded to them[64] ... Rognvald and his Normans devastated the land of Hugh between the Loire and the Seine because he had not received any land within France [Gallias].

[925] The Normans of Rouen broke the treaty which they had once made and devastated the districts of Beauvais and Amiens. Those citizens of Amiens who were fleeing were burned by a fire for which they were ill-prepared. So too was Arras suddenly ablaze from a fire

---

63 Seulf, archbishop of Reims (922–25).

64 There is some scepticism among historians whether land around Le Mans (Maine) so far south-west of Rouen could really have been given to William Longsword. It has been suggested that Flodoard at Reims simply got the area wrong and that instead of Le Mans he may have meant the area around Sées (Musset and Chanteux, 1973, 37–59 at 54–5).

that had sprung up. The Normans came as far as plundering Noyon and set fire to its suburbs. The inhabitants of Laon marched out accompanied by the inhabitants of the suburbs and drove the Normans back: they struck down those whom they could and liberated part of the suburb. The inhabitants of the Bessin, meanwhile, plundered the Norman territory beyond the Seine. When news of this had reached them, the Parisians and also Robert's very sons, together with several of Hugo's followers and with the inhabitants of certain fortresses, plundered that part of the district of Rouen which was held by the Normans, on this side of the Seine: they set fire to manors, stole cattle and even killed some of the Normans. In the meantime, Count Herbert, together with a few of the Franks, since there was still too little grass to be found for the horses, settled beyond the River Oise to prohibit the Normans from crossing. Once the Normans had heard about the devastation of their land, they hurried to return home. At last, Henry crossed the Rhine and took by force a certain town called Zülpich, which Gislebert's allies had been guarding.[65] And no longer did he delay to the south of Lotharius's kingdom, but returned to his own territory across the Rhine with the hostages that he had taken from Gislebert.[66] Count Helgaud and the other French coastal lords invaded those territories which had recently belonged to the Normans, next to their own and laid waste to them.[67]

Rudolf, meanwhile, returned from Burgundy to France and called a ban over the Franks to prepare themselves for war against the Normans. Once the military operation against the Normans had begun, Herbert, therefore, accompanied by the soldiers of the church of Reims as well as by Count Arnulf and the other French coastal lords, attacked that Norman post to which Rollo, the Norman leader, had sent over from Rouen one thousand Normans, a number greater than that of the inhabitants of the town itself.[68] It was this very same camp, situated on the coast and called Eu, that the Franks surrounded. They broke through the rampart by which the camp was surrounded in front of its walls and weakening the wall, climbed over. Once they had won possession of the town by fighting, they then slaughtered all the males and set fire to its fortifications. Some,

---

65 Henry, king of 'Germany' (918–36) and Gislebert, duke of Lotharingia (d. 939); Zülpich is near Cologne.

66 Lothar, king of the Franks (954–86).

67 Helgaud, count of Montreuil-sur-Mer (Pas-de-Calais).

68 Arnulf I, count of Flanders (918–65).

however, escaped and took possession of a certain neighbouring island. But the Franks attacked and captured it, although with a greater delay than when they had seized the town. After the Normans, who had been preserving their lives by fighting as best they could, had seen what had happened and had let slip any hope of survival, some plunged themselves into the waves, some to extricate themselves cut their throats and some were killed by Frankish swords, while others died by their own weapons. And in this way, once everyone had been destroyed and an outrageous amount of booty had been pillaged, the Franks returned to their own territory. King Rudolf, however, settled in the district of Beauvais, with Count Hugo and the people of Burgundy.

[927] Charles, therefore, together with Herbert requested a meeting with the Normans at the fortress which is called Eu. And there, [William] the son of Rollo recommended himself to Charles and affirmed his friendship with Herbert. Meanwhile, fears of the Hungarians' false rumour and of their flight, were stirred up throughout the kingdom [regnum] of Lotharingia and through France.[69]

[928] Count Herbert gained possession of Laon and there held a meeting [placitum] with the Normans: both he and Hugo, son of Robert, made an alliance of friendship with them. Nevertheless, Odo, son of Herbert, whom Rollo was holding hostage, was not returned there, until his father and several other Frankish counts and bishops had recommended themselves to Charles.

[933] William, the leader [princeps] of the Normans, recommended himself to the same king. And to him, the king gave the territory of the Bretons, which is situated on the sea-coast [terram Brittonum in ora maritima].[70]

[937] The Bretons retreated to their homeland after their prolonged expedition during which they had frequent encounters with the Normans, who had invaded the territory which had belonged to them, next to their own. They ended up the stronger in many of these battles and reclaimed the conquered territory.

69 The fight against the vikings coming from the north and west was at times compounded by the Saracen threat from the east.

70 This territory is normally identified as the Cotentin and Avranchin, areas which in 867 had been granted by King Charles the Bald to Salomon of Brittany.

[939] The English fleet was sent over by Athelstan, their king, to help King Louis: it crossed the sea and plundered the coastal territories of the Flemish.[71] And when none of the tasks, for which they had come, had been left undone, they crossed the sea once again and made for their own lands. King Otto held a meeting with Hugo, Herbert, Arnulf and William, the leader [*princeps*] of the Normans and having received their oaths of agreement, returned across the Rhine ...[72] The Bretons came into conflict with the Normans and won victory. And they are said to have captured one of the Norman fortresses. Several of Arnulf's men raided Herluin's territory and were killed by the same Herluin [of Montreuil].

[940] In the year 940, King Louis went to meet William, the leader [*princeps*] of the Normans, who came to see him in the district of Amiens and recommended himself to him. He gave him, moreover, the land which his father, Charles, had given to the Normans and from there, set out against Hugo. But since he refused to come to meet him, he returned to Laon ... Prince Hugo, son of Robert, joined forces with certain bishops from both France and Burgundy, and with Count Herbert, and William, the leader [*princeps*] of the Normans, and besieged the city of Reims. And on the sixth day of the siege, when almost all of the military force were in the process of deserting Archbishop Artold and were defecting to Herbert, this same count Herbert entered the city.[73]

[941] A son was born to King Louis, and the counts who had been sent out in advance, spoke with William and soon renewed the siege of Laon, thinking that the stronghold would be handed over to them.[74] But when the occupation that they had envisaged was not achieved, they returned home.

[942] Count Roger had come as a messenger on behalf of King Louis to William, leader [*princeps*] of the Normans, but died there. William gave a royal welcome to King Louis in Rouen. William of Poitou and the Bretons with their own leaders [*principes*] also came to the king. It was in this company therefore, that the king crossed the River Oise.

---

71 Athelstan, king of Wessex / England (924–39); Louis IV, king of France (936–54).

72 Otto I, king of Germany (936–73).

73 Artold, archbishop of Reims (931–40); Teutolo, archbishop of Tours (932–45).

74 According to Dudo and William of Jumièges, William Longsword became godfather to King Louis's son Lothar (Dudo, 199 and *GND*, i, 84–5).

Hugo and Herbert, however, along with Otto, duke of the Lotharingians, destroyed the bridges, smashed the ships and took up position
together with those men whose allegiance they had been able to
maintain, from the other side of the river.[75] After a dispute had been
stirred up among them by messengers, a truce was finally granted
from the middle of September until the middle of November. Hostages
were taken on both sides: the king even received Herbert's young son.
And even the king himself, as well as William and Hugo sent hostages to King Otto via Duke Otto. A great famine spread throughout
the whole of France and Burgundy, and the cattle died in such great
numbers that hardly any animals of this kind were left in these
regions.

[943] In the year 943, Count Arnulf summoned William, the leader
of the Normans, to a conference and in tricking him, brought about
his death.[76] King Louis, gave the land of the Normans to [Richard]
the son of William, who had been born by a Breton concubine, and
certain leaders [*principes*] entrusted themselves to his [the king's]
rule.[77] Others, however, entrusted themselves to Duke Hugo ...
Hugo, duke of the Franks, got involved in frequent encounters with
the Normans who had arrived as pagans or who were returning to
paganism: a large number of his own Christian footsoldiers were killed
by them. But once some of the Normans had been killed and the rest
driven into flight, Hugo himself gained control of the town of Evreux,
for the Norman Christians who were holding it were supporters of
his. Meanwhile on his way back to Rouen Louis met Turmod of the
Normans – who had reverted to idolatry and to the gentile religion
and was urging [Richard] the son of William and others to lay a plot
against the king – whom he killed together with the pagan king
Setric;[78] having entrusted Rouen to Herluin, he turned back to
Compiègne, where Duke Hugo was awaiting him, with his nephews,
the sons of Herbert, whose recapture was frequently being mooted.
First of all then their king received Bishop Hugo.[79] Otto, duke of the

75 Otto, duke of Lotharingia (944–55).

76 All sources agree that Count Arnulf I of Flanders instigated the murder of William
   Longsword in 943.

77 On this reference rests the identification of Sprota, William Longsword's wife
   'according to the Danish custom', as of Breton origin.

78 Flodoard is the only source to refer to Turmod (unidentified) and Setric (?Sigtrygg
   of Hedeby). Viking leaders were often called king by their men.

79 Hugo, archbishop of Reims (925–31, 940–46).

Lotharingians and Bishop Adelbero acted as mediators, as well as Duke Hugo who was particularly insistent on this course; namely that the abbots whom he had dismissed when he set out to the king, be restored to [the authority of] Bishop Artold; that he should make provision for another bishopric, and also that the honours for his brothers and relations, which they had held from the bishopric of Reims should be returned. Afterwards the other sons of Count Herbert were also received by the king. Likewise King Louis set out from Rouen and recaptured Evreux from Duke Hugo, and at Paris, weighed down by sickness, he lay ill for almost the whole of the summer.

Bishop Hugo captured and burned the fortification at Ambly, which the brothers Robert and Rudolf, having been expelled from Reims, were holding and from where they were making plundering raids over the bishopric of Reims. Herluin met Arnulf, gained victory and slaughtered the man who had killed William, leader [*princeps*] of the Normans, and sent his body to Rouen with its hands chopped off.[80] Again, the above-mentioned Bishop Hugo besieged the stronghold of Omont, which Dodo, brother of Bishop Artold held.[81] At length, having accepted his [Dodo's] small son as a hostage, he departed, as was the request of the king as well. Duke Hugo raised the king's daughter from out of the baptismal water, and the king granted him the duchy of the Franks, and placed the whole of Burgundy under his authority. This same Hugo made peace between the king and Arnulf, to whom the king had been hostile on account of William's murder. King Otto captured certain of Louis's followers who had been plotting against him and sent them to prison. This created friction between the kings.

[944] Hugo, duke of the Franks, concluded a pact with the Normans, with hostages given and received on both sides. After that he prepared a sortie with Herbert's sons, intending to meet with King Otto in the realm of the Lotharingians. But this same king had different ideas about his arrival and drew up a large army against a certain Duke Herman. Once peace had been made between Herluin and Arnulf, King Louis gave the castle of Amiens to this same Herluin.[82]

[944–45] Thereupon followed the ruin of the Bretons who were divided among themselves by the dissension of their leaders [*principes*]

---

80 He may have been Balzo, chamberlain of Count Arnulf I.

81 Omont (Ardennes, arr. Mézières).

82 Herluin, count of Montreuil-sur-Mer (d. 945); see also no. **53**.

Berengar and Alan:[83] they were scattered by the Normans, with whom they had made a pact, and weakened by much slaughter. Their city Dol was captured and their bishop was overwhelmed by the throng of the crowds who sought refuge in the church, and was killed. At last the Bretons with their strength restored entered the fray in which they seemed to be superior to the Normans. Finally, at the onset of the third engagement, a great multitude fell on both sides. But in fact the Normans, with victory on their side, massacred the Bretons and drove them from their territory. The Normans themselves, freshly arrived from the lands across the sea, invaded their territory.

King Louis set off into the land of the Normans with Arnulf and Herluin and with certain bishops from France and Burgundy. And so Arnulf went in advance of the king, scattered some Normans near Arques, who were in charge of its defence, and made preparations for the king's passage. Thus the king reached Rouen and was received in the city by the Normans. Some of their number went out onto the sea because they did not want to welcome him, the others were entirely under his sway. Duke Hugo with his men and certain leaders from Burgundy crossed the Seine, reached Bayeux and besieged the city which the king had given to him, in the hope that he would help him to subjugate this Norman people for himself. But the king, having been received by the Normans, instructed the duke to abandon the siege on the above-mentioned city. Upon his departure, the king entered the city. This act kindled trouble between the king and the duke. Furthermore, on his behalf the king received hostages from the people of Evreux, who had been subject to Hugo, and he was now unwilling to give them back to the duke.

In the year 945 while King Louis was still at Rouen, Queen Gerberga at Laon gave birth to a son, who was called Charles at his christening. The king returned to Laon, spoke with Arnulf, and when certain matters had been sorted out, returned to Rouen. Now Count Bernard of Senlis and Theobald of Tours, along with Herbert attacked the king's castle at Montigny during Easter.[84] They captured it, set it on fire and destroyed it. This same Bernard also fell upon the king's hounds and huntsmen, and carried off their horses and whatever else seemed good to him. He even ranged through Compiègne, a royal town, along with certain manors which were subject to this place.

---

83 Alan II Barbetorte of Brittany had fled to England c. 919 and returned in 936; he died in 952. Berengar was Judicael Berengar, count of Rennes.

84 Bernard of Senlis (d. c. 945).

King Louis gathered an army of Normans about him and laid waste
the district of Vermandois. And he took Herluin and his men with him
together with part of Arnulf's troops, Bishop Artold, whose men had
been driven out of Reims a short while ago and also Count Bernard
and Count Thierry, his nephew, and besieged the city of Reims.[85] The
crops round about were laid waste, villages were pillaged and generally burned to the ground and a good many churches were broken
into. For all those who were wounded while fighting at the gates or
about the walls on both sides, a significant number were also killed.
Duke Hugo finally joined battle with the Normans who had invaded
his territory. He routed them with excessive slaughter and expelled
them from his territories. After this he sent hostages from Reims to
the king, so that Rainald might attend a meeting with him on the
king's behalf. Upon his departure Duke Hugo dealt with him in such
a way that the king should receive hostages from Bishop Hugo and
abandon the siege of Reims, so that the same bishop at the agreed
meeting should come forwards, to give his opinion about all those
things which the king had asked of him. When these things were
provided for him along these lines, the king left the siege, fifteen days
after the city had been besieged. At around the time of St John's Mass
[24 June], therefore, Duke Hugo held a meeting with the king, via
agents. Nothing was brought to bear to secure a sure peace between
them and they only went as far as a bilateral treaty to last until the
middle of the month of August.

   And so, when this had been accomplished, King Louis, supported
by Herluin and some of his own personal retinue, set out for Rouen.
Lord Teutolo, bishop of the city of Tours and a venerable man, died.
He, while striving to broker peace between the king and the princes
[*principes*], and occupied by these endeavours whilst he returned from
Laon, was struck down with a bodily illness on that very journey.
And when he had breathed his last breath, a certain sign of light
appeared, flashing about through the air. It seemed to be a cubit in
length. Those who carried away his body were sufficiently served by
this light to drive away the shadows of the night. Having been
granted so great a consolation, they carried his body all the way to
Tours, a distance of some two hundred miles, so they say. The body
was duly buried in the monastery of Saint-Julian, which this same
holy man had founded with great piety, next to the tomb of Lord Odo.
Thereafter it was declared that the church itself was a sign of a divine
miracle.

85 Bernard, count of Rethel.

While King Louis remained in Rouen, Hagrold the Norman, who was pre-eminent in Bayeux, instructed him that he would come to him at an agreed time or place, if the king came to that place.[86] When the king finally came with a few men to the agreed place, Hagrold came armed with a crowd of Normans, and attacking, killed almost all of the king's companions. The king took flight on his own, followed by one faithful Norman. With this man he reached Rouen, where he was seized by other Normans whom he thought were loyal to him and was put in prison ... While Duke Hugo made efforts for the release of the king, the Normans sought out the sons of the king himself to be given over to them as hostages, for they would not let the king go under any other circumstances. Therefore messengers were sent to the queen for her sons. Sending the younger boy, she said that she would not send the elder.[87] The younger boy was thus handed over, and in order for the king to be released, Guy bishop of Soissons surrendered himself as a hostage.[88] Thus released from the Normans, the king was taken up by Prince Hugo. And Hugo, entrusting him to Theobald, one of his own men, set out to meet King Otto.

[960] Richard, the son of William, leader [*princeps*] of the Normans, married the daughter of Hugo, one time leader of the area beyond the Seine.[89]

11 Adémar of Chabannes, Chronicle

The chronicle of Adémar of Chabannes was written before 1034. The following passage is an important testimony of how people in Aquitaine viewed the settlement of the vikings in Normandy under the leadership of Rollo. It should be remembered that Rollo's daughter Gerloc/Adela married Count William III of Aquitaine (= William I of Poitou) and in due course provided money and monks from Saint-Cyprien at Poitiers to re-found the monastery of Jumièges. Indirectly, she may have been responsible for knowledge about early Normandy in south-west France.

Adémar de Chabannes, Chronique, ed. J. Chavanon (Paris, 1897), p. 139.

---

86 Harold was a viking leader based at Bayeux in the 940s. Both Dudo and William of Jumièges erroneously identify him with King Harold Bluetooth of Denmark (941–88) (Dudo, 239) and *GND*, i, 88–91.

87 The younger one was Charles, who died in 953.

88 Guy, bishop of Soissons (*c.* 937–73).

89 Emma, daughter of Duke Hugh, died without children after 968 (Fauroux, no. 3).

[Book III, c. 20] ... And at that time Rodulf, king of Burgundy, attacked Limoges with the bravest of enemy host.[90] And countless numbers of Normans [Normanni] assembled to oppose him. Once battle was joined in the region which is called Estresse, the pagans were devastated to their core and those who did escape held out little hope of reaching Aquitaine. So Rodulf thanked God for whose love he had staked his own life and returned with a great victory. And the Normans who had retreated to find their territory deserted, set up their own home [sedem] in Rouen with Rosso (= Rollo) as their leader. He had become a Christian and had made many of his captives Christian, whom before he would have had beheaded in honour of the gods whom he had worshipped. And he also distributed an infinite amount of gold to the churches of the Christians in honour of the true God in whose name he had been baptised.

12   Geoffrey Malaterra, Deeds of Count Roger and his brother Duke Robert

The Deeds of Count Roger of Calabria and Sicily and of Duke Robert Guiscard his brother was written c. 1090 by Geoffrey, a Norman, who had moved to southern Italy and worked at the court of Count Roger.

De rebus gestis Rogerii Calabriae et Siciliae Comitis et Roberti Guiscardi fratris eius auctore Gaufredo Malaterra, ed. E. Pontieri (Bologna, 1927), pp. 7–8; trsl. G. A. Loud.

[Book I, c. 1] The land of Normandy is in Gaul, but it was not always called Normandy. Once it, and everything that appertained to it, was part of the royal fisc of the king of the Franks, which was called by the general name of France [*Francia*]; up to the time when a very brave leader called Rollo sailed boldly from Norway with his fleet to the Christian coast, accompanied by a strong force of soldiers. He ravaged Frisia and other maritime areas to the west, and finally reached the port where the River Seine flows into the sea. His great fleet sailed up this river into the more inland areas of France, and seeing how fertile this area was, more so than the other regions which they had crossed, he conceived a desire to seize it and take it for his own. For it is a land with rivers full of fish and woods full of wild animals, fertile and suitable for corn and other crops, with rich

---

90 Rudolf I, king of Burgundy (888–911); the site of the battle is probably Estresse near Beaulieu.

meadows to feed cattle, and thus very likely to excite the greedy. For this reason they landed on each bank and began to make the inhabitants of the province subject to his rule.

[Book I, c. 2] However, the king who was at that time ruling over France – I think it was Louis II – was at first furious when he learnt that enemies had invaded the frontiers of his empire.[91] He raised an army, marched against the enemy and appointed a duke to expel them from his lands. But then he realised that this could not be done without great casualties among his men. Fearing the uncertain events of war and wishing to spare bloodshed among his followers, he took counsel and concluded a peace treaty. Accepting the service which they offered to him, he granted them the bulk of the land which they had invaded as a benefice [*beneficium*]. The land which had been granted to them stretched [westwards] from the area of Ponthieu on its eastern border, and was next to the English Channel, which lay between it and Britain on its northern side and bounded its western extent also. On its south-west frontier there was the area of Maine, and then the border went as far as Chartres, from Chartres it went to Abbeville and Beauvais, up to Ponthieu. Duke Rollo received this land outlined above from the king of the Franks as a hereditary fief [*haereditali feudo*]; he then distributed it among his followers depending on how close he was to them, reserving the most valuable land for his own use. Since we have now given a brief description of the land which they held, it seems proper to say something about the character of this people.

[Book I, c. 3] They are a most astute people, eager to avenge injuries, looking rather to enrich themselves from others than from their native fields. They are eager and greedy for profit and power, hyper-critical and deceitful about almost everything, but between generosity and avarice they take a middle course. Their leaders are, however, very generous since they wish to achieve a great reputation. They know how to flatter, and are much addicted to the cultivation of eloquence, to such an extent that one listens even to their young boys as though they were trained speakers. And unless they are held in thrall by the yoke of justice, they are a most unbridled people. When circumstances require they are prepared to put up with hard work, hunger and cold; they are much addicted to hunting and hawking, and they delight in fancy clothes and elaborate trappings for their horses

91 Not King Louis the Stammerer (d. 879), but his son King Charles III the Simple.

and decorations on their other weapons. They derive the name of their land from their own name: *north* in the English language means 'the northern region' [*aquilonis plaga*], and since they come from the north they are called Normans and their land Normandy.

13   The Life of Gruffydd ap Cynan

The anonymous author of the Life of Gruffydd ap Cynan wrote not long after King Gruffydd's death in 1137. As part of the account of the ancestry of King Gruffydd's maternal grandfather, the author claims that Rollo, called Rodulf, was the brother of King Harold Haarfaga. The story is interesting because it gives a Welsh/English perspective on the origin of the Normans in France.

A Medieval Prince of Wales: The Life of Gruffydd ap Cynan, ed. and trsl. D. S. Evans (Llanerch, 1990), p. 56.

The third brother, namely Rodulf (= Rollo), voyaged with his fleet to France, where he settled and overcame the French through warfare, and subdued a large part of France which is now called Normandy, because the men of Norway inhabit it; they are a people from Llychlyn; and that land was divided into twelve parts, according to the barons and leaders who first came to the part of France called Brittany or Llydaw. They built many cities there: 'Rodum' [Rouen], from King Rodulf its founder, which was named as Rome from Romulus, and Remys from Remus; and many other cities and castles and strongholds did he build. From him came the Norman kings who subdued England in battle, namely King William and his two sons, who succeeded him, William Long-Sword, and Henry and Stephen his nephew, who were contemporaries of king Gruffydd.[92]

14   Snorri Sturluson, *Heimskringla*, Saga of Harald Fairhair

Snorri wrote *c.* 1220 and recorded the Scandinavian tradition of the origin of the Norman dukes. Rollo is identified as the Norse Hrolf/Rolf the Ganger, son of Ragnvald, jarl of Möre, and Hild, daughter of Rolf Nevja. Whereas the prose part of the sage is thirteenth-century, the skaldic poem of Rollo's mother Hild is more or less contemporary to his outlawry.

From the Sagas of the Norse Kings by Snorri Sturluson, trsl. E. Monsen and A. H. Smith (Oslo, 1967), pp. 35–6; the translation of Hild's poem is by Jesch, 1991, 163–4.

92 William Rufus, king of England (1087–1100), is not otherwise known as William Longsword.

[c. 24] ... Ragnvald the Jarl was King Harald's dearest friend and the king valued him highly.[93] Ragnvald had for his wife Hild the daughter of Rolf Nevja, and their sons were Rolf and Tore. He also had bastard sons, called Hallad, the next Einar and the third Rollaug. They were full grown when their legitimate brothers were still children. Rolf was a great viking; he was grown so big that no horse could bear him and he therefore walked everywhere; he was called Rolf the Ganger. He harried much in the eastern countries. One summer when he had come to Viken, he learned of this he became very wroth, for he had strongly forbidden robbery in the land.[94] At the *thing*, therefore, King Harald declared Rolf to be an outlaw in Norway. But the king was so wroth that her asking availed her naught. Then quoth Hild:

> The name of Nevja is torn
> Now driven in flight from the land
> Is the warrior's bold kinsman.
> Why be so hard, my lord?
> Evil it is by such a wolf,
> Noble prince, to be bitten;
> He will not spare the flock
> If he is driven to the woods.

Rolf the Ganger afterwards crossed the sea to the Hebrides and from there went south-west to France;[95] he harried there and possessed himself of a great jarldom; he settled many Norsemen there, and it was afterwards called Normandy. From Rolf are descended the jarls of Normandy. Rolf the Ganger's son was William, the father of Richard, the father of another Richard, the father of Robert Longsword, the father of William the Bastard, king of England, from whom are descended all the later kings of England ...[96]

---

93 Harold, king of Norway (*c.* 872–930); Ragnvald was earl of Möre, a western province of Norway.

94 Viken, region near Oslo.

95 For the settlement of Ragnvald's sons in the Orkneys and Hebrides, see Morris, 1985, 210–42; Crawford, 1987, 63–9.

96 Interestingly the nickname 'Longsword' is here used not for William but for his great-grandson Robert the Magnificent.

II: THE NORMANS IN NORMANDY

Introduction

By 1066 Normandy had established itself as one of the most stable
and successful principalities in France. Rollo's dynasty had eliminated
all rivals and taking advantage of rivalries between neighbouring
powers had achieved a measure of independence from the French
kings. In order to maintain their relative independence the dukes
channelled their financial and military resources into defending their
frontiers, with great success. Effective ducal control over defence,
finances, administration and justice was the key to the Rollonid
success. How the dukes coped with their ever extending kin, how they
kept control over the building of castles, and how they maintained
law and order are the main questions addressed here. Attention is also
paid to the abundance of evidence concerning Norman women and
children.

After William Longsword (c. 928–43), successive rulers maintained a
careful balance within the ducal kin between legitimate and illegitimate offspring, allowing siblings to participate in the delegated
exercise of ducal power.[1] Nevertheless, rivalry between different kin
groups inevitably arose because of the dukes' multiple marriages.
Most of them had at least one mistress, to whom they were married
'according to Danish custom' and by whom they had offspring, as well
as one or two wives to whom they were married in the Christian
way.[2] Thus William Longsword had a concubine called Sprota and a
legitimate wife, Leyarda of Vermandois. Richard I (943–96), son of
Sprota, first married Emma, a Frankish Christian noblewoman, but he
had no children by her. Thereafter he married Gunnor, a woman of
Danish origin, who was already his mistress. She was the mother of
most of his children, but he had at least one other concubine who bore
him some children. Richard II (996–1026), Gunnor's son, married two

---

1 For the rivalries within the ducal clan, see Searle, 1988 (Part 3: Kinship by choice,
93–120; Part 4: The house of the Richards, 121–58, and Part 5: Predatory kinship,
159–92).

2 Eames, 1952, 195–208 and *GND passim*; see also the genealogical charts 1–4.

legitimate wives in succession (Judith of Brittany, and Papia) and had sons by both, as well as a series of illegitimate children by a variety of (unnamed) women. Richard III (1026–27), Judith's son, had a legitimate wife who bore him no children and a son (Abbot Nicholas of Saint-Ouen, d. 1092) and several daughters by one or more mistresses. Richard III's brother Robert the Magnificent (1027–35) had several children by at least two mistresses: Herleva bore him William the Conqueror and one or more mistresses were the mother(s) of his daughters. The Conqueror (1035–87) himself is exceptional in that he is not known to have had any children other than those by his wife, Matilda of Flanders. Of his sons, the eldest, Robert Curthose (duke of Normandy 1087–1106, d. by 1134), had Sibyl of Conversano, an Italian woman, as his wife and one son William Clito by her, plus several children by a variety of concubines. The second, William Rufus (king of England 1087–1100) never married and is generally believed to have been homosexual. The youngest, Henry I (king of England 1100–35, duke of Normandy 1106–35) had two children by his English wife Matilda II, William Adelin (d. 1120) and Empress Matilda (d. 1167), and at least twenty illegitimate children by a succession of concubines some of whom are known by name.

Rivalry within the ducal kin was common and posed continuous dangers to the man who was duke, whose office was and remained indivisible (see below). One way of dealing with the threat to ducal power by kinsmen (brothers in particular) was for the duke to selectively delegate some authority to brothers and half-brothers. Richard I's half-brother Rodolf of Ivry (Sprota's son) was his most trusted adviser and also advised his son Richard II. His second son Robert became archbishop of Rouen (989–1037) and advised three generations of dukes (Richard I, Richard II and the brothers Richard III and Robert the Magnificent). Richard II's son Malger (by Papia), and thus a half-brother of Richard III and Robert the Magnificent, succeeded Robert as archbishop of Rouen (1037–54/55). However, Richard II's other son by Papia, William of Arques, another half-brother of Richard III and Robert, caused problems by challenging the succession to Robert the Magnificent. He based his claim on the illegitimacy of William (the Conqueror) and his own legitimate descent from Richard II. Any half-brothers, especially those with whom they shared a father, posed threats to their position as heir and successor before they succeeded to the ducal office. Amicable relations between ducal half-siblings were more common among those who shared a mother. Maternal half-brothers often rose to important positions in

Normandy. Count Rodolf of Ivry, Sprota's son, has already been mentioned. Others are William the Conqueror's half-brothers who were sons of his mother Herleva by Herluin of Conteville: Odo, later bishop of Bayeux (d. 1097), and Robert, later count of Mortain (d. *c.* 1095). Henry I's illegitimate son Robert, earl of Gloucester, ultimately became the greatest advocate for his half-sister Empress Matilda, Henry's designated successor, in her struggle against King Stephen.

An effective way of placating male kin was through the distribution of secular and ecclesiastical offices, and the rise of the title of duke, first found in charters of Richard II, is directly linked to that duke's creation of the office of count for his rebellious brothers: Godfrey, who became count of Eu and probably also of Brionne [16], William of Hiémois, later count of Eu [15], and Robert, count of Mortain or Avranches. If Richard II were to call his siblings 'count' he needed a more exalted title for himself.[3] As time passed and the ducal kin expanded, the principality remained under the control of one man, the duke. In this process it was of crucial importance that the office of duke was indivisible: only one son at the time (usually the eldest) could succeed as duke, normally after he had been designated as heir and successor by his father.[4] All dukes produced sons and many of them survived, so that there was no shortage of male heirs, even though William the Conqueror faced stiff opposition because of his illegitimate birth. The dramatic exception was the tragic death of William Adelin in the White Ship disaster of 1120, which deprived King Henry I of his only legitimate son and forced him to accept his daughter Matilda as his heir. Thus problems about the succession should in theory have been rare; in practice, however, there were plenty of them as the chronicles of William of Jumièges and William of Poitiers testify.

Many important aristocratic families sprang from siblings or half-siblings of dukes, not least because of the influence that the duchesses who were the mothers of those siblings could sometimes exercise. Little research has been done into the role of the Norman duchesses, but what we know is indicative of pragmatic authority. Two examples may suffice here. Countess Gunnor (a girl of noble Danish origin according to Dudo [26], but a forester's daughter from the Pays-de-Caux according to Robert of Torigni [28]) survived not only her husband Richard I by more than three decades but most of her sons

3 Douglas, 1946, 129–56.

4 Garnett, 1994, 80–110.

and daughters as well. Her life between *c.* 950 and 1031 spanned a crucial period of political growth in Normandy. Gunnor's own contribution to that growth is difficult to assess, but judging by the prosperous marriages of her daughters (Emma married two consecutive kings of England: Aethelred II and Cnut; Hadvisa was married to Geoffrey of Brittany and Matilda to Odo of Blois-Chartres), by her own attestations in ducal charters up to the 1020s and by other evidence she was a formidable person.[5] Skilled in languages and with an excellent memory, she was probably one of the informants of the historian Dudo of Saint-Quentin about the early history of Normandy [26]. Her contribution to the restoration of the cathedral of Coutances, not very far from Mont-Saint-Michel, must have helped her son Richard II's policy of ducal expansion in western Normandy [8]. During her long widowhood she was frequently at the side of her sons, and she, presumably, deputised for the duke on occasion. In a poem called *Moriuht* written around 1026, Warner of Rouen, a contemporary of the chronicler Dudo of Saint-Quentin, alleges that Gunnor's intervention led to the manumission (freedom from slavery) of Moriuht's wife Glicerium and of their unnamed daughter. Warner's pen portrait reveals a woman of understanding and diplomatic skill, possessing a sense of humour rare in medieval female portraits [27]. Gunnor was also instrumental in the marriages of her sisters and nieces, who became the female ancestors of many Anglo-Norman families with large estates on both sides of the Channel [28]. The other clear example of authority of a ducal spouse comes from the second half of the eleventh century and centres on Matilda of Flanders, wife of William the Conqueror. The couple's charters reveal Matilda as her husband's deputy as mediator or judge, as his regent in Normandy, and as co-judge in dispute settlements [18], while her mediation between her husband and her eldest son Robert illustrates the perennial role of the medieval aristocratic mother in (political) settlement between rival fathers and sons [56].

Their ability to suppress military opposition within Normandy depended on the dukes' control over castellans, the men in charge of fortifications and castles.[6] The control over castles in Normandy, however, should be viewed in the context of control over castles in France north of the Loire. The proliferation throughout this area of

5 Fauroux nos 14 bis (1012) – 21 (1015–17), 29 (1015–c. 1025), 32 (1021–25), 43 (1015–26) and 47 (1017–26).

6 Yver, 1955, 28–115 and Bates, 1982, 114–16.

fortifications during the tenth and eleventh centuries had a tendency to consolidate the local power of the aristocracy at the same time that the fortifications also strengthened a territorial principality's defence. In some regions of northern France the noble castle became an effective centre of tax collection and jurisdiction. By and large Normandy (and much of the land north of the Loire) did not experience so drastic a breakdown of authority and public power remained either in the duke's hand or was acknowledged as having been delegated by him. Such a view is clearly expressed in William the Conqueror's laws, written down in the time of his sons:

> No one in Normandy might dig a fosse in the open country of more than one shovel's throw in depth nor set more than one line of palisade, and that without battlements or alures [wooden walkways on the top]. And no one might make a fortification on rock or island and no one might raise a castle in Normandy and no one in Normandy might withhold the possession of his castle from the lord of Normandy if he wishes to take it into his hand.[7]

This law referred to castles newly built in the Conqueror's time, but probably applied equally to the time of his predecessors when certain ducal fortications were entrusted by the duke to a magnate, usually for his lifetime. Good examples are the fortifications entrusted by Richard II to Gilbert I Crispin (see below) or by William the Conqueror to his cousin Guy of Brionne in the 1040s. However, there were also fortifications that had been built by local families. The castle of Laigle was one of the earliest in Normandy, built by a certain Fulbert *de Beina* at the time of, but not necessarily with the permission of, Duke Richard II.[8] Other pre-1066 non-ducal castles are known at Vernon, Gaillefontaine, La Ferté-en-Bray, Breteuil and Moulins-la-Marche.[9] Complications could arise when the distinction between ducal castles and private castles became blurred, a situation that was more common on the frontiers than elsewhere. In border areas a shift in the balance of power might easily lead to a castellan transferring allegiance to a neighbouring territorial prince. Again the example of the castle at Tillières (see below) offers the best illustration for this phenomenon.

Whereas the comital positions in Normandy were reserved for members of the ducal family, the lower ranks of castellans and vicomtes were occupied by local noble families such as the Crispins (so-called

7 Haskins, 1918, 282; the translation is by Brown, 1984, 153.

8 Thompson, 1995, 177–99 at 177–9.

9 Bates, 1982, 114.

because of their crisp hairstyle), who were vicomtes and castellans of Tillières, a castle on the River Avre built by Richard II [24]. The custody of Tillières was entrusted to the Crispins from the time of its construction c. 1005 onwards, but the overall control of it shifted between the dukes of Normandy and the kings of France due no doubt to the changing policy of its castellans.[10] At some stage during Duke Robert the Magnificent's reign it was in the hands of King Henry I (1031–60), as we know from William of Jumièges's account of how Robert's son William regained it,[11] and what happened before then can be reconstructed thanks to the survival of one Norman soldier's tale in a narrative history of the Normans in Italy [30]. Serlo of Hauteville, the only one of Tancred of Hauteville's many mercenary sons who did not go to Italy, took part in the defence of Tillières as one of Duke Robert's soldiers. During the siege he decapitated one of the French assailants and carried the dead man's head around for all to see. Serlo's act is a prime example of the aggressive Norman triumphalism which soldiers displayed in times of war, though William the Conqueror's apologists were careful not to draw attention to it in their chronicles.

Most castles were built on strategic sites on hilltops and near rivers along the borders, for example (from north to south) at Eu and Aumale on the River Bresle, Neaufles and Gisors on the River Epte, Ivry, Dreux and Tillières on the River Avre, with Alençon, Domfront and St James along the southern border. The geography of the site as well as architectural ingenuity determined the great variety of fortifications. The best-known, but not necessarily the most wide spread, were the motte and bailey type castles so well known from the Bayeux Tapestry.[12] More common were the earthwork enclosures surrounded by wooden palisades such as the one found at Grimbosq (Calvados) and at many places in the Pays-de-Caux. Larger fortifications were those built by the dukes themselves and which functioned as their palaces at Caen and Fécamp. The architecture is seldom described in narrative sources, which reveal interesting details only in passing, as in the story of William of Eu who was held captive in the tower of Rouen

---

10 *GND*, ii, 22–3 and Green, 1984, 47–61.

11 *GND*, ii, 100–1.

12 Bates, 1982, 115 and Le Maho, 1976, 83–7; for Caen, see M. de Bouard, *Le Château de Caen* (Caen, 1979) and for Fécamp, see A. Renoux, *Fécamp: du palais ducal au palais de Dieu. Bilan historique et archéologique des recherches menés sur le site du château des ducs de Normandie (IIe siècle A.C. – XVIIIe siècle P.C.* (Paris, 1991).

until he escaped from an upstairs window, the early eleventh-century tower in question was that of the ducal castle of Rouen [15].

Whereas strongholds were built for the defence of towns, some towns came into existence on account of fortifications. The origin of bourgs, market quarters adjacent to existing towns (Coutances), to new towns (Mortain), or to monasteries is an interesting Norman phenomenon because the dukes encouraged their growth by granting freedom to their inhabitants and by encouraging the division of market income between the local lord (or in the case of a monastery, the abbot) and themselves. The widescale building programmes of castles, bourgs and churches in eleventh-century Normandy testify to the wealth amassed by its dukes and the aristocracy, both secular and ecclesiastical.[13] The numerous references to payments in cash, alongside payments in kind, also illustrate the ready availability of silver coinage [18].[14] At the same time it shows that taxation was gathered with, perhaps, more efficiency and enforcement than in other principalities of France.

Military superiority and economic wealth can only flourish in an environment where law and order prevail, an ideal situation to which any territorial prince aspired but which few could achieve (except on the pages written by their apologists). I have already discussed in the previous chapter how emergency laws were enacted by Rollo, after the defence of Rouen had been entrusted to him and his viking followers. His legislation, presumably, combined Frankish and Scandinavian elements. Most historians now accept that the Frankish customs gradually took over, although a few Scandinavian ones never disappeared. We have already encountered exile as a ducal right that was of Scandinavian origin, whether as an indigenous survival or imported from the Danelaw. Its frequent use by the duke to get rid of disobedient, rebellious or otherwise internal troublemakers shows ducal authority in practice, especially by Robert the Magnificent and William the Conqueror. However, the very fact that they had to resort to these measures also illustrates their failure in keeping rebels within their territory under control. It is perhaps no surprise that the periods of most exiles coincide with the aftermath of serious internal disturbances, the minority of William the Conqueror in the late 1030s and early 1040s being the most notorious. As we will see in Chapter V, exile also partly explains the appearance of Normans elsewhere in

13 Musset, 1959, 285–99.
14 Bates, 1982, 96–8.

Europe. Serlo of Hauteville [30] was apparently banned by Robert the Magnificent, while Hugh Bunel, accused of the murder of Mabel of Bellême, left with his three brothers of his own accord [86]. Arnold of Echauffour was exiled in the early 1060s and left together with his son William. Dukes sometimes changed their minds under pressure of circumstance, however. Arnold of Echauffour is a case in point. According to Orderic Vitalis, Duke William was persuaded to recall him c. 1063 for a planned invasion of Maine along with Ralph of Tosny and Hugh of Grandmesnil. They were all men from the southern border area whose local knowledge William could presumably not afford to lose. Arnold, having visited Apulia, 'where his friends and kinsmen enjoyed rich possessions', returned to Normandy 'laden with wealth and ... a costly mantle' which he gave to the duke.[15] Those who left the country without the permission of the duke found themselves disinherited as though they had been exiled, as is illustrated by the case of Baudri, son of Nicholas, who went off to Spain. He too, however, was reinstated under an amnesty announced during the Conqueror's last and fatal illness in 1087.[16]

Exile and unauthorised departure from Normandy were matters that concerned only the free and wealthy members of Norman society. Very little is known about the lower classes and the unfree. Evidence for serfdom or slavery in Normandy is hard to come by, but Lucien Musset has shown that it did exist, albeit on a much smaller scale than elsewhere in France. The relative freedom of most Normans may be attributable, he suggests, to the invasions of Rollo and his contemporaries, not on the grounds that they brought traditions of freedom with them from Scandinavia, but on the grounds that raids on coastal areas of France caused depopulation. Freedom may have been offered to newcomers in order to repopulate the land.[17]

A glimpse of the harsh treatment applied by the duke to 'disobedient' peasants is provided by William of Jumièges at the start of his history of the reign of Duke Richard II (996–1026). One of the first acts of Richard II's reign was the suppression of an otherwise unattested peasants' revolt:[18]

15 Orderic, ii, 104–6.

16 Orderic, iv, 100.

17 Musset, 1988, 5–24. Barthélemy (1992, 233–84 at 252–3, n. 114), however, is sceptical about Musset's hyphothesis and points out that there are sufficient examples of serfdom and other forms of social dependence to consider the situation in Normandy as not significantly different from the rest of the north of France.

18 *GND*, ii, 8; the peasant revolt is discussed in Arnoux, 1992, 45–51.

> Throughout every part of Normandy the peasants unanimously formed many assemblies and decided to live according to their own wishes, such that in respect both of short cuts through woods and of the traffic of the rivers with no bar of previously established right of way, they might follow laws of their own. In order to ratify these new decrees, each of the rebellious peasants' groups chose two envoys who brought the decisions for confirmation to an assembly held in the middle of the province.

Written from the perspective of the duke, that account suggests rebellion. Another, more likely, interpretation is that free farmers and peasants joined together protesting against new or increasing demands on their time and labour. The building of castles, the guarding of castles and other such duties are unlikely to have formed part of their fathers' or grandfathers' obligations to the duke. In order to enforce such demands and prevent further uprisings Duke Richard II, together with his uncle Count Rodolf of Ivry, harshly punished the culprits by cutting off their hands and feet. No ducal lawcodes have survived, but on the basis of scraps of information in chronicles and charters historians now broadly agree that Norman custom was formed and crystallised during the reign of William the Conqueror and more precisely between 1047 and 1077.[19]

In the context of Norman law and justice something needs to be said about the exceptional position of women as part of the legal process. Normandy is the first principality for which we have evidence that women could act as legal witnesses. According to the Le Très ancien coutumier, the oldest known Norman lawcode, compiled in 1199, there was a recognised role for 'good women and legal matrons' who were appointed by the duke to testify in cases involving virginity, rape and contested births.[20] Although it is now impossible to trace when this female office was established, we can catch a glimpse of it in a case concerning a disputed child, which was heard in the late 1060s, but was recorded in a charter from Jumièges dated to the early 1080s [18]. The only woman mentioned among the witnesses, apart from the Conqueror's wife Matilda, was Alberada, wife of Robert *Insule*. Her presence may be explained if we accept that she was just such a 'good woman or legal matron' called in to verify the claims of the two parties in the dispute, the real and the substitute mother of the child. Norman sources also provide glimpses of the use that was made of children as witnesses in legal transactions. The children, all boys, are

19 Tabuteau, 1988, 224–5.

20 *Coutumiers de Normandie*, ed. E. J. Tardif (Rouen, 1881), pp. 40–1.

mentioned among the witnesses of monastic grants made by the duke.[21] They were young when they were required to attend such ceremonies, often under ten, the idea being that they would testify to the grants when they grew older. To make sure they would not forget the occasions, the duke or the boy's father would slap them in the face or otherwise mildly maltreat them; the boys were meant to remember the pain and hence the day's significance [19]. Such *aides-mémoire* were important in an illiterate society, where much depended on oral testimony.

It hardly needs stressing that Norman society included women and children as well as their menfolk, but they have not reeived the scholarly attention they deserve. Apart from documents quoted above, the monastic chronicles and hagiographical texts from Normandy are surprisingly forthcoming about their lives. One miracle story from Asnebecq, recorded at Saint-Wandrille, describes how children were playing in the forecourt of a castle when suddenly one of the little girls fell ill [21]. Through the intervention of St Vulfran, invoked by the girl's mother on the advice of her chaplain, the girl recovered and resumed playing. Such instances are important reminders that family life went on in castles we normally exclusively associate with warfare. Virtually unknown to scholars is the story of the anonymous married woman from the area of Lisieux who after several suicide attempts was committed to the care of the nuns of Saint-Amand at Rouen [23]. Once in the nunnery she saw her chance and almost managed to kill herself by hanging in the church's nave. She was saved, through the intervention of St Amand and the presence of mind of one of her carers.[22] The story throws some exceptional light on the tasks nuns were expected to perform, which evidently included caring for mentally unstable women. Abbess Marsilia, the author of the text, is herself remarkable for having written down the story as a contribution to the hagiographical dossier compiled by the monks of Saint-Amand in Flanders. Marsilia's letter is one of the very few surviving literary works by women in Normandy.

Many women of noble origin who became widows retired to monasteries and spent their final days in contemplation. Le Bec made provision for noblewomen very early on after its foundation in the 1030s. Heloise, Abbot Herluin's mother, joined her son and his monks and

21 Tabuteau, 1988, 149–50.

22 Platelle, 1967, 83–106; Van Houts, 1999, 56–7.

helped doing menial jobs such as cooking and baking. On one such occasion the oven caught fire and the kitchen burnt down. Fortunately, Heloise was unharmed [16]. Eve Crispin (née Montfort-l'Amaury) and Basilia of Gournay (née Fleitel) both died in their ninetieth year in 1099 at Le Bec, where they had lived with Basilia's niece Ansfrida.[23] There is no evidence that any of the Norman duchesses retired to a nunnery or monastery and we know for sure that Matilda I did not retire to Sainte-Trinité at Caen although she had founded this herself. However, their daughters did. Matilda I's daughter Cecilia was offered to Sainte-Trinité as an oblate and became abbess there [39]. In her widowhood, Empress Matilda, daughter of King Henry I of England, spent the last years of her life at Le Bec's priory of Notre Dame des Prés near Rouen.[24]

Contrary to common assumptions, monks often remained in touch with their family and in particular with their mothers. If a mother came to live at her son's monastery they obviously saw each other regularly, but even if this did not happen monks would stay in contact. Eadmer of Canterbury tells a story about a monk at Christ Church Canterbury (perhaps himself) who regularly paid a sum of money to his mother for her upkeep. One day, the monk discovered that he had lost the money and told Archbishop Lanfranc, who kindly gave him another sum with which he could pay his mother. Though the story is set in post-conquest Canterbury, such an event could have taken place in Le Bec, where Lanfranc had been a monk for many years [25].

15   William of Jumièges, Deeds of the Dukes of the Normans

William of Jumièges in his Deeds of the Dukes of the Normans describes how the dukes dealt with their paternal kin. The first text deals with the conflict (c. 1000) between Duke Richard II and his half-brother William of Hiémois, whom he afterwards made count of Eu (c. 975 to after 1040). The second one concerns Duke William the Conqueror and William of Arques, half-brother of his father Duke Robert the Magnificent, who did not accept William as Duke Robert's successor in 1035 and rebelled c. 1051. Noteworthy in this extract is the support given by King Henry I of France (1031–60) for William of Arques and not for Duke William.

GND, ii, 8–11, 102–5.

23 Porée, i, 183–4.
24 Chibnall, 1991, 151–4.

[Book V, c. 3] At the same time the insolence of some wicked men made William one of the duke [Richard II]'s brothers by the same father [Richard I], arrogant and rebellious. ~~By the friendship of his brother he had received the county of Hiémois as a gift, so that he could provide him with military support,~~ but misled by the cunning of evil men, he ~~despised his lordship and refused the obedience due from fealty.~~ After the duke had rebuked him several times through messengers and William had obstinately refused to back down, the duke, on the advice and with the support of Count Rodulf, ~~made him prisoner and kept him in custody in the tower of the city of Rouen, where he made amendment for his rebellion for five years.~~[25] Some of William's retainers, who had continued his rebellion, were killed in successive battles and others were exiled from their lands. Finally, after five years William with the help of one of his followers escaped from the tower by climbing down a very long rope hung from the highest window. During day time he hid himself in order not to be found by those looking for him, while at night he journeyed. Finally, he wondered whether it would be better for him to risk his life and seek his brother's forgiveness than without any hope of success, to ask help from some other king or count. One day, while making his way in this state of mind, he encountered the duke who was hunting in the valley of Vernon.[26] He threw himself on the ground at his feet, and miserably asked for forgiveness for his misdeeds. ~~The duke, instantly moved with compassion and with the support of Count Rodulf raised him from the ground and upon hearing his brother's own account of his escape he not only forgave him his faults but from that moment~~ onwards also benevolently loved him as his favourite brother. ~~Not long afterwards he entrusted him with the county of~~ Eu, and gave him in marriage a very beautiful girl called Lescelina, daughter of a nobleman called Turketil.[27] She bore him three sons: ~~Robert, who after his death was his heir to the county,~~ William count of Soissons and Hugh bishop of Lisieux.[28] After the unrest had calmed down the land of Normandy rejoiced in peace under the duke.

---

25 Rodulf, count of Ivry died after 1011 (Fauroux, no. 13).

26 Vernon (Eure).

27 Nothing is known about Turketil, whose name suggests that he was of Scandinavian origin (Adigard des Gautries, 1954, 322–3).

28 Robert, count of Eu (d. c. 1090), William, count of Soissons (c. 1057–c. 1076), Hugh, bishop of Lisieux (c. 1049–77).

[Book VII, c. 4 (7)] ... For after the death of Judith, Duke Richard II took another wife named Papia who bore him two sons, Malger the archbishop and William of Arques.[29] This William obtained from the duke [William], then flourishing in his adolescence, the county of Talou, meant as a fief for which he was to be his vassal. Haughty because of his noble birth William built the stronghold of Arques on top of that hill, and assuming arbitrary power, and secure in royal support, he dared to instigate a rebellion against the duke. The duke sought to turn him from his madness and summoned him, by way of messengers, to come in order to show his allegiance. In great confidence, however, having scorned the embassy, he fortified himself ready for rebellion. The duke then gathered his troops of Normans and instantly set off to tame his arrogance. At the foot of the hill he erected mounds for a siege-castle, which a strong force of warriors turned into an impregnable stronghold. He himself then withdrew after he had left behind sufficient food. At once King Henry [I of France 1031–60], who was not unaware of these events, summoned an army and did not hesitate to come and fortify the stronghold on the hill. He ordered his troops to set up their camp at Saint-Aubin.[30] When the duke's soldiers heard of the king's arrival they sent out some of their number in an attempt to draw away from the royal army some of the enemy, whom they, while lying in ambush, would capture by surprise. When the enemy thus arrived, the Normans succeeded in drawing away a considerable part of the army and as if in flight they led the French into a trap. For suddenly the Normans who seemed to be fleeing, turned round and began violently to cut down the French, so that during that encounter Count Enguerrand of Abbeville among many others was stabbed to death and Hugh Bardulf with many others was taken prisoner.[31] When the king learned this he sent food into the fortification for which he had come, and full of grief for his lost soldiers he shamefully retreated. Not long afterwards William and his men, who were weakened by starvation, freely yielded the stronghold and left his native land as an exile.

29 Judith, daughter of Duke Geoffrey of Brittany died in 1017. Papia came from the
   Pays-de-Caux in the north of Normandy.

30 Saint-Aubin-sur-Scie (Seine-Mar., c. Offranville).

31 A good example of the use of simulated flight as a military tactic.

16   Gilbert Crispin, Life of Herluin of Bec

Gilbert Crispin's Life of Herluin was written between 1109 and 1117 at Westminster where Gilbert, a former monk of Le Bec, had become abbot. Le Bec was founded by Herluin c. 1030 after he said farewell at the age of forty to his secular career as a soldier in the service of Count Gilbert of Brionne, son of Count Godfrey, who was an illegitimate son of Duke Richard I. After Herluin had founded the monastery his mother came to join him. The author draws on oral tradition at Le Bec, where Herluin in his eighties died in 1070.

The Works of Gilbert Crispin, ed. A. Sapir-Abulafia and G. R. Evans (London, 1986), pp. 185–90, 193; my revised trsl. from S. Vaughn, *The Abbey of Bec and the Anglo-Norman State* (Woodbridge, 1981), pp. 68–71, 73).

[C. 3] His [Herluin's] father was descended from the Danes who first ruled Normandy; his mother was related closely by blood to the dukes of Flanders. His father was named Ansgot, his mother Heloise. Count Gilbert of Brionne, grandson of Richard I of Normandy through the duke's son, Count Godfrey, had Herluin brought up fittingly at his home among all the nobles of his court. Herluin was especially suited to arms, and bore them with no small courage.

[C. 4] All the elders of all the great families in the whole of Normandy considered him among the chosen. They praised him for his fighting, for all his military skill, and for his physical fitness. He turned his mind from shameful practices and bent his whole effort to the honourable deeds which great men of the court do. At home and in the field he was not loth to be the most outstanding of his fellow soldiers.

[C. 5] Through these virtues he had obtained the singular favour not only of his lord, but also that of Robert [the Magnificent], duke of the whole country; and among the lords of the regions outside Normandy he won a very fine reputation and friendly access to their courts. Allow me to omit the many other things which he did in the course of gaining a name in the world; but about the strength of his mind, the constancy of his faith, and the boldness under arms, I cannot be silent.

[C. 6] Because on some occasion he unjustly suffered an injury done to him by his lord, detesting him, he withdrew the advantage of his service and went far away from Gilbert's court. It was at this time that Count Gilbert himself, provoked by the lawlessness of certain of the most powerful men in Normandy, collected a great band of soldiers, being fiercely keen to avenge his own injuries. Gilbert was a

man ferocious of mind, immensely powerful, and ~~greedy for~~ a
~~matchless reputation, inasmuch he was the close relative of such great~~
~~dukes.~~ So that he might show his strength, he sent word to his
enemies through envoys that he would seek revenge, saying when
this would be, not just before the day of battle, but several days
beforehand.

Gilbert's rebellion

[C. 7] So at the agreed time both sides prepared for hostilities, which
could not be conducted without huge bloodshed for both parties;
furthermore it was impossible to avoid war without sacrificing their
dignity. But when Herluin, the courageous man whose biography I
have undertaken, had discovered this, he straightway forgot the
insults he had suffered. Taking with him twenty select soldiers, he
went to the appointed contest, though he did not join his lord but
remained far apart from that company.

[C. 8] For in opposition to his own and his men's safety, he affirmed
the pledge of his loyalty and sought the danger of death, asking no
benefit from Gilbert in exchange. Enough has been said for it to be
clearly recognised what sort of man he was. Through this example I
do not speak to deserters from the fight, who are released by fear to
let others die, but to those who are led by cupidity to kill their lords
and destroy their country. I put this forward not so much to recom-
mend military glory as the preservation of fealty.

[C. 9] When the duke had led his force along the side of a high
mountain, he saw behind him twenty armed men following at a distance
on the plain. Dreading some enemy activity, he ordered his men to go
immediately and find out who they were. The duke's men approached
Herluin's and when they learned the cause, approving Herluin's high-
mindedness, reported back to the duke. The duke, marvelling that such
great service should be rendered in return for injury, at once granted
Herluin access to the court again. At the same time he restored with a
fuller esteem everything that was Herluin's by right.

[C. 10] The aforesaid messengers, coming to the province of Duke
Robert on the night before battle, delayed the fight which threatened
at dawn the next day, swearing by the law and by their sacred faith
that they would lay down their arms and await the decision of war on
the decree of his court. And so both parties, neither of which was
superior to the other, abandoned killing by arms. Divine Providence
preserved Herluin, its strong timber, for every good and useful work.

The supreme Creator did not wish Herluin to be twisted any further this way and that by the violence of the world's winds, nor be wet with tears from fruitless emotions.

[C. 11] Herluin was already over thirty-seven years old and his situation in this life most agreeable, when at last his mind began to burn with love of the divine,

[C. 12] and to cool and gradually each day to freeze from love of the world. Turning his eyes of his heart away from outside objects towards himself, he went more regularly to church, prayed devoutly, and often broke into tears, putting aside everything that was trifling. He was now less frequently at the court, where he was retained by one purpose only, that he could work to acquire for God estates of his own.

[C. 13] This he obtained by extracting them from his own lord through the great constancy of his service. Often he would spend the night right up to daybreak praying in churches, and in the morning was the first to be in the court at his lord's table. Since he did not wish to be frugal in front of his friends, he would devise many inconveniences to account for his absence, and would often pass the whole day in fasting.

[C. 14] In training his body to arms he did not display the same zeal as before, revealing the inner turmoil of his heart, which he still hid with earnest deception. His mind was pained, and distracted in further directions through his thoughtful meditations. It was his deepest wish to abandon the practice of knighthood and all other worldly things. Indeed he did not know where he ought to go or what kind of life to adopt.

[C. 15] It was rare in Normandy at that time to find anyone who could point out or blaze the right path. Priests and great bishops married freely and carried arms, just like laymen. They all still lived in the manner of the old Danes. But just as the wind bloweth where it listeth, so whom his anointing toucheth and teacheth all things. Therefore, renouncing knighthood, dressed in a cheap cloak, with beard and hair unshorn, for a long time he served among the courtiers with the intention I spoke of.[32] ...

[C. 17] Acting over a loss sustained by one of his fellow countrymen, which tended towards the man's ruin, Count Gilbert gave Herluin a

32 Note the implication that soldiers would have had their hair shorn and been shaven.

mission to go to Duke Robert of the Normans, for whom anything done about this was a matter of importance and to lay a charge against the person arising from the affair.[33] But Herluin, that man of peace, completely refused to be the bearer of schemes damaging to anyone. Count Gilbert remained steadfast in his decision, urging and threatening Herluin, saying that one who was his intimate friend should convey word of his resolve to Gilbert's own lord.

[C. 18] It was now up to the soldier, placed in such a position, to show whether he preferred to serve a heavenly or an earthly lord. But as soon as he acted for the cause of the Lord on high, Herluin thereupon broke the link by which he was held under the service of an earthly lord. Renouncing his embassy totally, he went away from the court. But Count Gilbert, not doubting in the least that Herluin would go to Duke Robert, after a few days went to the court wishing to know what the duke's response was. When, however, Gilbert learned that his message had not been carried to Robert, he became enraged at Herluin, to whom he had given this mission, and ordered that whatever property he and his men held should be taken away.

[C. 19] Immediately all his possessions were seized, yet Herluin did not care; but his paupers also had their possessions destroyed and for this reason he was very concerned. Therefore, pierced by the complaints and tears of these poor men, he returned to his lord after a few days had elapsed and with no regard for himself pleaded the cause of the innocent sufferers.

[C. 20] The whole court was summoned to gather and he was harshly brought to trial. The accusations were put forward. With humble but satisfactory logic Herluin refuted and dismissed them. The spirit of God, who replied to the judge in the case, kept silent on those points over which the judge was rather hostile and concentrated on certain other wrongs, knowing what lay hidden beneath. 'Let those things of mine', Herluin said, 'which I received from here, all be divided up, but let their own property be restored to the poor, who have not deserved your anger, since they have committed no crimes.'

[C. 21] The lord who was much possessed by pride in his earthly loftiness, was moved to mercy and taking Herluin to one side,

33 This is probably an example of the feudal obligation of messenger service, especially considering the prompt retaliation by Count Gilbert and the summons to Herluin to appear before his lord's court. For a discussion of this incident, see Tabuteau, 1988, 300, n. 95.

diligently enquired about his change of mind and the purpose of his words. Herluin answered him briefly amidst copious tears: 'In loving the world and being obedient to you I have neglected God and myself exceedingly until now.

[C. 22] In caring totally for the cultivation of my body, I accepted no instruction for my soul. Therefore I pray, if I ever deserved well of you, that you allow me to spend the rest of my life in a monastery with your love for me intact. Give to God with me what I owed.' This was how the long consultation ended. Moved to heartfelt tears, the duke could not bear to hear him talking any more and rushed away to his chamber.

[C. 23] He had much human affection towards that soldier of his, while Herluin cherished much towards his lord. Herluin was scarcely able to ask his release from him, but divine love, strong as death prevailed.

[C. 24] At last the duke granted to his most grateful follower the opportunity for which he had longed, for himself and all his people. Hitherto he had loved Herluin as one obedient to him and now he began to love him as a lord and willingly obeyed him.

[C. 25] Detaining Herluin at his house for several days with many honours the duke sent him away with due acclamation handing over to his power and authority everything Herluin's brothers held of their paternal right.[34] His brothers had been born equal to him in rank but because Herluin had proved worthier and more eminent in true nobility than they, it was not thought wrong or injurious for it to be taken from them by law and placed under his ownership.

[Herluin then becomes a monk, founds a monastery and in due course his mother joins him there]

[C. 42] His noble mother [Heloise] dedicated herself to similar service in that place for God's sake and consigned to Him the estates which she held. She performed the duty of a handmaid, washing the garments of God's servants and doing most scrupulously all the extremely hard work imposed on her.

[C. 43] One day when she was baking bread to help the labour of God's servants, by some chance the house caught fire on all sides. A

34 This is an interesting example of the system of *parage*, joint tenure by co-heirs.

man ran shrieking to report to the abbot that the building had burnt
down and that his mother had been consumed in the flames. Herluin,
however, although bathed in tears, raised his hands to God. 'I thank
you, God', he said, 'that the fire has taken my mother as she was
assisting your servants.' Strong in the love of God, his steadfastness,
which had been pounded by the battering-rams of the devil, could not
sag. Ignorant of this, the Enemy brought hammers and fires, which
had not the slightest effect in overcoming this patient man, but
cleansed and shaped him for the crown of glory. Nevertheless the lady
suffered no harm in that conflagration.

17   William of Poitiers, Deeds of Duke William

William of Poitiers, former chaplain of William the Conqueror, describes
how Duke William established law and order in Normandy. No lawcode has
survived, except for a tract from 1091 compiled by his sons which lists a few
customs.

The Gesta Guillelmi of William of Poitiers, ed. and trsl. R. H. C. Davis and M.
Chibnall (Oxford, 1998), p. 81.

[Book I, c. 48] And so this man [Duke William], worthy of his pious
father and his pious ancestors, even while he was active in arms did
not cease with his inward eye to gaze in awe on the eternal majesty.
For whether conquering in external wars or suppressing sedition,
rapine and brigandage, he served his country, where Christ was worshipped, so that the more peace was enjoyed the less were sacred
institutions violated. Nor could it ever be said that he undertook a
war where justice was lacking. In this way do Christian kings of the
Roman and Greek peoples protect their own, repel injuries, and fight
justly for the palm of victory. For who will say that it behoves a good
prince to suffer rebellious brigands? By his strict discipline and by his
laws robbers, murderers, and evil-doers have been driven out of
Normandy.[35] The oath of peace which is called the Truce has been
most scrupulously observed in Normandy, whereas in other regions it
is frequently violated through unbridled wickedness.[36] He listened to
the cause of widows, orphans and the poor, acting with mercy and

35 William the Conqueror's Norman laws are only preserved in a document from
   1091, which refers to confiscation of land and moveables but not explicitly to exile
   (Haskins, 1918, 282 section 1 and 283 section 13).
36 William the Conqueror had introduced the Truce of God in 1047 at a council in
   Caen.

judging most justly.[37] Since his fairmindedness restrained greed, no one, however powerful or close to him, dared to move the boundary of a weaker neighbour's field or take anything from him. Villages, fortified places, and towns had stable and good laws because of him, and everywhere people greeted him with joyous applause and sweet songs.

18   Charter from Jumièges on a substituted child

A charter from Jumièges, dated to 1080x4, documents the extraordinary case of a substituted child, which took place in the late 1060s, in a complicated property dispute. The document, which still survives as an original, is written in the first person by Rainald, a royal chaplain who ultimately passed on some of the property to Jumièges.

Bates, no. 162, pp. 530–3; trsl. based on J. Boswell, *The Kindness of Strangers: The Abandonment of Children in Western Europe from Late Antiquity to the Renaissance* (New York, 1988), pp. 447–8.

... In the days of Richard, count of the Normans, and of his son Robert, and of William, son of Robert, there was a chaplain of theirs at Bayeux named Ernald, a man rich in goods and lands both inside and outside the city, which he had bought with his own gold and silver. When he died, during the reign of William, duke of the Normans, Stephen, Ernald's nephew, inherited according to the laws of succession the estate of his uncle by grant of Duke William. This Stephen had a little son by a widow of Bayeux, called Oringa, the sister of a Norman called Ambarius. When the child died, the ingenious woman without Stephen's knowledge rented a child from a woman called Ulberga who lived in the village of Martragny [Calvados, c. Creully] paying her ten shillings a year. Stephen believed the child his and made him heir of his property, that is, of the houses he had at the Gate of the Trees inside the city and of 12 acres of land at Gold Spring outside the city and of some fields from which he derived income. Then after first his wife and later he himself passed away, the said woman [Ulberga] from Martragny not receiving the rent she was accustomed to getting for her son, demanded the return of the child, but could not get him back from the relatives of Stephen's wife. Word of her claim reached Duke William, who by now had become king, and his wife Matilda, in the village of Bonneville.[38] The king arranged

---

37 A good example follows hereafter, no. **18**.

38 Bonneville (Eure) where the duke regularly held court.

to have a hearing to determine whether the woman should regain her child. King William, Archbishop John, Roger de Beaumont and a number of others decided that the woman claiming the boy should regain her son by means of the ordeal of hot iron if God should preserve her unharmed.[39] King William and his wife Matilda sent me, Rainald the clerk, to Bayeux to witness the ordeal. William the archdeacon, now abbot of Fécamp, Gotselin the archdeacon, Robert *Insule* with his wife Alberada, Evremar of Bayeux and quite a few other outstanding citizens went with me at the king's behest. When the ordeal was carried out in the small monastery of Saint-Vigor the woman reclaiming her son was unharmed by the judgement of God, as I and the other named witnesses observed.[40] And when the king learned this from me and the other witnesses, he laid claim to Stephen's estate and gave it to the queen, who gave me, with the approval of the king, the houses and 12 acres I mentioned before and the fields and all of Stephen's allodial property. To Geoffrey the clerk surnamed Masculin, I gave one field from the estate in return for which he is to look out for my interest in court, if necessary, and whenever during the year I come to Bayeux he is to provide me, the first night with wine and beer and good bread, according to custom, and to feed my horses, and for this I have the witness of my lady the queen to advance me up to 100 shillings in the city if I should need them. And this field I gave to Vitalis the clerk that he should serve me … All these things which I have described can be verified by Vitalis the clerk who was with me throughout.

19   Charters from Rouen cathedral and from Saint-Pierre at Préaux

Two early eleventh-century Norman charters from Rouen cathedral, before 1026, and from Saint-Pierre at Préaux, 1035 show how as an *aide-mémoire* children who acted as witnesses for grants of land were slapped or otherwise maltreated, so that later on in life the memory of the physical abuse would jog their memory of the transaction.[41]

Fauroux nos 10 and 89.

---

39 John, bishop of Avranches (1060–67), archbishop of Rouen (1067–79) and Roger of Beaumont, son of Humphrey of Vieilles (d. after 1090).

40 Probably Saint-Vigor-le-Grand (Calvados, c. Bayeux).

41 The practice is discussed in Tabuteau, 1988, 149.

[Rouen cathedral charter.]

[Four men had been sent by Duke Richard II to Archbishop Robert of Rouen (989–1037) to enforce the restoration of land to the cathedral] ... That day they took a meal with the archbishop in a forest called *Blanca* where they whipped many small boys [*puerulos*] and refreshed [them] well in record and memory ...

[Saint-Pierre at Préaux charter]

... Humphrey, founder of this place with his sons Roger, Robert, William [the Conqueror], who moreover received a blow from his father [Duke Robert the Magnificent] for the sake of memory.[42] Richard of Lillebonne who carried the greaves, that is the hose, of Duke Robert received another blow, and when asked why Humphrey had given him such a great blow, he [Humphrey] answered: 'Because you are younger than me and perhaps you will live a long time and you will be a witness of this business when[ever] there is need.' Moreover, Hugh, son of Count Waleran [of Meulan] received a third blow.

20 Orderic Vitalis, Ecclesiastical History (on the character of the Normans)

Orderic Vitalis, a monk of half-English half-French origin at Saint-Evroult, wrote his Ecclesiastical History between *c.* 1110 and *c.* 1142. The following two passages in his work describe the Normans as he saw them as a warlike nation. The second passage quoted here was written during the period that King Stephen of England laid claim to Normandy against Henry I's daughter Empress Matilda after her father's death in 1135.

Orderic, v, 25–7 and vi, 455–7.

The Normans are an untamed race, and unless they are held in check by a firm ruler they are all too ready to do wrong. In all communities, wherever they may be, they strive to rule and often become enemies to truth and loyalty through the ardour of their ambition. This the French and Bretons and Flemings and their other neighbours have frequently experienced; this the Italians and Lombards and Anglo-Saxons have suffered to the point of destruction ... From his [Antenor's] son Danus this people of Trojan origin took the name of Danes. They were from the first a cruel and warlike people and were governed by powerful kings; but they rejected the faith of Christ for a

42 Humphrey of Vieilles founded Saint-Pierre at Préaux *c.* 1035.

very long time. The mighty leader Rollo with the Normans, was of this race; and they first conquered Neustria which is now called Normandy after the Normans. For in the English [*anglice*] language 'aquilo' means 'north' and 'homo' 'man'; Norman therefore means 'man of the north', and his bold roughness had proved as deadly to his softer neighbours as the bitter north wind to flowers. For up to now [1120s–1130s] natural ferocity and love of fighting for its own sake have existed together in the same race, and the Normans do not suffer the country people and peaceful officials to live quietly in their own homes.

After the Normans, who are innately warlike and bold, had realised that the crimes of their guests were stirring up trouble, they took up arms in their anger and pursued them through villages and woods and, it is commonly alleged, put more than seven hundred to death with fire and sword … If the Norman people would live according to the law of God and be united under a good prince they would be as invincible as were the Chaldeans under Nebuchadnezzar and the Persians and Medes under Cyrus and Darius and the Macedonians under Alexander, as their many victories in England and Apulia and Syria amply testify. But because strife divides them among themselves they take arms to rend each other; though they conquer other peoples they defeat themselves, and as their hostile neighbours look on with scorn they belabour and mercilessly butcher each other, so that their mother Normandy·is constantly in tears.

21   The Discovery and Miracles of St Vulfran

The Discovery and Miracles of St Vulfran, written at Saint-Wandrille *c.* 1053–54, contains interesting stories illustrating the lives of women and children. The one quoted here is related by the (anonymous) author at the time that he was a chaplain with Roger of Beaumont, lord of Asnebecq (Orne).

Inventio et miracula sancti Vulfranni, ed. Dom J. Laporte, Mélanges publiés par la Société de l'Histoire de Normandie, 14e s. (Rouen, 1938), pp. 70–1.

[C. 67] The aforesaid father [St Vulfran] not only flourishes in the glory of his virtue here with us who live close to his body restoring health to those who ask for it, but he also helps those in remote and faraway regions who approach him in faith and are helped kindly and swiftly. While we have experienced many [miracles] I shall commit to writing for posterity only one of them which I witnessed myself. The small daughter of a nobleman of that region was innocently playing, as is the custom of that age, in the forecourt [*platea*] of the fortification [*castellum*] called Asnebecq. Suddenly and miraculously, however, she was struck by paralysis and having lost her sight and speech, to the amazement of those who were present, she fell to the ground. When her mother had heard the news she arrived wailing and crying, took her small miserable daughter in her arms and brought her within the walls where she dwelled, while talking to her, stroking her and offering food without, however, [receiving] any reaction. Deeply upset she then sent for me, her clerk, and [asked] whether I knew of any medicine or way to treat the sick child. Although at first I said that I was not a doctor and knew nothing of medicines, she kept on pressing me for advice, so I told her that she might make an offering [*votum*] for the sick girl and persuaded her that she might devoutly promise a candle in honour of St Vulfran, whose virtue is renowned in our region on account of his many miracles. What more? Immediately she ordered through a messenger that an offering [*votum*] be made and while the candle was being made she folded the bent tow [= wick of the candle] around the dying girl.[43] As soon as she had finished this, the sick girl opened her eyes and responded to her mother's talking, happily accepted the food offered to her and, to the amazement of everyone, got up and went outside to play with the other children. With great joy her mother, remembering her promise, had a candle made for the church of St Vulfran at Saint-Georges [d'Asnebecq] just as the aforesaid clerk had told her to do.

22 The Miracles of Fécamp

The Miracles that Happened at Fécamp, first written between 1059 and 1088.
A. Sauvage, 'Des miracles advenus en l'église de Fécamp', *Mélanges de la Société de l'histoire de Normandie*, 2e s. (Rouen, 1893), pp. 24–5.

[C. 17] A certain man from Melun, Osmund, decided to go to Fécamp and urged his wife Maria that on account of her love for him, her husband, she ought to accompany him.[44] The wife, however, was a very proud and mischievous woman who spurned her husband's request,

---

43 For the custom of measuring an ill person and using the thread as the wick of a candle of the appropriate length, see R. Finucane, *Miracles and Pilgrims: Popular Belief in Medieval England*, 2nd edn (Basingstoke, 1995), pp. 95–6.

44 Melun (Seine-et-Marne).

refuted his devotion and plan for the pilgrimage, and – as is the custom of disgraceful women – began to argue [with him] in a loud voice: 'You', she said, 'ought to feed your children and look after your family instead of wishing to go to Fécamp more because you are stirred by vain curiosity rather than inspiration for religion and devotion.' In spite [of her objections] the steadfast and sensible man, who unlike Adam who agreed with Eve, strengthened by a virile mind, detested and rejected the expressions of bad advice, went on his planned journey determined to persevere and [fulfil] his holy wish and arrived at the monastery of the Holy Trinity at Fécamp. Meanwhile after her husband's departure heavenly vengeance struck Maria as an example and lesson for all other women and she was punished with the severity of a just judgement. For her blasphemous mouth, the organ through which the proud Maria had shamelessly uttered outrageous language against God and her husband, elongated rigidly in a distorted and deformed way so that it became fixed to both her ears … When Maria realised her present punishment and confessed her past sin, namely that she had refused to follow her husband, she came with another friend to Fécamp, entered the church of the Holy Trinity and taking off the ring from her finger as a pledge of justice put it on the altar for the sacrosanct Trinity. After she had done this she began to pray and with loud cries and laments readily acknowledged the severity and the judgement of the Eternal Judge. The woman's mouth, which had become misformed by her foul and proud words, healed as a result of the modest and humble confession as an instant medicine and was restored to its former beauty in the presence of many onlookers.

23   Marsilia of Saint-Amand at Rouen, Letter to Abbot Bovo II of Saint-Amand (Elnone)

Marsilia, abbess of Saint-Amand at Rouen, wrote in 1107 an account of a miracle to Abbot Bovo of Saint-Amand in Flanders. The miracle concerns a woman from Lisieux who had attempted suicide while staying with the nuns to whom she had been entrusted for her own safety.

Historia mulieris suspensae ad vitam revocatae descripta a Marsilia abbatissa Rotomagensi…, AA.SS, 1 Febr., 902–03; Platelle, 1967, 104–6.

… In the year of the Lord's Incarnation 1107 in the district of Lisieux a certain distinguished woman incurred such great cruelty of the ancient enemy, not so much because her own sins required it, but rather so that the glory of God in his holy bishop [St Amand] might

become more widely known, so that at first she was disturbed by
malignant and varied illusions of thoughts. Then, when she had lost
her natural perception, she deliberated what she might do on her own
when everyone was absent, namely that she might lay hands on
herself and cut short her life in some way, whether by hanging from
a noose or by submersion in a river. And she would have done that,
except that her husband's unexpected arrival often prevented her from
doing so. For she had been lead astray by a certain foolish woman,
who was restless and talkative, and approached her with deceitful
speeches indoors, outside and in the street, reporting that her husband regarded her with hatred, and that he esteemed another woman
more and preferred her in carnal union. Soon the woman believed in
the lie, just as once Eve believed in the serpent, and she fell into a
depression which worked towards death. And unmindful of God and
the Christian faith, she was always contriving and labouring towards
this in all ways, that she might put an end to her miserable life by
whatever kind of diabolical act. But divine compassion, which wishes
no one to perish, prevented her, so that this deed might not happen in
order to multiply the praise and glory of His Holy Confessor Amand.
And when her husband had learned of such a great disgrace, he
consoled her repeatedly with pleasant words and consolations, so that
she might come to her senses from this diabolical thought, and that
she might cheer herself and her relatives who were saddened by her
troubles. Her response to the words of encouragement was full of
miserable desperation when she said: 'This won't help me, but direct
me to go to hell with the devil, to whom I am predestined and given.'
No compliments, no promises, no threats could prevent her from
uttering such worthless words from her mouth.

Then when beneficial counsel had been sought, they brought the sick
woman to the nunnery of the blessed Amand, to whom this type of
virtue is believed especially to be conferred by the Saviour, that no
demonic strength may be able to resist him ... Yet, when several
people of sound faith and of either sex, who gathered to her for the
sake of visiting and encouragement, urgently asked her that she
might protect herself with the sign of the salutary cross, she did not
agree. But repeating that which is related above, the statement of un-
happiness, she complained more intently. Why should she prolong the
delay for going to the pitfall of death? When certain religious and
men of wiser intelligence approached her more closely and comforted
her more privately, she responded with adequately composed speech,
that she was completely delivered to the infernal flames and sulphurous

punishments, and while detained in this world she would experience that just part of these punishments, and she expected the remainder not long afterwards. Then it was decreed by these men, who were of complete faith and keener in intellect, that she should be blessed by water poured from a chalice and that the next day she would be delivered at once through the hands of priests with the invocation of the name of Christ and of his virtue and power. She was immensely astounded when she intelligently heard and understood these things and she began to be more intensely oppressed and to draw frequent breaths. Then with everyone looking on, with diabolical cunning she pretended to behave modestly on the outside, although on the inside she raved with devilish insanity.

And so when evening had come, she was brought beyond the choir and she stood before the altar on which St Amand had been accustomed to celebrate masses. Then when the darkness of night was coming on, those who had brought her and who were appointed to watch over her as her guardians withdrew. O cunning of the devil, O guile of the ancient serpent in the destruction of the human race. For immediately the unhappy woman, when she discovered an opportune moment to kill herself, deceitfully suggested to her guardians that from this time they might rest after the guard duty and the labours which they had devoted to her, and that they, exhausted by such great inconvenience, might now yield to sleep. She even pretended that she was very much wearied and wished to rest with them. Indeed, already seven days and just as many nights had passed since she had been brought there. And when a bed had been prepared and arranged decently enough, she had given herself as if to sleep for a little while, and looking around she perceived that no one would be at hand. Only wearing her smock she furtively climbed up a wall which seemed high. And she twisted part of her head veil around the top of a column in the wall. Indeed, from the remaining part she prepared an ordinary noose in an amazing manner. Putting her neck into it and jumping straight down, she bent her neck with such great force that a spurt of blood poured forth from her throat and stained a part of the facing wall. Already the midnight had passed when one of the guards woke and got up. She did not find the woman in her bed and after she had checked the whole church she discovered the spot where she was hanging. Shocked by the great horror, she realised that the body was rigid and thoroughly lifeless.

On the spot she made noise with a great clamour announcing by shouting what had happened. When these things had been heard, all nuns were called together and with a clamour arising from all sides they lamented the miserable dead woman. St Amand was invoked with many sighs and tears, that he should not allow the dignity of this place to perish, but compassionately would think it worthy to come to the aid of those who were running to him. Then when a light had been lit, the neck of the hanging woman was pulled from the noose, and the lifeless cadaver was thrown down on the floor of the church. Three of the sisters who were bolder and more experienced since it was night went for the archdeacon and in tears they asked him what to do. He gave the following response and advice to them: that before dawn might break, the body should be removed from the church and thrown into a pit in whatever manner. And the archdeacon followed closely after these women who returned and with the nuns crying out and standing there, he stood nearby, wondering at the great cunning of diabolical deceit. Meanwhile, when some of the nuns came nearer, one of them noticed renewed breath quivering in the woman's chest, and saw the face slowly regaining colour and, indeed, the eyes slowly opening; and then the woman drew a deep breath. Yet, the nuns standing there examined this most diligently and with a hugh clamour they called for the help of St Amand their patron and beating their breasts they multiplied the wishes of their prayers. While these things were being done, they recognised immediately that by the virtue of the omnipotent God and by the intervention of their glorious and admirable Bishop Amand, the soul had returned to the body. Yet, on that day and on the following night after the woman had been resurrected, she remained without the service of her voice and such was the force of her great strength that four people could scarcely hold her down.

At dawn of the next day her first words were truthfully: 'Holy Lady pious mother of God, Mary, help me.' And then her mouth opened to the praise of our Saviour and at his esteemed Confessor and with manifold congratulations to the omnipotent God she rendered prayers of thanks. Thus, after this had happened a certain priest was summoned and she made a full confession concerning her past sins and she was given absolution humbly. Then she added: 'I give thanks to you lord Jesus, you who resurrected me by your favour, by the merits of St Amand my lord, you freed me from the hands of the most pernicious enemy and from the infernal abyss. I believe faithfully in you with the Father and the Holy Spirit, I adore you and I renounce all displays and traps of Satan.' When this wonderful miracle resounded far and wide, the glorious and wonderful God was magnified in his holy bishop through whom He worked so many signs miraculously. For just as formerly when placed in the world he resurrected by prayer a robber, who was fixed to a gibbet and was dead, so now in heaven, living with Christ, he recalled to life by his precious merits the miserable woman who died by hanging, for the praise of our lord Jesus Christ, who is alone and everywhere, with the Father and Holy Spirit, God lives and reigns through infinite ages of ages.

24   Milo Crispin, On the origin of the Crispin family

Milo Crispin wrote the miracle story 'How the holy virgin appeared to William Crispin the elder and on the origin of the noble Crispins' in the first half of the twelfth century while he was a monk at the monastery of Le Bec.

Miraculum quo b. Mariae subvenit Guillelmo Crispino seniori; ubi de nobili Crispinorum genere agitur, ed. Migne, *PL*, 150, cols 735–44.

… since nowhere examples of her [the Holy Virgin's] appearance can be found in writing even though many continuously take place and of which the majority is not remembered, of these we wish to mention one which is worthy to be remembered and which on account of its importance cannot be left to oblivion. In it the most holy mother of God shows willing affection towards those who in distress flee to her, for she saved a noble man devoted to her, called William with the nickname Crispin, who in great anxiety appealed to her clemency from the instant danger of death, but before we describe this miracle it seems sensible to explain who this William was and where his and his family's nickname came from.

Before the Normans led by Duke William conquered England, there was in Neustria, which is now called Normandy, a famous man named Gilbert, of renowned origin and nobility who because of the shape of his hair was the first to be known as 'Crispin'.[45] For in his early youth he had hair that was brush-like and stiff and sticking out, and in a manner of speaking bristling like the needles of a pine tree which always stick out. This gave him the nickname Crispin from 'crispus pinus', 'pine hair'. This bristling hair can still be seen on those who descend from this Gilbert. And it is from him that many Norman families take that nickname. This Gilbert, who, as we said, was the

---

45 Gilbert I Crispin was castellan of Tillières (Eure). For the Crispin family, see
   Green, 1984, 49–50. See also below, no. **30**.

first to bear the nickname Crispin, took as wife a sister of Fulk d'Aunou the elder, named Gunnor, who bore him three sons:[46] Gilbert Crispin, [William] the man on whose account we began to write, and Robert, as well as two daughters Emma, the mother of Peter of Condé, and Esilia, the mother of William Malet who after a military career in his old age became a monk of Le Bec and having honourably lived for several years according to the monastic rule, as befits such a man, found a good rest.[47] Robert Crispin, the youngest brother, having left Normandy wandered through many provinces until he arrived at Constantinople where he was welcomed with honour by the emperor and made a name for himself with all, and where also, as is said, he died of poison due to the envy of the Greeks.[48] Gilbert Crispin, the eldest of the three brothers, received from Duke William the castle of Tillières in hereditary custody, which his heirs still hold until this day. The aforementioned William Crispin, the middle brother, of noble origin, of outstanding manners and the most famous soldier, first among the Normans, who, as we said, brought with happy fortune glory from his father Gilbert the first of the Crispins to his whole family. And like the Fabii, or the Anicii or Manlii carried the tokens of fame [*insignia*] among the Romans, so the Crispins knew even greater fame among the Normans and the French. But this William, so it is said, was the best known of all in his time; with military fame and with outstanding ability he rose above almost all his contemporaries. His famous prowess made many envious and turned most vicious enemies against him. At that time the French, led by Walter the old [*Vetulus*], count of Pont Isère, who claimed that all the land between the rivers Epte, the Andelle and the Seine was his, organised numerous expeditions across the River Epte and plundered the Vexin;[49] therefore William, duke of the Normans, who later became king of England, called the aforesaid William Crispin, his most outstanding soldier, to the castle of Neaufles and he gave him – and his son after him, as we know, until this day – the castle and the vicomté of the Vexin to hold in hereditary right against the French incursions and to

46 Fulk d'Aunou contributed ships to the invasion of 1066, see no. **37**.

47 For the Malet family, see Hart, 1996, 123–66 and Keats-Rohan, 1997b, 13–55, who on pp. 21–2 points out that William Malet (d. 1071) was the husband and not the son of Esilia. She suggests that Milo meant the son called Robert Malet who was a distinguished fighter in William the Conqueror's time and an important Domesday Book landholder.

48 For Robert Crispin, see also nos **79** and **80**.

49 Walter III, count of Pontoise and Vexin (1035–63) (Bates, 1987, 41).

curb their presumption.[50] There William established his home, his household [*familia*] and his garrison to ward off French invasions. This enraged the French who erupted into such hatred against him that they eagerly longed for his death.

Having explained the origin of the nickname Crispin, we will now turn to the subject which I learned from truthful reporters and which we will set out in a simple manner. And this case is worthy to be remembered and fitting for the Holy Virgin who for the human race after God is most lovable and through the ages most laudable ... This noble man [William], as we have said, had been appointed a marcher lord [*marchisus*] by Duke William at Neaufles against the French who had crossed the River Epte and had devastated the Vexin with raids of plunder. And there he settled with his household to guard the castle. He revisited, however, the land he had elsewhere in Normandy in the district of Lisieux on several occasions and having settled his business he returned to Neaufles.[51] On his return journeys he never passed Le Bec without visiting and talking to the venerable father Herluin. One day he met Father Herluin who specifically recommended him to the Holy Virgin. After this blessing and having embraced the abbot and the monks, he hastened with his companions home to the castle which had been entrusted to his custodians. But the French, who from their own area had come across the Epte, had heard that William Crispin had crossed the Seine and was about to leave Normandy, gathered together and kept an eye out for his return in the hope that one day on his return they would be able to lay an ambush in the wood in order to capture and maim him. Arriving at this spot, not far from his castle, Crispin passed the wood where the French, prepared to kill him, were hidden. They quickly spotted him and emerging from their hiding place audaciously attacked him. All his companions left William alone and took to flight. William wishing to take the lead in the flight, was hindered by the density of the wood and so was intercepted, because he could neither flee nor offer resistance. Then he fell from his horse and forced by circumstances he landed on a root of a fallen tree just next to him. Some say that the reins with which he guided his horse had caught the branch of a nearby tree, others, however, who augmented the miracle story, say that he

---

50 Neaufles (Eure, c. Gisors). The appointment cannot be dated more precisely than between 1035 and 1054 (Green, 1984, 49).

51 For the lands near Lisieux, see Green, 1984, 54–5.

caught it [the branch] with his hands. Thus stuck there William Crispin lifted his heart to God and appealed to His Mother ...[52]

After the prayer to God and with his whole mind devoted to His glorious mother Mary and with great grief of a contrite heart, without having uttered a single sound, anxious in mind about his imminent death, suddenly on his left appeared as his saviour a shining maiden with a happy face, dressed in royal style with a white mantle around her. With her right hand she pulled the mantle over him while her veil covered almost his whole body for the vestment came down from the middle to just over his thighs. However, because he wore red stockings he hunched up and made himself small and curled his whole body in an attempt to hide his calves and feet under the mantle of the royal girl, but he failed. The enemy arrived and the force of the lances and the tips of the swords came close and by prodding the leaves, branches and fruit they almost reached his feet and all over his body but without actually touching him. Through the defence of the Holy mother of God he was made invisible for his enemies who in complete amazement said: 'Where did he go?', 'What has happened to him?' 'The ground can't have swallowed him alive?', 'Here he came, there he was, where did he flee and where did he disappear?' 'Here is his horse that we followed; since we cannot find him it is really up for grabs.' But some of the more sensible men answered that they had not come to steal a horse, but, if possible, to kill their enemy. After they had investigated [the site] for a long while, without finding him, towards the early evening they went home utterly confused. Then the most devout Lady said: 'The Holy Virgin tells you that she is always ready to help those who in mortal danger invoke her help.'

Crispin's companions who had taken flight out of fear of the enemy, came home with the sad news for the castle that their lord had been captured or killed. Intense grief engulfed all, incomparable wailing filled the whole castle when suddenly they saw William Crispin arriving on horseback and with great joy they came up to him and welcomed him happily ...

This William Crispin had a wife named Eve who suited him well on account of her origin and manners.[53] She bore him Gilbert, the

---

52 Here follows a long prayer to the Holy Virgin.

53 Eve, sister of Amaury II of Montfort l'Amaury, is mentioned several times in the letters of Anselm, abbot of Le Bec and later archbishop of Canterbury (*The Letters of Anselm of Canterbury*, trsl. W. Frölich, 3 vols (Kalamazoo, 1990–94), i, nos 22, 98, 118 and 147).

aforementioned abbot of Westminster and many others.[54] This Eve, born of French origin and born from noble ancestors, after she married the aforementioned William, adapting herself to his tastes, grew fond of the monastery of Le Bec above all other churches and with all her might embraced the abbot and the monks, admiring them with deep devotion, as if they were her own children. Clothes and all that she possessed in precious ornaments she handed over for the use of the church and the brethren. She loved the mother of God and her monastery of Le Bec with her whole heart. After the death of her husband William, she converted to the service of God and lived in saintly widowhood while fasting, keeping vigils, praying intensely as much as her sex and age allowed her, spurning meat and blood until the end of her life and giving alms to the poor.[55] After some years she was veiled by Archbishop William of Rouen and till her death remained subjected to the monastery of Le Bec where she was buried next to her husband.[56]

Their grandson, by their son William, William Crispin III, by sincere love drawn towards the monastery of Le Bec admired her with fitting love. This William was related by blood to the count of Anjou and hence was his relative. He sometimes went to him as to a friend. And William fought for him as much as he could when the count was engaged in warfare against some of his own men who in his county rebelled against him.[57] One day meeting the enemy he launched attacks on them, but they turned their backs on him either out of fear to flee or by way of trickery so that by enticing him further away they could capture him. After he had pursued them for a while he became separated from the rest of his men. When the enemy saw that he pursued them on his own, one of them turned his horse and hit [William's] horse and stuck his lance in it. Seeing that his horse was mortally wounded William quickly tightened the reins, turned round and speedily tried to return to his own men. With a loud voice he invoked the Holy virgin: 'Holy Mary of Le Bec, help me.' Thus shouting he arrived at a ditch which he crossed and where in search of security he fell down, half dead. The same William Crispin used to tell this great miracle story in honour of God and his holy mother,

---

54 Gilbert, monk of Le Bec and abbot of Westminster (c. 1085–1117/18) is the author of the Life of Herluin (no. **16**).

55 William Crispin died in Abbot Herluin's time, so before 1078 (Porée, i, 182).

56 Eve died in 1099 at the age of more than 90 years (Porée, i, 183, n. 2).

57 Around 1135.

namely that with the horse more or less dead and with blood pouring
out here and there from its flanks it carried him for almost two miles
to a small village. He said that his horse had hardly any speed, but he
found it never so speedy. After this William was captured and held in
chains in his cell for a long time, forced by fear and anger, he vowed
that if God freed him from this tribulations he would go to Jerusalem.
Not long afterwards, free from jail, he took the cross, the sign to go to
Jerusalem. Soon he changed in word and deed so that he suddenly
seemed another man. All who saw him were amazed. When the time
for departure had been set at Michaelmas [29 September] he asked
God and His Mother whether if he died on the journey or if he died
before departure he could be carried to Le Bec to be buried among his
ancestors. In his goodness God granted him his wish. Weak through
illness he died on the vigil of Michaelmas and as he had wished in case
death overtook him on the day he would have departed, his body was
carried to His Lady the Holy Mary of Le Bec and he was buried
among his fathers. With so many blessings the Holy Mother of God
led the Crispin family and many others of their kin and lineage to her
neighbourhood, so that with stronger faith and ardent love for her
they would invoke her support in times of distress in order that
through her intercession they would be worthy of the grace of her son
our lord Jesus Christ who lives with the Father and the Holy Spirit
for ever and ever. Amen

25 Eadmer of Canterbury, History of Recent Events

Eadmer in his History of Recent Events in England tells how Archbishop
Lanfranc gave money to a monk of Christ Church Canterbury (Eadmer
himself?) for the care of his mother.

Eadmeri Historia novorum in Anglia, ed. M. Rule (London, 1884), pp. 14–15;
Eadmer's History of Recent Events in England: Historia Novorum in Anglia, trsl.
G. Bosanquet (London, 1964), pp. 14–15.

One of the brethren of the monastery at Canterbury was accustomed
to receive from Father Lanfranc thirty shillings every year for the
benefit of his mother. On one occasion he was on Lanfranc's instructions given five shillings, part of the thirty, as the money was paid
periodically by instalments. This money tied up in a cloth he, while
talking to his mother, slipped, as he thought, into her hand; but her
mind intent on other things, she did not notice what her son was
doing. So the money fell to the ground; and mother and son parted

and went their different ways. Afterwards the woman sent a message
to her son, anxious to know what had happened about the money
which he had promised to bring her. Astonished, he got her to come
to him and hearing what had happened was distressed, not so much at
the loss which his mother had suffered but rather from fear that the
archbishop, when this came to his knowledge, would be vexed at his
carelessness and be to some extent less kindly disposed towards him.
Meanwhile the good father, coming into the cloister, sat down there
as he was accustomed to do. Noticing that the brother was distressed
as he returned from talking with his mother, when they were alone,
he enquired privately what the reason for his being so was. On being
told, with a look of the utmost kindness, as was always his way in
dealing with those in trouble, he said: 'Is that the cause of your
distress, my dearest son? Why, God must purposefully have given
that money to someone else whose need of it was perhaps greater than
your mother's. Keep quiet and take care not to say a word about it to
anyone. That what has happened may not trouble you in the least, in
place of those five shillings I will have seven shillings given to you
today for your mother. But, as I have said, see that no one knows of
it.' Indeed it was his way when giving to give gladly what was to be
given and not let anyone tell of the gift or who was the giver.

26 Dudo of Saint-Quentin, History of the Dukes of the Normans (on Gunnor)

Dudo 288–9; trsl. with some borrowings from *Dudo of St Quentin, History of
the Normans*, trsl. E. Christiansen (Woodbridge, 1998), pp. 163–4.

[Book IV, c. 125] ... As has been recounted, France had been cleared
of the poison of destructive hostility. The complaints and sufferings of
aggressive disasters had faded and the interests of the Frankish realm
had been primed and established everywhere. The victory of the peace
they had been seeking was dictating the future. The reputation of the
most blessed Duke Richard, as illustrated by his well-known merits,
was aglow and grew to new heights. The merit of his blessedness was
lavishly broadcast throughout all the other kingdoms. But during this
period, Emma, his wife, daughter of the great Duke Hugo, died childless.[58] And grieved by the suffering caused by his loneliness, he sent
word to Hugo, the brother of his dead wife, to send him some of the

---

58 For Emma, see also above, no. **10**; Richard offered to hand back her dower.

members of the household to collect what his sister had possessed by her female right [= dower] for the holy Church and the poor. Duke Hugo sent word back to Richard the noble duke to say that whatever he in his goodwill supplied, he did so freely. And so Richard, the duke most generous in his liberality, distributed gifts of great richness throughout all the churches of Normandy and France, and also generously gave away what was his own to the poor for the sake of his spiritual well being. Finally, driven by the underlying frailty of human pleasure, he fathered two sons and as many girls by his mistresses. One of these sons was called Godfrey and the other William.[59] In time, he got together with a virgin of brilliant dignity, called Gunnor, born from a very famous family of Dacian nobles.[60] She was the most beautiful of all Norman maidens, most cautious in civil and foreign affairs [civilium forensiumque rerum eventibus], schooled in the art of feminine skills, gently persuasive with a copious store of eloquence, abundantly enriched by a hoard of capacious memory and recollection, and fortified by an abundance of all good qualities.[61] He happily chose her and agreed to a prohibited union. Now his noblemen, knowing that she had been born from the noblest seed of a famous family and reflecting a lot on both a successor and heir and on a safe future for the people, addressed Richard, the very powerful duke, with submissive voice and downward glance: 'Since you are, lord and most powerful duke, the most prudent of all the Franks, Normans, Burgundians and of indeed all the kingdoms in the scrutiny of your clever mind, we are completely astonished that you have not thought out who is to rule the people after your own lamentable demise and death, a people now subject to your most powerful authority. For we are afraid of the possible catastrophe caused by your future loss and are scared that after the mournful loss of you as leader, foreign peoples will trample us, deprived of an adviser and an heir.' Then Richard replied: 'I have always led the realm with your soundest counsel and I have done good when I have been able. Now explain to me in detail what you have decided upon in your heart in response to this matter.' And they answered: 'In our opinion, it is the providence

59 Godfrey was the father of Gilbert of Brionne (see above, no. 16); William is William of Eu, see no. 15. A third illegitimate son was Robert, count of Avranches, see Potts, 1992, 23–37.

60 In the oldest manuscripts she is not named, see *Dudo of St Quentin*, trsl. Christiansen, p. 224, n. 460.

61 Christiansen (*ibid.*), whose translation I have copied here, has pointed out that much of this sentence is borrowed from Martianus Capella, Lady Rhetoric.

of the highest divinity which has joined this Dacian woman, whom you cherish, to you, so that an heir for this land is born from a father and a Dacian-born mother to be its defender and strongest adviser. For she was born from magnificent stock, is beautiful to look at and attractive, cautious and prudent in counsel, devoted in her feelings, disciplined in emotion, restrained in her advice, mild in her dealings with people, hard working and wise in all matters. Immediately join this woman to you in the contract of inextricable marital union so that, with the approach of your death threatening, the land under your authority may be ruled safely and firmly by this woman's health-bringing offspring.' The very virtuous Duke Richard was therefore willingly in favour of this counsel. Once the bishops had met with the clergy and the governors with the people, he married her in a legitimate contract and from her in the course of time, fathered five sons and three daughters.[62]

27 Warner of Rouen, *Moriuht* poem

The early eleventh-century poet Warner of Rouen dedicated his *Moriuht* poem to Archbishop Robert of Rouen and his mother Countess Gunnor. Like Dudo before him, Warner does not mention Gunnor by name. It is unknown whether Moriuht, a poet from Ireland, and those associated with him are historical persons. The poem, however, attributes an important role to Gunnor as dowager countess in manumitting Moriuht's wife Glicerium. Whether this event is pure fiction or not, Gunnor herself was certainly active in her role as countess even after her husband Duke Richard I's death.

Warner of Rouen, Moriuht: A Norman Latin Poem from the Early Eleventh Century, ed. and trsl. C. J. McDonough (Toronto, 1995), pp. 73, 85–7, 87–91, 95, 105–7.

[Lines 1-12] To Lord Robert, supported by the purple of the archbishop, and to his mother, lady extraordinary, Warner, confidently trusting with certain hope, [wishes] life for both through [our] Lord, now and after death. The continuing life of Robert bestows glory on the Franks; he is a king, outstanding, renowned, and dutiful.[63] Through God's dispensation, you are the eminent pillar, a completely reliable citadel for the good, which will not quickly tumble. The former [Robert] reigns over the Franks, who glory in the arms of war. With

---

62 Richard II, Archbishop Robert of Rouen, another Robert, Malger, count of Corbeil, and a fifth unnamed son; Emma who married the kings Aethelred and Cnut, Hadvise who married Count Geoffrey of Brittany and Matilda who married Count Odo of Blois and Chartres.

63 Robert the Pious of France (996–1031).

any benevolence you rule over the Normans, warlike in [their] bloody slaughter. The two children of Richard are the mainstays of the world.[64]

[Lines 193–202] And while from his [Moriuht's] lips he gave voice to the halloed words, with his eyes twisting this way and that and with shaking hands, from a point opposite [to him], there is carried [the pronouncement]: 'Your beloved sweet-heart is alive. Further go more quickly to Rouen than an energetic person [?]. There your beloved grieves over the subject of her passion she has lost. [There] the beautiful nanny goat waits for her goat. She strolls to the port to see her beloved Moriuht, exploring every boat from all angles. As she has not located you, it is her wish to unite herself to a viking, declaring that [her] lord Moriuht is dead.'

[Lines 221–80] At this point it is proper to hear of the quality and greatness of a poet! This sage Moriuht became notorious in his style of dress. Before his penis Ravola wore an animal skin, behind [he wore] in front of his buttocks a black covering of a goat and his right shoe was made by sewing it together with an ass' hide, and in the same manner, his left [shoe]; all the way up to his buttocks [he was] naked and, to relate further, his genitals were visible in their entirety, and the black hairs of his arse and groin. In addition, his anus also constantly gaped so openly when he bent his head and looked down on the ground, that a cat could enter into it and rest [there] for an entire year, passing winter in company with his consort cat, that in the vast forest of his groin a stork could build its nest and a hoopoe could have a place of his own. This illmade man, made an object of mockery before people, was, like a ghost, a source of terror to children.

So, Moriuht came to the leading person in the kingdom, who lived on after the kingship of her celebrated, outstanding, wealthy and dutiful husband, I mean, of course, to [our] lady the countess.[65] Before her feet he fell down, tearfully relating his [tale]: 'You are, in our eyes, our father, mother and what remains of life [for me]. Now, I beseech you, confer your skilled advice on Moriuht. The sorrow of it all! Moriuht's beloved goat has been taken as plunder by the vikings and sold in your territory. You must restore her to me in my pitiful state. I beg you, since I have suffered countless dangers over sea and

64 These are the children of Richard II, Richard III and Robert the Magnificent, rather than the children of Richard I as McDonough (p. 111 commentary on line 11) suggests.

65 *regnum* (kingdom) and *sceptra* (kingship) might be translated, respectively, as 'realm' and 'rule'.

your land, as you see for yourself. Night and day I stay awake and swollen with passion I do not sleep, so that Moriuht whom you see, who is devoted to you, is considering death.' That is to say, this inept orator, who is considered eminent, does not follow logically the matters [and] deportment demanded by the art of rhetoric. For if versed in rhetoric, he would not have related those wretched points in composing his own [ad]dress in the presence of clever people. But since it is not our task to censure Moriuht (what does a man have to do with a monster?), I shall proceed with my story on my own.

At these words, the understanding lady smiled for a moment and buried her beautiful face beneath her headband. After some time, she uncovered her face and in a friendly manner addressed the Irishman as follows: 'You are an Irishman by country [of origin], as is evident in your appearance. Set a limit on your tears; your sweet ornament will be restored if she is [anywhere] in the whole land of ours. Go with speed through our realm and seek out your source of joy. When you have found her, be sure to report everything to me. If she happens to have been sold and is being kept in that service, I shall personally restore [her] to you, but I will give [her] back [to you] at a price.' On every side, everyone laughed at these words of their lady [and] then Moriuht withdrew from the lofty throne.

Around this monstrosity, young men and boys began to chant, 'Baldy, try to find [your] goat, little baldy, try to find [your] goat.' A second time he gave a return to the gods and appeased them and from the shrine he heard a voice: 'Your beloved is in Vaudreuil.[66] This port is not far distant from the city of your lady; rather frequently, it is full to bursting with the merchandise of wealth [supplied] by vikings.' Moriuht approaching this harbour confident about his wife, with his eyes surveyed every ship. When he did not see her there, moving through all the dwelling-places he caught sight of his spouse in a certain abode that belonged to a pauper. This woman, applying herself urgently over the iron comb of her owner's loom was leading a wretched life, like a slave. The shoulder of the ill-fated girl was bare and bare [too] were her beautiful breasts. By the evidence of these was Glicerium recognised.

[Lines 323–32] Finally, Moriuht arrived at the city still singing, conveying on his shoulders the great joy [of his life]. He was rewarded with his wife but he continued to be gloomy in his look,

---

66 Vaudreuil (Eure, c. Pont de l'Arche), is an inland port on the River Eure where it meets the Seine.

[for] the best was distressed on account of his goat's offspring. Just as the clever lady asked the Irishman Moriuht what was the matter, he mentioned that his child was missing. Inquiries were made about the child and she was ransomed with a quarter of a coin and with a portion of half a cooked loaf of bread. When [the child] had been brought, Moriuht is received with very great joy by his nanny-goat and his precious little kid.

[Lines 481–98] At this point, I could impose a limit on Moriuht's exploits, but Moriuht's far-flung reputation constrains me still. In the season of winter, the cuckoo sings in the woods, 'I am calling you, Moriuht, coo, coo, coo, coo, Moriuht.' for indeed, Moriuth, stay alert so that your goat, as she lies at her ease, does not, as may happen, say that a gentle bull is present alongside you, who is to become your successor by licking the buttocks of your beloved goat. Standing erect with his knees crouched, he repeatedly smacks his lips [?]. Be on your guard, Moriuht, that you do not lie down backwards, as may happen, [beware] that a bull does not come and lick your buttocks, friend.

I shall impose a limit on my abusive remarks, that I may not contaminate my pen and the poetic talent of my mind by making such statements. I wish now that Moriuht, a vessel of damnation, may disappear, and that [tale] he brought to the distinguished table of the bishop. As a result it now happens that through his tippling he has become a leech. Alas! lying flat on his back in the act of vomiting he is carried [away].

May you, Archbishop, fare well [and] I pray that through all time [my] Lady may prosper, a source of glory for the realm, [and] brilliant sources of light for their subjects.

28 Robert of Torigni, Deeds of the Dukes of the Normans (on Gunnor)

Robert of Torigni inserted many genealogies of Anglo-Norman families into his version of the *Gesta Normannorum Ducum*, Book VIII, *c.* 36–7, written in the late 1130s. All genealogies ultimately stem from Countess Gunnor of Normandy (*c.* 960–1031), her sisters Sainsfrida, Wevia and Duvelina, and unnamed nieces (her sisters' daughters).

GND, ii. 267–9.

[Book VIII, c. 36] ... Because we have referred to Countess Gunnor on account of Roger of Montgomery's mother, her niece, I should like to write down the story as reported by people of old of how Gunnor came to be Duke Richard's wife. One day when Duke Richard was told of the celebrated beauty of the wife of one of his foresters, who lived in a place called Equiqueville near the town of Arques, he deliberately went hunting there in order to see for himself whether the report he had learned from several folk was true.[67] While staying in the forester's house, the duke was so struck by the beauty of his wife's face that he summoned his host to bring his wife, called Sainsfrida, that night to his bedchamber. Very sadly the man reported this to Sainsfrida, a wise woman who comforted him by saying that she would send in her place her sister Gunnor, a virgin even more beautiful than her. And thus it happened. Once the duke perceived the trick he was delighted that he had not committed the sin of adultery with another man's wife. Gunnor bore him three sons and three daughters, as is set out above in the book containing the deeds of this duke. When, however, the duke wished his son Robert to become Archbishop of Rouen, he was told by some people that according to canon law this was impossible, because his mother had not been married. Therefore Duke Richard married Countess Gunnor according to the Christian custom and during the wedding ceremony the children, who were already born, were covered by a cloak together with their parents. Thereafter Robert could be appointed archbishop of Rouen.[68]

[Book VIII, c. 37] Apart from Sainsfrida, Gunnor had two sisters, Wevia and Duvelina. The latter, with the help of the countess, who was a very wise woman, married Turulf of Pont-Audemer. He was the son of someone called Torf, after whom several towns are called Tourville to the present day. Turulf's brother was Turketil, father of Ansketil of Harcourt. Turulf had by his wife Humphrey of Vieilles, father of Roger of Beaumont. The third of Countess Gunnor's sisters married Osbern of Bolbec, by whom she bore the first Walter Giffard, and then Godfrey, father of William of Arques ...

67 Saint-Vaast d'Equiqueville (Seine-Mar., c. Envermeu).
68 In 989.

29 Robert of Torigni, Deeds of the Dukes of the Normans (on Empress Matilda)

Robert of Torigni's interpolations in the *Gesta Normannorum Ducum* on Empress Matilda, daughter of King Henry I and Matilda II, who was a benefactress of Le Bec. Most of Robert's information on the empress must have come from her own mouth.

GND, ii, 217–19, 245–7.

[Book VIII, c. 11] By his wife Matilda II, queen of the English, he [Henry I] had a son called William and a daughter who shared her mother's name and also her character.[69] As a girl of not more than five years old she was sought in marriage by Henry, the fifth to be king and the fourth august emperor of the Romans and the Germans, who having won her hand welcomed her, escorted by famous men, bishops and counts acting as envoys, laden with innumerable presents from both her parents, to his realm, where at Utrecht the following Easter they were betrothed.[70] After the betrothal she was crowned on St James's Day at Mainz by the archbishop of Cologne [Frederick, 1100–31] assisted by his bishops, especially the bishop of Trier [Bruno, 1102–24], who reverently held her in his arms while she was consecrated. He commanded that having been a consecrated queen, she should be carefully educated, until the appropriate time for the marriage, and that she should learn the language and behave according to the customs of the Germans ... .

[Book VIII, c. 27] The same Empress Matilda sufficiently demonstrated her wisdom and religious devotion to the present and future generations when she was lying ill in Rouen. She distributed not only her incomparable imperial treasures, brought with her from Italy, but also those that royal, or rather her father's, magnificence had bestowed on her from the inexhaustible treasuries of the English, to the churches of several provinces, to religious of both sexes, to the poor, widows and orphans. She gave them with so devout a hand that she did not even hesitate to dispose of the silk mattress on which she had slept during her illness, but sold it and ordered the money she received to be given to lepers. In her liberality she was especially generous to the abbey of Le Bec, more than to any other or indeed all

---

69 William Adelin died in the White Ship disaster in November 1120; Empress Matilda died in 1167 and was buried at Le Bec.

70 Matilda was eight, not five, years old when the betrothal took place in 1110, see Chibnall, 1991, 17.

other monasteries in Neustria.[71] She bestowed on Le Bec several gifts, which were precious on account of their material as well as their make. Byzantium itself would have reckoned them most dear. They are most valuable till the end of time, an example of the diligence and affection of the empress for the monastery; and moreover it would be superfluous to describe them individually or give their names in order to impress the memory of this perfect and illustrious lady upon the hearts of its monks. It was an immense delight even for the noble guests – and these have often contemplated the treasures of noble churches – to view her gifts. Even a Greek or Arab traveller in this part of the world would enjoy the same pleasure in seeing them. We are convinced, and indeed it is right to be, that the most just Judge of all will repay her a hundredfold, not only in the future, but even in the present world, what she with joy, devotion, and generosity gave to her servants. There is no doubt about her present reward for, by God's mercy, she recovered after her illness and her health was fully restored; and the breath of her reviving health wholly refreshed her monks, the monks of Le Bec, who had striven in constant toil of prayer for her health before and above all other people's and almost been worn out in their endeavour.

[Book VIII, c. 28] We should not like to pass in silence, or rather, neglect to write down in 'letters an inch long' for future generations, that before she recovered she had won over her father's permission to be buried in the monastery of Le Bec. At first he refused saying that it was inappropriate for his daughter, an empress who more than once had worn the imperial crown while being led by the hands of the pope through the city of Romulus, the capital of the world, to be buried in a monastery however renowned for its religious observance and reputation, but that she should surely be carried to Rouen, the metropolis of Normandy, to be buried in the main church alongside her ancestors Rollo and his son William Longsword, who had conquered Neustria by force of arms. Having received the king's answer, she sent him another message telling him that she would never be happy again unless her wish in this matter could be fulfilled. O woman of admirable virtue and prudent counsel, who spurned worldly pomp for the burial of her body! For she knew it is better for the souls of the deceased to be buried at a place where prayers are very frequently and devoutly offered to God. Convinced by the devotion of an empress and the prudence of a daughter, the father,

71 For a list of her gifts to the abbey, see Porée, i, 650–1, 653.

who himself used to surpass others by his virtue and devotion, yielded and granted her wish and request to be buried at Le Bec. But by the will of God, as we have said above, she recovered and her health was completely restored ...

30 Geoffrey Malaterra, Deeds of Count Roger and his brother Duke Robert

Geoffrey Malaterra's The Deeds of Count Roger of Calabria and Sicily and of Duke Robert Guiscard his brother was written c. 1090 by Geoffrey, a Norman, who had moved to southern Italy and worked at the court of Count Roger.

De rebus gestis Rogerii Calabriae et Siciliae Comitis et Roberti Guiscardi fratris eius auctore Gaufredo Malaterra, ed. E. Pontieri (Bologna, 1927), pp. 24–5; trsl. G. A. Loud.

[Book I, c. 38] However, lest anybody think that those who had not come to Apulia with the other brothers but had remained in Normandy were less worthy than their siblings, something ought to be said about Serlo.[72] He was considered to be one of the more outstanding soldiers [*milites*] in Normandy, and so, when he was wronged by a certain powerful man, he sought revenge and killed him. Not wishing to suffer the resulting anger of Count Robert [the Magnificent 1027–35], the son of Richard II and father of the renowned William, king of the English, he fled into Brittany. He remained there for some time, where he was universally esteemed for his valour. He sent envoys to secure peace from Count Robert, but when he could not obtain this he launched a number of damning raids into Normandy.

[Book I, c. 39] On one particular occasion this same Count Robert was besieging a castle called Tillières on the border between France and Normandy.[73] A certain French soldier [*miles*] left the fortification every day seeking single combat with men from the Norman army, and vanquished many challengers. The count became afraid of the loss of men, and forbade anyone to go out to meet him. He told his men that although they were avoiding a dangerous task they could plead in mitigation that they were not doing this through fear but

---

72 Serlo, son of Tancred of Hauteville, cannot be traced in documents from Normandy; for his background and family see no. **71**.

73 See above, no. **24**. The incident took place before Tillières was ceded again to the Normans, *GND*, ii, 100–1.

because of their prince's prohibition. Serlo, who was at this time living in Brittany, was told of this, and could not stomach the shame brought upon his people. So, accompanied by two squires, he went to Tillières, and outside its gate he offered a challenge to single combat, waiting on horseback with his lance at rest. The man who was used to cutting down others was roused to anger and, splendidly equipped, rode furiously out, shouting at him; he demanded to know who the challenger was, and urged him to retire and save his life. Serlo revealed his name, but refused to withdraw, and when they fought together the man who had cast down others was himself overthrown by his mighty spear. Many people from both sides were looking on, but none of them knew who Serlo was; however, as the victor he was given a glorious reception by the Normans. He paraded through their camp with the severed head on his lance, but said not a word to his own people, and hurried back to Brittany. The count therefore sent an envoy with orders to find out who he was and summoned him to come and see him. The announcement was made that he was Serlo, son of Tancred, and that he had gone to Brittany because an order had been given to drive him forth from his own people and he wished to avoid the anger of the prince whom he had offended. He would willingly remain in exile, even as a pauper, in obedience to the prince's order, until the latter's anger had been appeased. The count was filled with remorse, and being unwilling to do without such a man any longer, told Serlo to come to him. He hastened to meet the count who received him back into his grace, and granted him the kiss of peace. The possessions which he had lost were restored to him; he was enriched with a wife who herself was well-endowed with property, and the count treated him as one of his followers [*familiares*].

[Book I, c. 40] It is by no means absurd to say something worthy of record about Tancred, the father of these great sons. During his youth he was dedicated to military endeavours and passed through a number of different regions and princely courts. He was anxious to secure praise through his exploits, and during the time when he was one of the household [*familia*] of the count of the Normans, Richard II, the fourth in the line from Duke Rollo, he not only gained a great reputation but also made his fortune. One day the prince went out hunting. He was much addicted to such a sport, as is the way of wealthy men. He flushed out a boar of extraordinary size, of the type known as a *sanglier*. It was, however, his custom, as it is with other powerful men, that when he himself had flushed out some game, it should be left to him, and nobody else should dare to kill it. The hounds were rushing after the boar and the count was following on behind more slowly, because the forest foliage was extremely thick. The boar was afraid of being attacked from behind, and so when it found a rock it used this as bulwark to guard its rear, and then it put forward its head with its tusks to protect itself from the dogs. Since these hounds lacked the hunter's assistance, the boar had soon inflicted many wounds upon them with its sharp tusks when, quite by chance, Tancred arrived. Seeing the carnage among the hounds he rushed to help them, even though he was well-aware of the prince's custom. On seing him, the boar ignored the dogs and charged towards him. Tancred was confident of his strength and waited for it, sword on high. He did not just inflict a wound upon it, but drove the sharp point right thought his tough forehead down into its heart, and left the hilt sticking out next to the head – indeed out of the whole long length of his sword only the hilt was left outside the boar's body. So it was vanquished; but Tancred, leaving the sword in its forehead, took himself a long way off, to ensure that the count would not find out who had done this. Coming upon the dead boar, the count was amazed. He ordered his companions to find out whether anyone was wounded; then the sword was discovered, stuck in the boar's forehead, and this blow caused amazement. The count asked whose sword it was and, to prevent whoever had done this concealing his exploit, he pardoned him. When it was discovered that Tancred was the culprit, he was much praised by the count and the others, and though already much-prized, he was thereafter even more highly honoured. From then he served in the count's court with ten soldiers [*milites*] under him.

III: THE NORMANS AND BRITAIN: THE NORMAN CONQUEST

Introduction

The story of the relations between Normandy and England which culminated in the Norman Conquest of 1066 begins with the pact negotiated between Duke Richard I and King Aethelred II of England (978–1016) in 991, whereby both parties bound themselves to friendship and non-aggression. Although the text does not refer explicitly to each ruler's dealings with the vikings, who were still roaming the Channel, the peace was clearly meant to prevent the duke and the king from sheltering each other's Scandinavian enemies or allowing them to trade their spoils in each other's harbours:

> And Richard is to receive none of the king's men, or of his enemies, nor the king any of his, without his seal.[1]

In 1002 the pact was followed by a marriage alliance. King Aethelred II married Duke Richard I's daughter by Gunnor, named Emma. When in 1013 King Svein of Denmark seized the throne of England the royal couple with their children Edward, Alfred and Godgyfu took refuge at the Norman court. Three years later Aethelred died and within another year Emma had married Cnut, son of her husband's successor King Svein, who in 1016 had become king of all England.[2] Edward and Alfred, known as the aethelings – a name for English royal sons – with their sister Godgyfu remained in Normandy waiting their time to return to England. After two unsuccessful attempts, including one in 1036 when Alfred was captured and killed, Edward was recalled by his half-brother Harthacnut, son of Emma and Cnut, and went to England.[3] Within a year Harthacnut was dead and Edward came to the throne. Edward's subsequent marriage with Edith, daughter of the mighty Earl Godwin, brought the Godwin family into an even more powerful position [31].

---

1 *EHD*, i, no. 230, pp. 823–4; Keynes, 1991, 81–113; also below p. 223 no. 2.

2 For Emma's position, see Stafford, 1997, 215–20.

3 Keynes, 1990, 173–206.

Earl Godwin had risen to power under King Cnut not least because of his marriage to the king's sister-in-law Gytha, of Danish origin. Amassing steadily extensive lands, especially in Wessex and East Anglia, Godwin turned into the most powerful earl of England. He was one of the King Edward's fiercest critics with regard to the Norman advisers he had brought with him from the duchy. In 1050 after King Edward had appointed one of them, Robert, bishop of London, as archbishop of Canterbury against the wish of the locals, who favoured a kinsman of Godwin, he found himself faced by a formidable Godwinian alliance. Godwin and his sons Harold and Tostig went into exile and Queen Edith was temporarily banished to a nunnery. With Flemish support Earl Godwin returned and persuaded the king to ban the Norman influence from his court (Archbishop Robert left Canterbury and retired to his old monastery of Jumièges in Normandy) and to take back his wife. The royal marriage remained childless and the lack of an heir ultimately led to the contested succession of 1066.[4] The childlessness was variously explained. Some people claimed that the royal couple remained virgins and thus never consummated their marriage, while others maintained that the queen was sterile. Whatever the reasons may have been, it became increasingly obvious that no children would be born and that, therefore, the succession to the throne needed to be resolved by finding a successor. During his time as king, Edward made several promises to several different candidates, playing them off against each other while at the same time keeping his options open.[5] Among the candidates were Edward, grandson of King Aethelred II, who had fled to Hungary in 1016 but was recalled by King Edward in 1057. He died in mysterious circumstances in London. Prince Edward's son Edgar from then onwards was the only descendant in the direct male line, and it was to him, a young boy of twelve, that the English nobility turned in 1066. Much more powerful were the sons of Godwin, Harold and Tostig, brothers-in-law of the king. There is evidence that the queen had a preference for Tostig, while the king may have preferred Harold.[6] Late in 1065 Tostig was exiled from England as a result of his failure to control the Northumbrian aristocracy and thus was disqualified as potential royal heir. When in early January of the next year King

4 Barlow, 1970, 81–5; Stafford, 1997, 72–3, 260–1.

5 Barlow, 1970, 214–40.

6 *The Life of King Edward who rests at Westminster*, ed. and trsl. F. Barlow (Oxford, 1992), p. lxv and Stafford, 1997, 270–2.

Edward was approaching death, he is said to have promised the throne to Harold who, with Edith, was present at the king's side. Thus it was Harold who was elected and crowned king on 6 January 1066. Criticism of Harold as king is scarce but can be detected in some English sources based on direct or indirect information on Harold's accession of the throne or his actions as king [49, 50].

The Norman version of the succession dispute is, not surprisingly, different. Before Archbishop Robert's disgrace, so the Norman story goes, the archbishop had been sent to Normandy to convey a message to Duke William to tell him that he would be King Edward's heir and successor. In the same year, 1051, Duke William, by then married and himself the father of a son, and thus obviously fertile, may have come to England to receive a similar message himself. No Norman source refers to such a visit, only the D version of the Anglo-Saxon Chronicle mentions it.[7] The Norman sources also tell us that in 1064 or 1065 Harold was sent to Normandy to repeat King Edward's promise of the English throne to Duke William. William of Poitiers, followed by Orderic Vitalis, adds that an agreement was struck with regard to the castle of Dover and that it was sealed by a marriage alliance [32, 33]. The English sources are silent, except for some post-conquest accounts, such as Eadmer of Canterbury, who claims that the real reason for Harold's visit was to negotiate for the release of Harold's brother Wulfnoth and nephew Hakon who had been hostages in Normandy since 1051 [44]. The claims from both sides seem contradictory, but are not necessarily so. Most historians agree that it is likely that in the early 1050s some promise was made to William of Normandy with regard to the succession. It is, however, unlikely that a renewal of such a promise was the reason for Earl Harold's visit even though the question of the succession may have come up between Duke William and Earl Harold. All sources date from after the events of 1066 and their authors, whether English or Norman, wrote with hindsight naturally selecting those stories which would 'prove' whatever argument they wished to put forward.

Whatever the precise circumstances of the run up to King Edward's death were, Duke William assumed that Harold was his ally and that in the event of the king's death, Harold would not obstruct his (William's) coronation. When, however, on 5 January 1066 Edward died, Harold was elected and on the next day, the day of the king's funeral, he was crowned king. The indecent haste is mentioned by

7 Anglo-Saxon Chronicle 'D' 1052 (for 1051).

most chroniclers and the account from Bury St Edmunds is especially important because it presumably derives from Abbot Baldwin (1065–97/98) who as the royal physician had attended King Edward in his last illness [49]. Apparently, on his deathbed the king had promised the throne to Harold and this annulled any earlier promise. Duke William protested against Harold's betrayal, as he saw it, since Harold had promised to be faithful to him and had now broken his word. Harold was branded a perjurer by the Normans, who petitioned Pope Alexander II (1061–73) and appealed for his (moral) support.[8] He sent the Norman duke a banner as a sign of his approval. The papal gesture was interpreted as a sign that God permitted the use of force to get rid of Harold and obtain the throne of England. William then, armed with papal approval, recruited a large invasion army which was gathered together in the course of the summer of 1066 [32, 33]. Some military leaders who had given him their support met together on 18 June at Caen on the occasion for the blessing of the abbey church of Sainte-Trinité.[9] There the duke and duchess offered their child Cecilia as an oblate to the nunnery, even though she did not enter until 1075.[10] For this event the poet Fulcoius of Beauvais wrote an interesting poem comparing William the Conqueror with the biblical hero Jephthah. Both were illegitimate sons who against all odds won a victory over their enemies and both had offered their daughters to God before the battle as war sacrifices [39]. The poem, interestingly, puts across the grief of the mother at the sacrifice: a clear reference, it seems, to some contemporary notion that Duchess Matilda had not agreed readily with her husband's decision to use their daughter for such a purpose. The army gathered at the mouth of the Dives in August and by the middle of September the duke had moved his fleet up north to Saint-Valéry-sur-Somme from where it departed for England on 28 September.

Meanwhile King Harold had been called north by the invasion of his brother Tostig, the exiled earl of Northumbria, with King Harold Hardrada of Norway (1047–66). After Tostig had left England he had first sought refuge in Flanders, where he assembled a fleet. Having attempted an invasion of the south coast of England he retreated and opened negotiations with the king of Norway, who himself had grievances against the new king of England. The two joined forces

8 Garnett, 1986, 91–116 at 110–11.

9 Fauroux, no. 231.

10 Orderic, iii, 8–10; Van Houts, 1989a, 39–62 at 42.

and landed on the Yorkshire coast in the summer of 1066. The invaders won the first battle of Fulford Bridge but then lost the second one at Stamford Bridge on 25 September, where both Tostig and Harold Hardrada were killed. On his way south, King Harold disbanded his army and was then told that William the Conqueror had invaded Sussex. In London he hastily put together a new army and marched to the south coast where, just north of Hastings, battle was joined on Saturday 14 October [40–3].

By the end of that 'day of destiny for England', in William of Malmesbury's words, the greater part of the English earls had been killed together with their king and his brothers and other lesser nobles and soldiers [48]. The English suffered defeat and William marched on north to Canterbury. From there he circled round London, went west and arrived at Winchester where the treasury and Queen Edith were. Laden with English money and probably with the queen's consent he turned round and marched for London. On his way there, at Berkhamsted, he received the submission of the English, including Prince Edgar, who had been acclaimed king by some of the nobility. Then on Christmas Day he was crowned in Westminster Abbey by Archbishop Ealdred of York, although it was another four years before Pope Alexander II allowed his legates to crown him, again, with a papal crown at Winchester as a sign of international acknowledgement of the ultimate Norman victory that most of England had been subdued. What gave William his victory at Hastings was the result of a combination of factors: his superb military skills (especially his use of cavalry during the battle itself), financial backing from his nobility and monasteries, international diplomacy which gave him papal support, and a good sense of timing. But above all, he was lucky in that King Harold had been lured north by Tostig and King Harold Hardrada. Had Harold not fought two battles within one month before Hastings, he might well have won.

Little is known about the English victims, for so few contemporary English sources have survived, if they had been written at all.[11] What little we know has to be pieced together from twelfth-century sources and from contemporary continental 'press' reports. All over the western world William the Conqueror's victory was noted but not with universal approval. Apart from the French annalists, most other European commentators denounced William for his use of violence, the bloodbath

11 Van Houts, 1996a, 167–80.

he had created at Hastings and the dubious grounds on which he justified his case. Some claimed that Pope Alexander II's adviser, Cardinal Hildebrand later Gregory VII, had dirtied his hands by associating himself with a murderer.[12]

Domesday Book testifies to the violence and extortion used by the Normans to acquire land. The endless litigation between monasteries and Norman despoilers illustrates the loss of land to the newcomers.[13] As far away as Bavaria the annalists knew that the indigenous population of England paid a high price, with their loss not only of the lives of dear ones but also of land [38]. Frutolf of Michelsberg in particular singles out the lot of widows, some of whom were forced to marry William's followers. Their estates were part of the reward system by which the Conqueror handed out land in return for services rendered. For the men marriage provided an additional argument to legitimise their hold over the land. Firstly, it was by right of battle that the Normans claimed possession. Secondly, legitimate marriage gave them added security for themselves and their offspring who in turn could inherit the land legally. A significant number of women took refuge in nunneries to avoid marriage by coercion. That Frutolf's account, written down in Bavaria, was no exaggeration is shown by Lanfranc's letter to Bishop Geoffrey of Coutances in which he asks advice on what to do with the women in nunneries who had taken refuge there 'out of fear for the French', but who later wished to leave the monasteries [36]. Both Lanfranc and the king felt that such women should be allowed to leave the nunneries because they had not entered the convent for religious reasons.[14]

Not only Normans but Flemish, Bretons and northern French immigrants got a share of the spoils. Younger sons especially took part in the grabbing of land. Robert of Rhuddlan's success in post-conquest England was somewhat helped by his earlier stay as one of King Edward's Norman soldiers, but even so his ultimate death at the hands of the Welsh was in the eyes of some a just punishment for Norman greed [51].

The traumatic effect of the English defeat reverberated through the next hundred years of historiography. Long-buried memories surfaced up to three generations after 1066 based on oral stories handed down

---

12 Van Houts, 1995, 851–3.

13 Fleming, 1998, 53, 68–86.

14 Stafford, 1994, 221–49 and Van Houts, 1999, 137–8.

from father to son to grandson and in the female line as well. On the
whole the English reaction is expressed through the mouths of ecclesiastical authors, monks and secular priests who wrote during the
second generation after the Conquest, that is in the first half of the
twelfth century. Then a torrent of chronicles, quite exceptional in
number, cascaded forth. Words of despair and resignation, acceptance
and self-punishment poured from their pens. The mood was one of
self-castigation: surely the English must have sinned unwittingly for
them to be punished by God with subjection to the Normans. Of all
the English authors, William of Malmesbury is the most vocal in his
self-analysis of why the English were punished [48]. Elsewhere I
have discussed the fact that three of the historians writing about post-
conquest England – Orderic Vitalis, William of Malmesbury (both
monks) and Henry of Huntingdon (archdeacon) – were the products
of mixed marriages of an English mother and a Norman/French father.
To what extent are these sons repeating childhood stories told by their
English mothers about the past in England?[15] Against this background it is significant to note the blend of characterisations of Normans
as warriors and supremely skilled in military matters with the self-
castigating moralisations of the sinful nature of the English. These
attributes are transmitted to us by the non-fighters in society: women
(the mothers of the chroniclers) and monks/priests as chroniclers.

The question of the impact of the Conquest, posed in the early twelfth
century, has remained the heart of historiographical debate ever
since.[16] The short-term consequences were pictured in the charters
and Domesday Book, which show massive changes of landholding at
the top but relatively little change at the bottom: peasants and smaller
tenants all stayed put. William initially took over the Anglo-Saxon
earldoms left vacant by the deaths of earls at Hastings. In 1067 William
fitzOsbern received extensive lands in the west, and Chris Lewis has
tentatively suggested that he was taking over the former Wessex
estates that had belonged to Harold before he became king. After his
death in February 1071 he was succeeded by his son Roger. Kent was
entrusted to Bishop Odo of Bayeux, half-brother of the Conqueror,
but he can also be found in other counties (Hertfordshire, Surrey,
Buckinghamshire and probably Middlesex as well) that had belonged

15 Van Houts, 1999, 138–9; Clark, 1978, 223–51.

16 Chibnall, 1999 for an excellent overview; Douglas, 1977, 57–77 is good on the
   sixteenth and seventeenth centuries and Stafford, 1994, 221–34 highlights aspects
   of the nineteenth-century debate.

to Leofwine, younger brother of Harold. In East Anglia the lands of Gyrth, Harold's other brother, were given to Ralph the Staller (d. 1069), one of King Edward's continental protégés who was succeeded by his son Ralph of Gael (exiled in 1075). Northumbria was restored to the pre-conquest Earl Morcar with Mercia similarly given back to Earl Edwin. Soon, however, rebellions forced William to split up several of the larger provinces. The rebellion of 1068 in Mercia led to its division between Hugh of Avranches in Chester and Roger of Montgomery in Shrewsbury. In 1075 when William fitzOsbern's son Roger and Ralph of Gael, possibly with the support of Earl Waltheof, one of the few indigenous earls, demanded the restoration of the larger territories given to their fathers in 1067, they were exiled and in 1076 Waltheof was executed.[17] Subsequently East Anglia was cut up into smaller portions. At the same time William the Conqueror also began to fill ecclesiastical vacancies with continental candidates.

The first bishop to die during his regime was Bishop Wulfric of Dorchester (1053–67) who was replaced with Remigius, almoner of Fécamp, who had contributed ships to the Conqueror's fleet [37]. A few years later he moved the see from Dorchester to Lincoln. Apart from two brothers, who succeeded each other as bishop in Durham (see below), few bishops were expelled from office. King William waited for natural causes like illness or death before he appointed new bishops. On the whole most sitting bishops collaborated with the Normans, an attitude that was probably understandable considering the fact that many pre-conquest bishops had been continental appointees of King Edward anyway. William, bishop of London (1051–75), for example, was a Norman. The ethnic diversity of the Anglo-Saxon Church's hierarchy may unintentionally have prepared the bishops for such collaboration.[18] Bishop Giso of Wells (1061–88) had been one of Edward's appointees and had not hidden his criticism of King Harold [50], while the Anglo-Saxon veteran bishop Wulfstan of Worcester (1062–95), a close ally of King Harold, supported the Conqueror from the submission at Berkhamsted in the autumn of 1066 onwards [47].[19] Of the pre-conquest bishops only a few were deprived of their office: Archbishop Stigand was ultimately deposed on canonical rather than political grounds due to the fact that he held several sees in plurality; his brother Aethelmaer of Elmham (1047–70) followed him presumably

17 Lewis, 1990, 207–24.

18 For important reflections on this topic, see Keynes, 1996, 206–13.

19 For Giso, see Keynes, 1996, 204–71 and for Wulfstan, see Mason, 1990, 131–42.

on the grounds of kinship. Two other brothers, Aethelric (1041–56, d. 1072) and Aethelwine (1056–71), bishops of Durham, were imprisoned as a result of rebellion. The elderly Bishop Aethelric of Selsey was also deposed though for reasons now unknown. His disgrace, however, did not prevent the Conqueror from demanding his services during the trial at Penenden Heath (one of the famous post-conquest land inquests), when he ordered the old man to be taken by carriage to the court session to give his expert advice on English law.[20]

The case of abbots was different. Their willingness to collaborate was distinctly less marked than that of most bishops. Many identified their monasteries' interests with those of the Anglo-Saxon royal house and actively resisted William's supremacy. That East Anglia in particular became a hotbed of Anglo-Saxon resistance was due not least to the many abbots who held out against the Conqueror. Ultimately the openly critical abbots were reconciled with William, for example Abbots Brand of Peterborough (1066–69) and Thurstan of Ely (?1066–72/ 73). Others, like Abbot Wulfketel of Crowland (c. 1061–85/86) and Aelfwine of Ramsey (1043–79/80), quietly helped the old English aristocracy behind the scenes. With the exception of Ramsey, where Aelfwine's successor was an English monk from St Augustine's at Canterbury, all abbots were replaced with continental monks after their natural deaths. With the new abbots came new practices – changes in the liturgy and the removal of some local saints from liturgical calendars – as well as, in due course, new buildings. Some Romanesque architecture can be found in pre-conquest churches, with Westminster Abbey being the most famous example. In the 1120s, however, as William of Malmesbury in his 'Deeds of the Kings of the English' (Book III, c. 246) famously points out, the whole of England was covered in buildings erected 'in a style unknown before' [48].

One of the most obvious features of Norman conquest was the military architecture. Although Anglo-Saxon England had known fortified manors and some stone fortifications, stone motte and bailey structures of the type springing up in north-western France were unusual.[21] After the conquest King William ordered the construction of many castles all over England. Domesday Book shows how whole quarters of towns like Cambridge, Winchester, Wallingford and Exeter were destroyed to make way for them. In Norwich the Domesday com-

20 Barlow, 1979, 113–14.
21 Pounds, 1990, 3–71; Strickland, 1996, 369–73.

missioners justified non-payment of tax by some bordars (holders of a cottage in return for a small service) on the grounds that their poverty was caused by the loss of their houses due to the building of the castle.[22] Not only in towns but in the countryside castles appeared as garrison places for William's troops. Particularly in the border areas with Wales [51] and with Scotland and along the Channel coast, fortifications were built at, for example, Chepstow, Rhuddlan, York and Durham, and Dover. Also, existing wooden, or sometimes stone-built, Anglo-Saxon fortified manors were used by the newcomers as foundations for strongholds. One such example is Goltho manor in Lincolnshire. The first traces of construction can be dated to the ninth century when a defence work against the vikings was constructed, then in the tenth century the wooden structures were encircled by an earthwork defence. Between the end of the eleventh and the beginning of the twelfth century this was partially destroyed to make way for a motte and bailey castle.[23]

Continuation of Anglo-Saxon government and administrative struc-tures remained the long-term consequence of the Norman conquest of England. Thus the hundred and shire courts, the sophisticated taxation system and the jobs attached to these institutions flourished under foreign domination. In this respect the Norman adaptation of indi-genous Anglo-Saxon institutions is comparable to the vikings' adapt-ation of Frankish institutions in Normandy as well as the Norman acceptance of Lombard, and sometimes Byzantine, offices in southern Italy. Some innovations occurred, notably in knight service and military tenure, that is, the system according to which landholders receive lands to which obligations were attached, the most onerous being military service. Historians disagree to what extent these developments were precipitated by the military organisation of the Conquest itself. Marjorie Chibnall, for example, argues that post-conquest English knight service was a result of the particular circum-stances of the Conquest and that it has no parallel in pre–1066 Normandy. John Gillingham, however, prefers to see continuation of Anglo-Saxon military obligations, some of which were attached to the holding of land, beyond 1066 albeit with some slight modifications. Whereas James Holt has suggested that the Conqueror devised a completely new system for England after 1066 that did not become

22 Van Houts, 1996b, 9.
23 Beresford, 1981, 13–36.

fully operational until the time of his sons William Rufus (1087–1100) and Henry I (1100–35).[24] Debates on the nature of the Norman conquest of England, its immediate causes and effects and its long-term consequences will continue for many generations to come. The selection of texts that follows is meant to stimulate such debates, not to stifle them.

Norman and other continental narratives

31   The Discovery and Miracles of St Vulfran

The Discovery and Miracles of St Vulfran was written *c.* 1053–54 at the monastery of Saint-Wandrille in Normandy. The chapter printed below contains important evidence for the sort of information about King Edward (his alleged consecration as king as a boy, his title of king while in Normandy) that was available in Normandy before 1066.

Inventio et miracula sancti Vulfranni, ed. Dom J. Laporte, Mélanges publiés par la Société de l'Histoire de Normandie, 14e s. (Rouen, 1938), pp. 29–31.

[C. 18] Aethelred, king of the English, took Richard [II]'s sister Emma in marriage, and had two sons, Edward and Alfred, whom he wanted to educate in their native tongue.[25] Edward was the elder of the two, though still no more than a soft and callow youth. With the blessing of his father, and the approval of the people of the realm, he was anointed and consecrated as king. Not long afterwards (when his above-mentioned father had passed from the land of the living), Cnut, king of the Danes, the son of King Svein, brutally invaded the kingdom of the English with a naval force.[26] And for the rest of his life he ordered his affairs using a strong sense of virtue as the bench-mark of his judgement. And so it came to pass that the aforementioned young boys fled across the sea to their uncle, Richard. They were kindly received by him and generously brought up as if they were his sons. For as long as he lived, they were held in the highest regard in the land of the Normans. King Cnut meanwhile, naturally fierce and strong in arms, tightened his grip on the kingdom which he had seized. After friendly negotiations with her brother Richard, Cnut took Emma, the widowed queen of the aforementioned King Aethelred, to be his

---

24 Chibnall, 1982, 65–77; Gillingham, 1981, 53–64; Holt, 1983, 89–106.

25 King Aethelred II (978–1016) married Emma, daughter of Richard I of Normandy and Gunnor in 1002. There was also a daughter Godgyfu.

26 Cnut, king of England (1016–35) and Denmark (1019–35).

lawful wife. He had by her a son Harthecnut, and also a daughter
Grumith [= Gunhild].[27] When Grumith had reached a marriageable
age, she married Henry [III], emperor of the Romans and the Saxons,
with much nobility, as befits a royal daughter, in great secular splendour. She only produced a daughter for him, because she herself died
shortly afterwards. When this daughter came of age, she spurned
carnal union in favour of the heavenly consort. And taking up her
sacred veil, she dedicated her virginity to God, the king of all.[28] A
long time passed under three kings, namely Cnut, whom I spoke
about earlier, his son Harold whom his concubine Aelfgifu bore, but
also Hardecnut his legitimate son.[29] Edward, nephew of the glorious
leader Richard, returned to his father's kingdom with the support of
the Normans.[30] And, after many events which would take too long to
recount, he remained on the throne for a long time. He also accepted
as wife the daughter of Godwin, great leader of his land, who had
already cruelly killed his [Edward's] brother Alfred along with many
others by a trick.[31] He exalted the men of both orders [= ecclesiastical
and secular] whom he had brought with him from Normandy with
numerous offices [*honoribus*] and enriched them with gold and silver.
But let's pass over these things and return to the story.

32 William of Jumièges and Orderic Vitalis, Deeds of the Dukes of the Normans

The *Gesta Normannorum Ducum* was written *c.* 1060 and updated with an
account of the Norman Conquest not later than early 1070 by William, a
monk of Jumièges. William's text is a piece of propaganda justifying William
the Conqueror's actions. His text was revised and updated *c.* 1113 by Orderic
Vitalis, a monk of Saint-Evroult, who toned down the pro-Norman sentiments and added material which for William's original public had been common knowledge. William of Jumièges's account is printed in roman with
Orderic's revisions printed between square brackets and in italic.

GND, ii, 159–73.

27 Harthecnut, king of Denmark and king of England (1040–42); Gunhild married
   King Henry III of Germany in 1036 and died in 1038.
28 Beatrix, later abbess of Quedlinburg.
29 Harold Harefoot, king of England (1035–40) was Cnut's son by his concubine
   Aelfgifu of Northampton.
30 Edward the Confessor, king of England (1042–66).
31 Edward married Edith, daughter of Earl Godwin in 1045. Alfred was killed by
   King Harold at the instigation of Earl Godwin in 1036; he died at Ely.

[Book VII, c. 13 (*Orderic's version chapter 31*)] Edward, king of the
English, by the will of God having no heir, had in the past sent
Robert, archbishop of Canterbury to the duke [William], to appoint
him heir to the kingdom given to him by God.[32] But he also, at a later
date, sent to him Harold, the greatest of all earls in his realm in
wealth, honour and power, that he should swear fealty to the duke
concerning his crown and, according to the Christian custom, pledge
it with oaths.[33] When Harold set out on this mission, sailing across
the sea he landed in Ponthieu, where he fell into the hands of Guy,
count of Abbeville, who instantly captured him and his men and
threw him into prison.[34] When the duke heard this he sent envoys and
under pressure had him set free. After Harold had stayed with him for
some time and had sworn fealty to him about the kingdom with many
oaths he sent him back to the king with many gifts. [*He made Harold
stay with him for some time and took him on an expedition against the
Bretons. Then after Harold had sworn fealty to him about the kingdom with
many oaths he promised that he would give him his daughter Adeliza with
half the kingdom of England. Later he sent him back to the king with many
gifts but kept as hostage his handsome brother Wulfnoth.*][35] At length,
having completed his fortunate life, Edward departed from this world
in the year of the Lord 1065.[36] Whereupon Harold immediately seized
Edward's kingdom, thus perjuring the fealty he had sworn to the duke.
The duke then instantly dispatched messengers to Harold urging him
to renounce this act of folly and with worthy submission keep the
faith which he had pledged with an oath. But Harold not only
disdained to listen, he even unfaithfully turned all English people
against him. [*After Gruffydd, king of the Welsh, had been slain by the
enemy's sword, Harold married his beautiful widow, daughter of the well-
known Earl Aelfgar.*][37] At that time a star appeared in the north-west,
its three-forked tail stretched far into the southern sky remaining
visible for fifteen days; and it portended, as many said, a change in
some kingdom.

32 Robert, bishop of London (1044–51) and archbishop of Canterbury (1051–52) died
   at Jumièges in 1055.

33 Harold, son of Earl Godwin, king of England (Jan.–Oct. 1066).

34 Guy, count of Ponthieu (1053–1100).

35 Wulfnoth was released from captivity in 1087.

36 Edward died on 5 January 1066.

37 Gruffydd ap Llywelyn (d. 1063); his widow was Ealdgyth (or Edith), daughter of
   Earl Aelfgar of Mercia, who later married Harold Godwineson.

[Book VII, (c. 32)] [*Furthermore the duke sent Earl Tostig to England, but Harold's fleet forcefully drove him away, so Tostig, prevented from entering England safely or returning to Normandy because of a contrary wind, went instead to King Harold Fairhair of Norway and begged him for support as a suppliant. The king granted Tostig's request with pleasure ...*][38]

[Book VII, c. 14] When the duke who by right should have been crowned with the royal diadem, observed how Harold daily grew in strength, he had a fleet of up to 3000 ships hastily put together and anchored at Saint-Valéry in Ponthieu, full of vigorous horses and very strong men armed with hauberks and helmets.[39] Thence with favourable wind and sails billowing aloft, he crossed the sea and landed at Pevensey, where at once he built a strongly entrenched fortification. He entrusted it to his warriors and speedily went to Hastings, where he quickly raised another one. Harold hastening to take him by surprise gathered innumerable English forces and, riding through the night, arrived at the battlefield at dawn.[40]

[Book VII, (c. 34)] [*William, thus safe again, turned all his furious energy against the English. When he observed how Harold daily grew in strength, he ordered a fleet of up to 3000 ships hastily, but with care, to be put together and anchored it collectively at Saint-Valéry in Ponthieu. He gathered an immense army of Normans, Flemish, French and Bretons and when the fleet was prepared he landed the vessels with vigorous horses and very strong men armed with hauberks and helmets. The fleet was thus ready, with a following wind and sails billowing aloft he crossed the sea and landed at Pevensey, where at once he built a strongly entrenched fortification which he entrusted to his valiant warriors. Thence he speedily went to Hastings, where he built another one. Meanwhile, when the Normans invaded the kingdom which Harold had seized, Harold was involved in a war against his brother Tostig in which he slew his own brother as well as King Harold of Norway who had come in support of Tostig. This battle, during which almost the complete Norwegian forces were slain by the English, took place on Saturday 7 October.*[41] *Thereafter Harold victoriously returned to London, but he was not able to rejoice in fratricide or security for long, because soon an envoy arrived with the news of the Norman invasion.*]

38 Tostig, son of Godwin and brother of Harold, formerly earl of Northumbria, was killed at Stamford Bridge in 1066.

39 Saint-Valéry-sur-Somme (Somme).

40 The battle took place on Saturday 14 October at a site approx. 8 miles north-west of Hastings, now called Battle.

41 The battle of Stamford Bridge took place on 25 September.

[Book VII, (c. 35)] [*When he was told that a more aggressive enemy presented himself in another part of the country, he prepared himself again for yet another combat. For he was a brave and valiant man, very handsome, pleasant in speech, and a good friend to all. However, his mother and other loyal friends tried to dissuade him from war; and his brother Earl Gyrth said to him:[42] 'My dearest brother and lord, you should let your prowess temper your valour. You have only just returned worn out after the war against the Norwegians; and now you are hastening to fight once more against the Normans. Rest, I beg you. You ought to contemplate carefully what you pledged by oaths to the duke of the Normans. Take care that you do not commit perjury and by this crime destroy yourself as well as the flower of our people and bring everlasting shame to our posterity. I have sworn no oath and owe nothing to Duke William; therefore I am ready to join battle boldly with him for my native soil. But you, my brother, should wait in peace wherever you like for the outcome of this war lest the liberty of the English should perish through your ruin.' After these words Harold flew into a violent rage. He despised the counsel that seemed wise to his friends, taunted his brother who loyally gave him advice, and when his mother anxiously tried to hold him back, he insolently kicked her. Then for six days he gathered innumerable English forces. Hastening to take the duke by surprise he rode through the night and arrived at the battlefield at dawn.*]

[Book VII, c. 15 (c. 36)] The duke, taking precautions in case of a night-attack, ordered his army to stand to arms from dusk to dawn. Early in the morning [*of Saturday*] he arranged his legions of warriors in three divisions and without any fear advanced against the dreadful enemy. Battle was joined at the third hour and the slaughter [*on both sides*] continued until the late evening. Harold himself was slain, pierced with mortal wounds, during the first assault. When the English learned that their king had met his death, they greatly feared for their own lives and turned about at nightfall and sought refuge in flight. [*When thus the Normans saw the English fleeing they pursued them obstinately through the night till Sunday to their own harm. For high grass concealed an ancient rampart and as the Normans fully armed on their horses rode up against it, they fell, one on top of the other, thus crushing each other to death.[43] It is said that almost 15,000 men perished there. Thus on 14 October Almighty God punished the countless sinners on both sides in diverse*

42 Gyrth, son of Earl Godwin and brother of Harold was killed at the battle. His mother was Gytha, a sister-in-law of King Cnut.
43 The so-called 'Malfosse' incident.

ways. For while madness was raging among the Normans God slaughtered many thousands of Englishmen, who long before had unjustly murdered the innocent Alfred and on the previous Saturday without mercy had slain King Harold, Earl Tostig and many others. The following night the same Judge avenged the English and plunged the fierce Normans into the abyss of destruction. For they had been guilty of coveting the goods of other men contrary to the precept of the law, and as the Psalmist says: 'Their feet were swift to shed blood'[44] and so they encountered grief and wretchedness in their ways.]

[Book VII, c. 16] The most valiant duke returned from the slaughter of his enemy to the battlefield at midnight. Early next morning [*on Sunday*] having looted the enemy and buried the corpses of his own dear men, he set out for London. It is said that in this battle many thousands of English perished; this being God's retribution for their unjust murder of Alfred, King Edward's brother. The very fortunate war-leader, supported by excellent counsel, came to a first stop at Wallingford, where turning away from the city he crossed the river and ordered his troops to pitch camp there. From there he moved on to London, where upon entering the city some scouts, sent ahead, found many rebels determined to offer every possible resistance. Fighting followed immediately and thus London was plunged into mourning for the loss of her sons and citizens. When the Londoners finally realised that they could resist no longer, they gave hostages and surrendered themselves and all they possessed to the most noble conqueror and hereditary lord. Thus triumph being complete, despite the manifold perils, our most illustrious duke, to whom our written tribute cannot do enough justice, on Christmas Day, was elected king by all magnates, both of the Normans and the English, anointed with holy chrism by the bishops of the realm, and crowned with the royal diadem in the year of our Lord 1066. [*The site, where, as we mentioned above, the combat took place is therefore called Battle to the present day. There King William founded a monastery dedicated to the Holy Trinity, filled it with monks of Marmoutier founded by Saint Martin near Tours, and endowed it with the necessary wealth to enable them to pray for the dead of both sides ...*][45]

---

44 Cf. Ps. 13:3.

45 Battle Abbey's foundation, though promised early by William the Conqueror, did not in fact take shape until well into the 1070s.

33   William of Poitiers, Deeds of Duke William

William of Poitiers, formerly a chaplain of William the Conqueror, wrote his
biography of William between 1071 and 1077. He had not been present during
the crossing or the invasion of England in 1066, but his story is based on
eyewitness accounts of others.

The Gesta Guillelmi of William of Poitiers, ed. and trsl. R. H. C. Davis and M.
Chibnall (Oxford, 1998), pp. 101–3, 103–5, 105–7, 109–11, 111–17, 123, 127,
131, 133, 135, 139, 159–61, 179–81.

[II, c. 1] A true report came unexpectedly, that the English land had
lost its king [Edward] and that Harold [Godwineson] was wearing
its crown. And this mad Englishman could not endure to await the
decision of a public election, but on the tragic day when that best of
all men was buried, while all the people were mourning, he violated
his oath and seized the royal throne with acclamation, with the
connivance of a few wicked men. He received an impious consecration
from Stigand, who had been deprived of his priestly office by the just
zeal and anathema of the pope.[46]

Duke William, after taking counsel with his men, determined to
avenge this injury with arms, and claim his inheritance by force of
arms, although many of the greater men argued speciously that the
enterprise was too arduous and far beyond the resources of Normandy. At that time Normandy had in its counsels, besides the bishops
and abbots, outstanding men of the secular order, shining luminaries
who were the pride of that assembly: Robert count of Mortain, Robert
count of Eu, the brother of Hugh bishop of Lisieux (of whose life we
have written above), Richard count of Evreux, son of Archbishop
Robert, Roger of Beaumont, Roger of Montgomery, William fitz-
Osbern, Hugh the vicomte.[47] It was thanks to their wisdom and their
efforts that Normandy could be kept in safety; supported by these the
Roman republic would not have needed two hundred senators, if she
had preserved her ancient power in our own time. However, we have
ascertained that in every debate all gave way to the wisdom of their
prince, as if by divine inspiration he foreknew what was to be done
and what avoided ...

[II, c. 2] It would take too long to narrate in detail how under his
prudent direction ships were built and equipped with arms, men,

46 Stigand held the sees of Canterbury and Winchester in plurality and was deposed
   in 1070.

47 For these magnates of William, see Hollister, 1987, 219–48.

provisions, and the other things necessary for war, and how all Normandy eagerly bent to the task. No less wisely did he determine who should govern and protect Normandy during his absence. Foreign knights flocked to help him in great numbers, attracted partly by the well-known liberality of the duke, but all fully confident of the justice of his cause.

After forbidding all plunder, he supported 50,000 men-at-arms at his own expense while unfavourable winds delayed him for a month at the mouth of the Dives. Such was his moderation and wisdom that abundant provision was made for the soldiers and their hosts, and no one was permitted to seize anything. The cattle and flocks of the people of the province grazed safely whether in the fields or on the waste. The crops waited unharmed for the scythe of the harvester, and were neither trampled by the proud stampede of horsemen nor cut by foragers. A man who was weak or unarmed could ride singing on his horse wherever he wished, without trembling at the sight of squadrons of knights.

[II, c. 3] At that time the see of St Peter at Rome was occupied by Pope Alexander [1061–73], a most worthy man who was obeyed and consulted by the universal Church, for he gave just and salutary replies ... Seeking approval of this pope, whom he had informed of the business in hand, the duke received a banner with his blessing, to signify the approval of St Peter, by following which he might attack the enemy with greater confidence and safety. Also he had recently made a friendly pact with Henry [IV], emperor of the Romans, son of the emperor Henry [III] and grandson of Emperor Conrad [II], by the terms of which Germany would, if requested, come to his aid against any enemy. Svein, king of the Danes, also pledged his faith to him through ambassadors; but he was to show himself the faithful friend of the duke's enemies, as you will see in reading in what follows of the harm he did ...

[II, c. 6] Presently the whole fleet, equipped with such great fore-sight, was blown from the mouth of the Dives and the neighbouring ports, where they had long waited for a south wind to carry them across, and was driven by the breath of the west wind to moorings at Saint-Valéry. There too the leader, whom neither the delay and the contrary wind nor the terrible shipwrecks nor the craven flight of many who had pledged their faith to him could shake, committed himself with the utmost confidence by prayers, gifts and vows, to the protec-tion of heaven, meeting adversity with good counsel, he concealed (as far as he could) the loss of those who had been drowned, by burying them in secret; and by daily increasing supplies he alleviated want. By divers encouragement he retained the terrified and put heart into the fearful. He strove with holy prayers to such a point that he had the body of Valéry, a confessor most acceptable to God, carried out of the basilica to quell the contrary wind and bring a favourable one; all the assembled men-at-arms who were to set out with him shared in taking up the same arms of humility.[48]

[II, c. 7] At length the expected wind blows; voices and hands are raised to heaven in thanks, and at the same time a tumult arises as each one encourages the other. The land is left behind with all speed and they embark eagerly on the hazardous journey. Their haste is so great that, as one calls for his squire and another for his companion, most, heedless of their dependants or friends or their necessary baggage, hurry forward fearful of being left behind. The duke meanwhile, eager and vehement, admonishes any laggards he can see and urges them to embark in the ships.

But for fear that they might reach the shore to which they were bound before dawn and run into danger in a hostile and unknown landing place, he has an order proclaimed by a herald that when they reach the open sea they should all rest at anchor for a short watch of the night not far from his ship, until they see a lamp lit at his masthead, and hear the sound of a trumpet as a signal to sail on ...

[II, c. 8] Carried by a favourable breeze to Pevensey, they disembarked easily from the ships, without having to offer battle. In fact, Harold had gone away to Yorkshire to fight against his brother Tostig and Harold, king of the Norwegians. It is not surprising that his brother, incensed by his injuries and eager to regain his confiscated lands, should have brought foreign arms against Harold, while his sister,[49] so unlike him in morals but unable to take up arms against him, fought him with prayers and counsel; for he was a man soiled with lasciviousness, a cruel murderer, resplendent with plundered riches, and an enemy of the good and the just. This woman of masculine wisdom, who knew what was good and revered in her life, wished William, who was wise, just and strong, to rule over the English, since her husband, King Edward, had chosen him as his successor by adoption in place of a son.

48 The church at Saint-Valéry-sur-Somme.
49 Queen Edith, widow of King Edward and sister of King Harold, died in 1075.

[II, c. 9] *The battle between Duke William and Harold, king of the English*
The Normans, rejoicing after they had landed, occupied Pevensey with
their first fortification, and Hastings with their second, as a refuge for
themselves and a defence for their ships. Marius and Pompey the
Great, each eminent for his astuteness and achievements, deserved a
triumph, the former having brought Jugurtha in chains to Rome, the
latter having forced Mithridates to take poison; but though daring to
lead a whole army into enemy territory, each was chary of putting
himself into danger away from the main army, with only a legion. It
was their custom, as it still is the custom of leaders, to send out
scouts, but not to go themselves on reconnaissance, being more concerned with preserving their own lives than with making provisions
for the army. But William was quick to investigate the region and its
inhabitants with a company of no more than twenty-five knights.
When he returned on foot because of the difficulty of the path (not
without laughter, though the reader may laugh) he deserved genuine
praise, for he carried on his own shoulders both his own hauberk and
that of his own follower, William fitzOsbern, renowned for his bodily
strength and courage, whom he had relieved of his iron burden...

[II, c. 14] Meanwhile, experienced knights who had been sent out
scouting, reported that the enemy would soon be there. For the furious
king [Harold] was hastening his march all the more because he had
heard that the lands near to the Norman camp were being laid waste.
He thought that in a night or surprise attack he might defeat them
unawares; and, in case they should try to escape, he had laid a naval
ambush for them with an armed fleet of up to 700 ships. The duke
hastily ordered all who could be found in the camp (for a large number
of his companions had gone off foraging) to arm themselves. He himself
participated in the mystery of the Mass with the greatest devotion, and
strengthened his body and soul by receiving in communion the body
and holy blood of the Lord. He hung around his neck in humility the
relics whose protection Harold had forfeited by breaking the oath he
had sworn on them.[50] Two bishops who had accompanied him from
Normandy, Odo of Bayeux and Geoffrey of Coutances, were in his company, together with numerous clerks and not a few monks.[51] This clerical
body prepared for combat with prayers. Anyone else would have been

---

50 These were almost certainly the relics which William later bequeathed to Battle
   Abbey (Van Houts, 1996a, 167–8).

51 Odo, bishop of Bayeux (1049/50–1097) was William's half-brother; Geoffrey, bishop
   of Coutances (1048–93).

terrified by putting on his hauberk back to front. But William laughed at this inversion as an accident and did not fear it as a bad omen ...

[II, c. 16] Now this is the well-planned order in which he advanced behind the banner which the pope had sent him. He placed foot-soldiers in front, armed with arrows and cross-bows; likewise foot-soldiers in the second rank, but more powerful and wearing hauberks; finally squadrons of mounted knights, in the middle of which he himself rode with the strongest force, so that he could direct operations on all sides with hand and voice ... For huge forces of English had assembled from all the shires. Some showed zeal for Harold, and all showed love of their country, which they wished to defend against invaders even though their cause was unjust. The land of the Danes (who were allied by blood) also sent copious forces. However, not daring to fight with William on equal terms, for they thought him more formidable than the king of the Norwegians, they took their stand on higher ground, on a hill near to the wood through which they had come. At once dismounting from their horses they lined up all on foot in a dense formation. Undeterred by the roughness of the ground, the duke with his men climbed slowly up the steep slope ...

[II, c. 19] ... The English fought confidently with all their might, striving particularly to prevent a gap being opened by their attackers. They were so tightly packed together that there was hardly room for the slain to fall. However, paths were cut through them in several places by the weapons of the most valiant knights. Pressing home the attack were men from Maine, Frenchmen, Bretons, Aquitainians, above all Normans whose valour was outstanding. A certain young Norman knight, Robert the son of Roger of Beaumont, nephew and heir of Hugh count of Meulan through Hugh's sister Adeline, while fighting that day in his first battle performed a praiseworthy deed, which deserves to be immortalised; charging with the battalion he com-manded on the right wing, he laid the enemy low with the greatest audacity ...[52]

[II, c. 22] Those who took part in this battle were Eustace count of Boulogne, William son of Richard count of Evreux, Geoffrey son of Rotrou count of Mortagne, William fitz Osbern, Aimeri vicomte of Thouars, Walter Giffard, Hugh of Montfort, Ralph of Tosny, Hugh of Grandmesnil, William of Warenne, and many others of military

52 Robert of Beaumont, who was only fifteen years old at the time, died in 1118.

distinction and great renown, whose names deserve to be remembered in the annals of history among the very greatest warriors ... Against Harold, who was such a man as poems liken to Hector or Turnus, William would have dared to fight in single combat no less than Achilles against Hector, or Aeneas against Turnus ...

[II, c. 25] So, after completing the victory, William returned to the battlefield and discovered the extent of the slaughter, surveying it not without pity, even though it had been inflicted on impious men, and even though it is just and glorious and praiseworthy to kill a tyrant. Far and wide the earth was covered with the flower of the English nobility and youth, drenched in blood. The king [Harold]'s two brothers were found very near to his body. He himself was recognised by certain marks, not by his face, for he had been despoiled of all signs of status. He was carried into the camp of the duke, who entrusted his burial to William surnamed Malet, not to his mother, though she offered his weight in gold for the body of her beloved son.[53] For he knew it was not seemly to accept gold for such an transaction. He considered that it would be unworthy for him to be buried as his mother wished, when innumerable men lay unburied because of his overweening greed. It was said in jest that he should be placed as guardian of the shore and sea, which in his madness he had once occupied with his armies ...

[William then went on to Romney, Dover, Canterbury, 'Broken Tower', Wallingford]

[II, c. 33] ... To his magnates he taught conduct worthy of him and of his dignity, and as a friend counselled equity. He warned them to be constantly mindful of the eternal King by whose aid they had conquered, and that it was never seemly to overburden the conquered, who were Christians no less than they themselves were, lest those they had justly defeated be goaded into rebellion by their injuries. He added that it was not honourable to act disgracefully when abroad in such a way as to bring dishonour to the land where one was born or brought up. He restrained the knights of middling rank and the common soldiers with appropriate regulations. Women were safe from the violence which passionate men often inflict. Even those offences indulged with the consent of shameless women were forbidden, so as to avoid scandal. He scarcely allowed the soldiers to drink in taverns,

---

53 William Malet was of half-English and half-Norman origin (Hart, 1996, 123–66). For Harold's burial, see also nos **35** and **46**.

since drunkenness leads to quarrels and quarrels to murder. He forbade strife, murder, and every kind of plunder, restraining the people
with arms and the arms with laws. Judges were appointed who could
strike terror into the mass of the soldiers, and stern punishments
were decreed for offenders; nor were the Normans given greater
licence than the Bretons or the Aquitainians ...

He set a limit that was not oppressive to the collection of tribute
and all dues owed to the royal treasury. He allowed no place in his
kingdom for thefts, brigandage, or evil deeds. He ordered that mer-
chants should go freely in the harbours and on all highways, and
should suffer no harm. He did not approve of the pontificate of
Stigand, which he knew to be uncanonical, but thought better to await
the pope's sentence than to depose him hastily. Other considerations
persuaded him to suffer him for the time being and hold him in
honour, because of the very great authority he exercised over the
English. He was considering placing in the metropolitan see a man of
holy life and great renown, a master in expounding the word of God
who would know how to furnish a suitable model for his suffragan
bishops, and how to preside over the Lord's flock, and who would
wish to procure the good of all with vigilant zeal.[54] He also gave
thought to making provisions for other churches. All the first acts of
his reign were righteous ...

[II, c. 44] He celebrated Easter Sunday [1067] at the abbey of the
Holy Trinity at Fécamp, most reverently honouring the Saviour on
the feast of His resurrection, with a great gathering of venerable
bishops and abbots. Humbly standing near the choirs of the religious
orders, he compelled crowds of soldiers and people to leave their
games and come to divine service. The stepfather of the king of the
Franks, the mighty Count Ralph, was present at this court, together
with many French nobles.[55] These men, like the Normans, looked with
curiosity at the long-haired sons of the northern lands, whose beauty
the most handsome youths of 'long-haired Gaul' might have envied;
nor did they yield anything to the beauty of girls.[56] Indeed as they
looked at the clothes of the king and his courtiers, woven and encrusted
with gold, they considered whatever they had seen before to be of

---

54 Lanfranc, monk of Le Bec, abbot of Caen (1063–70), archbishop of Canterbury
   (1070–89).
55 Ralph IV, count of Amiens, Valois and the Vexin (1038–74), father of St Simon of
   Vexin, see below, no. **56**.
56 Cf. no. **47**.

little worth. Similarly they marvelled at the vessels of silver and gold, of whose number and beauty incredible things could truthfully be told. At a great banquet they drank only from such goblets or from horns of wild oxen decorated with the same metal at both ends. Indeed they noted many such things, fitting the magnificence of a king, which they praised on their return home because of their novelty. But they recognised that far more distinguished and memorable than these things was the splendour of the king himself ...

34   Baudri of Bourgueil, Poem for Adela

Baudri, abbot of Bourgueil (1089–1107) and archbishop of Dol (1107–30), wrote his poem 'To Countess Adela' for William the Conqueror's daughter Adela, countess of Blois-Chartres, before 1102. It purports to describe Adela's chamber and the tapestries hanging on its four walls. One of these depicts the story of the Norman Conquest, but it is unlikely that Adela's tapestry is the same as the Bayeux Tapestry, which can be securely located at Bayeux. This does not preclude the possibility that the poet was inspired by the Bayeux Tapestry or that Adela had a similar embroidery in her house.

Trsl. M. W. Herren, in S. A. Brown, *The Bayeux Tapestry: History and Bibliography* (Woodbridge, 1988), Appendix III, pp. 168–70, 174–5, 177. The line numbers correspond with *Baldricus Burgulianus, Carmina*, no. 134, ed. K. Hilbert, Editiones Heidelbergenses, 19 (Heidelberg, 1979), pp. 155–7, 161–2, 163–4.

In short the brilliance of the tapestry was so great,/ you might say they excelled the splendour of Phoebus./ Moreover, you could reckon by reading the script of the titles/ that new and true stories are contained in the hanging./ 235/ Now it was seen that Normandy brought forth a child,/ William by name, a leader of men./ His own people soon drove him out of his native land/ and squandered his paternal rights.[57]/ But soon the Prince, by dint of his exceptional strength,/ overcame them and subjected them to his laws./ 240/ He moved through the successive ranks, beginning with consul;/ soon he will be beyond the ranks: to emperor from duke./ Behold the sky flashes, now flashes the reddening comet;/ with spreading rays it glitters towards the people./ But lest you think we have sung falsely about this star,/ 245/ we all have seen it ten times more./ In itself it was more remarkable than other stars,/ and if it had not been long, it would have been another moon./ Indeed it was seen to trail lengthy traces/ and scatter its rays far behind./ 250/

57 Cf. no. **39**, lines 37–8.

The older generation is dumbfounded and marvels,/ and what they see they pronounce to be great signs./ Mothers suckling their darling babes/ strike both breast and mouth and dread new portents./ A younger generation seeks answers from its elders,/ 255/ and inquisitive boys hang on the lips of old men./ What the sign betokens they know not – though they say they know;/ it is allowed to the many to invent much./ Look, now the Norman power has summoned its court;/ 260/ William himself, sitting in an exalted place,/ orders the court to sit, as was proper according to custom./ After the throng of elders and youths fell into hushed silence,/ speaking as befitted a ruler, he said:/ 265/ 'I shall explain straightaway why I have summoned you hither,/ my lords; only suppress your tumult./ My legates, whom I sent recently/ to claim the English realms for me, have returned./ The English realms come under my sway by right/ of consanguinity, as the kingdom now has no heir./ 270/ Moreover, while he was dying, my kinsman/ made me his heir and gave it in writing./ Legates came, swore that the kingdom was my due;/ we too believed their promised faith./ 275/ We bade them and our emissaries to hasten quickly/ to bear our agreement to the king./ They found that the king had succumbed more quickly/ than I wanted, or than was necessary, believe me./ What would the lawless spirit of the English not presume?/ 280/ They have presumed to deny my rights./ A certain perjurer was also sent to us/ to usurp the crown that is our due.[58]/ He swore allegiance to me with his own hand;/ how he lies now: then he gave his pledge./ 285/ Hear my legates.' He orders the legates to speak;/ they give witness to the same./ The nobles direct their eyes and ears towards them as they speak;/ then they carefully note the words of the consul./ The hero, struck by the plight of his kingdom/ 290/ and his honour, added that he should claim his rights:/ 'In uncertain affairs, one may ask what must be done,/ noble lords; now I do not hesitate to reply./ I know clearly what I shall do; but I beseech you to want what I want./ Our orders are still to be imposed./ 295/ But I know that you will laud the same course; what I applaud and approve, may you likewise approve. I am not the sort to let sworn debts be reneged, nor am I one to fear the trumpets of Mars./ Rather, I am the kind with whom an enemy soon shares its own./ 300/

That is, if I am content to let them share./ Before now, my lords, it was not part of your honour/ to be held in contempt of your own property./ Bold Normandy overturned the forces of Maine/ and

58 Earl Harold during his visit to Normandy in 1064/65.

completely subjected the people./ 305/ Your power now rules Apulia's claims and even bridles them,/ and Rome's ferocity trembles at your name./ A thousand men hope to be our Guiscard/ and grow feverish at the sound of his name./ Shall I tell you how you beat down the fierce Gauls /310/ and the number of times that you blunted their swords?/ Or was the whole of Brittany able to withstand you?/ For the Angevins themselves dread your swords./ Indeed, our clemency spared Bourgueil;/ our cavalry drove back the Angevins at the Loire./ 315/ So let the perjuring Englishman feel your accustomed might;/ don't let his madness check you in weakness./ Up to now, my lords, you have addressed me by the title of consul./ now consider my consular title to be that of king;/ Let me have the name of king; you, your wealth,/ 320/ and while there is the chance, expand your estates./ England is rich with all good things as you know;/ the people are most unwarlike, an effeminate race./ We lack nothing, save only ships./ Therefore, each of you must supply the vessels we need./ 325/ Let all of you be ready in the fifth month,/ nor let your idleness allow the winds to delay us./ I myself shall supply stores and arms for our fighters;/ I myself, if you wish, shall fight as a soldier rather than as a duke.'/ ...

[The battle is in progress]

Spirits depart through many kinds of wounds./ Mars favours both sides and smiles on both;/ no matter which party falls lifeless in battle/ Death quickly follows: now these perish, now those./ Death arrives, hastening with swords of his own./ 455/ Unless I am wrong, the sisterly Fates must have wearied:/ many a man fell, though his thread was not broken!/ Many a dying man departs unbidden to the kingdom below,/ and the Fates hasten a thousand with their hands./ Victory without injury is granted to neither side./ 460/ and the dry earth runs with blood of the slain./ At last, lest the celestial omens proved false,/ the merciful deity inclines to the Normans./ A shaft pierces Harold with deadly doom;/ he is the end of the war: he was also its cause./ 465/ He had girded his shameful head with royal gold/ and violated his kingdom with perjuring hand./ The English army trembles, God himself increases their fear;/ a whole legion suddenly gives way in fight./ Nor afterwards could so great a host be reassembled;/ 470/ the impetuous band flees, cast headlong./ Many a one strangles as his vital force is cut;/ many perished on their own swords./ Arms do injury to all; those who are able lay down their arms;/ the soldier who was fighting just now departs unarmed./ 475/

Now the Normans loosen the reins and harry the backs/ of the fleeing; swift horses crush many./ The cause of the triumph at hand
quickens the Normans;/ a slain king and dread dishearten the English./
The Normans are roused, so that war may be avoided in future;/ 480/
the English are dispirited by death all around them./ The Norman
attacks more savagely than a young tiger;/ the Englishman falls
everywhere more meekly than a lamb./ Just as the wolf, compelled to
the sheepfold by keen hunger,/ knows not how to spare the innocent
flocks,/ 485/ But does not cease until he has destroyed every one,/ so
the cruelty of the Normans does not grow cool. But by God's mercy,
night interrupted the war and the slaughter,/ and gave the English
opportunity for safety and flight./ No night was more welcome to the
English than this one,/ 490/ wherein they might take counsel for
their woes. At night they take whatever position chance offers them:/
some occupy caves, others find shelter in bushes./ The nobles, though
weakened, seize the towns,/ and build fences and walls./ 495/ It was
already daylight when the duke orders the standards of victory/ to be
brought forward, and he addresses his men:/ 'O race unbroken, O
people ever most invincible,/ whom the clear sign of heaven summon
to rule,/ Although the great fury of war, the task of night'/ 500/ ...

The nobility, people, cities, towns and country likewise/ establish the
duke as king over themselves./ William, who was a consul, has now
become a king;/ a star trailing blood announced the event./ A king
obtained a kingdom, a duke a dukedom,/ 555/ and so he obtained the
title of a caesar.[59] He alone, while he lived, ruled a double office/ and
was more exalted than all caesars and dukes./ No duke was better, no
king ever braver;/ as king he wore a crown, as duke he bore the arms
of a duke./ 560/ The wealth of the king, his glory, his wars and
triumphs —/ each could be seen on the tapestry./ I would believe that
the figures were real and alive,/ if flesh and sensation were not wanting in the images./ Letters pointed out the events and each of the
figures in such a way/ 565/ that whoever sees them can read them, if
he knows how./ If you could believe that this weaving really existed/
you would read true things on it, O writing paper./ But you might also
say: 'What he wrote ought to have been;/ a subject like this was
becoming to this goddess/ 570/ He wrote by arranging matters which
behoved/ the beauty of this Lady — and they are worthy of her.'/

59 Many of the poems composed for William the Conqueror after 1066 contain a
   reference to the possibility that he might one day become emperor (Van Houts,
   1989a, 43).

35   Guy of Amiens, Song of the Battle of Hastings

Bishop Guy of Amiens wrote the Song of the Battle of Hastings probably in
1067. He was not an eyewitness but relied on others for information. In 1068
he accompanied Duchess Matilda to England as her chaplain. Some modern
historians doubt the authenticity of the poem and argue in favour of an early
twelfth-century date in which case the author is unknown.

The Carmen de Hastingae Proelio of Guy, Bishop of Amiens, ed. and trsl. C. Morton
and H. Muntz (Oxford, 1972), pp. 37–9; for the debate on the authenticity,
see Davis, 1978, 241–61; Van Houts, 1989a, 39–62 and Orlandi, 1996, 117–27.

[Lines 575–96] The mother of Harold, in the toils of overwhelming
grief, sent even to the duke himself, asking with entreaties that he
would restore to her, unhappy woman, a widow and bereft of three
sons, the bones of one in place of three; or, if it pleased him, she would
outweigh the body in pure gold.[60] But the duke, infuriated, utterly
rejected both petitions, swearing that he would sooner entrust the
shores of that very port to him – under a heap of stones! Therefore,
even as he had sworn, he commanded the body to be buried in the
earth on the high summit of the cliff; and forthwith a certain man,
part Norman, part English, Harold's comrade [*compater*] willingly
did his behest;[61] for he swiftly took up the king's body and buried it,
setting over it a stone, and he wrote as epitaph: 'By the duke's commands, O Harold, you rest here a king,/ That you may still be
guardian of the shore and sea.'/ The duke lamenting amidst his people
over the buried bones, distributed alms to the poor of Christ. And
with the name of duke laid aside, and the king being thus interred, he
departed from that place, having assumed the royal title ...[62]

36   Lanfranc of Canterbury, Letter to Bishop Geoffrey of Coutances

This letter from Lanfranc, archbishop of Canterbury (1070–89), to Bishop
Geoffrey of Coutances (1048–93) asks advice as to the status of the women
who had taken refuge in English nunneries; dated 1077–89.

The Letters of Lanfranc, archbishop of Canterbury, ed. and trsl. H. Clover and M.
Gibson (Oxford, 1979), no. 53, p. 167 where the addressee is wrongly identified as Bishop Gundulf of Rochester.

60 Countess Gytha, wife of Earl Godwin, left England for Flanders in 1068 (see no.
40).

61 William Malet, see above no. **33**.

62 This is clearly an exaggeration; William did not became king until Christmas 1066.

Archbishop Lanfranc sends his respectful greeting to the reverend
Bishop G[eoffrey]. Concerning the nuns about whom you wrote to
me, dearest father, I give you this reply. Nuns who have made profession that they will keep a rule or who, although not yet professed,
have been presented at the altar, are to be enjoined, exhorted and
obliged to keep the rule in their manner of life. But those who have
been neither professed nor presented at the altar are to be sent away
at once without change of status, until their desire to remain in
religion is examined more carefully. As to those who as you tell me
fled to a monastery not for love of the religious life but for fear of the
French, if they can prove that this was so by the unambiguous
witness of the nuns better than they, let them be granted unrestricted
leave to depart. This is the king's policy and our own. May the Lord
almighty preserve your life according to his own good pleasure.

37   The Ship List of William the Conqueror

The Ship List of William the Conqueror lists the contributions of ships and
soldiers made by his magnates in 1066. The list dates from c. 1067–72 and
was probably drawn up at the abbey of Fécamp.

Trsl. from the Latin edn in Van Houts, 1987, 175.

When William, duke of the Normans, came to England to acquire the
throne, which by right was owed to him, he received from William
fitzOsbern the steward sixty ships; from Hugh, who later became earl
of Chester, the same [number]; from Hugh of Montfort fifty ships
and sixty soldiers; from Romo [= Remigius], almoner of Fécamp,
who later became bishop of Lincoln,[63] one ship and twenty soldiers;
from Nicholas, abbot of Saint-Ouen fifteen ships and one hundred
soldiers; from Robert, count of Eu, sixty ships; from Fulk of Aunou
forty ships;[64] from Gerald the steward the same number; from William,
count of Evreux [he received] eighty ships; from Roger of Montgomery sixty ships; from Roger of Beaumont sixty ships; from Odo,
bishop of Bayeux, one hundred ships; from Robert of Mortain one
hundred and twenty [ships]; from Walter Giffard thirty [ships] and
one hundred soldiers. Apart from these ships which all together

---

63 This is the only source for Remigius's position as almoner of Fécamp. He was
   bishop of Lincoln from 1067 to 1092 and he transferred the see from Dorchester to
   Lincoln in 1072.

64 It is interesting to note that Fulk of Aunou had been in southern Italy where in
   1057 he witnessed the first surviving charter for Robert Guiscard (Ménager, no. 4).

totalled one thousand, the duke had many other ships from his other men according to their means. The duke's wife Matilda, who later became queen, in honour of her husband had a ship prepared called 'Mora' in which the duke went across. On its prow Matilda had fitted [a statue of] a child who with his right hand pointed to England and with his left hand held an ivory horn against his mouth.[65] For this reason the duke granted Matilda the earldom of Kent.[66]

38   Bavarian annals, 1066

Annals of Nieder-Altaich

The Annals of Nieder-Altaich on the Danube, written in 1075, contain the following entry under the year 1066.

Annales Althahenses maiores, ed. W. de Giesebrecht and E. L. B. ab Oefele, *MGH SS*, 20, 817–18.

That summer the Aquitainians fought a naval battle with the Anglo-Saxons and having defeated them, subjected them to their rule. Those who were present at the battle told us that 12,000 men on the side of the winners died.[67] How many died on the side of the victims can hardly be comprehended in figures. Some people also explained that the terrible, long-tailed comet had previously blazed forth because so many thousands of people perished that year.

Frutolf of Michelsberg

Frutolf of Michelsberg in Bavaria wrote in Bamberg at the end of the eleventh century.

Frutolfs und Ekkehards Chroniken und die Anonyme Kaiserchronik, ed. F. Schmale, and I. Schmale-Ott (Darmstadt, 1972), p. 78.

In the same year England was miserably attacked and finally conquered by William the Norman, who himself was made king. Soon thereafter he sent almost all the bishops of the kingdom into exile and the nobles to their death; he forced the middle-rank knights into servitude and the wives of the Anglo-Saxons into marriage with the newcomers.

65 *The Bayeux Tapestry*, ed. D. Wilson (London, 1985), plate 42 shows a similar illustration (in mirror image).

66 There is no other evidence for such a grant.

67 The oral informants may have been fleeing Anglo-Saxons who took service with the Byzantine emperor and on their way passed the monastery of Nieder-Altaich on the Danube (Van Houts, 1995, 841–2).

39 Fulcoius of Beauvais, *Jephthah* poem

Fulcoius of Beauvais wrote his poem probably in 1075 to celebrate the formal
entry of Cecilia, daughter of William the Conqueror and Matilda of Flanders,
into the nunnery of Sainte-Trinité. She had been promised as an oblate in
June 1066 as a sacrifice for her father's impending invasion of England. The
poem is a clever paraphrase of the biblical story of Jephthah, who offered his
daughter in return for victory (Judg. 12:34 ff.).

M. Colker, 'Fulcoii Belvacensis epistolae', *Traditio*, 10 (1954), 191–273 at
245–6, no. 11; trsl. A. Orchard.

'I came to see the wonders of which I had heard,
but more wonderful than those I had heard are the things I tell.'
At this time a queen lived; from the south she came:
Behold, two kings come again in this one king,
father and son. Who? Solomon and David./   5
In whom? Pray tell. In King William. Who, pray?
That man is a David, 'strong in hand', as the English bear
                                                          witness,
the same a Solomon, 'peacemaker', as the same bear witness.
He beats back, he withdraws, he heals where he wounds;
both peace and war obey him sympathetically:/   10
they sing over again how much Jephthah's victory costs.
That is what William is doing, who does not know how to
                                                spare himself:
Jephthah would not spare his daughter, nor the king his life.
      Let Jephthah's daughter not be passed over now improperly
Jephthah, about to wage battle, about to come back the victor,/ 15
vowed that he would put on his dear altars whatever he
                                                      first met:
'victory has vanquished the vow', he says.
First of all there had gone out, lest anyone is looking for more
                                                          sadness,
carrying cymbals, bring grief through her joy,
his only daughter. As she sings, the daughter badly makes a
      fool of her father./   20
      Let Jephthah's daughter not be passed over now improperly
When her father saw her, the pitiable man rent his clothes:
as he remembers his promise, he plainly forgets his prize,
repeating: 'Oh, oh me! Daughter, you trap yourself and me.'
When she asks why the victor weeps, and he explains,/   25
the maiden urged him not to act, but the pact is made,

and by her death she will let her people and her parent live.
    Let Jephthah's daughter not be passed over now improperly
The only daughter begs: send me away for three months, a
                              breathing space,'
So she can grieve for her virginity and her life./   30
She brought together fine examples with collected dances
and, if he could, he would have brought together a thousand,
when maidenly dances were joined in lovely meadows:
she produces a lament; a hundred songs reply:
    ('Let Jephthah's daughter not be passed over now
                              improperly'):/ 35
Since Jephthah was cast out, he heartily arms his heart;
since Jephthah was cast out, he has been disposed to war.
He was not an equal heir, since he is an unequal son.
But the Ammonites and the Israelites are disturbed:
there is no one to lead the Jews and bring them back;/   40
among the Hebrews there is no one worthy of triumphs except
                                    Jephthah.
    Let Jephthah's daughter not be passed over now improperly
First spurned, Jephthah was afterwards recalled;
they grant a cohort to the one they would not grant a consort.
Jephthah knew when he entered the battle   45
that the first to come out would leave as a victim.
'I am the only daughter of my father and my wholly wretched
                                    mother.
I came out first; I entered the vow that he vowed.
Let him not consider anything of me, but let him pay the debt.
    Let Jephthah's daughter not be passed over now improperly.'/ 50

English narratives

The **Anglo-Saxon Chronicle** is a convenient name for a series of annals which survive in slightly different versions in a number of manuscripts. For the English story of the Norman conquest of England versions C, D and E are the most important. Version C is contained in MS London BL Cotton Tib. B. i; it is written in a mid-eleventh-century hand, might originate from Abingdon and breaks off in 1066. Version D, in MS London BL Cotton Tib. B. iv, is written in various hands of the early twelfth century. Its origin is difficult to establish because it contains a number of Scottish interpolations, especially with regard to Queen Margaret of Scotland. Otherwise the version focuses on northern English events around York, which may indicate its place of origin or it may represent another set of interpolations. The text breaks off in 1079. The only version to continue well into the twelfth century is E. This occurs in MS Oxford Bodl. Lib. Laud Misc. 636, a Peterborough manuscript written up to the middle of the twelfth century. The text up to 1061, and probably up to 1121, may represent a version as composed in St Augustine's at Canterbury. But all the way through, the E version contains Peterborough interpolations. As sources for the Norman conquest of England it is important to remember that C is clearly a contemporary document, while versions D and E contain interpolations which cannot be dated securely. Despite these uncertainties the Anglo-Saxon annals are the closest we can come to more or less contemporary English views on the arrival of the Normans. The dates listed are those in the manuscripts; the ones between square brackets are the correct ones.

Two of the Saxon Chronicles Parallel: A Revised Text, ed. C. Plummer and J. Earle, 2 vols (Oxford, 1892–99); a new multi-volume diplomatic edition is under way: *The Anglo-Saxon Chronicle: A Collaborative Edition*, ed. D. Dumville and S. Keynes (Woodbridge, 1983–); trsl. from *English Historical Documents 1042–1189*, ed. D. Douglas and G. W. Greenaway (London, 1968), pp. 139–47.

⁕ 40   Anglo-Saxon Chronicle, version C

[1065] ... And they [the Northumbrians] adopted Morcar as their earl,[68] and Tostig went overseas and his wife with him, to Baldwin's country, and took up winter quarters at Saint Omer.[69] And King Edward came to Westminster at Christmas and consecrated the minster he had himself built to the glory of God and St Peter and all God's saints. The consecration of the church was on Holy Innocents' Day [28 December]. And he died on the eve of the Epiphany [5 January 1066], and was buried on the Feast of the Epiphany [6 January] in the same minster – as it says below:

> Now royal Edward, England's ruler
> To the Saviour resigns his righteous soul
> His sacred spirit to God's safe keeping

68 Earl of Northumbria (1065–67). He was captured at Ely in 1071 and kept in captivity in Normandy until after 1087.
69 Earl Tostig's wife was Judith, half-sister of Count Baldwin V of Flanders (1035–67).

In the life of this world he lived awhile
In kingly splendour strong in counsel.
Four and twenty was his tale of winters
That ruler of heroes lavish of riches
In fortunate time he governed the Welshmen
Ethelred's son; ruled Britons and Scots
Angles and Saxons, his eager soldiers.
All that the cold sea waves encompass
Young and loyal yielded allegiance
With all their heart to King Edward the noble.
Ever gay was the courage of the guiltless king
Though long ago, of his land bereft
He wandered in exile, over earth's far ways
After Cnut overcame Ethelred's kin
And Danes had rule of the noble realm
Of England for eight and twenty years
In succession distributing riches.
At length he came forth in lordly array
Noble in goodness, gracious and upright
Edward the glorious, guarding his homeland
Country and subjects – till on a sudden came
Death in his bitterness, bearing so dear
A lord from the earth. And angels led
His righteous soul to heaven's radiance.
Yet the wise ruler entrusted the realm
To a man of high rank, to Harold himself
A noble earl who all the time
Had loyally followed his lord's commands
With words and deeds and neglected nothing
That met the need of the people's king.

And Earl Harold was now consecrated king and he met little quiet in it as long as he ruled the realm.

[1066] in this year Harold came from York to Westminster at the Easter following the Christmas that the king died, and Easter was then on 16 April. Then all over England there was a sign in the skies such as had never been seen before. Some said it was the star 'comet' which some call the star with hair; and it first appeared on the eve of the Great Litany, that is 24 April, and so shone all the week. And soon after this came Earl Tostig from overseas into the Isle of Wight with as large a fleet as he could muster, and both money and provisions were given him. And then he went away from there and did damage everywhere along the sea-coast wherever he could reach, until he came to Sandwich. When King Harold who was in London was informed that Tostig his brother was come to Sandwich he assembled a naval force and a land force larger than had ever been assembled before in this country, because he had been told as a fact that Count William from Normandy, King Edward's kinsman, meant to come here and subdue this country. This was exactly what happened afterwards. When Tostig found that King Harold was on his way to Sandwich he went from Sandwich and took some of the sailors with him, some willingly and some unwillingly, and then went north and ravaged Lindsey and killed many good men there. When Earl Edwin and Morcar understood about this they came there and drove him out of the country, and then he went to Scotland, and the king of Scots gave him protection, and helped him with provisions, and he stayed there all of the summer.[70] Then King Harold came to Sandwich and waited for his fleet there, because it was long before it could be assembled; and when his fleet was assembled he went to the Isle of Wight and lay there all that summer and autumn; and a land force was kept everywhere along by the sea, though in the end it was no use. When it was the Feast of Nativity of St Mary [25 August] the provisions of the people were gone and nobody could stay there any longer. Then they were allowed to go home, and the king rode inland, and the ships were brought up to London and many perished before they reached there. When the ships came home, Harold, king of Norway, came by surprise north into the Tyne with a very large naval force – and no little [ ][71] or more – and Earl Tostig came to him with all those he had mustered just as they had agreed beforehand, and they both went with all the fleet up the Ouse towards York. Then King Harold in the south was informed when he disembarked that Harold, king of Norway, and Earl Tostig were come ashore near York. Then he went northwards day and night as quickly as he could assemble his force. Then before Harold could get there Earl Edwin and Earl Morcar assembled from their earldom as large a force as they could muster, and fought against the invaders and caused them heavy casualties and many of the English host were killed, and drowned and put to flight, and the Norwegians remained masters of the field. And this fight was on the eve of St Matthew the Apostle [21 September] and that was a

70 Edwin was earl of Mercia (d. 1070/71); Malcolm III Canmore, king of Scotland (1058–93).

71 Lacuna in the manuscript.

Wednesday. And then after the fight Harold, king of Norway, and Earl Tostig went to York with as large a force as suited them and they were given hostages from the city with provisions, and so went from there on board ship and had discussions with a view to complete peace, arranging that they should all go with him and subdue this country. Then in the middle of these proceedings Harold, king of the English, came on the Sunday with all his force to Tadcaster, and there marshalled his troops, and then on Monday went right on to York. And Harold, king of Norway, and Earl Tostig and their divisions were gone inland beyond York to Stamford Bridge, because they had been promised for certain that hostages would be brought to them out of all the shires. Then Harold, king of the English, came against them by surprise beyond the bridge, and there they joined battle, and went on fighting strenuously till late in the day. And there Harold, king of Norway, was killed and Earl Tostig, and numberless men with them both Norwegians and English and the Norwegians fled from the English. There was one of the Norwegians there who withstood the English host so that they could not cross the bridge or win victory. And then an Englishman shot an arrow but it was no use, and then another came under the bridge and ran him through the hauberk. Then Harold, king of the English, came over the bridge, and his host with him and there killed large numbers of both Norwegians and Flemings and Harold let the king's son Edmund go home to Norway with all the ships.

⁋41   Anglo-Saxon Chronicle, version D

[1065] ... And King Edward came to Westminster at Christmas and consecrated the minster he had built there to the glory of God and St Peter and all of God's saints. The consecration of the church was on Holy Innocents' Day [28 December]. And he died on the eve of the Epiphany [5 January 1066], and was buried on the Feast of the Epiphany [6 January] in the same minster ... And Earl Harold was now consecrated king and he met little quiet in it as long as he ruled the realm.

[1066] In this year Harold came from York to Westminster at the Easter following the Christmas that the king died, and Easter was then on 16 April. Then all over England there was seen a sign in the skies such as had never been seen before. Some said it was the star

'comet' which some call the star with hair; and it first appeared on the
eve of the Great Litany, that is 24 April, and so shone all the week.
And soon after this came Earl Tostig from overseas into the Isle of
Wight with as large a fleet as he could muster, and both money and
provisions were given him. And King Harold his brother assembled a
naval force and a land force larger than any king had ever assembled
before in this country, because he had been told that William the
Bastard meant to come here and conquer this country. This was
exactly what happened afterwards. Meanwhile Earl Tostig came to
the Humber with sixty ships and Earl Edwin came with a land force
and drove him out, and the sailors deserted him. And he went to
Scotland with twelve small vessels and there Harold, king of Norway,
met him with three hundred ships, and Tostig submitted to him and
became his man; and they both went up the Humber until they
reached York. And there Earl Edwin and Morcar his brother fought
against them: but the Norwegians had the victory. Harold, king of the
English, was informed that things had gone thus; and the fight was
on the vigil of St Matthew. Then Harold our king came upon the
Norwegians by surprise and met them beyond York at Stamford
Bridge, with a large force of English people; and that day there was a
very fierce fight on both sides. There was killed Harold Fairhair and
Earl Tostig, and the Norwegians who survived took to flight; and the
English attacked them fiercely as they pursued them until some got to
the ships. Some were drowned and some burned, and some destroyed
in various ways so that few survived and the English remained in
command of the field. The king gave quarter to Olaf, son of the Norse
king and their bishop and the earl of Orkney and all those who
survived on the ships, and they went up to our king and swore oaths
that they would always keep peace and friendship with this country;
and the king let them go home with twenty-four ships.[72] These two
pitched battles were fought within five nights. Then Count William
came from Normandy to Pevensey on Michaelmas Eve, and as soon as
they were able to move on they built a castle at Hastings. King
Harold was informed of this and he assembled a large army and came
against him at the hoary apple tree, and William came against him by
surprise before his army was drawn up in battle array. But the king
nevertheless fought hard against him, with the men who were willing
to support him, and there were heavy casualties on both sides. There
King Harold was killed and Earl Leofwine his brother and Earl

72 Olaf, king of Norway (1067–93) and Paul, earl of the Orkneys.

Gyrth, his brother, and many good men, and the French remained masters of the field, even as God granted it to them because of the sins of the people. Archbishop Ealdred and the citizens of London wanted to have Prince Edgar as king, as was his proper due;[73] and Edwin and Morcar promised him that they would fight on his side; but always the more it ought to have been forward the more it got behind, and the worse it grew from day to day, exactly as everything came to be at the end. The battle took place on the festival of Calixtus the Pope [14 October]. And Count William went back to Hastings, and waited there to see whether submission would be made to him. But when he understood that no one meant to come to him, he went inland with all his army that was left to him, and that came to him afterwards from overseas, and ravaged all the region that he overran until he reached Berkhamsted. There he was met by Archbishop Ealdred and Prince Edgar, and Earl Edwin and Earl Morcar, and all the chief men from London. And they submitted out of necessity after most damage had been done – and it was a great piece of folly that they had not done it earlier since God would not make things better because of our sins. And they gave hostages and swore oaths to him, and he promised them that he would be a gracious lord, and yet in the meantime they ravaged all that they overran. Then on Christmas Day, Archbishop Ealdred consecrated him king at Westminster. And he [William] promised Ealdred on Christ's book and swore moreover – before Ealdred would place the crown on his head – that he would rule all his people as well as the best of the kings before him, if they would be loyal to him. All the same he laid taxes on people very severely, and then went in spring overseas to Normandy, and took with him Archbishop Stigand, and Aegelnoth, abbot of Glastonbury, and Prince Edgar, and Earl Edwin, and Earl Morcar, and Earl Waltheof, and many other good men from England.[74] And Bishop Odo and Earl William [fitzOsbern] stayed behind and built castles here and far and wide throughout this country, and distressed wretched folk, and always after that it grew much worse. May the end be good when God wills!

[1067 (for 1068)] The king came back to England on St. Nicolas Day [6 December]. And during the day Christ Church at Canterbury

73 Ealdred, bishop of York (1044–69); Edgar the aetheling was the grandson of Edmund Ironside, son of Aethelred II, he died after 1125; for his career, see Hooper, 1985, 197–214.

74 Aegelnoth, abbot of Glastonbury (1053–77/78); Earl Waltheof later married Judith, niece of King William; he was executed for treason in 1076.

was burnt down. And Bishop Wulfwi died and is buried in his cathedral town of Dorchester.[75] And Eadric 'Cild' and the Welsh became hostile, and fought against the garrsion of the castle at Hereford, and inflicted many injuries upon them.[76] And the king imposed a heavy tax on the wretched people, and nevertheless caused all that he overran to be ravaged. And then he went to Devonshire and besieged the city of Exeter for eighteen days, and there a large part of his army perished. But he made fair promises to them, and fulfilled them badly; and they gave up the city to him because the thegns had betrayed them. And in the course of the summer Prince Edgar went abroad with his mother Agatha and his two sisters, Margaret and Christina, and Maerleswein and many good men with them, and came to Scotland under the protection of King Malcolm, and he received them all ... And Gytha, Harold's mother, and many distinguished men's wives with her went out to Flatholm and stayed there for some time and so went from there overseas to Saint Omer.[77] This Easter the king came to Winchester, and Easter was then on 23 March. And soon after that the Lady Matilda came to this country and Archbishop Ealdred consecrated her as queen at Westminster on Whit-Sunday [11 May].[78] Then the king was informed that the people in the North were gathered together and meant to take a stand against him if he came. He then went to Nottingham and built a castle there, and so went to York and built two castles, and in Lincoln and everywhere in that district. And Earl Gospatric and the best men went to Scotland. And in the meanwhile one of Harold's sons came unexpectedly from Ireland with a naval force into the mouth of the Avon, and ravaged all over that district. Then they went to Bristol and meant to take the city by storm but the citizens fought against them fiercely. And when they could not get anything out of the city they went to their ships with what they had won by fighting, and so went to Somerset and landed there. And Ednoth, the staller, fought against them and was killed there, and many good men on both sides. And those who survived went away.

75 His successor was Remigius of Fécamp.

76 Eadric Cild or 'the Wild' was a guerilla leader active in Herefordshire 1067–70 when he made peace with William the Conqueror; he is probably the same as Bishop Wulfstan's steerman called Eadric (Mason, 1990, 145–6 and Williams, 1995, 14–15).

77 Flatholm is an island in the Severn estuary; Saint-Omer is in Flanders.

78 William the Conqueror's wife Matilda of Flanders (d. 1083).

42   Anglo-Saxon Chronicle, version E

[1066] ... In this year the minster of Westminster was consecrated on Holy Innocents' Day [28 December 1065], and King Edward died on the eve of Epiphany and was buried on the feast of the Epiphany in the newly consecrated church at Westminster. And Earl Harold succeeded to the realm of England, just as the king had granted it to him, and as he had been chosen to the position. And he was consecrated king on the feast of the Epiphany. And the same year that he became king he went out with a naval force against William and meanwhile Earl Tostig came into the Humber with sixty ships and Earl Edwin came with a land force and drove him out and the sailors deserted him, and he went to Scotland with twelve small vessels and Harold, king of Norway, met him with three hundred ships, and Tostig submitted to him; and they both went up the Humber until they reached York. And Earl Morcar and Earl Edwin fought against them, and the King of Norway had the victory. And King Harold was informed as to what had been done, and what had happened, and he came with a very great force of Englishmen and met him at Stamford Bridge, and killed him and Earl Tostig and valiantly overcame all the invaders. Meanwhile Count William landed at Hastings on Michaelmas Day, and Harold came from the north and fought with him before all the army had come, and there he fell and his two brothers Gyrth and Leofwine; and William conquered this country, and came to Westminster, and Archbishop Ealdred consecrated him king, and people paid taxes to him, and gave him hostages and afterwards bought their land. And Leofric, abbot of Peterborough, was at that campaign and fell ill there and came home and died soon after, on the eve of All Saints [31 October].[79] God have mercy on his soul. In his day there was every happiness and every good at Peterborough, and he was beloved by everyone, so that the king gave to St Peter and him the abbacy of Burton and that of Coventry which Earl Leofric, who was his uncle, had built, and that of Crowland and that of Thorney. And he did much for the benefit of the monastery of Peterborough with gold and silver and vestments and land, more indeed than any before or after him. Then the golden city became a wretched city. Then the monks elected Brand, the provost, as abbot because he was a very good man and very wise and they sent him to Prince Edgar because the local people expected that he would be king, and the prince gladly gave assent to it. When King William heard about this he grew very

79 Leofric, abbot of Peterborough (1052–66).

angry, and said the abbot had slighted him. The distinguished men
acted as intermediaries and brought them into agreement, because the
abbot was one of the distinguished men. Then he gave the king forty
marks of gold as settlement. And he lived a little while after this –
only three years. Then all confusions and evils came upon the
monastery. May God take pity on it.

[1067] The king went overseas and took with him hostages and
money and came back the next year on St Nicholas Day [6 December
1067]. And that day Christ Church at Canterbury was burnt down.
And he gave away every man's land when he came back. And that
summer Prince Edgar went abroad, and Maerleswegen and many
people with them and went into Scotland. And King Malcolm
received them all and married the prince's sister.

43   John of Worcester, Chronicle

John of Worcester wrote his chronicle before 1140 at Worcester. He used a
now lost version of the Anglo-Saxon Chronicle which he expanded extensively. His account is particularly valuable for its details on Tostig's
involvement in Northumbria and his exile in 1065.

The Chronicle of John of Worcester, vol. ii *The Annals from 450–1066*, ed. R. R.
Darlington and P. McGurk; trsl. by J. Bray and P. McGurk (Oxford, 1995),
ii, pp. 597–607.

[1065] The reverend man, Aethelwine, bishop of Durham, raised the
bones of St Oswine, once king of the Bernicians, from the tomb of the
monastery situated at the mouth of the River Tyne 415 years after
their burial, and placed them with great honour in a shrine.[80] Harold,
the vigorous earl of the West Saxons, ordered a great building to be
erected in Wales, in a place called Portskewet, in July, and he
commanded that large supplies of food and drink should be gathered
there so that his lord, King Edward, could stay there sometimes for
the chase. But Caradog, son of Gruffydd, king of the South Welsh
(Gruffydd, king of the North Welsh, had killed him a few years earlier
and invaded his kingdom), went there on the feast-day of St Bartholomew the Apostle [24 August] with all the men he could raise, and
slew virtually all the workmen with their overseers, and took away all
the goods which had been stockpiled there.[81] Then after the feast of St

80 Aethelwine, bishop of Durham (1056–71).
81 Caradog of Deheubarth (1055–81).

Michael the Archangel, on Monday 3 October the Northumbrian thegns Gamelbearn, Dunstan, son of Aethelnoth, and Glonieorn, son of Heardwulf, came with 200 soldiers to York, and on account of the disgraceful death of the noble Northumbrian thegns Gospatric (whom Queen Edith on account of her brother Tostig had ordered to be killed in the king's court on the fourth night of Christmas by treachery), Gamel, son of Orm, and Ulf, son of Dolfin (whose murder Earl Tostig had treacherously ordered the preceding year at York in his own chamber, under cover of a peace-treaty), and also of the huge tribute which Tostig had unjustly levied on the whole of Northumbria, they on that same day, slew first his Danish housecarls, Amund and Reavenswart, hauled back from flight, beyond the city walls, and on the following day more than 200 men from his court, on the north side of the River Humber.[82] They also broke open his treasury, and having taken away all his goods, they withdrew. After that almost all the men of the earldom united to meet Harold, earl of the West Saxons, and others whom the king at Tostig's request had sent to them to restore peace, at Northampton. There first, and later at Oxford, on the day of the feast of the apostles Simon and Jude [28 October], while Harold and very many others wished to make peace between Earl Tostig and them, all unanimously spoke against it and they outlawed him and all who had encouraged him to establish his iniquitous rule. And after the feast of all Saints [1 November], with the aid of Earl Edwin, they drove Tostig out of England; he and his wife then approached Count Baldwin of Flanders, and spent the winter at St Omer. After this, King Edward began to weaken by degrees but at Christmas he held his court, as best as he could at London, and had the church which he himself raised from the foundations consecrated in honour of St. Peter, the prince of the apostles, with great splendour on the day of the Holy Innocents [28 December].

[1066] The glory of the English, the peaceable King Edward, son of King Aethelred, after governing the Anglo-Saxons for twenty-three years, six months, and twenty-seven days, in the fourth indiction, on Thursday, the eve of Epiphany, met his death at London, and was royally buried the next day, most bitterly lamented, not without tears by all who were present. When he was entombed, the underking [*subregulus*] Harold, son of Earl Godwin, whom the king had chosen before his demise as successor to the kingdom, was elected by the

82 The root cause of the Northumbrian unrest was the unwillingness of the northerners to accept direct rule from the south (Williams, 1995, 32–3).

primates of all England to the dignity of kingship, and was
consecrated king with due ceremony by Ealdred, archbishop of York
on the same day. He soon, when he had undertaken the government of
the realm, destroyed iniquitous laws and set about establishing just
ones; becoming patron of churches and monasteries, cultivating and
venerating at the same time bishops, abbots, monks and clerks; showing himself pious, humble and affable to all good men; detesting
malefactors, for he ordered the earls, ealdormen, sheriffs and his own
officers generally to seize thieves, robbers, and disturbers of the
realm, and to exert themselves by land and sea for the defence of the
country. In that same year, on 24 April, a comet was seen, not only in
England but also, so they say, throughout the whole world, blazing
for seven days in great splendour.

Not much later Earl Tostig returning from Flanders landed on
the Isle of Wight, and having forced the islanders to pay tribute and
maintenance, departed and raided the coast as far as the port of
Sandwich. When King Harold, who was then staying in London,
learnt this, he ordered a large fleet and a force of cavalry to be
assembled and he himself prepared to go to the port of Sandwich.
When this was reported to Tostig, he retreated, taking some of the
seamen with him, whether they wished to go or not, and steered his
course towards Lindsey, where he burnt many townships, and did to
death many men. When he learnt this Edwin, earl of the Mercians,
and Morcar, earl of the Northumbrians, hurried up with an army, and
expelled him from that region. Retreating thence, he went to
Malcolm, king of the Scots, and remained the whole summer with
him. Meanwhile, King Harold came to the port of Sandwich and there
he awaited his fleet. When it had been drawn up, he went to the Isle
of Wight and, because William, duke of the Normans, cousin of King
Edward, was preparing to come to England with an army, he watched
all summer and autumn for his arrival, against which he also placed
his infantry at strategic places around the coast. And so, with the
approach of the nativity of St Mary [25 August] as food was running
out, both the fleet and the infantry returned home.

When these things had been done, Harold Fairhair, king of the
Norwegians, brother of St Olaf the king, landed unexpectedly at the
mouth of the River Tyne with an extremely strong fleet; that is more
than 500 great ships. Earl Tostig joined him with his fleet as he had
previously promised, and on a swift course they entered the mouth of
the River Humber; sailing thus up the River Ouse, they landed at a
place called Ricall. When King Harold learnt of this, he speedily

undertook an expedition to Northumbria. But before the king arrived there, the two brother earls, Edwin and Morcar, with a great army joined battle with the Norwegians on the north bank of the River Ouse, near York on Wednesday the eve of St Matthew the apostle's day, and fighting manfully in the first thrust of the battle, they laid many low. But after the struggle had continued for a long time, the English were unable to withstand the Norwegian attack. Not without some small loss they turned to flee, and many more of them were drowned in the river than fallen in battle. But the Norwegians gained the mastery in that place of death and, having taken 150 hostages from York, they returned to their own ships having left in York 150 hostages of their own. But on the fifth day after this, that is on Monday 25 September, Harold king of the English with many thousands of well-armed fighting men marched to York and met the Norwegians at a place called Stamford Bridge. He put to the sword King Harold and Earl Tostig and the greater part of their army, and after a most bitter battle gained total victory. However, he permitted Harold's son Olaf, and the earl of Orkney, Paul by name, who had been sent off to guard the ships with part of the army, after first taking hostages and oaths from them, to return freely to their own land with twenty ships and the remainder of the army.

While these things were happening and the king supposed all his enemies had been destroyed, he was informed that William, duke of the Normans, had landed his fleet at a place called Pevensey with an innumerable multitude of mounted soldiers [*equites*], slingers, archers and foot soldiers, for he had brought strong auxiliaries from the whole of Gaul with him. Whereupon the king at once moved his army to London in great haste, and although he knew that all the more powerful men from the whole of England had already fallen in two battles, and that half of his army had not yet assembled, yet he did not fear to go to meet his enemies in Sussex with all possible speed, and nine miles from Hastings, where they had earlier built a fortress for themselves, before a third of his army had been drawn up on Saturday 22 October he joined battle with the Normans.[83] But because the English were drawn up in a narrow place many slipped away from the battle-line and very few of a constant heart remained with him. However, from the third hour of daylight until dusk he resisted his enemies most stoutly, and defended himself by fighting so strongly and vigorously that he could scarcely be slain by the enemy line. But afterwards, when very many had fallen on both sides, he himself fell, alas,

83 The correct date is 14 October.

at dusk. Earls Gyrth and Leofwine, his brothers, also fell and the more noble of almost all England, but Duke William returned to Hastings with his own men. Harold reigned nine months and as many days.

When they heard of his death, Earls Edwin and Morcar who had slipped away from the battle with their men, came to London and took their sister Queen Edith and sent her to the city of Chester.[84] However, Ealdred, archbishop of York and those earls, with the citizens of London and the seamen wished to raise to the throne the atheling Edgar, grandson of King Edmund Ironside, and promised to enter battle with Duke William. But while they prepared to go down into battle, the earls withdrew their support from them and returned home with their army. Meanwhile, Duke William laid waste Sussex, Kent, Hampshire, Middlesex and Hertfordshire and did not cease from burning townships and slaying men until he came to the township called Berkhamsted. There Archbishop Ealdred, Wulfstan, bishop of Worcester, Walter, bishop of Hereford, the atheling Edgar, Earls Edwin and Morcar, and the more noble citizens of London, with many others, came to meet him, and having given hostages, made him their submission, and swore fealty to him.[85] He himself made a treaty with them, but none the less he permitted his army to burn and plunder townships. Therefore, as the Christmas feast was approaching, he came to London with his whole army that he might be raised to the throne there. Because Stigand, primate of all England, was accused by the apostolic pope of not having received the pallium canonically, William was consecrated with due ceremony by Ealdred, archbishop of York, on Christmas Day itself, which in that year fell on a Monday, at Westminster first swearing, as the same archbishop required of him, on oath before the altar of St Peter the Apostle, in the presence of clergy and people that he would defend the holy churches of God and their rulers too, and would govern the whole people subject to him justly, and by royal provision would establish and maintain right law, and totally forbid rapine and unjust judgements.

44   Eadmer of Canterbury, History of Recent Events

Eadmer, an English monk at Canterbury and Archbishop Anselm's secretary, wrote his History of Recent Events in England c. 1093–c. 1119. He attributes

---

84 This Queen Edith was the widow of King Harold Godwineson and not King Edward's widow.

85 Wulfstan, bishop of Worcester (1062–95); Walter, bishop of Hereford (1060–79).

Earl Harold's visit to Normandy in 1064/65 to a mission organised to negotiate the release of his brother Wulfnoth and nephew Hakon who had been
held hostage in Normandy since the early 1050s.

Eadmeri Historia novorum in Anglia, ed. M. Rule (London, 1884), pp. 6–9;
Eadmer's History of Recent Events in England: Historia Novorum in Anglia, trsl.
G. Bosanquet (London, 1964), pp. 6–10.

So Wulfnoth, son of Godwin, and Hakon, a son of his [Godwin's] son
Svein, were given as hostages and were despatched to Normandy to
the guardianship of Duke William, a son of Robert, son of Richard
[II], brother of the King [Edward]'s mother [Emma]. After these
events Godwin, a bitter enemy of the Church of Canterbury (for he
stole from that church her manor of Folkestone having first bribed
Archbishop Eadsige),[86] shortly afterwards died an evil death and
Harold his son became possessed of the earldom of Kent in succession
of his father. He soon afterwards asked leave of the king to go to
Normandy to set free his brother and nephew who were being held
hostages, and when so freed, to bring them back home. The king said
to him: 'I will have no part in this; but, not to give the impression of
wishing to hinder you, I give you leave to go where you will and to
see what you can do. But I have a presentiment that you will only
succeed in bringing misfortune upon the whole kingdom and
discredit upon yourself. For I know that the duke is not so simple as
to be at all inclined to give them up to you unless he foresees that in
doing so he will secure some great advantage to himself.' Harold,
trusting his own judgement rather than the king's, embarked on
board ship taking with him his richest and most honourable men,
equipped with a lordly provision of gold, silver and costly raiment.
But soon the sea grew stormy and those on board were terrified, as
the ship was tossed by the violence of the towering waves. At last
she was driven with all that she had on board into a river of
Ponthieu which is called Maye.[87] There, in accordance with the local
custom, she was adjudged captive by the lord of the land and the
men on board were put under strict arrest.[88]

86 Eadsige, bishop of Canterbury (1038–50).

87 Eadmer is the only source of information on the exact location where Harold
landed.

88 The right of shipwreck was the prerogative of the territoral rulers in western
Europe (king, duke or count), who could claim ownership of any shipwreck
(including its cargo and sailors) on their coast. Thus such a ship could not be
claimed by the local owner of the beach. The custom goes back to the period of
viking invasions and may well have been introduced by Scandinavians who settled
in coastal areas, as was certainly the case in Normandy (above, p. 20).

So Harold was held a prisoner. But he managed to bribe one of the common people with a promise of reward and sent him secretly to the duke of Normandy to report what had happened to him. The duke thereupon promptly sent messengers to the lord of Ponthieu and told him that, if he wished to have his friendship for the future as he had had in the past, Harold and his men must be sent to him as quickly as possible and that free of any charge against him.[89] The other refused to let his prisoner go; whereupon he received a second peremptory message that he must send Harold; and, if not, he could rest assured that William, duke of Normandy, would come in arms to Ponthieu to release him. So then he sent Harold and his men, but not without first having taken from them all the most valuable belongings which they had brought with them. In this way Harold came to William and was received with all honour.

When William had been told why Harold had set out from England, he replied that his mission would certainly be successful or it would be his own fault if it was not. Then he kept Harold with him for some days and during that time cautiously revealed to him what he had in mind. He said that King Edward, when years before he was detained with him in Normandy, when they were both young, had promised him and had pledged his faith that if he, Edward, should ever be king of England, he would make over to William the right to succeed him on the throne as his heir. William went on to say: 'If you on your side undertake to support me in this project and further promise that you will make a stronghold at Dover with a well of water for my use and that you will at a time agreed between us send your sister to me that I may give her in marriage to one of my nobles and that you will take my daughter to be your wife, then I will let you have your nephew now at once, and your brother safe and sound when I come to England to be king. And, if ever I am with your support established there as king, I promise that everything you ask of me which can reasonably be granted, you shall have.' Then Harold perceived that here was danger whatever way he turned. He could not see any way of escape without agreeing to all that William wished. So he agreed. Then William, to ensure that all should thenceforth stand firmly ratified, had relics of saints brought out and made Harold swear over them that he would indeed implement all which they had agreed between them, provided he were not before then taken from this life, a chance to which all mortal men are subject. When all this had been done, Harold took his nephew [Hakon] and returned home. There, when, on being

89 Guy, count of Ponthieu (1053–1100).

questioned by the king he told him what had happened and what he had done, the king exclaimed: 'Did not I tell you that I knew William and that your going might bring untold calamity upon this kingdom?'

Shortly after this Edward died; and, as he had before his death provided, Harold succeeded him on the throne. Thereupon there arrived in England a messenger from William asking for Harold's sister in accordance with the agreement which had been made between them. He also reproached him for not having kept his other promises in violation of his oath. To this Harold is said to have made the following reply: 'My sister, whom according to our pact you ask for, is dead. If the duke wishes to have her body, such as it now is, I will send it, that I may not be held to have violated my oath. As for the stronghold at Dover and the well of water in it, I have completed that according to our agreement although for whose use I cannot say. As for the kingdom, which then was not yet mine, by what right could I give or promise it? If it is about his daughter that he is concerned, whom I ought, as he asserts, to take to be my wife, he must know I have no right to set any foreign woman upon the throne without having first consulted the princes. Indeed I could not do so without committing a great wrong.' So the messenger returned home and reported these anwers to his master. He, on hearing this reply, sent a second time and in all friendliness urged Harold, if he let the rest go, at any rate to keep his promise so far as to marry the duke's daughter, and, if not, he could rest assured that the duke would make good by force of arms his succession to the throne which had been promised him. Harold's answer was that he would not do the one and did not fear the other.

Then William, incensed at this, conceived high hopes of a war of conquest resulting from this unjust conduct of Harold's. Accordingly he fitted out a fleet and set sail for England. A furious battle was joined; Harold fell in the thick of the fray and William as conqueror possessed himself of the kingdom. Of that battle the French who took part in it do to this day declare that, although fortune swayed now on this side and now on that, yet of the Normans so many were slain or put to flight that the victory which they had gained is truly and without any doubt to be attributed to nothing else than the miraculous intervention of God, who by so punishing Harold's wicked perjury shewed that He is not a God that hath any pleasure in wickedness.

So William became king. What treatment he meted out to those leaders of the English who managed to survive the great slaughter, as it could do no good, I forbear to tell. From the time that he gained this victory, which was on the 14th of October [1066], William remained unconsecrated until Christmas Day when he was consecrated king by Ealdred of blessed memory, archbishop of York, and a number of English bishops. Although the king himself and everyone else knew well enough that such consecration ought to be performed by the archbishop of Canterbury as being his special and peculiar privilege, yet seeing that many wicked and horrible crimes were ascribed to Stigand, who was at that time archbishop of Canterbury, William was unwilling to receive consecration at his hands, lest he should seem to be taking upon himself a curse instead of a blessing.

Now, it was the policy of King William to maintain in England the usages and laws which he and his fathers before him were accustomed to have in Normandy. Accordingly he made bishops, abbots and other nobles throughout the whole country of persons of whom, since everyone knew who they were, from what estate they had been raised and to what they had been promoted, it would be considered shameful ingratitude if they did not implicitly obey his laws, subordinating to this every other consideration; or if any one of them presuming upon the power conferred by any temporal dignity dared raise his head against him. Consequently all things, spiritual and temporal alike, waited upon the nod of the king.

45   Henry of Huntingdon, History of the English People

Henry, archdeacon of Huntingdon, wrote his History of the English People between c. 1129 and 1154, using the Anglo-Saxon Chronicle as his main source.

Henry, Archdeacon of Huntingdon, Historia Anglorum (History of the English People), ed. and trsl. D. Greenway (Oxford, 1996), pp. 381–97.

[Book VI, c. 25] In King Edward's twenty-second year [1063–64], when after the death of King Henry [I], his son Philip [I, 1060–1108] reigned, William duke of the Normans subjected Maine to himself. Now Harold, who was making the crossing to Flanders, was driven by a storm into the province of Ponthieu. He was captured, and the count of Ponthieu handed him over to William duke of Normandy. Harold swore to William, on many precious relics of the saints, that he would marry his daughter and after Edward's death would preserve England for William's benefit. On his return to England, he who had been received with great honour and many gifts, chose to commit the crime of perjury. In the following year, Harold and Tostig went on campaign into Wales. The people of that country were subjugated to them and gave hostages. Afterwards they killed their king, Griffith, and took his head to Harold. Then Harold set up another king there. It happened in the same year that in the king's presence in the royal hall at Windsor, as his brother Harold was serving wine to the king, Tostig grabbed him by the hair. For Tostig nourished a burning jealousy and hatred because although he was himself the first born, his brother was higher in the king's affection.[90] So driven by a surge of rage, he was unable to check his hand from his brother's head. The king, however, foretold that their destruction was already approaching, and that the wrath of God would be delayed no longer. Such was the savagery of those brothers that when they saw anyone's vill in a flourishing state, they would order the lord and all his family to be murdered in the night, and would take possession of the dead man's property. And these, indeed, were the injustices of the realm! So Tostig, departing in anger from the king and from his brother, went to Hereford, where his brother had prepared an enormous royal banquet. In which place he dismembered all his brother's servants and put human leg, head, or arm into each vessel for wine, mead ale, spiced wine, morat, and cider. And he sent to the king, saying that when he came to his farm he would find enough salted food, and that he should take care to bring the rest with him. For such immeasurable crime the king commanded him to be outlawed and exiled.

[Book VI, c. 26] In Edward's twenty-fourth year [1065–66], when the Northumbrians heard of these events, they drove out Tostig, their earl, who had brought much slaughter and ruin upon them. Killing all his household, both Danes and Englishmen, they took his treasure and arms in York. Then they set up Morcar, son of Earl Aelfgar, to be earl over them. He marched with that people and with the men of Lincolnshire, Nottinghamshire, and Derbyshire, as far as Northampton, and his brother Edwin came out to meet him with the men of his earldom and many Welsh with him. Then Earl Harold came to them. So they sent him to the king, and messengers with him, requesting that they might have Morcar as earl over them. The king granted this, and sent Harold back to them at Northampton, who confirmed it to them. But meanwhile they did not spare that district, burning and plundering and killing. When they had gained their petition, they took away with them many thousands of men, thus rendering that part of the kingdom poorer for many years to come. Tostig and his wife went away to Baldwin count of Flanders and wintered there.

90 It is usually thought that Harold was the elder of the two brothers.

[Book VI, c. 27] In the year of grace 1066, the Lord, the ruler, brought to completion what he had long planned for the English nation. For he delivered them up for destruction to the violent men and cunning Norman people. After the basilica of St Peter's at Westminster had been dedicated on the day of the Holy Innocents, and later, on the eve of the Epiphany, King Edward had left the world, and had been buried in the same church (which he himself had built and had endowed with many possessions), some of the English wanted to advance Edgar the atheling as king. But Harold, relying on his forces and his birth, usurped the crown of the kingdom. Then William, duke of Normandy, was provoked in his mind and inwardly incensed, for three reasons. First, because Godwin and his sons had dishonoured and murdered his kinsman Alfred. Second, because Godwin and his sons had, by their cunning, exiled from England Bishop Robert and Earl Odda and all the Frenchmen.[91] Third, because Harold, who had fallen into perjury, had wrongfully usurped the kingdom which by law of kinship ought to have been William's. So summoning the Norman leaders, he sought aid in the conquest of England. William FitzOsbern, the duke's steward, was among those who came to advise the duke. He asserted that an expedition to conquer England would be very difficult and the English nation was very strong, and argued vehemently against the few who wished to go to England. Hearing this the nobles were very glad, and gave him their word that they would all agree with what he was going to say. So he went into the duke's presence ahead of them, and said, 'I am prepared to set out on this expedition with all my men.' Therefore all the Norman leaders were obliged to follow his word. A very large fleet was prepared at the port called Saint-Valéry. Hearing this, King Harold, who was a fierce warrior, set out to sea with a naval force to oppose Duke William. Meanwhile Earl Tostig came into the Humber with sixty ships. But Earl Edwin came with an army and put him to flight. Fleeing to Scotland, Tostig met Harold, king of Norway, with 300 ships and very gladly submitted to him. Then they both came up the Humber as far as York, and Earls Edwin and Morcar fought against them near the city. The site of this battle is still pointed out on the south side of the city. But King Harold of Norway and Tostig with him took possession of the glorious prize of Mars. When Harold, the English king, heard this, he met them with a strong force at Stamford Bridge. A battle began that was more arduous than any that

91 Odda, earl of Devon.

had gone before. They engaged at dawn and after fearful assaults on both sides they continued steadfastly until midday, the English superiority in numbers forcing the Norwegians to give way but not to flee. Driven back beyond the river, the living crossing over the dead, they resisted stoutheartedly. A single Norwegian, worthy of eternal fame, resisted on the bridge, and felling more than forty Englishmen with his rusty axe, he alone held up the entire English army until three o'clock in the afternoon. At length someone came up in a boat and through the openings of the bridge struck him in the private parts with a spear. So the English crossed, and killed King Harold and Tostig and laid low the whole Norwegian line, either with their arms or by consuming with fire those they intercepted.

[Book VI, c. 28] Harold, king of the English, returned to York on the same day with great joy, and while he was dining he heard a messenger say to him 'William has invaded on the south coast, and has built a castle at Hastings.' So the king, hastening down without delay, drew up his lines on the flat land of Hastings. Then William nobly led out five companies of knights against his enemy, and when they were terrifyingly deployed he delivered a speech to them, as follows:

[Book VI, c. 29] 'I address you, O Normans, the bravest of peoples, not because I am uncertain of your prowess, or unsure of victory, which could never, by any chance or impediment, escape you. If, on a single occasion, you had been unable to gain victory, you would perhaps need to be exhorted, so that your prowess might shine forth. But what exhortation can your natural and inevitable conduct require? O most valiant of mortals, what could the French king, with that whole nation stretching from Lotharingia as far as Spain, accomplish in wars against our ancestor Hasting? Hasting took for himself as much as he wanted of France, and as much as he wanted the king to have, that he allowed him. He held it as long as he pleased, and when he was satisfied, he relinquished it, striving for yet greater things. Did not Rou [= Rollo] my ancestor, the first duke and originator of our race, together with your ancestors, defeat the French king in battle at Paris, in the heartland of his realm? And the only hope of safety for the French king was as a humble petitioner, to offer both his daughter and the land you call Normandy. Did not your fathers capture the French king in Rouen, and hold him until he gave up Normandy to the boy Richard, your duke, with the condition that in every conference between the king of France and the duke of Normandy, the duke would be armed with his sword, while the king would not be allowed to carry a sword nor even a small knife? Your fathers put the great king under compulsion, and established this perpetual decree. Did not the same duke lead your fathers as far as Mirmande near the Alps and waging war at will force the duke of the city to release his son-in-law? And lest it should seem enough to have conquered men, he himself overcame the devil in the flesh wrestling with him and overthrowing him, and binding his hands behind his back, and as victor of angels he left him defeated. But why do I tell stories of what happened long ago? When in my time you fought at Mortemer, did not the French prefer headlong flight to battle, spurs to spears? When Ralph the high commander of the French was killed, were you not, in taking possession of fame and spoils, maintaining the force of habit the good that is natural to you? Ah! let any of the Englishmen whom our Danish and Norwegian ancestors have conquered in a hundred battles, come forth and prove that the nation of Rou, from his time until now, have ever been routed in the field, and I will withdraw in defeat. Is it not shameful to you that a people accustomed to defeat, a people devoid of military knowledge, a people that does not even possess arrows, should advance as if in battle order against you, O bravest? Are you not ashamed that King Harold, who has broken the oath he made to me in your presence, should have presumed to show you his face? It is amazing to me that you have seen with your own eyes those who by execrable treachery beheaded your kin, together with my kinsman Alfred, and that their impious heads should still stand on their shoulders. Raise your standards, men, and let there be no measure or moderation to your righteous anger. Let the lightning of your glory be seen from the east to the west, let the thunder of your charge be heard, and may you be the avengers of most noble blood.'

[Book VI, c. 30] Duke William had not yet concluded his speech when all his men, boiling with unbelievable anger, charged forward in their lines with indescribable force against the enemy, and left the duke, speaking to himself. Shortly before the warriors entered the battle, one man, named Taillefer, played a game tossing swords in front of the English nation and while they all gazed at him in astonishment, he killed an English standard-bearer.[92] He repeated this, a second time. The third time in the act of doing it again, he was himself killed,

92 The Song of the Battle of Hastings is alone among the early sources referring to this minstrel (*The Carmen de Hastingae Proelio of Bishop Guy of Amiens*, ed. and trsl. C. Morton and H. Muntz (Oxford, 1972), line 399, p. 26).

and the lines fell upon him. Then began deathbearing clouds of arrows. There followed the thunder of blows. The clash of helmets and swords produced dancing sparks. Harold had placed all his people very closely in a single line, constructing a sort of castle with them, so that they were impregnable to the Normans. So Duke William instructed his people to simulate flight, but as they fled they came to a large ditch, cunningly hidden. A great number of them fell and were trampled. While the English were continuing in pursuit, the principal line of Normans broke through the central company of the English. When those who were pursuing saw this, they were obliged to return over the said ditch, and the greater part of them perished there. Also Duke William instructed the archers not to shoot their arrows directly at the enemy, but rather in the air, so that arrows might blind the enemy squadron. This caused great losses among the English. Twenty of the most valiant knights gave their word to one another that they would break through the English line and snatch away the royal banner, which is called the 'Standard'. When they went to do this, several of them were killed. But some of them, making a way with their swords, carried off the standard. Meanwhile the whole shower sent by the archers fell around King Harold, and he himself sank to the ground, struck in the eye. A host of knights broke through and killed the wounded king, and Earl Gyrth and Earl Leofwine, his brothers, with him. And so the English army was shattered. Then William, taking possession of this great victory, was received peacefully by the Londoners, and was crowned at Westminster by Ealdred, archbishop of York. Thus occurred a change in the right hand of the Most High, which a huge comet had presaged at the beginning of the same year. Whence it was said:

> In the year one thousand, sixty and six
> The English lands saw the flames of the comet.

The battle took place in the month of September, on the feast day of St Calixtus [14 October]. In that place King William later built a noble abbey for the souls of the departed, and called it by the fitting name of Battle.

[Book VI, c. 31] In the following year [1067], King William crossed the sea, taking with him hostages and treasure. And he came back in the same year, and divided the land among his warriors. But Edgar the atheling, with many soldiers, went to Scotland and betrothed his sister Margaret to Malcolm, king of Scots. King William gave the earldom of Northumbria to Earl Robert, but the inhabitants of the province killed him and 900 men.[93] Then Edgar the atheling came to York with all the people of Northumbria, and the townsmen made peace with him. Then the king arrived with his army, and sacking the city, he made great slaughter of the treacherous people. But Edgar returned to Scotland.

46   The Waltham Chronicle

The Waltham Chronicle was written by an anonymous author *c.* 1177 and based on the author's conversations, in the 1120s, with the then eighty-year-old Turkill, who had been sacristan of Waltham Abbey in 1066. In that capacity he had overseen the delayed burial of King Harold, the abbey's patron, at Waltham. He may also have been the author's source for the details of the collection of Harold's body by the canons Osgod and Aethelric from the battlefield near Hastings, although those regarding his mistress Edith seem legendary.

The Waltham Chronicle, ed. and trsl. L. Watkiss and M. Chibnall (Oxford, 1994), pp. 45, 51–7.

[c. 20] After the death of this most saintly king [Edward], therefore, Earl Harold was elected king by unanimous consent, for there was no one in the land more knowledgeable, more vigorous in arms, wiser in the laws of the land or more highly regarded for his prowess of every kind. So those who had been his chief enemies up to this time could not oppose this election, for England had not given birth to a man as distinguished as he in all respects to undertake such a task. So after being crowned king by Stigand, archbishop of Canterbury, he could not have hated what he previously favoured.

  And, indeed, he now showed a greater affection for the church at Waltham than before, and began to adorn it further with many fine gifts; indeed, he never thereafter visited that place without wanting to bestow many gifts upon it.[94] I heard this from the lips of the old sacristan Turkill whom I was privileged to see two years before he died and later to be present with the brethren at his burial. But it was only for a short time after he became king that he was patron of our church, for he was cunningly tricked by the perfidious Normans because he had refused to marry the daughter of William of Normandy. Returning from Battlebridge, a name the place received from

93 Robert de Commines succeeded Gospatric as earl of Northumbria (d. 1069).
94 Earl Harold had refounded Waltham Abbey *c.* 1060.

the battle itself, where with his brother Tostig he had slaughtered a large number of enemies, he nobly triumphed over the forces of the enemy. Then with a few companions, for almost all his men had departed to different regions, he returned to Waltham. There he received a message about the landing of the Normans, news that was only too true, and straightway he decided to go and meet them, allowing nobody to stop him. In fact, everyone advised him to wait for Tostig, Gyrth and Bondi, and the rest who had gone back home, but he was headstrong and trusted too much in his own courage;[95] he believed he would be attacking a weak and unprepared force of Normans before reinforcements from Normandy could increase their strength ...

[c. 21] ... After the unhappy outcome of the battle, with its bad omen for those who fought in it, the man who can recall the verse 'O you who pass by, look and see if there is any sorrow like my sorrow' will be able to appreciate what feelings of anguish and sorrow the brethren Osgod and Aethelric had to endure, who had followed the king's doomed fortunes from afar that they might see his end. Compelled by necessity, however, though their fear made them hesitant, they approached the duke, humbling themselves before his feet. Tearfully they addressed and entreated him: 'Noble duke, we are your servants, bereft of all solace (would that we were bereft now of our lives!) were sent here to observe the outcome of the war by our brethren whom the dead king had appointed to the church at Waltham, but our master who provided for us has, because of your victory, been taken from us. He used to console us, and it was under his protection, indeed, and through his endowments that those whom he established in the church served God. We ask you, master, indeed we urge you, through the grace bestowed upon you by the divine will, and for the salvation of the souls of all who have lost their lives in this present cause of yours, to allow us at your good pleasure to remove and take with us without let or hindrance the body of our lord the king, the founder and originator of our church, together with the bodies of the men who, out of reverence for the place itself, have chosen a place of burial amongst us. We ask this that the standing of the church might be established more firmly under the protection, and its continuance be assured.'

Accordingly the glorious duke showed them compassion characteristic of a mind that is merciful and more prone to listen because of victory, for the Lord had permitted him his triumph over his enemy.

95 Bondi the Staller, a Midlands thegn and one of King Edward's stallers (d. after 1066).

He therefore granted them their requests, rejecting the gold offered to him, considering it of no consequence. He continued, 'If you need anything towards the expenses for carrying out the funeral ceremony, or have any needs at all for your journey, we are giving orders for these to be fully satisfied. We grant you peace and complete freedom from molestation by the knights of our army in all you have to do.'

And so the brethren were strengthened by feelings of extraordinary joy. They hastened to the dead bodies and, though turning them over on this side and that, they were unable to recognise the body of the king. This is because the body of a man when dead and drained of blood does not usually have the same appearance as when alive. They decided that there was only one solution, for Osgod himself to return home and to bring back with him the woman whom the king had loved before he became ruler of the English. This was Edith, surnamed 'Swanneshals', which in the vernacular means 'Swan-neck'. She had at one time been the king's concubine, and knew the secret marks on the king's body better than the others did, for she had been admitted to a greater intimacy of his person.[96] Thus they would be assured by her knowledge of his secret marks when they could not be sure from his external appearance. The reason for this was that, when the mortal blow was struck, whatever royal insignia he wore were immediately carried off to the duke so as to be evidence that the king had been slain. This was the ancient custom, and is still, I believe, modern practice, that when kings are captured or their fortresses taken, those who are the first to strip off the king's helmet and offer it to their king, or who are the first to take the king's standard when a fortress is captured (especially when the keep of an important castle is taken) are given large rewards.[97]

When Osgod had brought the woman she pointed out the king's body amongst the heaps of dead from several identifying marks. The body was placed by the brethren themselves upon a bier, and many of the company of Norman warriors paid their respects to the body all the way to Battlebridge, as it is now called, and so did a large number of Englishmen who had heard of the imminent defeat of their men and had caught them up, because the English had never experienced fellowship with the Normans before. They brought the body to Waltham and buried it with great honour, where, without doubt, he has lain at rest until the present day, whatever stories men may invent that

96 Edith Swanneshals was King Harold's concubine and mother of most of his children.

97 I know of no other reference to this custom.

Harold dwelt in a cave at Canterbury and that later, when he died, was buried at Chester. I can now in my old age remember that I was present when his body was translated for the third time, occasioned either by the state of building work in the church or because the brethren out of devotion were showing reverence to the body. It is generally well-known, and we have heard men of old testify, that men saw with their own eyes, and touched with their own hands, the marks of the wounds visible on the very bones. But his life had ended, and that noble king, having ruled the English for a short time only of a year and [some] months, went the way of all flesh and was gathered unto his fathers.

47   William of Malmesbury, Life of Wulfstan

William of Malmesbury wrote the Life of Wulfstan, bishop of Worcester (1062–95), between c. 1124 and c. 1143. His account is based on the, now lost, vernacular life composed by Coleman between 1095 and 1113.

The Vita Wulfstani of William of Malmesbury, ed. R. R. Darlington (London, 1928), pp. 13, 22–4; *Three Lives of the Last Englishmen*, trsl. M. Swanton (New York-London, 1984), pp. 100, 108–10.

Thus his [Wulfstan's] fame spread throughout England, to the point where the most powerful nobles among the English eagerly sought his friendship and held it most steadfastly. It offered a safeguard in prosperity, a refuge in adversity, a support at all times. Among them Harold, already thinking himself capable of greater power and laying claim to the kingdom by his noble conduct, esteemed him above all men. So much so that when on a journey he would not hesitate to go thirty miles out of his way in order to find relief from the burden of his cares in conversation with Wulfstan. Harold was so given over to his will and guidance that although Wulfstan might be ashamed to command, Harold was never reluctant to obey. The saint returned the earl's esteem no less. He received his confession benevolently, and was the faithful mediator of his prayers to God ...

Five years after the episcopacy had been conferred on Wulfstan, King Edward met his end, leaving England a monstrous seed-bed of discord, for on the one hand Harold, and on the other Duke William of Normandy, claimed it as of right. And then whether by good will or taken by force, Harold gained the crown and virtually the whole kingdom. Only the great and turbulent people of Northumbria were not prepared for the time being to submit. They declared that it was

not right for the bold north to submit to the soft south. Their desire
for strong rule and their great courage were roused by the king's own
brother Tostig, a man of no ignoble spirit, he had chosen to apply his
great ardour to the pursuit of peace. He was subsequently killed in
that same province, together with Harold king of Norway whom he
had brought in to help him and who suffered the penalty of his rashness. But this was later. At that time in fact Harold travelled there
determined not to break their stubbornness with arms, but hoping
that he might settle it by gentler remedies, bringing the saintly man
[Wulfstan] with him. For the fame of his holiness had penetrated to even
the most remote people, and it was believed that there was no arrogance he could not soften. Nor, in the event, was the opinion disappointed. For on account of the reverence in which the bishop was held,
that race who could never be broken by force of arms, and so great-
hearted from the time of their forefathers, readily conceded an oath of
allegiance to Harold. And they would have maintained it, if Tostig, as
I have said, had not turned them aside from it. Well, the bishop, good,
mild, and gentle though he was, did not indulge the sinners with soft
words, however, but accused them of vices, grinding his teeth with
threatening words. By way of prophecy, he announced to them frankly,
if it carried on they would pay the penalty in suffering. Nor did his
human wisdom or his gift for prophecy ever easily deceive him. Both
on that journey and repeatedly on other occasions, he had foreknowledge of and gave forewarning of many things. He even openly called
to Harold's attention the calamity which would befall him and England,
unless they took care to correct their evil ways. For almost everywhere
in England at that time people lived an abandoned way of life, and,
with peace and abundance of pleasures, debauchery flourished. He
attacked all who were depraved, especially those who had let their hair
grow long.[98] If any of these yielded him his head, he would cut away
the unrestrained locks with his own hand. For this purpose he had a
little knife, with which he used to scrape muck from his nails or dirt
off his books. Having thus culled the first-fruits of their locks, he would
charge them of their obedience to even up the remainder of their tresses
to match. If anyone thought to refuse he would openly accuse him of
softness, openly warn him of misfortune. It would come to pass that
those who were ashamed to be what they were born and imitated the
flowing tresses of women, would prove no better than women in the
defence of their homeland against foreigners. As much became evident
with the coming of the Normans that same year. Who can deny it? ...

98 Cf. no. **33**.

In due course Duke William of Normandy came to England, and meeting with Harold in battle, killed him, slaughtering the English and laying claim to sovereignty in the kingdom for himself. At this the truth of the prophet's words was evident, for the wretched people of the province were so helpless that after the first fight they never joined together *en masse* in an attempt to stand up for liberty. It was as if the whole strength of the country had fallen with Harold. Henceforth King William never did anything to annoy the holy man. Instead he honoured him with great reverence, indeed, both loving him as a father and speaking of him as such. Coming on more favourable times, therefore, Wulfstan restored to their proper use many possessions of the church of Worcester which formerly the insolence of the Danes, and latterly the power of the Archbishop Ealdred, had stripped from it. Thus the king regarded him with favour; thus such holiness invited the concern of leaders of affairs; thus was religion revered by one whom others fear.[99]

48 William of Malmesbury, Deeds of the Kings of the English

William of Malmesbury started writing his Deeds of the Kings of the English at the request of Queen Matilda II and therefore before her death in 1118. Later, he revised the text several times.

William of Malmesbury, Gesta regum Anglorum, ed. and trsl. R. A. B. Mynors, R. M. Thomson and M. Winterbottom (Oxford, 1998); this translation is based on *The Church Historians of England*, trsl. J. Stevenson, 5 vols in 8 (London, 1853–58), 3, pt 1, 213–17, 227–8, 230 and 231–5.

[Book II, c. 228] ... The king [Edward], in consequence of the death of his relative [Edward, son of Edmund] losing the hope of his first choice, gave the succession of England to William count of Normandy. He was well worthy of such a gift, being a young man of superior mind, who had raised himself to the highest eminence by his unwearied exertion. Moreover, he was the nearest blood relation as he was the son of Robert, the son of Richard the second, whom we have already mentioned as the brother of Emma, Edward's mother. Some affirm that Harold himself was sent to Normandy by the king for this purpose; others, who knew Harold's more secret intentions, say that being driven thither against his will by the violence of the wind, he imagined this device in order to extricate himself. This, as it appears nearest the truth, I shall relate.

99 For King William's relationship with Bishop Wulfstan, see Mason, 1990, 105–6, 131–42.

Harold being at his country seat at Bosham went for recreation on board a fishing boat, and for the purpose of prolonging his sport, put out to sea; when a sudden storm arose he was driven with his companions on the coast of Ponthieu. The people of that region, as was their native custom, immediately assembled from all quarters and those who were unarmed and few in number were as it easily might be quickly overpowered by an armed multitude and bound hand and foot. Harold, craftily meditating a remedy for this mischance, sent a person whom he had allured by very great promises, to William to say that he had been sent into Normandy by the king for the purpose of expressly confirming, in person, the message which had been imperfectly delivered by people of less authority, but that he was detained in fetters by Count Guy of Ponthieu and could not execute his embassy; that it was the barbarous and untamed custom of the country that those who had escaped destruction at sea, should meet with perils on shore; that it well became a man of his dignity not to let this pass unpunished; that to suffer those to be laden with chains, who appealed to his protection, detracted somewhat from his own greatness; and that if his captivity must be terminated by money, he would gladly give it to Count William, but not to the contemptible Guy. By this means Harold was liberated at William's command and conducted to Normandy by Guy in person.

The count entertained him with much respect, both in banqueting and in vesture, according to the custom of the country; and the better to learn his disposition and at the same time to try his courage he took him with himself in an expedition which he at the time led against Brittany. There, Harold well approved both in ability and courage won the heart of the Norman. And, still more to ingratiate himself, he of his own accord, confirmed to him by oath the castle of Dover, which was under his jurisdiction, and the kingdom of England after the death of Edward. Wherefore honoured both by having his daughter, then a child, betrothed to him, and by the confirmation of his ample patrimony, he was received into the strictest intimacy. Not long after his return home, the king [Edward] crowned at London on Christmas Day and being there seized with the disorder of which he was aware that he would die, commanded the church of Westminster to be dedicated on Innocents Day. Thus, full of years and glory, he surrendered his pure spirit to heaven and was buried on the day of the Epiphany in the said church which after he had arrived in England had built in that kind of style which now almost all attempt to rival at enormous expense.

The people of the West Saxons which had reigned in Britain 571 years from the time of Cerdic and 261 from Egbert ceased altogether to rule. For while the grief for the king's death was yet fresh, Harold on the very day of the Epiphany seized the crown extorting their consent from the nobles. Though the English say that it was granted to him by the king, I allege it was more through regard to Harold than through sound judgement that Edward should transfer his inheritance to a man of whose power he had himself always been jealous. Although, not to conceal the truth, Harold would have governed the kingdom with prudence and with courage in the character he had assumed, had he assumed it lawfully. Indeed, during Edward's lifetime he had quelled by his valour whatever wars were excited against him, wishing to signalise himself with his countrymen and looking forward with anxious hope to the crown. He first conquered Gruffydd, king of the Welsh as I have before related in battle; and afterwards, when he was again making formidable efforts to recover his power, beheaded him, appointing as his successors two of his own adherents that is the brothers of this Gruffydd, Bleddyn and Rhiwallon, who had obtained his favour by their submission.

The same year Tostig arrived in the Humber from Flanders with a fleet of 60 ships and infested with piratical depredations those parts which were adjacent to the mouth of the river. But being quickly driven from the province by the joint force of the brothers Edwin and Morcar he set sail towards Scotland where meeting with Harold Harvagra king of Norway then meditating an attack on England with 300 ships he put himself under his command. Both then with united forces laid waste the country beyond the Humber and falling on the brothers reposing after their recent victory and suspecting no attack of the kind, they first routed and then blockaded them in York. Harold, on hearing this proceeded thither with all his forces and each nation making every possible exertion a bloody encounter followed. But the English obtaining the advantage put the Norwegians to flight. Yet, however reluctantly posterity may believe it, one single Norwegian for a long time delayed the triumph of so many and such great men. For standing on the entrance of the bridge, which is called Stamford Bridge, after having killed several of our party, he prevented the whole from passing over. Being invited to surrender with the assurance that a man of such courage should experience the amplest clemency from the English, he derided those who entreated him and immediately with a stern countenance reproached them as a set of cowards who were unable to resist a single individual. No one approaching nearer as they thought it inadvisable to come to close quarters with a man who desperately rejected every means of safety, one of the king's followers aimed an iron javelin at him from a distance. Transfixed with which as he was boastfully flourishing about and too incautious from his security, he yielded the victory to the English. The army immediately passing over without opposition destroyed the dispersed and flying Norwegians. King Harvagra and Tostig were slain. The king's son with all the ships was kindly sent back to his own country.

Harold elated by his successful enterprise, vouchsafed to give no part to his soldiers on which account many, as they found opportunity stealing away, deserted the king as he was proceeding to the battle of Hastings. For with the exception of his stipendiary and mercenary soldiers he had very few of the people with him. This was the reason why circumvented by a stratagem of William's he was routed with the army he headed after possessing the kingdom nine months and some days. The effect of war in this affair was trifling. It was brought about by the secret and wonderful counsel of God; since the English never again in any general battle made a struggle for liberty as if the whole strength of England had fallen in the person of Harold who certainly might and deserved to pay the penalty of his perfidy even though it were by the instrumentality of the most unwarlike people. Nor in saying this do I at all derogate from the valour of the Normans to whom I am strongly bound both by descent and by the advantages I enjoy. Still those persons appear to me to err who augment the numbers of the English and underrate their courage, for while they thus design to extol the Normans they in fact degrade them. A mighty commendation indeed that a very warlike nation should conquer a set of people who were obstructed by their multitude and fearful through cowardice. On the contrary, they were few in number and brave in the extreme. And who throwing aside every regard for their personal safety laid down their lives for their country. But, however, as these matters await a more detailed narrative, I shall now put a period to my second book that I may return to my composition and my readers to the perusal of it with fresh ardour.

[Preface to Book III] Incited by different motives both Normans and English have written of William. The former have praised him to excess, alike extolling to the utmost his good and his bad actions, while the latter out of national hatred have laden their conqueror with undeserved reproach. For my part as the blood of each people flows in

my veins I shall steer a middle course: where I am certified of his
good deeds I shall openly proclaim them; his bad conduct I shall touch
upon lightly and sparingly though not so as to conceal it, so that
neither shall my narrative be condemned as false nor will I brand that
man with ignominious censure almost the whole of whose actions
may reasonably be excused if not commended. Wherefore I shall
willingly and carefully relate such particulars of him as may be matter
of incitement to the indolent of example to the enterprising useful to
the present age, and pleasing to posterity ...

[Book III, c. 238] I feel no regret at having inserted this for the
benefit of my readers. Now I shall return to William. For since I have
briefly, but I hope not uselessly, gone over the transactions in which
he was engaged as count of Normandy for thirty years, the order of
time now requires a change in the narrative that I may as far as my
inquiries have discovered detect what is false and declare the truth
relating to his regal government.

When King Edward died England, fluctuating with doubtful favour,
was uncertain to which ruler she should commit herself: to Harold,
William or Edgar. For the king had recommended Edgar also to the
nobility as nearest to the sovereignty in point of birth concealing his
better judgement from the tenderness of his disposition. Wherefore,
as I have said above, the English were distracted in their choice
although all of them openly wished well to Harold. He indeed when
once dignified with the crown thought nothing of the covenant
between himself and William, but he said that he was absolved from
the oath because his daughter to whom he had betrothed had died
before she was marriageable. For this man though possessing numberless good qualities is reported to have been careless about abstaining
from breach of trust if he might by any device whatever elude the
reasonings of men on this matter. Moreover he supposed that the
threats of William would never be put into execution because the
latter was occupied in wars with neighbouring princes and so he and
his subjects gave full indulgence to their fancied security. And indeed
had he not heard that the king of Norway was approaching he would
neither have condescended to collect troops nor to array them. William,
in the meantime began mildly to address him by messengers to expos-
tulate on the broken agreement to mingle threats with entreaties and
to warn him that before a year expired he would claim his due by
sword and that he would come to that very place where Harold
supposed he had firmer footing than himself. Harold again rejoined

what I have related concerning the marriage of his daughter and added that he had been presumptuous on the subject of the kingdom in having confirmed to him by oath another's right without the universal consent and edict of the witan and of the people. Again that a rash oath ought to be broken for if an oath, or vow, which a maiden under her father's roof made concerning her person without the knowledge of her parents were adjudged invalid, how much more invalid must that oath be which he had made concerning the whole kingdom, when he was himself only a subject under the king's authority and compelled by the necessity of the time and without the knowledge of the nation. Besides it was an unjust request to ask him to resign a government which he had assumed by the universal kindness of his fellow subjects, a thing which would neither be agreeable to the people nor safe for the military ...

[Book III, c. 239] In the meantime Harold returned from the battle which he had waged against the Norwegians, happy in his own estimation at having conquered, but not so in mine as he had secured the victory by fratricide. When the news of the Norman's arrival reached him, reeking as he was from battle, he proceeded to Hastings though accompanied by very few forces. No doubt the fates urged him on as he neither summoned his troops nor had he been willing to do so would he have found many ready to obey his call so hostile were all to him, as I have before observed, from his having appropriated the northern spoils entirely to himself. He sent out some persons, however, to reconnoitre the number and strength of the enemy. These, being taken within the camp, William ordered to be led amongst the tents and after feasting them plentifully to be sent back uninjured to their lord. On their return Harold inquired what news they brought. When after relating at full the noble confidence of the leader they gravely added that almost all his army had the appearance of priests, as they had the whole face with both lips shaven. For the English leave the upper lip unshorn suffering the hair continually to increase which Julius Caesar in his treatise on the Gallic Wars affirms to have been a national custom with the ancient Britons. The king smiled at the simplicity of the messengers observing with a pleasant laugh that they were not priests but soldiers strong in arms and invincible in spirit. His brother Gyrth, a youth on the verge of manhood and of knowledge and valour surpassing his years caught up his words: 'Since', he said, 'you extol so much the valour of the Normans, I think it ill-advised for you who are his inferior in strength and desert to contend with him. Nor can you deny that you are bound to him by oath either willingly or by compulsion, wherefore you will act wisely if yourself withdrawing from this pressing emergency you allow us to try the issue of a battle; we who are free from all obligation shall justly draw the sword in defence of our country. It is to be appre-hended if you engage that you will be either subjected to flight or to death, whereas if we only fight your cause will be safe at all events, for you will be able to rally the fugitives and to avenge the dead.' ...

[Book III, c. 241] The courageous leaders mutually prepared for battle each according to his national custom. The English, as we have heard, passed the night without sleep in drinking and singing and in the morning proceeded without delay towards the enemy. All on foot armed with battle axes and covering themselves in front by the junction of their shields, they formed an impenetrable body which would have secured their safety that day had not the Normans by a feigned flight induced them to open ranks till that time, according to their custom, closely compacted. The king himself on foot stood with his brothers near the standard in order that while all shared equal danger none would think of retreating. This standard William sent after the victory to the pope. It was sumptuously embroidered with gold and precious stones and represented the form of a man fighting.

[Book III, c. 242] On the other hand the Normans passed the whole night in confessing their sins and received the communion of the Lord's body in the morning. Their infantry with bows and arrows formed the vanguard while their cavalry divided into wings were thrown back. The duke with serene countenance declaring aloud that God would favour his, as being the righteous side, called for arms. And presently when through the hurry of his attendants he had put on his hauberk back to front he corrected the mistake with a laugh, saying: 'The power of my duchy shall be turned into a kingdom.' Then beginning the song of Roland that the warlike example of that man might stimulate the soldiers and calling on God for assistance the battle commenced on both sides and was fought with great ardour neither side giving ground during the greater part of the day. Finding this, William gave a signal to his party that by a feigned flight they should retreat. Through this device the close body of the English opening for the purpose of cutting down the straggling enemy brought upon itself swift destruction. For the Normans facing about attacked them thus disordered and compelled them to flee. In this manner deceived by a strategem they met an honourable death in avenging their country, nor indeed were they at all without their own revenge for by frequently making a stand they slaughtered their pursuers in heaps. Getting possession of a hillock they drove down the Normans when roused with indignation and anxiously striving to gain the higher ground into the valley beneath where easily hurling their javelins and rolling down stones on them as they stood below, they destroyed them to a man. Besides by a short passage with which they were acquainted, avoiding a deep ditch, they trod under foot such a multitude of their enemies in that place that they made the hollow level with the plain by the heaps of carcasses. This vicissitude of first one party conquering and then the other prevailed as long as the life of Harold continued. But when he fell from having his brain pierced with an arrow, the flight of the English ceased not until night. The valour of both leaders was here eminently conspicuous.

[Book III, c. 243] Harold not merely content with the duty of a general in exhorting others diligently entered into every soldierlike duty, often would he strike the enemy when coming to close quarters so that none could approach him with impunity for immediately the same blow levelled both horse and rider. Wherefore, as I have related, receiving the fatal arrow from a distance he yielded to death. One of the soldiers with a sword gashed his thigh as he lay prostrate for which shameful act and cowardly action he was branded with ignominy by William and expelled from the army.

[Book III, c. 244] William too was equally ready to encourage his soldiers by his voice and by his presence; to be the first to rush forward, to attack the thickest of the foe. Thus everywhere raging, everywhere furious he lost three chosen horses, which were that day killed under him. The dauntless spirit and vigour of the intrepid general, however, still persisted though often called back by the kind remonstrance of his bodyguard. He still persisted, I say, till approaching night crowned him with complete victory. And no doubt the hand of God so protected him, that the enemy should draw no blood from his person though they aimed so many javelins at him.

[Book III, c. 245] This was a day of destiny for England, a fatal disaster of our dear country in the struggle for the change of its new lords. For it had long since adopted the manners of the English, which had been very various according to the times. For in the first years of their arrival they were barbarians in their look and manners, warlike in their usages, heathens in their rites, but after embracing the faith of Christ by degrees and in the process of time in consequence of the peace which they enjoyed they regarded arms only in a secondary light and they gave their whole attention to religion. I say nothing of the poor, the meanness of whose fortune often restrains them from overstepping the bounds of justice. I omit men of ecclesiastical rank, whom sometimes respect for their profession and sometimes fear of shame suffers not to deviate from the true path. I speak of princes who from the greatness of their power might have full liberty to indulge in pleasure, some of whom in their own country and others at Rome changing their habit obtained an heavenly kingdom and a saintly intercourse. And many during their whole lives in outward appearance devoted themselves to wordly affairs in order that they might exhaust their treasures on the poor or divide them amongst monasteries. What shall I say of the multitudes of bishops, hermits and abbots? Does not the whole island blaze with such numerous relics of its natives that you scarcely pass a village of any consequence but you hear the name of some new saint? And of how many have all notices perished through the want of records? Nevertheless in process of time the desire after literature and religion had decayed for several years before the arrival of the Normans. The clergy, contented with a very slight degree of learning could scarcely stammer out the words of the sacraments and a person who understood grammar was an object of wonder and astonishment. The monks mocked the rule of their order by fine vestments and the use of every kind of food.

Their nobility, given up to luxury and wantonness, went not to the church in the morning after the manner of Christians, but merely in a careless manner heard matins and masses from a hurrying priest in their chambers amid the blandishments of their wives. The common people left unprotected became a prey to the most powerful who amassed their fortunes by either seizing on their property or by selling their persons into foreign countries. Although it is characteristic of this people to be more inclined to revelling than to the accumulation of wealth. There was one custom repugnant to nature which they adopted, namely to sell their female servants when pregnant by them and after they had satisfied their lust they entrusted them either to public prostitution or foreign slavery. Drinking in parties was a universal practice in which occupation they passed entire nights as well as days. They consumed their whole substance in mean and despicable houses unlike the Normans and the French who in noble and splendid mansions live with frugality. The vices attendant on drunkenness which enervate the human mind followed.

Hence it arose that when they engaged William, more with rashness and precipitate fury than military skill, they doomed themselves and their country to slavery by one and that an easy victory. For nothing is less effective than rashness. And what begins with violence quickly ceases or is repelled. In fine the English at that time wore short garments reaching to the mid knee, they had their hair cropped, their beards shaven, their arms laden with golden bracelets, their skin adorned with punctured designs [= tattoos], they were accustomed to eat till they became surfeited and to drink till they were sick. These latter qualities they imparted to their conquerors as to the rest they adopted their manners. I would not, however, have these bad propensities ascribed to the English universally. I know that many of the clergy at that day trod the path of sanctity by a blameless life. I know many of the laity of all ranks and conditions in this nation were well pleasing to God. Be injustice far from this account, but as in peace the mercy of God often cherishes the bad and the good together, so equally does His severity sometimes include them both in captivity.

[Book III, c. 246] The Normans, that I may speak of them also, were at that time and are even now exceedingly particular in their dress and delicate in their food, but not so to excess. They are a race inured to war, and can hardly live without it, fierce in rushing against the enemy and where force fails of success ready to use the strategem or to corrupt by bribery. As I have said they live in large buildings with economy, envy their equals, wish to excel their superiors and plunder their subjects, though they defend them from others. They are faithful to their lords, though a slight offence renders them perfidious. They weigh treachery by its chance of success and change their sentiments with money. The politest however, of all nations, they esteem strangers worthy of equal honour with themselves. They also intermarry with their subjects. They revived, by their arrival, the rule of religion which had everywhere grown lifeless in England. You might see churches rise in every village and monasteries in the towns and cities built after a style unknown before. You might behold the country flourishing with renovated rites so that each wealthy man accounted that day lost to him which he had neglected to observe by some magnificent action. But having enlarged sufficiently on these points let us pursue the operations of William.

49   Herman of Bury St Edmunds, Miracles of St Edmund

The following paragraphs give the events of 1066 from the perspective of
Bury St Edmunds where King Edward's physician Baldwin had been made
abbot in 1065/66. Since he had attended the king's deathbed, the present
testimony, written towards the end of the eleventh century, is likely to reflect
his opinion. Gransden (1995, 1–52) suggests that the text was written not by
Herman the archdeacon but by another continental hagiographer, called Bertran.

Heremanni archidiaconi Miracula sancti Eadmundi, in *Ungedruckte Anglo-
Normannische Geschichtsquellen,* ed. F. Liebermann (Strasbourg, 1879), pp.
202–81 at pp. 245–6.

[c. 33] Afterwards, towards the end of his life he [King Edward] fell
ill at his royal palace of Westminster, which he himself had built, on
the vigil of Epiphany; his illness brought an end to his life and to
almost all of England. His burial having taken place in a royal manner
before the day's Mass on Epiphany, Harold son of Godwin, who had
seized the kingdom in a cunning way, promptly at the start of Mass
sat himself on the royal throne and so triggered off his own demise
for he was king for less than ten months. He liked to come to the
place of this martyr [Bury St Edmunds] and granted to the aforementioned father Baldwin the liberty of the monastery as other kings
had done before him, and he would with oaths have confirmed [the
grant] if Fate had not interfered. For, meanwhile, Count William of
Normandy, having gathered a fleet of numerous ships, came by boat
with as large a group of people as he could collect to the aforesaid
king in England and took possession of it as if he were the more
rightful successor of the good Edward, formerly his blood relation.
Rumour had it that King Edward of many good memories had already
promised the kingdom to the aforementioned Norman duke not only
on account of their blood relationship but also because he had no
children to succeed him. After his appetite for the English government
had been stimulated on these grounds and the Norman ships having
been sailed to Hastings, the battle in which the king of the English
died took place on the appointed day and the roles [of the kings]
were changed. The contest about the kingdom had been predicted by
a comet that had appeared the previous summer for almost eight days.

[c. 34] It is good to pause now briefly and summarise that as many
as fifteen kings have ruled England since the death of the precious
martyr Edmund, as the Chronicle testifies,[100] until the time of the first

100 An interesting reference to the Anglo-Saxon Chronicle.

William during whose reign the custom of the French took root and
English things began to change in various ways.

[c. 35] Thus in the year of the Lord 1066, 196 years after the death
of the precious martyr Edmund, the Norman count was crowned king
of the English and as count and king for as long as he lived he ruled
both countries in his way promoted to the rulership by the rightful
disposition of the Highest.

[c. 36] A certain Norman courtier of the aforesaid king, as is the
custom of that people who greedily lay their hands on all that they
see, seized a neighbouring manor of the saint [St Edmund] and
joined it to his own ...

50   Giso of Wells, 'Autobiography'

Giso of Wells's *Historiola* is a short text that may or may not be Giso's auto-
biographical account. If it is his own work it can be dated to the period before
his death in 1088. If, however, it is a fabrication, it probably dates from the
last quarter of the twelfth century.

S. Keynes, 'Giso, bishop of Wells (1061–88)', *ANS*, 19 (1996), 204–71; the
following translation, by S. Keynes, can be found on p. 267.

[c. 6] I even considered striking Earl Harold, who had despoliated
the church committed to me and whom I rebuked sometimes in
private and sometimes openly with a sentence of the same kind; but,
after King Edward's death in the year of the Lord's Incarnation 1065
[= 1066] and on taking up the government of the kingdom, he
promised not only to restore what he had taken away, but also to give
fresh donations. However, the judgement of divine vengeance overtook him on the twenty-first day after the victory which he obtained
over his namesake, the king of the Norwegians, when, having
recruited his army, he engaged in battle with William, duke of the
Normans, who had invaded the southern shore of his land, and was
slain, in the tenth month of his reign, and with his two brothers, and
a great slaughter of his people.

[c. 7] The duke, having obtained the victory, and when he had taken
up the government of the kingdom after him, and had heard from me
a complaint about the injury which had been done to me, surrendered
Winsham to the church, and confirmed it by a charter which specified
that the brethren, offering the sacrifice of praise to God in that

church, for the eternal welfare of himself and of his predecessors, should possess it inviolably, by hereditary right.

Wales and Scotland

51   The Life of Gruffydd ap Cynan

The anonymous author of the Life of Gruffydd ap Cynan wrote not long after King Gruffydd's death in 1137. The Life was originally composed in Latin, but now only a thirteenth-century Welsh translation survives. Gruffydd ap Cynan was king of Gwynnedd from 1081 to 1137. Most of his career was concerned with warfare against rival kings in Wales and the Norman settlers on the eastern borders of Wales. Both sides persuaded each other's enemies to join them. Hence warfare was the result of endlessly shifting alliances. King Gruffydd was of mixed Irish–Welsh parentage, born and brought up in Dublin (Ireland) and returned from there to Wales in the mid-1070s. With initial help from the Norman Robert of Grandmesnil (d. 1093), castellan of Rhuddlan, he established himself as king, but then turned against the Normans, occasionally having to retire to Ireland, as the following abstracts show.[101]

A Medieval Prince of Wales: The Life of Gruffydd ap Cynan, ed. and trsl. D. S. Evans (Llanerch, 1990), pp. 59, 62, 69–70, 74–8.

Forthwith he [Gruffydd] embarked in a ship, raised sails to the wind, voyaged by sea towards Wales, and arrived at the harbour of Aber-menai. At that time there were ruling over all Gwynnedd unjustly and contrary to right Trahaearn, son of Caradog and Cynwrig son of Rhiwallon, a petty king of Powys, and they had divided it between them.[102]

Then Gruffydd sent messengers to the men of Anglesey and Arfon, and the three sons of Merwydd and Llyn, Asser, Meirion and Gwgon, and other leading men to ask them to come in haste to talk to him. And without delay they came and greeted him, and told him, 'your coming is welcome'. Then he besought them with all his might to help him to obtain his patrimony because he was their rightful lord and in conjunction with him to repel fiercely with arms their usurping lords who had come from elsewhere.

When the meeting was over and the council dispersed, he again voyaged by sea towards the castle of Rhuddlan to Robert of Rhuddlan,

---

101 For the Norman version of these events, see Orderic, iv, 138–42; a modern commentary can be found in Lewis, 1996, 61–77.

102 Trahaearn, son of Caradog, lord of Gwynnedd (1075–81).

a renowned, valiant baron of strength, a nephew of Hugh earl of Chester, and he besought him for help against his enemies who were in possession of his patrimony.[103] And when Robert heard who he was, and for what he had come, and what his request was, he promised to support him ...

[Gruffydd established himself and then decided to attack the castle of Rhuddlan]

After a little time had then elapsed, urged by the leading men of the land, he mustered a large host and advanced towards the castle of Rhuddlan to fight with Robert the castellan and with the other fierce knights from France who had lately come to England and had subsequently come to rule the confines of Gwynnedd. After he had prepared for battle and raised his ensigns, he plundered the bailey and burned it and took much booty. Many of the mailed and helmeted knights of the French fell from their horses in fighting, and many footsoldiers, and hardly did a few of them escape into the tower. When the king of Ireland and his barons heard that things had happened so successfully for Gruffydd, their kinsman and foster-son, they rejoiced greatly ... Then there grew much evil and grief in Gwynnedd. And during that time, after a little while, Hugh earl of Chester and many other leaders, namely Robert of Rhuddlan and Warin of Shrewsbury, and Walter of Hereford, mustered the largest host ever of horsemen and footsoldiers.[104] And they brought with them Gwrgenau son of Seisyll and the men of Powys and traversed the mountains till they came to Llyn. In that cantref [a Welsh administrative district] they encamped for a week, causing destruction there daily and ravaging it and inflicting a great slaughter of corpses which they left behind. The land then remained desolate for eight years and the people of that land were scattered over the world despised and destitute. Many of them went into exile to other lands over many years, and hardly did any of them return to their land. And that was the first plague and fierce advent of the Normans first to the land of Gwynnedd, after their advent to England ...

[Gruffydd was kept imprisoned by the Normans at Chester from 1081 to 1093]

103 Robert of Rhuddlan was a Norman, the son of Humphrey of Tilleul and a cousin of Earl Hugh of Chester. Robert's brother was a fellow monk of Orderic Vitalis at Saint-Evroult, who brought back Robert's remains to Normandy c. 1093. He was well informed about Welsh affairs and no doubt Orderic's informant. Hugh son of the vicomte of Avranches was earl of Chester from 1070 to 1101.

104 Warin, sheriff of Shrewsbury; Walter de Lacy was lord of Hereford.

And as he was thus enjoying the use of his kingdom, Meirion Goch, his own baron, was stirred by the devil's arrow, accused him before Hugh earl of Chester, and betrayed him in this way.[105] He arranged that the two earls from France, namely Hugh mentioned above and Hugh earl of Shrewsbury son of Roger of Montgomery, should come, along with a multitude of footsoldiers as far as Y Rug in Edeirnion.[106] The traitor then betrayed him with these words: 'Lord', he said, 'two earls from the border greet you and beseech you to come safely with your foreigners to talk to them as far as Y Rug in Edeirnion.' Gruffydd, believing these words, came as far as the place of his tenancy. And when the earls saw him, they captured both him and his retinue and put him in the gaol of Chester, the worst of prisons, with shackles upon him, for twelve years. His foreigners, after they had been caught, had the thumb of the right hand of each of them cut off, and in that condition they let them go. And when that was heard, the others dispersed; for the Holy Word says: 'I will smite the shepherd and the sheep of the flock shall be scattered'.

And straightway after he had been captured Earl Hugh came to his territory with a multitude of forces and built castles and strongholds after the manner of the French, and became lord over the land. He built a castle in Anglesey, and another in Arfon in the old fort of the emperor Constantine son of Constance the Great. He built another in Bangor and another in Meirionnydd. And he placed in them horsemen and archers on foot, and they did so much damage as had never been done since the beginning of the world. And the cry of the people ascended unto the Lord and He listened to them.

[After several other skirmishes between the Welsh and the Normans, King William Rufus arrived in 1095]

When William Longsword, king of England, heard of the prowess of Gruffydd and his ferocity and cruelty against the French, he found it intolerable.[107] And he roused his whole kingdom against him and came as far as Gwynedd with an abundance of troops of horsemen and footsoldiers prepared to exterminate and destroy all the people completely so that there would not be alive as much as a dog. He also

---

105 Meirion Goch is probably the same as 'Meiriawn goch o Leyn' mentioned in other sources as Gruffydd's supporter.

106 Hugh, son of Roger of Montgomery, earl of Shrewsbury (1068–94), was himself earl of Shrewsbury from 1094 to 1098.

107 William Rufus, king of England (1087–1100), undertook two expeditions to north Wales. The second one took place in 1097.

intended to cut down all the woods and groves so that there would
not be shelter or protection for the people of Gwynnedd from then on.
And he, therefore, set up camp and pitched tents first in Mur Castell,
with some of the Welsh as his guides. When Gruffydd heard that, he
also mustered the host of all his kingdom, and marched against him,
in order to prepare ambushes for him in narrow places when he
should come down the mountain. And he became frightened of that
and took his host back through the middle of the land till he came to
Chester without inflicting any kind of loss on that journey to the
people of the land. He did not obtain any kind of profit or gain, except
for one cow; and he lost a great part of his horsemen and esquires and
servants and horses and many other possessions. Thus did he
[Gruffydd] completely avenge the presumption of the French.

Throughout that time, Gruffydd constantly engaged them, sometimes in front, sometimes behind, sometimes to the right, sometimes
to the left of them, lest they should cause any kind of loss in the
territory. And had Gruffydd allowed his men to mingle with them in
the woods, that would have been the last day for the king of England
and his Frenchmen. He, however, spared them as King David of yore
spared Saul.

After that was over, Earl Hugh of Chester, he who was mentioned
above, the root of all the evil like Antiochus of yore, mustered a fleet
and a mighty wondrous host for the land, with sadness and moaning
and grief remembering the men of the castle, the razing of his castles
and the slaughter of his horsemen. And the other Hugh, earl of
Shrewsbury, and his host also, joined with him, that they should come
together of one accord to avenge the losses which Gruffydd had
inflicted on them. Therefore, they voyaged with their host in their
fleet by sea as far as Gruffydd's territory with Oswain son of Edwin
and Uchtryd his brother and their force ahead of them.[108] And when
that became known, the men of Gwynnedd and Powys united to
oppose them and not submit. Therefore the lords of Powys, namely
Cadwgan and Maredudd his brother, moved taking their abodes with
them to Gruffydd.[109]

Then after taking counsel together they went to Anglesey both
they and Gruffydd and there they defended themselves as in a fortress
surrounded by the ocean. For to Gruffydd there had come sixteen

108 Oswain and Uhtred, sons of Edwin, are local lords. Gruffydd married Oswain's
    daughter Angharad (d. 1162).
109 Cadwgan (d. 1111) and his brother Maredudd, sons of Bleddyn (d. 1132) of
    Powys.

ships with long keels as a help to him from Ireland, and they were to fight at sea against the earls' fleet. When the earls heard that, they sent messengers to the ships which had come to assist Gruffydd, to ask them to fail him when he should be in the most dire straits, and to come to them in return for all the goods they wanted. And so it happened. After they had believed the deceit of the French, they all poured into the island and broke their pledge to Gruffydd.

And when Gruffydd knew that, he grieved and feared greatly for he knew not what counsel he should follow against his adversaries the French and the traitor-ships. Then, after he had consulted with Cadwgan ap Bleddyn, his son-in-law, they voyaged in a skiff until they came to Ireland, and left their people and possessions to the will of God and His protection, He who is accustomed to assist every man, when he is most hard-pressed, with an unfailing will.[110] And when their people knew that, they turned and fled, concealing themselves and hiding in caves in the earth, and swamps, and woods and groves, and fern-brakes, and wood-slopes and precipices, and bogs, and desolate parts and rocks and in all kinds of other places where they could hide for fear of the Jews, namely the French and other peoples who had come to attack them. for, as the Holy Word says, 'the people fell without a leader'. And without delay, the earls and their hosts pursued them gleefully that day until the evening along the length and the breadth of the island, ravaging it and killing the people and breaking the limbs of others. And night halted the chase.

The following day, behold, through the providence of God a royal fleet at hand, appearing without warning. And, when it was seen, the French and Danes, the traitors who had deceived Gruffydd became dejected. As the French were, however, always treacherous, they sent secretly there and then some of the Welsh who were in league with them to the men of the island, to ask them to come in haste to make peace, and to offer them safety; because they feared that the fleeing Welsh would overcome them on the one side, and the royal fleet on the other. And thus it happened. And thus did the French deceive the traitors of the Welsh, besieged on every side of the island, after the havoc they had wrought, which could be remembered by descendants after their forbears.

However, the fleet which they had suddenly seen was owned by the king of Llychlyn [Norway], whom God in his mercy had directed to Anglesey in order to free the people besieged by the foreigners; for

110 Gruffydd's daughter Gwenllian was married to Cadwgan ap Bleddyn.

they had called on their Lord in their suffering and grief, and God listened to them. After the king had been told through an interpreter what island it was, and who was master, what ravaging had been done, what pursuing, who were the pursuers, he shared their grief, and became angry and approached the land with three ships. The French, however, fearful like women, when they saw that, fought with their hauberks on, and sat on their horses as was their wont, and advanced towards the king and the force of three ships. The king and his force fearlessly fought against them, and the French fell down from up on their horses like fruit from fig trees, some dead, some wounded by the missiles of the men of Llychlyn. And the king himself, unruffled from the prow of the ship, hit with an arrow Hugh earl of Shrewsbury in his eye, and he fell a humped back to the ground mortally wounded from his armed horse, beating upon his arms. And from that incident the French turned in flight and presented their backs to the arrows of the men of Llychlyn. The king and his fleet sailed away from there, for he had come with much power to look at the islands of Britain and Ireland which are outside the world, as Virgil said that 'the Britons were entirely separated from the whole world'.

Therefore, Earl Hugh and others of the French, joyous because of the return of King Magnus, took with them the people of Gwynnedd and all their possessions entirely as far as the cantref of Rhos, for fear of the arrival of Gruffydd at any time.[111] And then were counted all the cattle and plunder of every owner, which were divided in half, and with the one half he proceeded to Chester.

There, however, were the perjured traitors from among the Danes, who had betrayed Gruffydd, awaiting the promises which Hugh had given them, captives of men and women, of young men and maidens. And he paid them as faithful to unfaithful, where divine providence affirmed for he had from afar assembled all the hags – toothless, humped, lame, one-eyed, troublesome, feeble, and offered them to them in return for their treachery. When they saw that, they weighed anchor and made for the deep sea towards Ireland. He who was ruler at that time caused some of them to be maimed and their limbs broken, and others were expelled ruthlessly from his entire kingdom.

And at that time, behold Gruffydd according to his usual practice coming from Ireland and he found his whole land desolate its people having gone to another place. He then sent emissaries to earl Hugh and made peace with him; and in that cantref three townships were

---

111 Magnus Barefoot, king of Norway (1092–1108). Three of his skalds produced poems celebrating this Welsh expedition (Jesch, 1996, 117–27).

given him. And there he spent his life for years in poverty and grief, hoping for the providence of God in time to come.

And then after years had gone by, he journeyed to the court of Henry, king of England, who succeeded his brother as king.[112] From him he got good-will, affection and recognition, through the intercession and diplomacy of Hervey, bishop of Bangor.[113] He gave him with peace and affection the cantrefs of Llyn, and Eifionydd and Arllechwedd, along with their people and possessions. And straightway, when Gruffydd returned from the court, he brought settled life to those lands, and for it thanked God, who casts down the proud rich from their chair, and elevates the humble in their stead, who makes the needy opulent, who abases man and elevates him.

However, from then on everything gradually prospered for Gruffydd, for his hope was in the Lord, and there slipped to him daily others from Rhos and their possessions with them, without the consent of the earl of Chester [Richard], and his people multiplied. In the following year he proceeded to Anglesey and its people with him and settled it, and then to the other commotes. In that way he got back through strength everything in Gwynnedd as did Maccabeus son of Mattathias of yore in Israel. And he brought all his people from exile in various parts, those who had gone into exile from the pursuit mentioned above, and he increased in Gwynnedd joyfully as happened in the case of the land of Israel and their return from the captivity of Babylon.

The earl was offended because his territory had been seized and over-run without his consent. And when the king of England heard that, it surprised him, and he opened his treasury, and gave abundantly to horsemen and footsoldiers, and brought with him the king of Scotland and the Scots and the men of the south.[114] He thus came to Gruffydd's territory and encamped at Mur Castell. Gruffydd also, from his experience of warfare, encamped against him on the ridges of the snow-clad Snowdon. And from there he negotiated with the king, and the king with him, through the space of some days, and they made peace. King Henry then returned to England, and Gruffydd to his territory.

And again after a period of time, King Henry came back with large hosts, and he encamped in the same place as mentioned above in the

112 After the death of Earl Hugh of Chester in 1101, Henry I, king of England (1100–35) took Cheshire and Shropshire under direct control. Hugh's small son Richard (d. 1120) did not become earl until 1115 (Lewis, 1996, 74).

113 Hervey, bishop of Bangor (1092–late 1090s) and bishop of Ely (1109–31).

114 King Alexander of Scotland (1107–24) accompanied King Henry I on his first expedition to Wales in 1114. Henry's second expedition took place in 1121.

mountain with the intention of uprooting the territory of Gruffydd and destroying it and killing and exterminating his people with the edge of the sword. When that was heard, after mustering a host, Gruffydd came against him according to his usual practice, and placed his abodes and villeins and the women and sons in the recesses of the mountains of Snowdon, where they did not suffer any danger. Therefore the king feared that he would fall into the hands of Gruffydd from the danger he was in, when he came down from the mountain, and having made peace with him he returned.

O God, the number of times the earls of Chester contrived to oppose Gruffydd, and could not do it. And the number of times the men of Powys and they could not. And the number of times the men of the deceiver Trahaearn, but they were not able to bring it to fulfilment.

52   William of Malmesbury, Deeds of the Kings of the English

William of Malmesbury began writing the Deeds of the Kings of the English at the request of Queen Matilda II before 1118. The following abstracts cover the immediate conquest years until the end of King Malcolm III's reign (1058–93).

William of Malmesbury, Gesta regum Anglorum, ed. and trsl. R. A. B. Mynors, R. M. Thomson and M. Winterbottom (Oxford, 1998); this translation is based on *The Church Historians of England,* trsl. J. Stevenson, 5 vols in 8 (London, 1853–58), 3, pt 1, pp. 236–7.

[Book III, c. 248] ... He [William] almost annihilated the city of York that sole remaining shelter for rebellion, destroying its citizens with sword and famine. For there Malcolm, king of the Scots, with his party there Edgar, Morcar and Waltheof with the English and Danish troops often brooded over the nest of tyranny. There they frequently killed his generals. Perhaps I should not be out of order were I severally to commemorate their deaths though I might risk the peril of creating disgust, while I should not be easily pardoned as an historian if I were led astray by the falsities of my authorities.

[Book III, c. 249] Malcolm willingly received all the English fugitives affording to each every protection in his power but more especially to Edgar whose sister [Margaret] he had married out of regard to her noble descent. On his behalf he infested the adjacent provinces of England with plunder and fire. Not that he supposed by so doing he could merely annoy William who was incensed that his territories were subject to Scottish invasions. In consequence William collecting a body of infantry and cavalry soldiers repaired to the northern parts of the island and first received into subjection the metropolitan city [York] which the English, Danes and Scots obstinately defended, its citizens being wasted with continued want. He destroyed also in a great and severe battle a considerable number of the enemy who had come to the succour of the besieged, though the victory was not bloodless on his side as he lost many of his people.[115] He then ordered both the towns and fields of the whole district to be laid waste, the fruits and grain to be destroyed by fire or by water, more especially on the coast as well on account of his recent displeasure as because a rumour had gone abroad that Cnut king of Denmark the son of Svein was approaching with his forces.[116] The reason for such a command was that the plundering pirate should find no booty on the coast to carry off with him if he designed to depart again directly, or should he be compelled to provide against want if he thought proper to stay. Thus the resources of a province once flourishing and the nurse of tyrants were cut off by fire, slaughter and devastation, the ground for more than thirty miles totally uncultivated and unproductive remains bare even to the present day. Should any stranger now see it, he laments over the once magnificent cities, the towers threatening heaven itself with their loftiness, the fields abundant in pasturage and watered with rivers, and if any ancient inhabitant remains he knows it no longer.

[Book III, c. 250] Malcolm surrendered himself without coming to an engagement and for the whole of William's time passed his life under treaties uncertain and frequently broken. But when in the reign of William [Rufus], the son of William, he was attacked in a similar manner, he diverted the king from pursuing him by a false oath. Soon after he was slain together with his son by Robert Mowbray, earl of Northumberland, while regardless of his faith he was devastating the province with more than usual insolence.[117] For many years he lay buried at Tynemouth, lately he was conveyed by Alexander his son to Dunfermline in Scotland.[118]

15 Probably a reference to William the Conqueror's march to York in 1069.

16 Cnut (d. 1086) did not become king until the death of his father Svein in 1075. The rumour may refer to Cnut's arrival with a large fleet off the coast of East Anglia as potential support for the rebellion of Earl Roger and Earl Ralph of Gael. They never landed but turned to Flanders instead.

17 King Malcolm was killed in 1093. Robert of Mowbray was imprisoned and his lands forfeited after his rebellion in 1095; he died several decades later.

18 Alexander, king of Scotland (1107–24), son of Malcolm III.

IV: THE NORMANS AND THEIR NEIGHBOURS

Introduction

Within a few decades of settling in Normandy the Scandinavian leaders had been integrated into the Frankish nobility.[1] Rollo married his daughter Gerloc (*Geirlaugh*) to Duke William III of Aquitaine, and first count of Poitou (*c.* 935–63). She took a Christian Frankish name and became Adela. Rollo's son William Longsword married into another neighbouring family when he took Leyarda of Vermandois as wife. There were no children from this marriage.[2] His concubine, Sprota, mother of Richard I, is said by Flodoard to have been from Brittany, which might mean that she was of Celtic, Scandinavian or Frankish origin. Her name suggests the latter.[3] According to William's *Plaintsong* written *c.* 943, his father Rollo may have already been married to a Christian woman 'overseas' (possibly Scotland) before he came to Normandy [9]. Once in Normandy Rollo associated himself with Popa, whose Frankish name suggests that she belonged to the indigenous aristocracy (from Bayeux). The swift association of the Scandinavian counts of Rouen with their Frankish noble neighbours is indicative of their wish to settle and root in western France. The marriage alliances also made them known in the neighbouring regions, as is illustrated by the local chroniclers who report on Rollo's dynasty. The willingness of the Scandinavians to become Christians in return for land and social acceptance is reported by most non-Norman historians. The Aquitainian Adémar of Chabannes highlights Rollo's willingness to convert to Christianity and shake off the pagan gods [11]. His younger contemporary in Burgundy, Rodulfus Glaber, also notes the pagan past but does not seem to know about Rollo [64]. For him William was the first count of Rouen.

Aquitainian and Poitevin contacts, established through Gerloc's marriage, with the Norman ducal family remained close. Richard I's

---

1 The best discussion of Normandy's relations with its French neighbours can be found in Bates, 1982, 65–85.

2 Adigard des Gautries, 1954, 305; *GND*, i, 58–9, 80–1.

3 *GND*, i, 78–9.

daughter Beatrice, who was illegitimate and thus not one of Gunnor's daughters, married the vicomte of Turenne [63]. The marriage resulted in divorce after which Beatrice returned to Normandy to become abbess of Montivilliers in the early 1030s.[4] While still married she may have alerted her nephew Duke Richard II to the capture of Emma, viscountess of Limoges, who had been kidnapped by vikings and kept prisoner for three years [62]. During this time a huge ransom was collected, mostly from church treasure, and paid to the captors, who then refused to let her go. Richard II's mediation with the vikings was successful and resulted in her release. Another example of Norman–Aquitainian relations can be found in charters resulting from yet another marriage arrangement. The abbots of Jumièges (in Normandy) and Bourgueil (in Aquitaine) decided to exchange land. Jumièges owned lands at Tourtenaye near Bourgueil, while Bourgueil held property near Vernon in eastern Normandy [61]. The Vernon estate had been part of the dowry of Leyarda, William Longsword's wife. After her death c. 979, the lands which she had taken with her when she married Count Theobald I of Blois-Chartres went to her daughter Emma, later duchess of Aquitaine. In turn Emma gave them to the abbey of Bourgueil. An exchange of land made sense for both monasteries – enabling them to cultivate estates nearer to home – and the abbots had no problems persuading their respective princes, William V of Aquitaine (995–1029) and Richard II, to agree. Not until the rise of Geoffrey Martel, count of Anjou (1040–60), did relations with these neighbours become more strained. A period of endemic warfare on the southern frontier of Normandy, and in particular in Maine, was the result and lasted on and off through the reigns of William the Conqueror [60] and those of his sons.

Relations with Burgundy were initiated by Richard I when he invited William of Volpiano, the Italian abbot of Saint-Bénigne at Dijon, to reform the Norman abbeys and in particular Fécamp. It was there that in 1001 William persuaded Richard II to replace the community of canons with Benedictine monks. Thirty years later, while on a visit, William of Volpiano fell ill and died at Fécamp [65]. Contacts with Burgundy were strengthened through the marriage of Richard III's sister Adeliza with Reginald I of Burgundy. Their second son Guy became a pretender to the Norman duchy during William the Conqueror's

---

4 Fauroux, no. 90, p. 233 where the foundation charter of Montivilliers has Duke Robert the Magnificent refer to her as '*quadam amita mea, nomine Beatrice*' (one aunt of mine called Beatrice).

reign. Adeliza survived many of her male contemporaries and, aged well into her seventies, was still able to confirm a gift of the castle of Le Homme to the nuns of Sainte-Trinité at Caen in 1075, even though she could not be present herself and was represented by her chaplain William.[5]

Nearer to Normandy we hear most, unsurprisingly, about the relations with the kings of France, themselves lords of central France around Paris. After the defeat of Louis IV (936–54) in Normandy during Richard I's minority, he and his Carolingian successors left the Norman duke alone [53]. The latter became a master in playing off against each other the two main rivals for the French throne: the Carolingian kings and the newly emerging Robertian family also known as the Capetians. As dukes of Paris they had already played a considerable part in supporting the Norman dukes against the Carolingian dynasty. In 960, before he had become king, Hugh Capet (king 987–96) gave his sister Emma in marriage to Richard I.[6] She died without children and Richard took his Danish mistress Gunnor as his lawful wife, without apparently upsetting his relations with his former in-laws [53]. In *c.* 1005 King Hugh's successor, King Robert the Pious (996–1031), settled a frontier dispute between Duke Richard II and Count Odo of Blois-Chartres [53], while twelve years later he welcomed Richard at the coronation ceremony of his eldest son Hugh [54]. He could also count on the Norman duke's support for military campaigns, of which the one against a rebellious vassal in Burgundy in the 1020s was described by William of Jumièges and alluded to in the poem *Moriuht*.[7] Friendly relations resulted in the exchange of gifts, one of which ended up in the royal palace of Compiègne where a would-be thief tried to steal the precious object [54]. Richard II's son Richard III (1026–27) distinguished himself in the above-mentioned Burgundian campaign but died too soon to capitalise on his position. His brother Robert the Magnificent (1027–35) succeeded him and during his reign relations with France changed.[8] First of all Duke Robert fell out with his great-uncle Archbishop Robert of Rouen (989–1037), who, presumably with King Robert the Pious's

5 *GND*, ii, 36–7; Musset, 1967, no. 21, pp. 128–9; Bates, no. 58. Bates, no. 59 (dated 1082) records the countess as still being alive and consenting to the fact that Countess Adelaide of Aumâle would hold the place for the rest of her (Adelaide's) life after which it would return to the nuns.

6 *GND*, i, 116–17, 128–9.

7 *GND*, ii, 36–9; Van Houts, 1998a, 622–3.

8 Bates, 1982, 59–62.

support, took shelter in France. As a result Duke Robert was reprimanded by Bishop Fulbert of Chartres [55]. Then a few years later, around 1030, Duke Robert in turn offered shelter to King Robert's son Henry when he was quarrelling with his mother Queen Constance, who supported his younger brother as royal heir.[9] Henry won and became king of France in 1031. Around this time, Orderic Vitalis later recalled, King Henry I gave the French Vexin to Duke Robert in gratitude for the duke's help, but the Vexin was to remain a bone of contention.[10]

The see-sawing history of the frontier castles of Tillières and Neaufles illustrates the guerilla warfare in the Vexin [24, 30, 53]. When in 1074 Simon succeeded his father as count of Vexin he was in a position to improve relations between the two rulers. Wiliam the Conqueror and Matilda had educated him, perhaps because Matilda as his kinswoman had offered to foster him [56]. He was considered a suitable husband for one of their daughters (Simon refused and became a monk instead), but not until he had returned land near Gisors to Rouen cathedral and tried to negotiate in the quarrel between King William and his eldest son Robert Curthose.[11] To escape the perils of diplomacy, Simon went on pilgrimage to Rome, where he died. From then on he was venerated as a saint.

The most controversial matter between France and Normandy was the nature of the feudal obligations between the two princes, a problem which became acute after 1066.[12] Around the year 1000 Dudo had put into words what the Norman dukes felt, namely that *c.* 911 King Charles the Simple had given Normandy as an allod, a hereditary fief without any strings attached, to Rollo and his heirs [4]. Such an interpretation no doubt reflects the political ambitions of Richard I and Richard II, but other evidence suggests that Dudo's interpretation was wishful thinking. The French considered Normandy to be a principality like, for example, Flanders, Aquitaine, Burgundy and Blois-Chartres, where despite their semi-independence the princes ultimately owed allegiance to their overlord, the king of France. That in practice the French kings could not always enforce these obligations is a different matter. For them the grant *c.* 911 had been a temporary

9 *GND*, ii, 54–7.

10 Orderic, iv, 76–7.

11 Bates, no. 229, pp. 720–1.

12 The literature on this topic is huge. For useful modern introductions, see Hollister, 1986, 17–58 and Chibnall, 1989, 5–19.

one that had become permanent. In their eyes it had never been an allod but always a fief of the French crown.

The situation became complicated after 1066 when William the Conqueror as duke of Normandy remained a subject of King Philip I of France (1060–1108), but as king of England had become his equal. The practical consequences were that William refused to do homage to the French king, a refusal repeated by his sons including Henry I. On the other hand, the refusal to kneel before the king and acknowledge him ceremonially as superior did not prevent William the Conqueror from sending Norman troops to the royal army at Cassel (Flanders) in 1071, which shows that the king/duke was willing to support his overlord against the usurper Robert the Frisian in Flanders. However, this example loses some of its force if we realise that William's wife Matilda, Robert's sister, was horrified by his attempted coup and that thus the maintenance of family honour rather than feudal obligation dictated Norman policy.

The reign of William's youngest son Henry I (1100–35) saw the lengthiest series of hostilities along the Norman–French border when neither Louis VI of France (1108–37) nor Henry I was prepared to give in.[13] It was during this time that a clever historian at Battle Abbey in England wrote The Short Account of William the Most Noble Count including a reinvented passage from Dudo's history. The Scandinavian Harold is said to have helped Richard I against Louis IV after which a pact was negotiated between the Danes and the French stipulating that the Norman dukes owed no fealty and no military service to the king of France in return for Normandy [57]. This was clearly a free and contemporary (twelfth-century) interpretation of past Norman–French relations, but nevertheless it forcefully reminds us of the strength of feeling at Henry I's court. From a slightly later date comes Henry of Huntingdon's reference to the same occasion when, he says, the duke of Normandy carried a sword while the king of France was not allowed a sword nor even a small knife [45]. Some softening of heart, however, occurred as a result of the brutal battle of Brémule in 1119, where Anglo-Norman troops defeated the French. As part of the peace negotiations Henry I agreed that his son and heir William Adelin would do homage to Louis VI for Normandy [58]. One year later the White Ship disaster ruined the diplomatic solution when it included William Adelin among its victims and consequently Normandy (and England) were without a legitimate male heir.

13 Hollister, 1986, 17–58.

An important document, the treaty between Henry I as king of England and Count Robert II of Flanders concluded in 1101, is illustrative of the relations between the king of France and his territorial princes as well as of the relations between the English king and the count of Flanders [66]. According to the treaty, Count Robert of Flanders would recruit and supply 1000 soldiers to King Henry I in return for an annual sum of money. The treaty also, almost incidentally, throws light on the relationship between the count of Flanders and his overlord, the king of France. For it states unambiguously that Henry I could count on Robert II's support only as long as Robert was not needed by the king of France. In other words, King Henry I knew that Robert of Flanders had in fact the same obligations to the king of France as the duke of Normandy had. At the time, in 1101, the duke was King Henry I's brother Robert Curthose. The clauses that relate to a potential summons by Henry I for Count Robert of Flanders's mercenaries to fight in Normandy clearly hint at Henry's ambitions to establish himself as duke of Normandy. This did not happen until 1106 when he defeated his brother at Tinchebrai. The document also shows Henry I's urgent need for mercenaries, probably because the feudal obligations of his men to provide him with soldiers in return for their lands did not work in practice. The 'feudal' system of military obligation was too unreliable a system of recruitment of troops for any military commander to count on. Instead a payment of tax, known as scutage, by which the king's men could substitute money for soldiers was preferred by king and men alike. King Henry had enough money to pay for mercenaries, for the English taxation system worked smoothly and efficiently and enabled him to hire soldiers regularly. The treaty had an additional advantage for the king of the English in that it prevented any English exile taking refuge in Flanders.[14] Thus the treaty put an end to the customary welcome English political exiles had experienced there throughout the eleventh century. For the count of Flanders, with limited financial resources available to him, the treaty guaranteed an annual income from England.

A glimpse of where and how the count recruited the mercenaries is provided by Lambert of Wattrelos's annals into which he inserted in 1153 a history of his own family [59].[15] According to this account Lambert's maternal uncle, also called Lambert, had served under Henry I and had been given land in Normandy after 1106 but before

14 Nip, 1998, 145–67.
15 Vercauteren, 1963, 223–45.

1118 when he, together with another member of the family, died during the conflict between King Henry I and Count Baldwin VII (1111–19) [58]. Wattrelos (Nord, arr. Lille, c. Roubaix) is situated in the north-western corner of France which was precisely the catchment area for the recruitment of mercenaries by the counts of Flanders.

France

53 William of Jumièges, Deeds of the Dukes of the Normans

William of Jumièges wrote his Deeds of the Dukes of the Normans in the late 1050s to *c.* 1070. Here follows his account of the relationship between consecutive French kings and Norman dukes. Well into the reign of Robert the Pious the Normans were supported by Scandinavian troops in their struggle against their French neighbours.

GND, i, 103, 111–13, 127–31; ii, 27–9, 143–5.

King Louis IV of France (936–54) and Duke Richard I

[Book IV, c. 3] [Count Arnulf I of Flanders (918–65) counselled King Louis IV to expel the Normans] He also said that the king ought to remember the abuses and insults of the Normans from which he and his father had suffered so long; and so as not to let this trouble drag on, the best advice was to brand the knees of young Richard, keep him under close observation, and impose such heavy taxes on Normandy that in the end the Normans would be compelled to return to Denmark, whence they had burst forth …

[Book IV, c. 7] Meanwhile Bernard the Dane feared that King Louis on his way back with Duke Hugh would inflict graver sufferings upon the Normans, so he sent messengers secretly to Harold, king of the Danes, who was still at Cherbourg, explaining to him that he himself had troops from the Cotentin and Bessin for an expedition on land and that Harold with a hostile force should organise attacks from the sea on Normandy.[16] This would compel King Louis to come and confer with Bernard against Harold, which would give Bernard an opportunity to avenge the blood of his friend William [Longsword's murder in 943] upon his enemies. King Harold swiftly responded to these

---

16 Harold, a viking leader in the Cotentin.

suggestions, pushed his ships out to the sea, raised his sails aloft, and with a north-west wind landed on the coast near the salt works of Corbon, where the Dives pours its rapid waters into the stormy sea.[17] As usual the news spread quickly and reached the ears of the Franks, to the effect that the heathens had occupied the coast with a large number of ships. Bernard the Dane and Rodulf Torta sent an embassy to King Louis telling him about this disastrous turn of events.[18] After gathering a powerful army, the king came as quickly as possible to Rouen. From there he instructed King Harold to come and meet him at Val d'Herluin, for he was eager to know why he was attacking the frontiers of his realm.[19] The proposition pleased King Harold tremendously, for he realised that the duke's death could now be avenged by an all-out effort. At the appointed day the two kings met and discussed for a long time the unjust murder of Duke William. It then happened that one of the Danes recognised Herluin, count of the town of Montreuil, among the bystanders, for whom the duke had died; inspired by friendship for the duke, the Dane instantly killed Herluin on the spot by driving his lance through him. Herluin's brother Lambert and other Franks, indignant at the murder and raised to fury, rushed forward to kill the Danes in an impetuous assault. But the heathens offered fierce resistance and in the heat of the battle, their swords pierced eighteen French leaders as well as innumerable other men whom they sent to fiery hell. Others hastened to conceal themselves in various hiding-places, and in fear and trembling sought refuge hither and thither. King Louis, too, escaped from King Harold by the swift pace of his horse, but fell into the hands of a certain soldier. The king promised him a large reward in order not to be handed over to his enemy, so that finally the soldier, won over by the king's tears, hid him secretly on an island in the Seine. When Bernard the Dane heard this from his scouts, he sent out his officials, who instantly put the soldier in chains. The soldier was compelled against his will to produce the king before them, having intended to release him in return for a reward. When the king was fetched from the island, he was confined in strict custody at Rouen on Bernard's orders ...

---

17 Corbon-en-Auge (Calvados).

18 Rodulf Torta's background is unknown. He was a benefactor of Saint-Ouen at Rouen and he was appointed governor of Rouen by King Louis IV.

19 Val d'Herluin is the unidentified site where Count Herluin of Montreuil (see below) was killed.

King Lothar of France (954–86) and Duke Richard I

[Book IV, c. 16] ... seeing that he [Duke Richard] was threatened by the many treacherous attempts of the king [Lothar] and the united fury of the counts of the Franks, the duke sent messengers to Harold, king of the Danes, requesting him to come to his support as soon as possible in order to repress the fury of the Franks with a host of heathens. The king not only rejoiced in welcoming the messengers, but sent them back to the duke laden with rich gifts and the promise to send support as quickly as possible.[20] Need I say more? At the king's orders ships were launched into the sea, the heathen youths made preparations for this expedition, and an innumerable army was provided with shields, hauberks, helmets and all sorts of weapons. And so at the appointed day the banners were raised, the sails billowed vigorously before the fresh breezes and after a prosperous and quick crossing of the sea they sailed their ships up the mouth of the River Seine. On the news of their arrival the duke set off with immense joy to meet them. Then he went on before them and they followed him, rowing their boats along the course of the Seine, and came swiftly to Jeufosse, where they lowered their anchors and planned an attack on the Franks.[21] And with a sudden shout they sprang from their boats and set all the surrounding countryside on fire. Men were carried off chained with their women, villages were pillaged, cities laid waste, and strongholds laid low: the land was turned into a desert. Throughout Theobald's country all were stricken with grief but no dog barked.[22] When there was nothing left to destroy, they went straight on and invaded the lands of the king, and all that they stole from the Franks they sold for a small price to the Normans. Normandy remained free of these heathen raids; France with no resistance, was carried off captive.

[Book IV, c. 17] While this was happening, a synod of bishops was held at Laon to discover the reason why the Christian people were afflicted by disasters. Finally, they sent one of them, the bishop of Chartres, to the duke to ask him why he, as a most Christian and devout man, meted out such detestable cruelty. When the duke had told the bishop of the treacherous acts of the king and Theobald and

20 This Harold is probably the same as Harold, the viking leader in the Cotentin.

21 Jeufosse (Seine-et-Oise, c. Mantes); viking fortifications there are known from Charles the Bald's reign (Nelson, 1992, 181, 185–6).

22 Theobald the Trickster, count of Blois and Chartres (943–77).

how the city of Evreux was stolen from him, the bishops promptly requested and obtained a truce from the heathen attacks.[23] During the truce the bishops were to escort King Lothar to a convenient place where, in a friendly spirit, he could pay satisfaction to the duke in every respect. When Theobald heard that the king was negotiating peace without consulting him, he feared that the weight of the whole war would fall on him and therefore sent a monk in haste to the duke. He told the duke that he utterly repented of the offences he had committed against him, and that he wished to come to his court and to give him back the city of Evreux. The duke was delighted by this news and promised him a safe conduct and granted him permission to come and see him. Theobald and his retinue arrived at the ducal court and there not only returned the city to the duke but also concluded a pact of friendship with him. Then, having received many gifts, he returned joyfully home. As the day of his meeting with the king approached our duke gave orders for the building of a stage of remarkable size in the heathen camp of Jeufosse. When King Lothar and his barons had arrived and stood on the stage, he made satisfaction to the duke and concluded a pact with him, and both swore oaths to keep it. After the duke had brought these negotiations to a happy conclusion, he converted very many of the heathens to the Christian faith by his holy words; and he sent those who decided to remain heathens to Spain, where they fought many battles and destroyed eighteen cities.[24]

[Book IV, c. 18] At that time his wife Emma, daughter of Hugh the Great, died without issue. Not long afterwards he married again, according to Christian custom, a very beautiful maiden called Gunnor of noble Danish origin. By her he fathered sons, Richard, Robert, Malger, and two others, as well as three daughters.[25] One of them named Emma married Aethelred, king of the English and on her he fathered King Edward and Alfred, who long afterwards was treacherously slain by Earl Godwin. The second daughter, named Hadvisa, married Count Geoffrey of the Bretons, who fathered on her Counts Alan and Odo. The third daughter, named Matilda, was the wife of Count Odo.[26]

---

23 The treaty of Gisors dates from 966.
24 Cf. below, no. **81**.
25 Of the two unnamed sons only Robert Danus is known from other sources.
26 Cf. above, no. **26**.

King Robert the Pious (996–1031) of France and Duke Richard II

[Book V, c. 12] When King Robert of the French heard about the shameless behaviour of the heathens towards the Bretons and how Duke Richard had summoned them to punish Count Odo's disobedience, he feared that France might be destroyed by them and called together the leaders of his realm for an assembly at Coudres, to which he also summoned the two warring princes.[27] There as each one listened to the reasons for the quarrel, their minds were pacified and they were brought to agree to a peace by which Odo would hold the castle of Dreux and in return the duke would receive the land he had seized with the stronghold of Tillières remaining permanently, as it was then, in the power of the duke and his heirs.[28] When the duke had solemnly agreed to this, he returned joyfully to his kings.[29] He rewarded them with gifts fitting for kings and allowed them permission to return home in triumph after they had promised to return to him whenever he was in need of their support. King Olaf, delighted by the Christian religion and despising the cult of the idols, was converted to the faith of Christ with some of his followers at the urging of Archbishop Robert; and he was washed in the water of baptism and anointed with the holy chrism by him.[30] He rejoiced in the grace he had received and returned to his kingdom. Later, he was betrayed by his own people and slain by perfidious men, and he entered the heavenly kingdom as a glorious king and martyr and now shines brightly among his own people with his miracles and virtues.

King Henry I of France (1031–60) and Duke William the Conqueror in 1054

[Book VII, c. 10] Ever since the Normans had begun to cultivate the lands of Neustria, the French had made it their custom to envy them; they incited their kings to turn against them and asserted that the Normans had taken away by force from their ancestors the lands now in Norman hands. King Henry, roused by malicious and envious suggestions of some men at his court, and provoked by the duke's

---

27 Coudres (Eure, c. Saint-André).

28 For the frontier castle of Tillières, see also nos 24 and 30.

29 Olaf and Lacman, viking leaders who called themselves 'kings' who had come to his support against Count Odo of Blois-Chartres.

30 William of Jumièges is the only authority for the fact that Olaf on his return journey to Norway, where he became king in 1014, was baptised at Rouen. He was slain at the battle of Stiklarstadir in 1030.

taunt, launched a double attack on Normandy, which he entered with
two armies; one consisting of chosen and valiant noblemen under the
command of his brother Odo he sent to subdue the Pays-de-Caux, he
himself led the other one with Count Geoffrey of Anjou [1040–60] to
overthrow the county of Evreux. As soon as the duke saw to what
extent he and his people were under attack, he, moved by deep and
noble grief, at once chose soldiers whom he quickly sent out to curb
the pillagers of the Pays-de-Caux. Escorted by some of his men he
himself set out for the king with the intention of inflicting punishment upon him if only he could draw away one of the royal retainers
from the king's force. Meanwhile the other Normans found the French
at Mortemer totally preoccupied with arson and rape of women.[31]
There at dawn battle was instantly joined and continued on both sides
with bloodshed until noon. Finally the defeated French took to flight
including the standard-bearer Odo, the king's brother. In that battle
the greater part of the French nobility was slain: the remainder was
kept in custody throughout various Norman villages. When the king
learned about their misfortune, he was full of grief about their deaths
and withdrawing from the Norman troubles he rapidly returned.

54   Helgaud, The Life of Robert the Pious

Helgaud wrote the Life of Robert the Pious c. 1033 at Saint-Benoît-sur-Loire.
This chapter describes the co-coronation of the king's eldest son Hugh on 9
June 1017 at Saint-Corneille-de-Compiègne. Hugh predeceased his father in
1025. The duke of Normandy is Richard II (996–1026).

Helgaud de Fleury, Vie de Robert le Pieux, ed. R. H. Bautier and G. Labory
(Paris, 1965), pp. 90–3.

At the palace of Compiègne the king [Robert the Pious] became the
victim of a noble [nobilis] robbery. The day of Whitsun approached
when the Holy Spirit, who replenishes all, purifies the hearts of the
faithful so that they please the Father and the Son in equal measure to
the Holy Spirit. On that day the glorous king, who was also a father,
was planning to appoint as a king his son named Hugh, a young man
of the greatest nobility and the goodness of the father and the son
which was well-known through the whole world caused almost
everyone to gather together to create him a king because they loved
that occasion. The good young man displayed the highest character,

31 Mortemer (Seine-Mar., c. Neufchâtel).

welcomed everyone, loved everyone, hated nobody and in turn was liked by all and always loved was held in high esteem by all in everlasting love. Early on the day that the wonderful blessing would take place, the father was happy on account of his son and filled with a great joy. On that day the father gave his son the following advice: 'Look, my son, always remember that today it is God who has given you a share in the government of his kingdom so that you may take delight in the ways [leading to] fairness and justice. What I ask is for God to allow me to watch this and you to act according to his will, which is always there for those who desire it.'

During the solemn ceremony one of the priests, whose mind was filled with bad thoughts, came forward to put them into action. The man of God had among his treasures a statue of a deer made of solid silver which he loved to display during solemn ceremonies. He had received this gift from Duke Richard of the Normans for secular use, but kind in words and kind of heart he gracefully did not refuse to put it to God's use. Attached to this ornament was a horn cup [*sciphum*] through which wine was poured for the celebration of Mass. Seeing the statue, the criminal and corrupt priest took it and hid it in his shoes; he looked hither and thither in vain to find someone to whom he could sell it or in what way he could destroy the statue of the deer. One has to believe that the objects were saved because of the merits of the pious king who loves God with his whole heart. For on the following Tuesday in the oratory [= chapel?] of Charles's tower,[32] while he was talking to one of his closest advisers, behold there came the thief; he stood before the altar, alternatingly praying in vain and drawing in long breaths, uncovered [the statue of the deer] from under the altarcloth together with the cup and left full of shame, the miserable man, unaware of whose eyes followed him. Having stopped his conversation the king silently walked to the altar together with his true friend and took his belongings, happily returned them to his servant, while forbidding his companion for as long as he lived to disclose the name of the thief and inflict shame on him.

32 The tower at the royal palace at Compiègne was built by King Charles the Bald (ed. Bautier and Labory, p. 62, n. 5 and Nelson, 1992, 247–8).

55   Fulbert of Chartres, Letters (concerning Normandy)

Here follow four letters from the collection of Bishop Fulbert of Chartres (d. 1028) which show the extent to which people from the diocese of Chartres did business with the Normans and also how Bishop Fulbert himself lent support to Archbishop Robert (989–1037) in his dispute with his nephew Duke Robert the Magnificent.

The Letters and Poems of Fulbert of Chartres, ed. and trsl. F. Behrends (Oxford, 1976), pp. 113–15, 117, 151, 227–9.

66 The canons of Chartres to Bishop Herbert of Lisieux (c. 1022–49/50): explaining why they have not paid their visitation dues and asking him to wait until Fulbert returns from Rome (late 1022–early 1023).[33] The churches involved are Bonneville-sur-Touques, Englesville-en-Auge, Roncheville and Saint-Julien-sur-Calonne, which in 1014 had been granted by Duke Richard II in penance for the destruction he had caused in the Chartres area (Fauroux, no. 15).

To the venerable bishop of Lisieux, Herbert, from the community of canons of St Mary's of Chartres, with many greetings and the support of their prayers. You order us, your excellence, to pay you the visitation dues for our churches which lie in your diocese. But we wish to inform your eminence of the truth of the matter, namely that the bishops of holy memory in whose diocese we have churches have always shown their loving and reverent devotion to our most holy Lady by not exacting from us, her unworthy servants, the payment that you demand. So we beg you not to accuse us of being unreasonable when we ask you in your kindness, father, to follow in the honourable footsteps of the holy fathers and not make us pay these dues for fear that you yourself might be blamed as the one who was first responsible for the loss that this causes us. We are inspired even more than this by no small desire for your own welfare, and we hope to see you entered in the list of benefactors of our blessed community, so that as we continually offer sacrifice to the Lord for them, and thus also for you, and recount in his presence your kind good works, we may declare that you too are worthy of being included in the book of heavenly life. Moreover, we do not think that it has escaped you, given the breadth of your knowledge, that our lord, Bishop F[ulbert], to whom we know that you are very dear, has gone to Rome. We mention this, for if it should please you in your generosity to grant our petition, we shall tell him about it when he returns, and he will be

33 For Herbert as bishop of Coutances, see no. 8.

very grateful for your good and judicious kindness. But if it should not please you to do so, we beg you at least to give us, your humble servants, time, since we are bound in this matter to seek the advice, on his return, of him on whose good pleasure our plans depend, and we also beg you in the meantime not to place our churches under any censure. May a long life of good works be yours, and please be so kind as to write and let us know the answer that comes from the oracle in the sanctuary of your breast. Again and again, may you fare well, now and always.

68 Hildegar to Siegfried, Duke Richard II's chaplain, reminding him that he promised to send him a horse (late 1022–early 1023).

Hildegar, Bishop Fulbert's disciple, to Siegfried, Count Richard's chaplain, even now with his greeting.[34] By not keeping faith with your words, you have deceived me for a long time, and I am distressed at finding myself deceived and overwhelmed with shame by your lies. It is not fitting for a person of your eminence and position to suffer the disgrace of being called a liar, and it would be a dreadful thing to fall into the sin of sacrilege, for as one reads: 'a priest's words are either true or sacrilegious'. So I beg you by the holy friendship that ought to exist between us to begin living up to your reputation for truthfulness and honesty by sending me now by the monk Walter the horse that you once promised me and rightly. Unless you do so, know that you will have utterly fallen from our love. With my conscience as my witness let me say that in asking you for this I am no more desirous of my own advantage than of yours, and of your honour too.

83 Bishop Fulbert to Duke Richard II of Normandy (*c.* mid-1023). Baldricus is the *Baldricus procurator* who witnessed Richard II's charter of 1014 for Chartres cathedral (see above, Letter 66).

To the venerable prince of the Normans R[ichard], from Fulbert, by the grace of God bishop of Chartres, with his greeting and the support of his prayers. You have performed many good services for the church of our Lady, St Mary. May God reward you through her intercession. In return for them we too are faithful vassals [*fideles*] of your soul and body, and we hope that we can always be so. But recently we received an unexpected message that your servant Baldricus has recalled the land that you gave us, forbidden the servant whom we placed in charge there to exercise any authority and seized his possessions, and imposed a new ban on our men by ordering them

34 Siegfried is not otherwise known.

to use the mill at Saint-Ouen which, so they say, is five leagues away from their holdings.[35] If these things, most excellent prince, were done at your command, which we by no means believe, we are very much grieved on your account, and we humbly beg that they may be corrected. May you in your wisdom instruct your servants not to give our men any further trouble and from now on to let us hold this land on the same terms as we received it from your most kind hand. May good health and strength be yours for many years.

126 Bishop Fulbert to Archbishop Robert of Rouen (after 5/6 August 1027). This letter ought to be seen against the background of the archbishop's disagreement with his nephew Duke Robert I the Magnificent, who succeeded his brother Duke Richard III (1026–27).[36]

To the venerable archbishop of Rouen, R[obert], from F[ulbert], a humble bishop, with his faithful prayers. I sympathise with you, holy father, over the injuries with which you have been unjustly afflicted, especially from one who owed himself and his all to your good faith. I am also deeply grieved over him who was our brother and fellow bishop as long as he stood upright, but who has now fallen into these great depths of crime and infamy.[37] But to you, father, it should be very comforting that though he has taken away your outward possessions, he could not take away those that are within; for by God's grace you have the charity by which you may recall one who goes astray, the reins of ecclesiastical sanction by which you may strike him. Use these as you should until he deserves absolution and is glad to say to you: 'thy rod and thy staff, they have comforted me'.[38]

56   The Life of St Simon of Vexin

The anonymous Life of St Simon, written at the beginning of the twelfth century, throws interesting light on the conflict between William the Conqueror and his son Robert Curthose as well as on Matilda, who is said to have been Simon's kinswoman and to have educated him. Simon became count of the Vexin but in 1077 gave up his countship and became a monk. He died at Rome in 1088.

Vita beati Simeonis, Migne, *PL*, 156, cols 1215, 1219, 1222.

35 Saint-Ouen is unidentified.

36 *GND*, ii, 46–9.

37 Unidentified bishop.

38 Ps. 22:4.

[C. 5] After Simon had hardly settled down to a measure of quietness at home, behold the most powerful king of the English William, who had educated him, requested that he quickly visit him. He added that he would neither receive him in a castle nor in a town unless in the depth of night and that he was in no way obliged to take a wife as long as he would hastily come to the meeting in Normandy. Then Simon, fearing the king's order, decided to leave without delay and carry out the order. Upon his arrival the king cheered up, called him secretly and said: 'Because I have long since known your faithfulness and love and because I raised you, I wish to increase feelings in you. I have chosen you as the future husband of my daughter who has been asked for in many conversations by the messengers of King Anfurcius of Spain and Robert of Apulia, adopting you as my son [for the purpose] of my inheritance.[39] My treasures shall be shared with you, my friends shall be your friends and my enemies yours. In response to these words the holy man, believing in the prosperity of the devil who surrounds the hearts of the elected with many snares, modestly thanked him saying: 'Great and generous is the benefice you have bestowed upon me since my youth, but ... Your worthiness, as has been written, descends in humility so that it will be exalted. My humility deserves to be crushed deeper, so that it will not be subjected to you by the deed of gratitude. There is one obstacle for us that is both ambiguous and severe and inspires me with cautious thoughts. My lady the queen, your wife, and I, as they say, are bound by ties of blood and close kinship in such a way that we have to ask wise men their advice if this marriage is at all possible and why.'[40] To which the king responded: 'If our people from the past and of old count our [degree] of blood relationship, it is necessary that the bishops, abbots and ecclesiastical wise men, who know the law and old custom, look round and search whether a gift of alms or the building of a monastery or anything of that kind deals with this problem legally.'[41] Simon, however, who always put his faith in God said: 'There still remains something that with your will needs to be agreed. With your permission I wish to go

39 William of Poitiers also mentions two brothers, kings of Spain (Sancho of Castile and Alfonso VI of Leon) requesting William the Conqueror's daughter in marriage (Cf. no. 60). This text is the only source for such a request from Robert Guiscard, duke of Calabria.

40 Matilda of Flanders was related by blood to Simon of the Vexin through Matilda's mother Adela, who was a daughter of King Robert the Pious.

41 These are interesting words put into the mouth of William the Conqueror, who himself built the monasteries at Caen as penance for his own marriage to Matilda, who was held to be related by blood to him.

to Rome and ask counsel and support from the holy apostles Peter and Paul and from the pope [Gregory VII, 1073–85] so that with spiritual permission obtained we can with confidence proceed what we decide to do.' Giving his consent the king said: 'Do whatever you think is right with God's favour and my will.' And with these words they took leave ...

[The marriage project comes to nothing]

[C. 11] ... Simon hastened to Normandy to visit the king and queen of the English who had educated him and upon his arrival he found the king fighting against his own son Robert.[42] Feeling compassion for both, Simon fled the peaceful region which had been transformed by the curse of pestilence. Some having heard of his fame in the world and many others, [consisting of] almost 1000 soldiers, came cheerfully towards him and devoutly pressed upon him some of their own gold or silver, a mule or a horse. Simon, however, outwardly showing gratitude but in his heart wishing for nothing, refused everything and looked at all of it in distaste. Finally, the king came to him and dealt in piety equally with the grieving and the happy to such extent that the queen, as is the custom of good women, choked on her words because of her tears. After sweet talks with both of them and their pleading with him to accept the relics, gold and silver and other presents they offered him, he rejected everything except for the relics ... Not knowing him, some of his companions who were with him took some excellent gifts secretly; thus evil having been done he decided to return to his monastery ...

[C. 14] ... The queen of the English, Matilda, wealthy and powerful, because she educated him and, as is said, because of their close kinship, sent a monk with gold and silver to Rome to pay for the burial of the man of God.

57 The Short Account of William the Most Noble Count

This account was written c. 1114–20 at Battle Abbey. The following paragraph purports to record a pact between the Danes and Richard I of Normandy, concluded after the siege of Montreuil-sur-Mer (see above, no. 53), which

---

42 The occasion may be tentatively dated to c. 1077, two years after Simon's visit to Rouen on the occasion of his restitution of land to the cathedral (Bates, no. 229), the record of which is signed by Robert as count.

allegedly also contained several clauses regulating the relationship between the Normans and the French. This section is almost certainly apocryphal and reflects the early twelfth-century anxieties about the precise obligations between the Norman duke, who after 1106 (Henry I) was also king of England, and the French king.

'The *Brevis relatio de Guillelmo nobilissimo comite Normannorum*, written by a Monk of Battle Abbey', ed. E. M. C. van Houts, in *Chronology, Conquest and Conflict in Medieval England*, Camden Miscellany, 34, Camden 5th s., no. 10 (Cambridge, 1997), p. 45.

[C. 16] … In this pact it was also agreed that the duke of Normandy shall not render any service to the king of France for Normandy or otherwise perform service, unless the king of France should grant him a fief in France [i.e. the royal domain] for which he would owe service. Therefore the duke of Normandy renders nothing to the king of France except homage for Normandy and fealty during his lifetime and for his earthly honour. Similarly, the king swears fealty during his lifetime and for his earthly honour to the duke of Normandy and there is no distinction between them except that the king of France does no homage to the duke of Normandy as the duke of Normandy does to the king of France. This liberty then was acquired by the Danes for their kinsmen the dukes of Normandy.

58   Suger of Saint-Denis, Life of Louis VI

Suger, abbot of Saint-Denis (1122–51), wrote the Deeds of Louis the Fat. In chapter 26 he describes the battles between Henry I, king of England and duke of Normandy, and King Louis VI of France (1108–37) in the years leading up to the battle of Brémule (1119) where the former defeated the latter. At issue was Henry's refusal to do homage to the French king on the grounds that as kings they were equals, even though as duke he was the French king's subordinate.

Suger, Vie de Louis VI le Gros, ed. and trsl. H. Waquet (Paris, 1929), pp. 182–200; *Suger, The Deeds of Louis the Fat*, trsl. R. Cusimano and J. Moorhead (Washington, 1992), pp. 111–18.

[C. 26] Unbridled conceit is worse than pride in this respect: a proud person believes there is no one superior to him, but a conceited person believes there is no one equal to him. To this person can be applied that saying of the poet: 'Caesar could not acknowledge a superior, nor Pompey an equal'; and since 'everyone who has power grows weary of a peer', Louis, king of the French, conducted himself toward Henry, king of the English and duke of the Normans, as toward a vassal ... for he always kept in mind the lofty rank by which he towered over him. But the king of the English, having regard for the nobility of his kingdom and the wonderful abundance of its wealth, soon grew tired of his lower standing. With help from his nephew, the palatine count Theobald, and from many disaffected men of the kingdom of the French, he strove to unsettle the realm and disturb its king, for he wished to withdraw from his lordship.[43]

The persistent plague of recurrent strife between them returned once more when the king of England joined efforts with Count Theobald and attacked the nearest border district of the king. The nearness of Normandy to the countryside of Chartres made them neighbours. They sent Count Stephen of Mortain, nephew of one [King Henry] and brother of the other [Count Theobald], at the head of the host to other districts, namely into Brie, for they were afraid that the king would suddenly seize that land in the absence of Count Theobald.[44] But the king chose to spare neither the Normans nor the men of Chartres and Brie. Finding himself somewhat encircled by these two enemies, he laid waste the lands of one and then the other, and with frequent fighting made known the heroic spirit of the royal majesty.

Through the excellent foresight of the kings of the English and the dukes of the Normans, the Norman border was tightly protected by an impressive line of new castles and by the channels of the unfordable rivers that flowed there.[45] Aware of all this but still aiming to cross into Normandy, the king made his way towards the border with only a small band of soldiers, for he hoped to do his planning in some secrecy. He cautiously sent ahead men disguised as travellers, but they wore chainmail beneath their cloaks and carried swords at their waists. They went down the main road to a village called Gasny an old settlement that would give the French an open and easy approach to the Normans.[46] The River Epte flowed around the middle of the village and provided safety for those inside, while no one on the outside of the village could cross the river upstream or downstream except at a distance. Suddenly the king's men cast off their cloaks and unsheathed their swords, but the villagers, seeing what was coming

43 Theobald IV, count of Blois and Chartres and II, count of Champagne (1125–52) was the second son of Adela, Henry I's sister and Count Stephen of Blois and Chartres.

44 Stephen, count of Mortain, later became king of England (1135–54).

45 For the frontier of Normandy, see Power, 1994, 181–202.

46 Gasny (Eure, c. d'Ecos).

surged forward vehemently with their weapons. The royal force, however, drove them back with a powerful attack of its own; and then, unexpectedly, when his men were almost worn out, the king hurried across the dangerous slope of a hill and brought them timely aid. He seized the village's churchyard and the church itself – which was fortified by a tower – but not without the loss of some men.

When he discovered that the king of England was nearby with a large host, something he generally had, he summoned his barons and urgently invited them to follow his lead. Quick to arrive were Count Baldwin of Flanders, a distinguished and courageous young man who was a true soldier, Count Fulk of Anjou, and many other leading men of the kingdom.[47] Having broken through the defensive barrier of Normandy, some of them fortified the village while others opened up to pillage and fires a land that long peace had made rich. They wreaked unbearable havoc in every direction with their raiding, something that usually did not happen when the king of the English was present.

Meanwhile the king of England quickly made preparations for the building of a castle and urged on the workmen. While King Louis left his own stronghold protected by a guard of soldiers, King Henry erected his castle on the hill nearest to it. From there he used his many soldiers and the arrows fired by his crossbowmen and archers to drive back his enemies. He planned to cut the French off from the foodstuffs the land produced and force them to plunder their own land out of a dire need to support themselves. But the king of the French let fire his own arrows and immediately paid him back in kind, just as if he were throwing dice with him. He hastily assembled his host, returned at dawn, and forcefully attacked that new castle, commonly called Mallassis, expending much effort while giving and receiving many heavy blows.[48] This is the kind of toll generally paid in this kind of marketplace, and he paid it like a man. He plundered and destroyed, and with true valour brought to nought whatever had been plotted there, adding to the excellence of his kingdom and the shame of his opponent.

Fortune is a powerful force that no one can escape, for as the saying goes: 'You will rise from teaching rhetoric to become a consul

---

47 Baldwin VII, count of Flanders (1111–19) presumably had been summoned by his overlord King Louis VI. This illustrates rather nicely that Baldwin's duty to the king of France took precedence over his agreement with the king of England to support him militarily (see below, no. **66**). Fulk V, count of Anjou, Touraine and Maine (1106–28, d. 1142).

48 Mallassis, near Gasny.

if fortune wishes, and if it wishes, you will fall from being a consul back to teaching rhetoric.' The king of England had been enjoying very good luck after a long and wonderful run of successes, but he now found himself disturbed by a different and luckless turn of events, like someone falling from the top of the wheel of fortune. From this region the king of France strove with all his power to make endless trouble and countless attacks upon him, as did the count of Flanders from the neighbouring region of Ponthieu and Count Fulk of Anjou from the region of Maine. The king of England suffered war damage inflicted on him not only by these men from outside his lands but also by his own vassals inside them, namely Hugh of Gournay, the count of Eu, the count of Aumale and many others.[49]

To crown his misfortune, he was even troubled by a piece of wickedness inside his very own household. Frightened thoroughly by a clandestine conspiracy of stewards and chamberlains, he changed beds often and dreading night's terrors regularly increased his armed guards. He also ordered that a shield and sword be placed before him every night while he slept. One member of the cabal, named H, was an intimate councillor who had been enriched by the king's generosity; but having become powerful and renowned, he became even more renowned as a traitor.[50] Caught taking part in this terrible plot, he was mercifully condemned to losing his eyes and genitals when he deserved to be choked to death by a noose. Living under conditions like these the king never felt safe; and despite his reputation for valour and greatness of spirit, he took the precaution of wearing his sword even in his house. And he also punished those whom he considered most faithful men if they went out of their homes without swords at their sides, making them pay a large sum as if it were a trifle.

During those days Enguerrand of Chaumont-en-Vexin, a valiant courageous man, boldly went forth with a band of soldiers and gallantly took hold of the castle called Andelys.[51] Its ramparts were being guarded by men who were secretly on his side. Relying on help from King Louis, he seized and fortified it with supreme confidence; and from there he brought under his full control all the land up to the River Andelle – everything from the River Epte all the way up to Pont-Saint-Pierre.[52] Then supported by a large company of soldiers

49 For the Norman attacks on troops of King Henry I, see Orderic, vi, 188–92.

50 Note that Suger only refers to him by his initial; he was probably Herbert the Chamberlain (Hollister, 1986, 214).

51 Les Andelys (Eure), the site of impressive fortifications.

52 Pont-Saint-Pierre (Eure, c. Fleury-sur-Andelle).

who outranked him in nobility Enguerrand went out on to the plain to confront the king of England. And in turning him back he mocked the king rudely and made use of the land within the above limits as his own. After a long delay the king of England decided to accompany Count Theobald and bring help from the region of Maine to those besieged in the tower of the castle of Alençon.[53] But he suffered a setback at the hands of Count Fulk of Anjou, losing many of his men, his castle, and, what made his loss the more inglorious, even the tower.

King Henry was troubled for a long time by losses like these, and his fortunes had sunk almost to the very bottom. But although a wanton man, he was a generous donor to churches and a liberal giver of alms. So, after he had been harshly whipped and chastised for some time, the divine mercy decreed that he be spared and mercifully lifted him up from the depths to which he had sunk. The wheel suddenly brought him back from the pit of misfortune to the summit of success, for the divine hand rather than his own abruptly pushed his antagonists who were higher up, and they began to plummet downward, plunging all the way to the very bottom. But this is the customary way of the Divinity, which mercifully extends the right hand of its clemency to men who have been abandoned by human help and are at the very brink of despair.

Count Baldwin of Flanders had been severely harassing King Henry with bitter attacks and frequent invasions of Normandy. On one occasion, when the count was making war with unrestrained spirit on the castle of Eu and the neighbouring coast, a sudden glancing blow from a lance struck him in the face. He disdained to take care of so small a wound, but did not disdain to die and in the coming to such an end, he saw fit to do a favour not only to the present king of England but all later ones as well.[54]

And then there was Enguerrand of Chaumont, a very daring man who had become overconfident in his attacks on King Henry. He did not flinch when he brought about the destruction of some land in the archdiocese of Rouen which belonged to the blessed Mary, Mother of the Lord, but a very serious illness laid him low. Having been tormented for a long time by continual bodily pain, which he deserved but could not bear, he departed this life, having learned too late what was due to the queen of heaven. There was also the case of Count Fulk of

---

53 Alençon (Orne).

54 Count Baldwin VII died at Eu from a wound received the previous year during the siege of Bures-en-Bray (Orderic, vi, 190–1). A Norman account of the battle of Brémule can be found in Orderic, vi, 234–43.

Anjou, who had earlier allied himself to King Louis by personal homage, many oaths, and even a large number of hostages. But Count Fulk now put greed before fealty and inflamed by treachery gave his daughter in wedlock to William, son of the English king, without consulting King Louis.[55] He falsely betrayed his sworn word to be an enemy of King Henry and joined himself to the English king by ties of friendship of this kind.

Campaigning from his own region, King Louis forced the land of Normandy to grow silent in his sight. Sometimes large, sometimes small, the size of his band of men did not matter when he delivered the land over to plundering. After some time his continual ability to harass the English king made him despise him and his men and pay no attention to them. But the king of England took note of the reckless and daring behaviour of the king of the French and gathering together many of his strongest men, one day suddenly sent out from their hiding place a force of soldiers in battle order against him. Setting fires that would leap up and throw him into disarray, King Henry made his armed soldiers dismount so that they might fight more effectively on foot, and wisely busied himself taking whatever military precautions he could.

King Louis and his men, however, deemed it unworthy to plan carefully for battle and rushed against their enemy in a bold but careless attack. The men of the Vexin, along with Burchard of Montmorency and Guy of Clermont, were the first to set their right arms to work.[56] This brave band cut down the first battle line of the Normans and chased their foes from the glorious field of combat, and with a powerful hand drove the first line of soldiers back on top of the armed foot soldiers. The French then decided to pursue the enemy but fell into disorder when they pressed against the Normans' surprisingly well aligned and positioned ranks. And as happens in these cases, they gave ground when they could not withstand the pressure from their foe's ordered row.

The sight of his army falling back astonished the king; but as he usually did in bad times, he relied on his own hardy fighting spirit to help himself and his men. He returned to Andelys as decently as possible, but without his wandering host sustaining great harm, and suffered for a while from the misfortune which his own foolishness had suddenly wrought upon him. But he became more courageous

---

55 William Adelin married Matilda of Anjou in June 1119. After his death in November 1120 Matilda retired to Fontevrault where she became abbess.

56 Guy, son of Hugh I of Clermont.

than he usually was in hard times and, as befits true men, more steadfast. To avoid being taunted any further by his enemies for not daring to enter Normandy, he called back his army, summoned those who were absent and invited the leading men of the kingdom to join him. He then notified the king of the English on what day he would enter his land to engage him in a very great battle, and hurry to fulfil his promise as if it were a sworn agreement. Leading a marvellous army he rushed into Normandy, ravaged the land and penetrating as far as Breteuil, captured the well-fortified castle of Ivry with fierce fighting and burned it with fire.[57]

He lingered in the land for a little while but found neither the king of the English nor anyone else on whom he might take adequate revenge for the insult he had suffered. So he turned his attention to Count Theobald, withdrew to Chartres and launched a powerful attack against the city, striving to burn it with fire. Then, all of a sudden, the clergy and townspeople came up to him bearing the tunic of the blessed Mother of God before them.[58] They devoutly begged that he be merciful and as chief protector of the church, spare them out of love for her, imploring that he not take revenge on them for a wrong committed by others. The king made the loftiness of his royal majesty bow before their pleas; and to prevent the noble church of the blessed Mary and the city from being burned down, he ordered Count Charles of Flanders to call back the army and spare the city out of love and reverence he bore the church.[59] But when they had gone home, they did not stop punishing the misfortune of a moment with a long constant and very heavy revenge.

59   Lambert of Wattrelos, Annals

In 1153 Lambert of Wattrelos (d. c. 1170) inserted his family history into his annals under the year in which he was born (1108). Two members of his family had taken service with Henry I, king of England and duke of Normandy: Lambert's maternal uncle Lambert and his own brother Baldwin. There is also a reference to a member of his family who was standard-bearer of William Clito as count of Flanders (1127–28).

Lamberti de Wattrelos, *Annales Cameracenses*, in: *MGH SS*, 16, 511–12; the toponyms have been identified by Vercauteren, 1963, 223–45.

---

57 Ivry-la-Bataille (Eure).
58 This was allegedly also done during Rollo's siege of Chartres, see above, no. **5**.
59 Charles the Good, count of Flanders (1119–27).

[1108] In this year I was born between Easter and Pentecost. Whose son and descendant I am, I will set out in simple terms for the various readers. I come from the area of Tournai, from the village of Néchin. In that land I received, by the grace of God, these parents: my father, called Alulfus and my mother Gisla. My father was the son of Ingebrand, soldier of Waterlo and of Havide of Néchin. My grandmother was Havide of Néchin who belonged to a local family of secular standing, for all my grandfather Ingebrand's possessions in Néchin came from her. My grandfather Ingebrand was a relative of Evrard of Waterlo. This Evrard of Waterlo had three sons by his wife Disdelde: Elbod, Baldwin and a third one whose name I cannot now remember. Elbod was the eldest and married the sister of Gossuin of Avesnes, the maternal aunt of Walter Puluchet. My grandfather Ingebrand had four sons, namely Ingebrand, Oghot, Gummar, Alulf, and one daughter who died unmarried; any one of them married a woman of secular standing. The eldest son Ingebrand married at Tournai; he, and his offspring, died before his father. Oghot married Gisla, the sister of Rabod of Dossemetz, and their son is Evrard, a soldier and powerful man of arms. Gummar married Mersinde, sister of Gummar of Saméon. She was the niece of the castellan of Tournai. Alulfus, as the youngest of all, married Gisla, the daughter of Radulf of Waterlo, who bore him six sons and four daughters. I stem from his flesh. Baldwin the eldest of them died during the siege of Soissons. He was already married. My grandfather Radulf, the father of my mother, was a very rich man, a relative of the aforementioned Evrard; he had [gap in text] ... brothers, ten of whom were slain by the enemy on the same day in the same battle. At home their deeds are still being recorded in an epic poem by jongleurs. My grandfather Radulf had several sisters who were married in the area of Ménin and they bore many children. This Radulf married a noble wife, Resinde, from Ménin-sur-Leie. She descended from ancient nobility in Flanders. She had eleven brothers, of whom four were castellans at the time of Count Robert [II, 1093–1111], the father of Baldwin. She brought with her into marriage male and female serfs, although I say that nobody ought to be a slave unless he has sinned, for the voice of God says: 'He who sins is the slave of sins.' She had so many brothers that it is suitable to say of them: 'The branches extended to the sea and their shoots reached the river.' From this stock many people stem, namely Lambert, abbot of Saint-Bertin and his sister, Gisla abbess of Bourbourg and her nephew Lambert, abbot of Lobbes, and Richard, standard-bearer of Count William the Norman who was

killed in the civil war with count Thierry,[60] and the famous soldiers of
Lampernisse and the grand people from Furnes, and the other noble
people who were blood relations. But let us return to my grandparents. Radulf and Resinde had four sons and four daughters: Tiard
and Lambert, who were soldiers, Richard the clerk and Evrard who
was the youngest and who died after a fall from his horse. My uncle
Lambert together with some of his friends went over to Henry, king
of England, who honourably kept him and his companions [in his
service]. Tiard, the eldest, later became mayor [alderman] of Waterlo.
He married an honest girl Emma, who bore him soldiers and clerks.
The very good king [Henry] handed over to Lambert many estates
in Normandy. However, he was wounded in the war between the king
of England and Count Baldwin of Flanders, took refuge in a church
and then died. My brother Baldwin was also present.[61] Richard, of
happy memory, having renounced his wordly affairs, went to Mont-
Saint-Eloi, where later by God's wish he respectfully became abbot
over the brothers and his body was buried there. Of the three daughters
of my grandparents, Godelide, the eldest, gave birth to Lambert and
Gummar, who both are regular [gap in manuscript: canons?] at
Watten. Disdelde gave birth to Radulf, a kind and devout man, who
later succeeded his uncle Richard as third abbot of Mont-Saint-Eloi.
From Gisla last but not least I, Lambert, spring who by the same
uncle Radulf [read Richard] was made a regular canon at the church
of Saint-Aubert, bishop of Cambrai; who has written down this gene-
alogy of his ancestors according to truthful oral reports and who by
the inspired grace of God has inserted this brief account [here].

Maine, Anjou and Brittany

60   William of Poitiers, Deeds of Duke William

William of Poitiers wrote the Deeds of William King of the English and
Duke of the Normans probably between 1071 and 1077. He was the former
chaplain of William the Conqueror and had first-hand knowledge of the
military affairs of the Normans on the southern border with Maine, Anjou
and Brittany.

---

60 William Clito, count 1127–8; Thierry of Alsace, count of Flanders (1128–68).

61 The events referred to here probably concern the siege of Bures-en-Bray in the
   autumn of 1118.

The Gesta Guillelmi of William of Poitiers, ed. and trsl. R. H. C. Davis and M. Chibnall (Oxford 1998), pp. 15–19, 55–7, 73–7.

[Book I, c. 11] After this William rendered a reciprocal service to the king [Henry I of France, 1031–60] with devoted loyalty, when asked by him for help in thwarting certain very powerful enemies. For King Henry, irritated by the insults of Geoffrey Martel, led an army against him, and with a strong force besieged and captured a castle of his called Mouliherne in the district of Anjou.[62] The French saw what in their envy they did not wish to see, an army led from Normandy alone which was bigger than the whole assembly of royal contingents brought or sent by many counts. While I was in exile in Poitiers, the fame won by the Norman count in that expedition to which our compatriots bear witness was spread abroad in Aquitaine.[63] They said he had excelled all in intelligence, assiduity and strength. The king decided to consult him freely and gave great weight to his opinion, preferring him to all others for his perspicacity in finding the best counsel. He reproached him for one thing only; that he exposed himself too much to the dangers, and often went off in search of combat, travelling openly with only ten men or less. He besought the Norman magnates not to engage in battle or the slightest skirmish in front of any town, fearing that, in showing his valour, the man whom he considered the strongest defence and the finest ornament of his realm might be slain ...

[Book I, c. 13] After that time Geoffrey Martel enjoyed giving his opinion that there was no knight or warrior under the sun equal to the count of the Normans. From Gascony and Auvergne powerful men sent or took to him thoroughbred horses known by their regional name. Likewise Spanish kings sought his friendship with these gifts among others ... If for serious reasons he [Duke William] was forced to abandon the friendship of anyone, he preferred to allow it to dissolve gradually, rather than breaking it off suddenly. We consider this to be in accordance with the judgement of wise men. The wicked withdrew wickedly; King Henry conceived a cruel enmity to him, persuaded by the eloquence of evil men. While the king was inflicting insupportable injuries on Normandy, William, to whom its defence belonged, marched against him, paying respect, however, to his former

62 Mouliherne (Maine-et-Loire); William of Poitiers is the only source for the battle which took place sometime in the late 1040s or early 1050s between Count Geoffrey of Anjou and William the Conqueror.

63 The author William of Poitiers refers to himself here.

friendship and the royal dignity. He took care not to engage battle with his army while the king was present, unless as a last resort. He restrained the Normans time and time again, not so much by command as by request, for their dearest wish was to defeat the king and tarnish his honour … .

[The battle of Varaville in 1057]

[Book I, c. 34] Once again the peace broke down, since the king demanded justice not so much for the damage as for the humiliation he had suffered; he undertook a new campaign against Normandy, after assembling a sizeable army, though less large than the previous one. The greater part of the kingdom was mourning, or fearing, the death or unworthy flight of its men, and was none too anxious to attack again, though very eager to have revenge. Martel the Angevin who, in spite of many failures was not yet broken, far from abstaining, brought the largest force he could collect by any means. It would scarcely have satisfied the raging hatred of this man if the land of Normandy had been utterly crushed and laid waste. Concealing all knowledge of their movements as far as possible, lest they should be confronted and repelled at the very moment of their attack by the champion whose strength they had already experienced, they crossed the Hiémois by forced marches and reached the River Dives, plundering as cruel enemies wherever they went. Once arrived, they were unwilling to turn back and dared not halt … For while they were delaying at the ford of the Dives, the duke himself came upon them with a small troop of men at a lucky moment spoiling for a fight. Part of the army had already crossed the river with the king. And behold! the redoubtable avenger hurled himself at the rest and slaughtered the plunderers, believing it a crime when the survival of his wounded country was at stake to spare the dangerous enemy captured on his own territory. Those intercepted on this side of the water were nearly all cut down under the eyes of the king, except for those who, stricken by terror, preferred to plunge into the torrent. But it was impossible to pursue those on the opposite bank with the sword of justice, for the high tide filled the channel of the Dives with an impassable barrier of water. Fearful and distressed at the death of his men, the king, with the Angevin tyrant, left the bounds of Normandy with all possible speed; for this man, valiant and renowned as he was in the art of war, realised in consternation that it would be madness to attack Normandy further.

[The Breton–Norman war around Dol in 1064 or 1065][64]

[Book I, c. 43] ... The leader of this audacious enterprise was Conan fitz Alan.[65] He had grown up to be an aggressive man; free from a tutelage he had long endured, he captured Eudo, his paternal uncle, imprisoned him in chains, and began to lord it with great truculence over the province which his father had left to him.[66] Then renewing his father's rebellion, he wished to be the enemy, not the vassal, of Normandy. Meanwhile William, who was his lord by ancient right as well as being lord of the Normans, established a castle called St James at the frontier between them, so that hungry predators would not harm defenceless churches or the common people in the remotest parts of his land by their pillaging raids. For Charles [the Simple], king of the Franks, had bought peace and friendship from Rollo the first duke of Normandy and ancestor of the later dukes, by giving him his daughter Gisla in marriage and Brittany in perpetual dependence. The Franks had asked for this treaty, as they no longer had the strength to resist the Danish axe with the Gallic sword. The pages of annals bear witness. Since then the Breton counts have never been able to free their neck from the yoke of Norman domination, even though they often attempted to do so, struggling with all their might. Because they were close blood relations of the dukes of Normandy, Alan and Conan treated them in an arrogant and boastful way.[67] Conan's daring had grown to such a point that he was not afraid to announce a date on which he would attack the frontiers of Normandy. This man, aggressive by nature and at an impetuous age, was bountifully served by the fidelity of a region which extended far and wide, and was crammed full of more fighting men than anyone could have believed ...

[Book I, c. 45] Undismayed by these terrifying practices, Duke William, on the day which he remembered Conan had fixed for his coming, went himself to the frontier to meet him. The latter, thinking that a thunderbolt was about to strike him, fled as fast as possible to

64 Keats-Rohan (1990, 157–72) discusses the rivalry between two groups of Bretons in the border area between Normandy and Brittany. One was centred on Duke William's Breton cousins, the descendants of Count Alan III of Rennes, while the other was grouped around the castellan of Dol, Ruallon I.

65 Conan II of Brittany, son of Alan III.

66 Eudo of Penthièvre, brother of Alan III.

67 Alan III's and Eudo's father Geoffrey had married Duke Richard I's daughter Hadvisa, while Duke Richard II had married Geoffrey's sister Judith.

fortified places, abandoning the siege of Dol, a castle in his own land.[68] This castle, hostile to the rebel, remained faithful to the just cause. Ruallon, the defender of the castle, tried to restrain Conan: he called him back in jest, begging him to stay for two more days and claiming that they would win the cost of the delay from him. The wretched man, frightened to death and hearing only the sounds of panic, carried on his way and fled further. The terrible leader who pursued him would have pressed the fugitive further, if he had not been aware of the manifest danger of taking a numerous force through uninhabited country, which was infertile and unknown. If any remnants of the previous year's produce were left in the impoverished land, the inhabitants had hidden them in safe places with their flocks. The crops were standing green in the fields. So, to avoid the sacrilegious looting of church goods, if any were found, he led back his army, which was exhausted by the lack of regular provisions. Moreover, he assumed magnanimously that Conan would come very soon to seek mercy and pardon for his crime. But he had scarcely crossed the frontiers of Brittany when he learnt that Geoffrey of Anjou had joined Conan with huge forces, and that both would be ready to give battle on the next day. And so the fight appeared more desirable than ever to him, for he knew that it would be more glorious to triumph over two enemies, both of them redoutable, in one conflict. This would give a manifold gain as the fruit of one victory.

But Ruallon, on whose territory the tents had been pitched, broke into complaints. He would have been grateful (he said) to have been rescued by William from the enemy's power if the damage were not to cancel out the gain; for if he were to pitch camp and await his enemy the region (which was very infertile and greatly exhausted) would be totally devastated. It made no difference to the peasants whether they lost the labour of the previous year to the Norman or Breton army. So far the expulsion of Conan had brought fame, but not the preservation of property. The duke replied that they must bear in mind that a hasty retreat might be considered dishonourable, but he promised full recompense in gold for any damage done. At once he forbade his men-at-arms to touch the crops and herds belonging to Ruallon. This command was obeyed with such restraint that a single sheaf of corn would have amply sufficed as compensation for all damage. The battle was awaited in vain, as the enemy fled further away.

68 Ruallon, castellan of Dol, became an ally of Duke William (*The Bayeux Tapestry*, ed. D. Wilson (London, 1985), plates 22–4 show the siege of Dol).

Aquitaine

61 Charter of Jumièges, 1012

This record shows the exchange of lands between the Norman monastery of Jumièges (Seine-Mar.) and the Aquitainian monastery of Bourgueil on the Loire in 1012. Monastic houses tried to consolidate their property in areas close by and release distant properties, situated too far away to be administered. They could only do so with the permission of their secular lords, respectively Duke Richard II of Normandy and William V of Aquitaine (995–1029).

Fauroux, no. 14, p. 90.

... Therefore in order that it be clear to all Christ's faithful, in the future as well as in the present, we have written down that we, Berno and Robert abbots of Bourgueil and Jumièges, have come together, with the agreement of our princes, William, duke of Aquitaine and Richard, marquis of the Normans, for the exchange and record thereof of two of our estates, one of which is called Longueville and belongs to Bourgueil and is situated in Normandy close to the abbey of Jumièges, and one which is called Tourtenay and belongs to Jumièges and is situated close to Bourgueil in the realm [*regnum*] of Aquitaine. And in order that this exchange will be permanent and unviolated and be upheld by the brothers of our congregations, and also by our bishops and princes and their canons and soldiers, and for the memory of future generations, we have had this [charter] written and order it to be signed as a chirograph.

62 Adémar of Chabannes, Chronicle

Adémar of Chabannes wrote his chronicle before 1034.

Adémar de Chabannes, Chronique, ed. J. Chavanon (Paris, 1897), pp. 148, 166–7, 177.

[Book III, c. 27] When Rosso [= Rollo] died his son William [Longsword] took his place. He had been baptised as a child and the whole throng of Normans who had lived next to France accepted the Christian faith, put aside their pagan language [*gentilem linguam*] and got used to speaking romance [*latino sermone*]. William was deceitfully murdered by Arnulf, count of Flanders [I, 918–65] and was succeeded by his son Richard [I of Normandy]. Himself thoroughly Christian, he built in that part of Normandy which used to be called the 'March' of France and Brittany the monastery of Mont-Saint-Michel,[69] where he installed monks. He did the same at the monastery of the Holy Trinity at Fécamp, where he was buried and where he established monks. Meanwhile, Louis king of the Franks had died and in his place ruled Lothar [king, 954–86], his son by Queen Gerberga.[70]

[Book III, c. 44] At that time, around the Festival of the Apostles and St Martial, Emma, viscountess of Angoulême, went to pray at the shrine of St Michael the Hermit and there, during the night she was taken captive by the Normans [= vikings] and detained for three years as an exile across the sea.[71] Immense weights of silver and gold were offered from the treasury of Saint-Martial for her ransom as well as a gold statue of the saint [sancti] archangel and other precious ornaments, which the vikings carried off in false trust, for they did not return the woman, until after many days Richard count of Rouen cleverly got hold of her through overseas embassies and returned her free to her husband Guy.[72]

[Book III, c. 55] At this time the aforesaid Normans invaded the Hibernian island of Ireland with a large fleet, something their fathers had never dared to do, together with their wives and children and the Christian captives, whom they had made their slaves, with the intention that with the Irish wiped out, they themselves could inhabit this very prosperous country. This land comprised twelve states with many bishoprics, a single king and a native language, but they wrote in Latin. The Roman St Patrick had converted them to Christianity, and had become the first bishop there. The land was surrounded by the sea on all sides. During the winter solstice there are barely two hours of daylight and during the summer solstice the night is of equal brevity. And so battle was joined for three days without a break and not one of the Normans [= vikings] escaped with his life.[73] Their wives threw themselves into the sea together with their children and drowned. Those who were captured alive were thrown to their death among the wild beasts. The king let one of the captives live because he recognised that he was a Christian captive and he showered him

69 Richard I replaced the community of canons with that of monks. For the frontier position of Mont-Saint-Michel in the eleventh century, see Potts, 1989, 135–56.

70 Gerberga was the widow of Gilbert of Lotharingia when she married King Louis IV.

71 Emma was the wife of Guy, vicomte of Angoulême.

72 Richard II, duke of Normandy (996–1026).

73 The battle of Clontarf (Ireland) took place in 1014 (Crawford, 1987, 67–8).

with gifts. However, Cnut, the pagan king of the Danes, upon the death of Aethelred, king of the English, deceitfully seized his kingdom and took in marriage the queen of the English, who was the sister of Count Richard [II] of Rouen.[74] Cnut became a Christian and held on to both kingdoms and he coerced as many of the Danish pagans as he could towards the faith of Christ.

63 The Miracles of Sainte-Foy

The Book of Miracles of Sainte-Foy at Conques, written c. 1050 by the monk Bernard, contains two miracles involving Norman women, Beatrice, daughter of Richard I of Normandy, and Godehilde, wife of Roger I of Tosny (d. c. 1040). After the death of her husband Godehilde married the count of Evreux.

Liber miraculorum sancte Fidis, ed. A. Bouillet (Paris, 1897), pp. 109–11, 128–9; translation based on P. Sheingorn, *The Book of Sainte Foy* (Philadelphia, 1995), pp. 128–9, 144–5.

[Book II, c. 6] As some pilgrims, natives of the Limousin, were travelling to Sainte-Foy, they passed near the castle of Ebalus, which is called Turenne.[75] By chance they met an inhabitant of that place, an enemy of theirs named Gozbert. He was a cleric, but only in name; by employment he was a secular fighting man. At once Gozbert invented a reason for taking them all captive. It happened that Lord Ebalus had been away. When Lady Beatrice, his wife (at that time, but soon to lose him through divorce), had heard of the capture, she ordered Gozbert that if he ever wished to have a friend in her, he should allow the pilgrims to leave immediately.[76] He must not detain the people he had forcibly arrested for even one hour within the walls of the castle. Gozbert did not dare to contradict entirely the orders of this lady ...

[He sets all, except one pilgrim, free and this man later escapes through the intervention of St Foy]

Otherwise he remained unchanged, fixed and immobile until the fugitive reached Lady Beatrice. On the next day she assigned escorts to accompany him until he passed far beyond the territories ruled from

74 King Cnut (1016–35) married his predecessor's widow Emma, daughter of Richard I and Gunnor.

75 Ebalus of Comborn, castellan of Turenne (Corrèze).

76 Beatrice was an illegitimate daughter of Richard I. Around 1035 she was appointed abbess of Montivilliers in Normandy by her nephew Duke Robert the Magnificent (Fauroux, nos 90 and 164).

the castle and was assured of resuming his journey in safety. Finally the freed man, whose name was Peter, arrived at Conques with his companions, and there he gave thanks to God for his release. Afterwards the joyful man returned home, but his bonds, which I said had remained hanging from his arms after the knots had been loosened, he left behind in witness of the miracle. Almost one year and a half after my second visit from Conques, some business took me to the court of William, count of Poitiers [= William V of Aquitaine, 995–1029]. There I saw the Lady Beatrice, who had been sent there by her brother Richard [II], count of Rouen. I eagerly entered into conversation with her; then and there I began to ask her about this miracle. Her words agreed with what I had been told by the monks at Conques. This shows how trustworthy their reports have been, if anyone should doubt the other things they told me.

[Book III, c. 1] Through the inspiration of the Holy Spirit, wonderful and highly astonishing miracles are accomplished ceaselessly at the tombs of the saints. It is by the power of the same spirit that the prodigious miracles of the renowned virgin and glorious martyr of Christ were shimmering through the vast reaches of the world. As is quite clearly evident in the preceding pages written by Bernard, St Foy's power was traversing the farthest regions of the universe and was leaving behind no one untouched by her gifts. Nor was any needy person rejected by her assistance, for she was favourably inclined to anyone who called on her with a devout faith and a trusting heart. But why am I saying this? In any case, let me not wait any longer to narrate in an orderly fashion the main point of the following events. There lived at that time in Normandy a soldier named Roger, who was renowned because of his noble lineage and very powerful because of the dignity of his high office.[77] His beautiful wife Gotelina was afflicted by a serious illness and lay at death's door. The leading men of the realm to whom she was related by blood were very dejected at the prospect of her death and had gathered at her house by the order of the great prince Richard [II of Normandy], as if they were about to hold her funeral. Relying on the careful knowledge they had gained from experience, they perceived all the signs of death in her face and they turned their thoughts wholly to the preparation of her grave. When

---

77 Roger I of Tosny founded Saint-Pierre at Conches c. 1035 and died c. 1040 (GND, ii, 94–5). His widow Godehilde married Count Richard of Evreux. As countess of Evreux she issued a charter for Conches (Gallia Christiana, xi Instrumenta, col. 130) no doubt in gratitude for her recovery from illness as related in the miracle story. For Roger of Tosny, see also no. 82.

they had almost completely despaired of her return to life, a bishop perhaps inspired by a breath from heaven, addressed her husband with words like these: 'We have just learned the quickly spreading news that in Aquitaine a very holy virgin and martyr named Foy shines brightly, working miracles completely unheard of and full of wonder. If you pledge your wife to Foy's very powerful mercy with vows, I believe that she will be snatched away from the impending jaws of death and will return to you fully healthy.' Thereupon Roger, who very much wanted his wife's recovery, arranged for a relic to be placed in the bishop's hands and he swore on the relic solemnly vowing Gotelina to the holy martyr. He also promised that he himself would conduct her to the abbey of Sainte-Foy with a great gift for the saint. Soon after this had been done, his wife let out a moan and opened her eyes wide as if returning from a long period of sleep. With an attentive gaze she began to scrutinise the faces of those standing nearby. And finally she asked why it was that she saw these princes standing near her and she moved her body which was already limp in death. And so little by little as her limbs grew warm she came back to life through the intercession of the holy martyr Foy. They were not able to go to St Foy's shrine because Roger feared that he would be ambushed and captured by his enemies. Because of Roger's evil deeds many people had been driven from his realm and they thirsted for his blood. Therefore Gotelina built a church in honour of the holy martyr Foy.[78] In this way she gave eternal renown to the saint's holy and healing name.

Burgundy

54 Rodulfus Glaber, History

Rodulfus Glaber wrote his History of France in the period c. 1030 to c. 1045–46. His information about Normandy derived from sources close to St William of Volpiano (960–1031), the monastic reformer from Dijon who reformed the monastery of Fécamp at the request of dukes Richard I and Richard II.

Rodulfus Glaber, Opera, ed. and trsl. J. France, N. Bulst and P. Reynolds (Oxford, 1989), p. 37.

[Book I, c. 21] Although after this the Normans ravaged many islands and provinces close to the sea, they never again descended on those parts ruled by the kings of the Franks, except at royal request.

78 Sainte-Foy a church near Saint-Pierre at Conches-en-Ouche (Eure, c. Evreux).

Soon afterwards, however, when the Normans had been converted to
the catholic faith, the French and many of the Burgundians made marriages with them in peace, and declared with one accord the existence
in word and fact of a kingdom under a single king. From this alliance
arose an outstanding line of dukes, first William [Longsword], then
those who took the name Richard after a father or grandfather.[79]
Rouen was the capital city of this ducal principality. These dukes
surpassed all men in military might, in desire for peace and liberality.
The whole of the province subject to their might lived as one clan or
family united in unbroken faith. Amongst these people anyone who, in
any transaction, took more than was just from another, or by lying
gave false merchandise, was regarded as equivalent to a thief and a
robber. The needy, the poor, and all the pilgrims were treated with
that constant care with which fathers treat sons. They made generous
gifts to the churches of almost the whole world. Thus each year
monks came to Rouen even from the famous Mount Sinai in the east
and took back with them many presents of gold and silver for their
communities.[80] Richard II sent one hundred pounds of gold to the
Sepulchre of Our Saviour at Jerusalem, and he aided with rich
presents all who wished to go there on holy pilgrimage.[81]

65   Rodulfus Glaber, Life of William of Volpiano

Rodulfus Glaber wrote his Life of William of Volpiano in 1031–36

Rodulfus Glaber, Opera, ed. and trsl. J. France, N. Bulst and P. Reynolds
(Oxford, 1989), pp. 271, 297.

[C. 7] Since, therefore, the fame of his sanctity was now spread far
and wide, the respected Richard [II], duke of the Normans, heard
about it and sent to him reverently petitioning that he should come to
him. After a while he came gladly to him as had been asked, and, as
was only proper, was honourably received. As a lover of all that is
good the duke refreshed by his most holy eloquence; and he asked him
to receive and adorn with the monastic order the church dedicated to
the name and honour of the Holy and undivided Trinity built in

---

79 Note that Rodulfus omits the name of Rollo.

80 The relics of St Catherine were said to have been handed by St Symeon of Mount
Sinai to Isembert, chaplain of Duke Robert the Magnificent and later first abbot of
Sainte-Trinité at Rouen (Fawtier, 1923, 357–68).

81 For a comprehensive survey of pilgrimages involving Normans, see Musset, 1962,
127–50.

ancient times at the place called Fécamp and honourably restored by
his father Richard [I]. In that place there was an inconsequential little
congregation of clerics living in carnal manner unfettered by the
burden of the Rule.[82] Discerning the devotion of his [Richard's] soul,
Father William promised that he, with the aid of God, would do what
he requested. They went together to that place, and the duke, along
with several bishops, solemnly and ritually committed to him the
dominion and care of the entire house. Then this man of the Lord
gathered to that place a group of monks under the Rule so numerous
in their persons and abounding in the study of virtue that they
exceeded three times the number of the past clerics. Seeing this, the
prince endowed the place with gifts of many presents and property.
He often told the abbot and the other brethren that they should seek
from him anything that they knew would be useful for them, because,
in his case, following the wish, there had come forth the ability ...

[C. 14] ... When in loving charity he was revisiting all his people, he
came to the monastery of Gorze which he had reformed, along with
others, on the monastic pattern, and took care to clear up all matters
which were outstanding; from there he came to Fécamp, which we
have already mentioned. After a few days he started to be afflicted
with sharp pains. When the celebration of the Nativity of the Lord
was approaching, receiving foreknowledge of the day of his calling by
Christ, he gathered the brothers to him and discussed with them
prudently and wisely all the matters which bore upon his responsibility, and the means by which they might be handled. And so, once
all, whether present or absent, had been strengthened by his blessing
and committed to God, he begged that a saving and lifegiving
departure should be granted to him. When all the week's celebrations
had been completed, without saying anything at all he lifted his eyes
only to God, directing himself to Him, so that his spirit should dwell
only on Him, for his happy soul was already looking to go suddenly to
the majesty of God in His glory from the vessel of the flesh. And so,
in the year of the Lord 1031, the fourteenth indiction, in the
seventieth year from the birth of this father and devotee of God, and
the forty-first after his arrival in Gaul from Italy, in the reigns of
Conrad [II] as emperor and Robert [the Pious] as king in Francia on
the holy day of the Lord's Circumcision and on the octave of His
Nativity, on the Friday morning as dawn of coming day banished the
darkness his happy and blessed soul passed from the world ... His

82 The canons were replaced by Benedictine monks c. 1000 (GND, i, 130–3).

holy body was buried with honour in the heart of the church of the Holy Trinity in the sight of the comings and goings of the brethren, so that each day they should have before their eyes as an example to them this father whom they had had as teacher to help them win the eternal reward of justice ...

Flanders

66 The Treaty between King Henry I of England and Robert II of Flanders, 1101

The treaty between King Henry I of England (1100–35) and Count Robert II of Flanders (1093–1111) was concluded at Dover on 10 March 1101 and renewed several times during the twelfth century. The 1101 treaty may well go back to one arranged between King William I of England (1066–87) and Count Baldwin V of Flanders (1035–67) which is mentioned by William of Malmesbury.[83] The 1101 treaty stipulates that the count of Flanders will provide annually 1000 soldiers to the king of England for fighting in England, Normandy or Maine in return for a yearly rent of £500. The document is particularly interesting because it shows not only the relationship between the king of England and the count of Flanders, but also both men's relationship with the king of France. He was overlord of the count of Flanders and the duke of Normandy, but not, of course, of the king of England. In 1101 Henry was king of England but his brother Robert Curthose was duke of Normandy. From 1106 onwards, after Duke Robert's defeat at Tinchebrai, matters became complicated when, as in 1066, the king of England was the same person as the duke of Normandy.

Diplomatic Documents Preserved in the Public Record Office, ed. P. Chaplais, i (1101–1272) (London, 1964), no. i. A full translation can be found in Van Houts, 1998b, 169–74.

Agreement between Henry, king of the English, and Robert, count of Flanders, concluded and written down at Dover on 10 March [1101] ...

[1] Robert, count of Flanders, pledged to King Henry with faith and an oath his life and the limbs that pertain to his body and the taking of his person that the king would have his [Robert's] life to his cost and that Robert will help him to hold and defend the kingdom of England against all men who are alive and can die, subject to the fealty [owed to] Philip king of the French. So that, should King

---

83 *William of Malmesbury, Gesta Regum Anglorum* , ed. and trsl. R. A. B. Mynors, R. M Thomson and M. Winterbottom (Oxford, 1998), i, pp. 728–9.

Philip wish to invade the kingdom of England against King Henry, Count Robert, if possible, shall persuade King Philip to stay put and request him in whatever way possible with advice and requests through faith and without ill intention or giving money that he should stay at home. But should King Philip come to England and bring the aforesaid count with him, Count Robert shall bring with him a minimum number of men so as not to prejudice his obligation [i.e. his fief] towards the king of France.

[2] And within 40 days of Count Robert having been summoned by the king [of England] by a messenger or letters, he shall have 1000 mounted soldiers [equites] in his harbours, ready to cross to England in support of King Henry, as quickly as possible. And the king shall find them ships and send them to either Gravelines or Wissant. And he shall send as many ships as are necessary for the soldiers in such a way that each of them shall have three horses with him [i.e. 3000 horses]; provided that if the king does not send enough ships in one go the remaining soldiers of the thousand shall wait at the harbour from the day the ships depart with the soldiers up to one whole month unless they themselves cross within that month. And Count Robert shall bear the cost of the shipping for all his own men and in particular for Count Eustace of Boulogne's men and all his other men, for whom he shall pay for the duration of the stay [in the harbour], and the crossing to and fro.

[3] And after the soldiers have arrived in England they shall pledge faith to King Henry or his envoys if so required, to this effect: that as long as they are on expedition in England they shall be at the king's disposal, that they shall not act so that he loses either land or men, but that they shall help him in faith to hold and defend the kingdom of England against all men.

[4] And should any other people [gens] come to England against the king when Count Robert has been summoned on the king's behalf within the aforementioned period and for his cause, the count himself shall come with the 1000 soldiers; unless he stays at home on account of a demonstrable illness of his body, or the loss of his land, or of a military summons from Philip, king of the French or of a summons issued by the emperor of the Romans throughout his lands; if Count Robert himself is there [in Flanders] at the time, the aforesaid summons on this account are not to be found without ill intention.[84] ...

84 The German emperor was overlord for the eastern, or 'imperial', part of Flanders.

[12] And if during that time King Philip invades Normandy against King Henry, Count Robert shall come to King Philip with 20 soldiers and the other [980] soldiers shall remain with King Henry in his service and fealty.

[13] The same Count Robert shall come to King Henry in Normandy as has been prescribed unless he is forced to stay [in Flanders] on account of severe illness of body or loss of his land or an expedition of the king of France or an expedition of the emperor of the Romans, as set out above. And if for this reason he has to stay, he will send, as we have set out, 1000 soldiers into Normandy in the king's service.

[14] And if the king wishes to have him with him in Maine, he shall come with 500 soldiers once a year and they shall join his household troops [*familia*] for one whole month;[85] if the king wishes to keep him longer he shall do so at the king's expense and with reimbursement of losses as is his custom with regard to the royal household troops [*familia*]. And the king shall do this from the moment they enter Normandy in order to go to Maine.

[15] That if Count Robert by summons of King Henry shall lead or send more than 1000 soldiers in Normandy or more than 500 in Maine, any men more than 1000 in Normandy or 500 in Maine shall be deducted from the count's next service; whichever of the two services, in Normandy or Maine, Count Robert performs to King Henry once a year will exclude the other service in the same year unless he performs it out of friendship.

[16] And if Count Robert is still on an expedition when he is summoned he shall have respite of three full weeks from the moment he returns, and he shall have the same respite if the summons arrives within 8 days after his return from an expedition. And if he is ill he shall have respite to send soldiers up to 15 days before sending them …

85 The royal household troops were a more or less standing elite army of professional soldiers as opposed to the casual mercenaries of the type to be recruited by Count Robert.

V: THE NORMANS IN THE MEDITERRANEAN

Introduction

The first presence of Normans in Italy was signalled in 999, when a group of Norman pilgrims came to the support of the local population in Salerno who were being attacked by Saracens.[1] Other Norman pilgrims became involved in the revolt of Melus of Bari against Byzantine rule in Apulia in the years 1017–18 [70]. According to early eleventh-century French chroniclers Adémar of Chabannes and Rodulfus Glaber [68, 69], one of the first Normans was a certain Rodulf, an exile, who might have been a member of the Tosny family.[2] As a direct result of this impromptu military involvement other Normans arrived in Italy, not any longer as pilgrims, but as mercenaries recruited by local princes. Among the latter were the princes of Salerno and Capua, the duke of Naples, the sons of Melus, who had a stronghold at Comino in the north of the principality of Capua, and even the monastery of Montecassino. Civil wars and outside pressure from Byzantium and the Saracens led to an insatiable need for soldiers to take part in the endemic fighting. In *c.* 1030 a group of Norman mercenaries led by a certain Rainulf acquired a more permanent foothold at Aversa. The investment of Rainulf as count of Aversa at around this time marked the beginning of the Norman principality there even though the indigenous prince Guaimar IV (d. 1052) was acknowledged as overlord until 1047 or later.[3] Meanwhile, in the early 1040s, the first of the sons of Tancred of Hauteville from the Norman Cotentin had arrived in Apulia and set themselves up as counts of Apulia: William the Iron Arm (1042–46), Drogo (1046–51) and Humphrey (1051–57) [71, 72].[4] Only charters from the latter two have

---

1 The classic study is Chalandon, 1907 on which most of the chronology is based. Indispensable are Hoffmann, 1969, 95–144 and Jahn, 1989.

2 Musset (1977, 50–1) identifies him as one of the witnesses of the Anglo-Norman treaty of 991, above p. 102 and also below, n. 28.

3 Chalandon, 1907, i, 76–82; Loud, 1985, 36–7. Guaimar IV is often named Guaimar V due to an erroneous modern assumption that there was a son of Guaimar II, called Guaimar III, who ruled after his father (Taviani-Carozzi, 1991, i, 366–7).

4 For the Hauteville family see also Orderic, ii, 98–104.

survived, one from Drogo and two from Humphrey.[5] Despite the persistent appearance in modern historiography of the sixteenth-century
myth that Tancred's wives were illegitimate daughters of Duke
Richard II of Normandy, there is absolutely no evidence for any blood
relationship between the Hautevilles and the Norman ducal family.
Therefore ducal kinship cannot be used as argument for Norman
expansion or Norman ducal imperialism.[6] After a series of spectacular
conquests including the defeat of the Lombards and Pope Leo IX at
Civitate in 1053, the youngest Hauteville son, Robert Guiscard, who
had arrived in 1046, expelled the Greeks from Calabria. In 1059 at
Melfi both Robert Guiscard and Richard of Capua made peace with
Pope Nicholas II to whom they swore oaths of fealty and promised to
pay an annual tribute [73].[7] Robert was made duke of Apulia and
Calabria, while Richard, count of Aversa, and son of Rainulf I, was
acknowledged as prince of Capua, having besieged and captured that
city in the previous year. In that same year, 1058, Robert Guiscard
had repudiated his first wife Alberada of Buonalbergo and instead
married Guaimar IV's daughter Sichelgaita, while Richard had earlier
married Robert Guiscard's sister Fresenda. The alliance of the Norman
rulers with each other, sealed with marriages, and with the pope,
sealed with promises of money, marked the beginning of Lombard
and papal acceptance of Norman supremacy in southern Italy. The
next decades saw a continuous influx of newcomers from northern
Europe, among whom the Normans were still the most numerous,
facilitating further expansion southwards. Sicily was conquered over a
period of more than thirty years from the first invasion in 1061,
followed by the conquest of Palermo in 1071–72, till the conquest of
the last Muslim stronghold in early 1091.[8] Different branches of the
same Hauteville family vied for supremacy and were not combined
until 1128 when Roger II, count of Sicily, acquired Apulia and
Calabria and crowned his success with the acquisition of the title of
king in 1130.

Why did the westerners, among whom the Normans were so numerous that we can speak of a Norman conquest, come to Italy?[9] Initially,
religious motivation was the driving force behind the stream of

5 Ménager, nos 1–3.

6 Szabolcs de Vajay, 1971, 129–47; Stasser, 1990, 49–64.

7 Loud, 1985, 38–85.

8 Matthew, 1992, 33–53.

9 Loud, 1981a, 13–34.

visitors who went as pilgrims. But being a pilgrim, a peaceful traveller whose aim is to receive salvation by visiting holy shrines, is a difficult and arduous business. The lure of reward could easily turn a pilgrim and innocent traveller into a temporary soldier and this is what seems to have happened in 999 and 1017–18. Reports sent back home then encouraged others to set out on a similar journey knowing that there was a demand for good soldiers [70, 71, 72]. Thus the second motivation was the rewards offered for mercenaries. Cash or payment in goods was initially the big attraction. Land is not mentioned in any of the early sources and is therefore unlikely to have been the Normans' main motivation. From the 1030s onwards the mercenaries may have begun to take advantage of the endemic internal strife by claiming lordships for themselves, as in Aversa, with the intention of remaining in Italy. The fertility of Campania, the area on the Mediterranean coast around Naples, with its vineyards, fruit trees, springs and plains, was an important aspect of the Normans' wish to settle permanently.[10] The settlement of Normans in southern Italy was thus a very gradual process of military support for local princes and a slow emancipation of soldiers who grew from subordinates to become local lords themselves. Intermarriage became another means of legitimising illegal occupation. Many Norman military leaders married into the Lombard local aristocracy. Robert Guiscard and two of his brothers married women of Guaimar of Salerno's kin. Not only high-ranking indigenous women found Norman husbands. Lower down the social scale Lombard females were also sought after. Local men too were attracted to Norman spouses as the early twelfth-century example of the son of Landulf of Graeca illustrates. His wife's dowry was arranged 'according to the customs of the Normans', an indication that the woman in question was Norman rather than Lombard.[11] Graham Loud is right in arguing that slow and gradual occupation turned the process of Norman infiltration into a mirror image of the viking occupation of Normandy which was also characterised by assimilation, adaptation and infiltration over a number of decades.[12] In this respect the Norman conquest of southern Italy is quite different from the Norman conquest of England which was completed within a period of twenty years.

10 Loud, 1996, 314–16.
11 Loud, 1996, 331–2.
12 Loud, 1981a, 15–16

There were other reasons, besides pilgrimage and mercenary activity, why the Normans came to Italy. Chronicles from Germany, France, Normandy and southern Italy also mention political exile from Normandy as an important reason [30, 68–9, 72, 74–5]. As we have seen above, in Chapter I, the Scandinavian custom of *ullac* was practised in Normandy even though we are not sure whether it was as a custom inherited from the first Scandinavian settlers or as a custom introduced in Normandy later from the Danelaw.[13] Anyway, as a result any murderer or thief in Normandy was directly at the mercy of the duke. Richard II, Robert the Magnificent and William the Conqueror all used exile, rather than execution, as a means of getting rid of troublemakers. Exile had the advantage that the perpetrators of crime physically disappeared from the scene and because their lives had been spared their kin would not demand revenge. In several cases we hear of exiles leaving the country accompanied by their brothers or sons, the very persons who otherwise might have been expected to continue the policies of the exiled member of the family. Graham Loud and Lucien Musset have pointed out that the peak of political expulsions coincided with periods of political instability in Normandy, particularly during the reign of Robert the Magnificent and the minority of his son William.[14] Gilbert Buatère, Osmond Drengot and Serlo of Hauteville were exiled from Normandy during Duke Robert's reign [30, 72, 74] while most expulsions date from the first half of Duke William's reign when Guimund of Moulins, William Werlenc, Robert Bigot and Robert of Grandmesnil, former abbot of Saint-Evroult, were driven into exile [75].[15] Others followed later. William Pantulf and Hugh Bunel when they left Normandy were accused of Mabel of Bellême's murder in 1077 [86]. Abbot Robert of Saint-Evroult, having been embroiled in a conflict with some of his monks, was exiled and later, deciding to remain in Italy, he called his sisters Judith and Emma to join him [75]. The fact that their brother's departure from Normandy might have been shameful did not prevent the girls, according to Orderic Vitalis, from contracting prosperous marriages. Judith married Roger I (d. 1101), brother of Robert Guiscard, but Emma's husband is unknown.

Political exile was an important reason but cannot account for the great numbers of Normans who left Normandy. By far the most

13 See above, p. 20.

14 Loud, 1981a, 19–20; Musset, 1985, 47–9.

15 Loud, 1981a, 19.

pressing reason for young men to leave their home never, it seems, to return again, was the lack of land and a share in the paternal inheritance due to overpopulation. This, at least, is the reason given by contemporaries in Italy as well as Normandy, for Amatus of Montecassino and Geoffrey Malaterra are unambiguous in quoting overpopulation as the main cause for emigration [71, 72]. The case of Tancred of Hauteville's offspring is often cited as the most famous example, even though its implication that all Normans came from families with twelve or more sons is a clear exaggeration. Tancred married twice and had five sons by his first wife and seven sons by his second. At least eight of them ended up in Italy because the family lands in the Cotentin were insufficient to support them and eventually their offspring. Although in Normandy, as elsewhere, *parage* determined that heirs should share their inheritance, there is a limit to the extent that estates can be divided and still remain a viable source for the upkeep of large families. In families with large numbers of daughters, as well as sons, enough needed to be held back to provide them with dowries.[16] In this respect it is interesting to note that the sources describing the Norman settlement in southern Italy give the same motive (overpopulation) as Dudo and William of Jumièges quote for the Scandinavian settlement of Normandy. Conversely, overpopulation has never been given as a reason for the Norman conquest of England even though William's success in recruiting such a large army was itself due to large numbers of (young) men enlisting in the hope of reward and land overseas. Considering the large numbers of younger sons of local families from north-western France there is good reason to suppose that shortage of good prospects at home stimulated the large-scale support from this constituency for the Norman invasion.[17]

The crusading movement offered another reason why people from north-western Europe went to the Mediterranean and spent some time in Italy. The First Crusade of 1096 attracted a sizeable Norman contingent in response to Pope Urban II's request for military support against the Muslims in the Holy Land. They were led by Duke Robert Curthose (1087–1106), William the Conqueror's eldest son and successor in Normandy, whose reputation as crusader far outweighed that as duke.[18] Other Normans appear in the crusading sources

16 Loud, 1981a, 17–18.

17 In general on the aristocratic diaspora, see Bartlett, 1993, 24–60.

18 David, 1920, 89–119, and for the legends around his crusading career, 190–201.

sporadically, like Hugh Bunel, the Norman who had been exiled for the murder of Mabel of Bellême [86]. The Norman presence among crusaders was, however, mostly an Italian–Norman presence dominated by the second generation of Hauteville offspring with a leading role for Bohemond I (d. 1111), son of Robert Guiscard, and his cousin (or nephew) Tancred (d. 1112). Otherwise the career of Ilger Bigod is interesting in that he, a member of the Norman Bigod family, attached himself to Bohemond I and became his military commander (*magister militum*) [86–7]. We know about him from stories circulating in the Anglo-Norman realm about his home visit during which he distributed relics consisting of some hairs of the Virgin Mary acquired at Antioch. Another group of Normans can be traced among the crusading force that liberated Lisbon in 1147. They are referred to as Normans as a distinct group from the English, Flemish and German crusaders who took part in the siege of Lisbon. The text of Priest Raol's account of the siege is interesting because it contains yet another example of a description of supposed Norman qualities [85].

The continuation of Norman emigration into Italy in the second half of the eleventh century also shows that many Norman mercenaries used Italy simply as a stepping stone for careers in countries further afield. Again the Norman exile Hugh Bunel is a good example. According to Orderic Vitalis, he felt uneasy in Italy because the long arm of William the Conqueror's 'police' might have been able to catch up with him and therefore he went to the Holy Land then occupied by the Turks [86]. Twenty-odd years later when the first crusaders arrived they seized on his language skills and he made himself useful as an interpreter at Jerusalem for William's son Robert Curthose. Other Norman mercenaries who passed through Italy on their way to Byzantium were Roussel of Bailleul and Robert Crispin as well as their companion Hervé whose precise origin is unknown [78–80]; all three ended up in the service of the Byzantine emperors. From a Byzantine perspective the Normans' main attraction was their military skill and in particular their expertise in fighting on horseback.[19] Closely connected was their capacity to teach others to fight in 'conrois', small units of cavalry whose fighting impact increased as a result of frequent training. In return for their military service the Normans received from the Greeks, as they had become accustomed to receive in Italy, moveable goods such as money, precious cloths and other oriental goods unobtainable in the west. Dissatisfaction

19 For what follows, see Shepard, 1992, 275–305; see also Hanawalt, 1995, 114–22.

with the lack of a more permanent reward led to several uprisings and rebellions whereby the Norman leaders would join the local population, such as their resistance against the Byzantine Greeks in Asia Minor. Anna Comnena is very clear on this when she describes how her father Emperor Alexius Comnenus (1081–1118) used a ruse to prevent the Turkish people, Roussel's ardent supporters, from obstructing his capture [78]. None of the Norman mercenaries in Byzantine service established permanent settlements in Byzantine-occupied territory, nor is there any evidence that they fathered offspring who continued Norman practices in the way the Normans did in southern Italy.

Some Normans had been engaged in warfare elsewhere around the Mediterranean before they arrived in Italy and Byzantium. In the late 1050s and early 1060s the expeditions organised by the Christian kings of northern Spain against the Muslims increased. They, like their colleagues elsewhere in Europe, needed skilled soldiers to fight battles against the infidel. Presumably messengers from Castile, Aragon and Barcelona were sent out to recruit personnel in northern Europe or, alternatively, family links between the princes of northern Spain, Aquitaine, Anjou and Normandy provided the network whereby potential recruits knew where the fighting was about to take place.[20] Such family links can be dated to the early eleventh century when Roger I of Tosny exiled from Normandy and in search of fighting ended up in northern Spain, where he was briefly married to Estefania, daughter of Ramon Borrell of Barcelona (d. 1018). Having visited the abbey of Conques in southern France, probably in the area of origin of his second wife, Godehilde, he returned to Normandy where he founded the abbey of Saint-Pierre at Conches [63, 82].[21] Thus, he never settled for good in Spain. Neither did Robert Crispin, the best-known Norman mercenary engaged in the battles of Argastro and Barbastro in 1064.[22] Robert, according to Amatus of Montecassino, was no great military success and had to flee the scene to save his life [83]. What exactly went wrong we do not know, but he thought it safer to go to Italy, where we find him at the court of

20 Keats-Rohan, 1993b, 1–51 at 30–9.

21 Godehilde's identification as daughter of Ramon Borrell of Barcelona by Keats-Rohan, 1993b, 33–5, is wrong; see Aurell i Cardona, 1993, 201–32 at 214–15.

22 Gaimar mentions also a member of the Giffard family at Barbastro (*L'Estoire des Engleis by Geffrei Gaimar*, ed. A. Bell (Oxford, 1960), line 6078, pp. 193 and 274, where the allusion to Barbastro is misunderstood by the editor (Keats-Rohan, 1993b, 19 and Defourneaux, 1949, 132–9).

Richard of Capua in June 1066.[23] This is interesting because as a Norman one might have expected him to answer Duke William's call to join his army to prepare for the invasion of England, knowledge of which was available at the papal court, and thus presumably at Montecassino, from March of that year.[24] That he did not return home may be a reason to suspect that he had left Normandy as an exile rather than a simple mercenary. A much later Norman fighter in northern Spain, who put down roots and settled, is Robert of Tarragona. He arrived *c.* 1114 and built up a small principality of which he nominally remained prince (*princeps*) until his death in 1155 [**84**].[25]

The French presence of mercenaries in Italy, Byzantium and Spain was recognised as predominantly Norman by contemporaries. Charter evidence and prosopographical studies have proved without any doubt that among the western European settlers in Italy, the Normans constituted the largest ethnic group. L. R. Ménager and Graham Loud estimate that as many as two-thirds or three-quarters of the immigrants came from Normandy.[26] Among them, men were by far the most numerous, although Rodulfus Glaber explicitly mentions women and children among the Norman migrants [**69**]. This fact offers another parallel with the Scandinavian settlement in Normandy. In both countries the lack of respectively Norman and Scandinavian women forced the men to accept indigenous women as wives and mothers of their children. Intermarriage in turn facilitated the process of settlement both in legal terms – landholding by conquest was legitimised through marriage – and in social and ethnic terms with the amalgamation of two cultures. There is a parallel here, too, with the Norman conquest of England where intermarriage had its legal and social advantages.[27]

23 Loud, 1981c, 121–2.
24 Van Houts, 1995, 850–3.
25 McCrank, 1981, 67–82.
26 Loud, 1981a, 20–2; Ménager, 1981, iv, 189–214, esp. 202–5.
27 Searle, 1980, 159–70.

Italy

67 Wipo, Deeds of Conrad II

Wipo wrote the Deeds of Conrad *c.* 1040 as chaplain of King Conrad II (1024–39). He describes the German king's first expedition into Italy in 1026 from a northern German perspective.

Wippo, Gesta Chuonradi II imperatoris, ed. and trsl. W. Trillmich and R. Buchner (Darmstadt, 1961); *Imperial Lives and Letters of the Eleventh Century*, trsl. T. E. Mommsen, K. F. Morrison (New York, 1962), pp. 79–80.

[C. 17] After peace had been made, therefore, between the Romans and the Germans, the emperor advanced into Apulia and subjected to himself Benevento and Capua and the remaining cities in this region, either by force or by voluntary surrender. And to the Normans, who, compelled by some necessity or other, had flocked together into Apulia from their country, he gave permission to live there, and he established a union of them with the princes to defend the borders of the realm against the treachery of the Greeks. When all other affairs came to pass happily and in good order for him, the emperor turned back and went again through Italy bypassing Rome.

68 Adémar of Chabannes, Chronicle

Adémar of Chabannes, based in Aquitaine, wrote his chronicle before 1034. His account of the first Normans going to Italy is confused, though it may be more trustworthy than has hitherto been thought.

Adémar de Chabannes, Chronique, ed. J. Chavanon (Paris, 1897), pp. 177–8.

[Book III, c. 55] … During the reign of Richard [II], count of Rouen and son of Richard [I] of the Normans, an armed band of Normans under the leadership of Rodulf went to Rome and with the tacit agreement of Pope Benedict [VIII, 1012–24] advanced on Apulia where they laid waste everything.[28] Basil [II, 976–1025] sent an army against them and after two clashes, and then a third, the Normans came out victoriously. In the fourth encounter with the people of Rus they [the Normans] were defeated, laid low and wiped out, and a great number of them were led off to Constantinople,

---

28 Rodulf was a Norman but his likely identification with Rodulf, son of Hugh, of Tosny (Musset, 1977, 50–1) is disputed by Hoffmann (1969, 136–7, 140–1). The date may be sometime in the second decade of the eleventh century.

where they spent the rest of their lives in prison.[29] Whence comes the saying: 'The Greeks captured the hare along with the cart.' For three years, then, the road to Jerusalem was closed. For on account of the anger of the Normans, whatever foreigners the Greeks came across, they led them off in chains to Constantinople, and let them suffer in prison there.

69   Rodulfus Glaber, History

Rodulfus Glaber wrote his History in the 1030s and 1040s in Burgundy. His account is important in that it underlines the protection of Rodulf the Norman by both the German king and the pope.

Rodulfus Glaber, Opera, ed. and trsl. J. France, N. Bulst and P. Reynolds (Oxford, 1989), pp. 96–103.

[Book III, c. 2] At that time the Hungarians, who lived along the Danube, together with their king, were converted to the faith of Christ. This king took the name of Stephen at his baptism and became a good catholic; the aforementioned Emperor Henry gave him a sister in marriage.[30] After that almost all those from Italy and Gaul who wished to go to the Sepulchre of the Lord at Jerusalem abandoned the usual route, which was by sea, making their way through the country of King Stephen. He made the road safe for everyone, welcomed as brothers all he saw, and gave them enormous gifts. This action led many people, nobles and commoners to go to Jerusalem. Then the Emperor Basil, who ruled the holy empire of Constantinople, ordered one of his satraps, known as the Catapan because he lives by the sea, to come and demand from the cities across the sea the tribute owing to the Roman empire.[31] The satrap obeyed willingly, and sent a Greek fleet to pillage Italian property. This went on for two years, and the Greeks conquered no small part of the province of Benevento.[32]

[Book III, c. 3] At this time a very brave Norman called Rodulf incurred the anger of Count Richard [II].[33] Fearing the wrath of his

---

29 The people of Rus were Scandinavian settlers of Russia. They may have been Varangians working on behalf of the Byzantine emperor in southern Italy.

30 Stephen of Hungary (1000–38); in 996 he married Gisela of Bavaria, sister of the later Henry II, king of Germany (1002–24).

31 Southern Italy.

32 Sometime between 1009 and 1017.

33 No Norman evidence for Rodulf and Richard II has survived.

lord, he fled with all those he could take with him to Rome, where he explained his position to Pope Benedict. The pope, seeing that he was a good soldier, began to tell him how angry he felt about the Greek invasion of the Roman empire, deploring the fact that there was no one in all his lands who could repel this foreign nation. When he heard this Rodulf promised to fight the enemy if the Italians would help him, for the distress of the country fell upon them rather than him. Pope Benedict then sent him and his men to the rulers of Benevento, ordering them to receive him in peace, accept him as permanent war-leader, and obey him loyally in battle. He went to the Beneventans, who received him as the pope had ordered. Then Rodulf, attacking those of the Greek administration who were collecting taxes from the people, plundered and killed all of them. Hearing of this, their colleagues, who had already conquered many cities and fortresses, collected their forces and took the field against Rodulf and his followers. In the battle the greater part of the Greeks were killed, and they were forced to evacuate some castles, which the victorious army of Rodulf occupied in their pursuit. In view of their losses, the Greeks sent to Constantinople asking for the speediest aid from those who charged them with this task. Immediately a fleet was formed which carried many more soldiers than had been sent before. In the meantime it had been rumoured abroad that a mere handful of Normans had triumphed over the arrogance of the Greeks, and because of this a great many of Rodulf's compatriots left their own country with their wives and children. Richard their count did not simply permit this, he pressed it on them. Travelling boldly they came to the part of the Alps known as 'Mount Jupiter', in whose narrow passes the local rulers, driven by greed, had placed barricades and set guards in order to extract tolls from those making the crossing: but when they had denied them passage, wanting payment first, as was customary, the Norman army became angry, broke down the barricades, killed the guards and forced a passage. This group brought Rodulf no small reinforcement. So both sides joined battle a second time with renewed strength; both suffered heavy losses, but the Normans emerged victorious. After a little while there was a third battle and each army withdrew to its own ground, exhausted. When Rodulf realised that his own countrymen were suffering heavy losses while the local population was useless in battle, he and a few companions went to see the Emperor Henry and explained to him the course of events.[34] The

---

34 Henry II, king of Germany (1002–24). The king undertook an expedition to Italy in 1021–22 at the request of Pope Benedict VIII who visited him. I see no reason

emperor received Rodulf well and gave him various gifts, for rumour
of his deeds had aroused Henry's curiosity.

[Book III, c. 4] Soon the emperor gathered a great army and set out
to protect the common weal. The Greeks, believing that Rodulf had
fled from the country, advanced smartly to the towns which he had
taken from them after his victories – but in vain; for they hastily
threw up a wall around the ancient city of Troia and filled it with a
great many men and women.[35] In the meantime the emperor, having
set out for Benevento, assaulted and captured all the towns and cities
which the Greeks had wrenched from his empire. When he came to
Troia the rebels in the city resisted him long and hard, hoping that in
the next summer, as the Greeks had promised, the Emperor Basil
would aid them. They added that Henry would be so humiliated that
he would take to his heels in terror before Basil. He laid siege to the
city with his army, setting out his machines to take it by storm. But
the besieged made a sortie under cover of night, carrying with them
torches smeared with pitch, and in this way they destroyed the
machines outside by fire. When he saw this, the emperor, blazing with
anger, ordered that stronger machines should be built and covered
with raw hide, and he commanded his men to guard them vigilantly.
At the end of the third month of the siege both sides were exhausted
by heavy losses (for the scourge of dysentery had sorely ravaged the
emperor's army). In the end the besieged took better counsel and
devised a way of avoiding ruin. One day they found a hermit dressed
as a monk (Italy abounds with such men), gave him a cross to carry,
and sent out after him all the young children of the city. So prepared,
with loud cries of 'Lord have mercy', he approached the emperor's
tent. When the emperor heard this he ordered that he be asked what
they wanted of him, and when the answer came that they were
begging mercy for the city he had afflicted, he replied: 'He who reads
men's hearts knows very well that their own fathers are the
murderers of these little ones, not I.' Weeping, he ordered that they
should return in safety to the city. They did as the emperor ordered.
The next day, at first light, they again trooped out of the city crying:
'Lord have mercy' as before, until the sound of their voices reached
the ears of the emperor. Immediately he left his tent, looked at the

---

to doubt Glaber's statement that Rodulf had accompanied the pope on the visit (in
1020).

35 The siege of Troia took place in 1022. Other sources suggest that Henry II failed
to take the town and abandoned the siege.

crowd of children, and was stirred by pity; being a just man, he used the words of the Lord, 'I have compassion on the multitude.' Now before all this happened he had said that if he managed to capture the city all its males would be hanged from the gibbet and everything else would be burnt and the walls razed to the ground. Then the emperor sent messages to the leaders of the city saying that if they wanted to gain his indulgence and placate his anger, they should themselves break down part of the walls of the city, which stood out stubbornly against his machines. Hearing this they eagerly did as they were told. After this the emperor ordered them to come out to him in peace, and repair the wall. Then, after he had taken hostages from all the inhabitants of that region, he returned to Saxony. The Normans, led by Rodulf, went back to their own land and were joyfully received by Richard their prince.[36]

70   William of Apulia, Poem on the Deeds of Robert Guiscard

William of Apulia wrote his poem on Robert Guiscard in the late 1090s.

Guillaume de Pouille, La Geste de Robert Guiscard, ed. M. Mathieu (Palermo, 1961), pp. 98–102, 154–6; trsl. by G. A. Loud.

[Book I, lines 1–79] After it had been pleasing to the Mighty King who orders the seasons as well as the kingdoms that the shores of Apulia, for so long possessed by the Greeks, should no longer be occupied by them, the people of the Normans, distinguished by their warlike soldiers, should enter and rule Italy, after expelling the Greeks. In the language of their native country the wind which carries them from the boreal regions from which they have departed to seek the frontiers of Italy is called 'north', and the word 'man' is used among them to signify 'homo'; thus they are called 'Normans', that is 'men of the north wind' [*homines boreales*].

Some of these men had climbed to the summit of Monte Gargano, to you, Michael the Archangel, to fulfil a vow which they had made.[37] There they saw a man clad in the Greek manner, called Melus.[38] They were amazed at the peculiar costume of this stranger, one which they

36 Rodulf's return to Normandy is dated to the year before Henry II died, thus to 1023.

37 A peninsula north of Bari, where the shrine of St Michael had been a pilgrimage site since at least the eighth century.

38 Melus and his brother-in-law Dattus rebelled against the Greeks in 1009 and 1017.

had never seen before, with his head tied up in a bonnet wrapped around it. On seeing him they asked who he was and where he came from. He replied that he was a Lombard, a citizen of noble birth from Bari, and that he had been forced to flee from his native land by the cruelty of the Greeks. When the Gauls sympathised with his fate he said, 'If I had the help of some of your people, it would be easy for me to return, provided that you are willing.' Indeed he assured them that with their help the Greeks could rapidly and with no great effort be put to flight. They promised him that they would swiftly provide this help, along with others from their country, to which they were about to return.

So after they had returned to their native land, they immediately started to encourage their relatives to come with them to Italy. They talked of the fertility of Apulia and of the cowardice of those who lived there. They advised them to carry with them only what was necessary for the journey; for they promised that once there they would find a wise patron, under whose leadership they would gain an easy victory over the Greeks. By such means they persuaded many to go; some because they possessed little or no wealth, others because they wished to make the great fortune they had greater still. All of them greedy for gain ...

[Book I, lines 400-68] After celebrating his funeral ceremonies Robert [Guiscard] returned to Calabria.[39] He immediately besieged the city of Cariati that by his capture he might terrify the other cities.[40] Then he learnt of the arrival of Pope Nicholas II [1059-61]; he abandoned the siege along with only a small escort, leaving there the larger part of his cavalry. He went to Melfi and there the pope was received with great honour. He had come to this region to deal with ecclesiastical matters.[41] For the priests, levites and all the clergy of this area were openly joining themselves in marriage. The pope celebrated a council there, and with the consent of a hundred prelates whom he had called to that synod, he exhorted priests and ministers of the altar to arm themselves in chastity; he told them and ordered them to be the husbands of the church, since it is unlawful for priests to be addicted to indulgence. He thus drove away from those parts all the wives of priests, threatening those who disobeyed him with

39 The author here refers to the death of Robert Guiscard's elder brother Humphrey which occurred in 1057.

40 Cariati (Rossano, prov. Cosenza).

41 Melfi (prov. Potenza); the Council of Melfi took place in July and August 1059.

anathema. At the end of the synod and on the request of many, Pope
Nicholas gave to Robert the ducal honour. Alone among the counts
he received the ducal title. He swore an oath to be faithful to the
pope.[42] Thus Calabria and all Apulia was conceded to him and rule
over the people of his native land in Italy …

As his reputation for power and bravery grew, he sent envoys who
carried his words to the excellent Gisulf, son of Guaimar, requesting
marriage with his noble sister, for he then lacked a spouse having
repudiated his first wife because of consanguinity.[43] From her had
been born Bohemond, a mighty son, who was later to become
powerful and be distinguished for his courage. To begin with Gisulf
disdained Robert's message, not that he could marry his sister to a
greater and more noble man, but because the Gauls seemed to him a
race fierce and barbarous, cruel and inhuman in mind, and the reputation of his first wife imposed a pause before one gave a second! Finally
the prince assented and gave his elder sister in marriage to you, Duke
Robert. She was called Sichelgaita, and the younger, Gaitelgrima.
Gaitelgrima afterwards married his nephew Jordan, the prince of
Capua, who equalled in his virtues both the duke and his father.[44] A
marriage of such grandeur much augmented Robert's noble reputation, and people who had previously had to be constrained to serve
him now rendered to him the obedience due to his ancestors. For the
Lombard people knew that Italy had been subject to his wife's grandfathers and great-grandfathers. She gave him three sons and five
daughters, these children of both sexes will in the future distinguish
themselves.[45]

42 See no. **73** which contains the text of Robert's pledge to Pope Nicholas.

43 Gisulf II of Salerno, was the son of Guaimar IV (1027–52); Robert's first wife was
Alberada of Buonalbergo to whom he may not have been related by blood. Robert
and Alberada's son was Bohemond I (d. 1111). Robert Guiscard's second marriage
took place in 1058 and thus preceded the treaty of Melfi.

44 Jordan I of Capua (duke, 1078–90), son of Richard I of Capua and Fresenda, sister
of Robert Guiscard.

45 The sons are Roger Borsa (duke, 1085–1111), Guy and Robert. At least seven
daughters are known: Helena (**77**), Mabel, Sibyl (**77**), Matilda (**77**), Cecilia,
Gaitelgrima (see Ménager, no. 58) and one unnamed one (Chalandon, 1907, i, 283);
see genealogical table, no. **7**.

71   Geoffrey Malaterra, Deeds of Count Roger and his brother Duke Robert

This text was written *c.* 1090 by Geoffrey, a Norman, who had moved to southern Italy and worked at the court of Count Roger.

De rebus gestis Rogerii Calabriae et Siciliae Comitis et Roberti Guiscardi fratris eius auctore Gaufredo Malaterra, ed. E. Pontieri (Bologna 1927), pp. 7–11; trsl. G. A. Loud.

[Book I, c. 3] ... In this province [Normandy] there is a city called Coutances, and in its territory there is a village named Hauteville;[46] called thus not so much because of the height of any hill upon which it is situated, but rather, so we believe, as an omen predicting the extraordinary fortune and great success of the future heirs of this village, who with the help of God and their own dynamism [*strenuitas*] raised themselves step by step to the highest of ranks. We do not know whether divine providence saw what was pleasing to it in the preceding generations, or foresaw it in their heirs who came after, or even both, but it raised these heirs to great estates so that, as was promised to Abraham, they grew into a great people and spread their rule by force of arms, making the necks of many people subject to themselves, as we shall explain little by little in what follows.

[Book I, c. 4]   There was a certain knight [*miles*] of quite distinguished family who possessed this village by hereditary right from his ancestors. He was called Tancred, and he married a wife called Moriella, who was notable both for her birth and good character, and as the years went by he received from her in lawful manner five sons, who were in the future to become counts: namely William, known as 'the Iron Arm', Drogo, Humphrey, Geoffrey and Serlo.[47] Their mother died while their father was still a young man and unsuited for celibacy, but this good man detested extra-marital unions and therefore married again, preferring to be contented with one legitimate union rather than soiling himself with the filthy embrace of concubines, mindful of the word of the apostle: 'to avoid fornication let every man have his own wife' [1 Cor. 7:2], and of what follows 'whoremongers and

46 Hauteville (Manche, c. Saint-Sauveur Lendelin).

47 William the Iron Arm, count of Apulia (1042–46), Drogo, count of Apulia (1046–51), Humphrey, count of Apulia (1051–57). Geoffrey, too, went to southern Italy where he became the ancestor of the counts of Loritello. Serlo stayed behind in Normandy but also spent some time in exile in Brittany (see no. **30**); Serlo's son, also named Serlo, joined his uncles in Italy.

adulterers God will judge' [Hebr. 13:4].[48] So he married Fresenda, a lady who in birth and morals was by no means inferior to his first wife. In due course he had from this union seven sons, who were of no less worth or dignity than their brothers mentioned above. We shall list their names here. First there was Robert, called from his birth 'the cunning' [*Guiscardus*], afterwards prince of all Apulia and duke of Calabria, a man of great wisdom, ingenuity, generosity and boldness. The second was called Malger, the third William, the fourth Aubrey, the fifth Hubert, the sixth Tancred, the seventh and youngest Roger, later the conqueror and count of Sicily.[49] Their mother raised her sons most carefully and affectionately, and she demonstrated such love to the ones who were not hers but born of her husband and his first wife that unless one had learnt from some third party one would not have known which was her own son and which was not. As a result her husband loved her all the more, and she was greatly esteemed by their neighbours. As the years were granted to them, the children grew from childhood and one by one reached the age of adolescence. They began to imbibe military skills, to practise the use of horses and weapons, learning how to guard themselves and strike down their enemies.

[Book I, c. 5] They saw their own neighbourhood would not be big enough for them and that when their patrimony was divided not only would their heirs argue among themselves about the share-out, but the individual shares would simply not be big enough. So, to prevent the same thing happening in future as had happened to them, they discussed the matter among themselves. They decided that since the elders were at that time stronger than those younger to them, they should be the first to leave their homeland and go to other places seeking their fortune through arms, and finally God led them to the Italian province of Apulia.

[Book I, c. 6] They learned that, as the result of various disputes, hostilities had broken out between two very famous princes, those of Capua and Salerno.[50] Since they discovered that on the road by which they came Capua was the nearer of these two places, they took them-

48 It has been wrongly argued that both Moriella and Fresenda were illegitimate daughters of Richard II; see Stasser, 1990, 55 and Szabolcs de Vajay, 1971, 130–1.

49 Robert Guiscard, count and duke of Apulia (1057–85); Roger I, count of Sicily (1072–1101).

50 Capua was ruled by the house of Pandulf until 1058, whereas Salerno was ruled by the house of Guaimar till 1076.

selves to its prince, ready to fight for hope of gain. They remained there for a short time, accepted his wages, and vigorously carried out their duties. But, realising how stingy the prince of Capua was, they abandoned him and changed sides to enter the employ of the prince of Salerno. He received them as was fitting, because their military reputation had already made them extremely well-known throughout Apulia, and particularly since they had deserted the prince's enemy and joined him. Their loyalty to him was encouraged with generous gifts and they wreaked havoc on the Capuans with all sorts of frequent raids, terrorising the whole province as though some dreadful epidemic had broken out. Revenging the injuries suffered by the prince of Salerno far and wide, they continued to do this indefatigably and so curbed those in rebellion against the prince that all the districts round about were reduced to peace ...

[Book I, c. 7] A Greek called Maniakes, whom the emperor at Constantinople had placed as governor of those parts in Calabria and Apulia which belonged to him, planned to lead an expedition to conquer Sicily and sought help from all sides.[51] Thus on the emperor's behalf he requested the prince of Salerno, who was well-disposed to the emperor, to send him the men through whom he was reputed to have conquered his enemies, that they might aid the holy empire. He promised to reward them generously. The prince seized the opportunity to get rid of them in an honourable way, and immediately agreed to this request. He urged them to do this, and to persuade them he promised them rewards. He made speeches to them; he even promised them [the help] of his own men. They finally made the necessary preparations and went to join Maniakes, not however so much because of the prince's order but rather seduced by the hope of securing the rewards which they had been promised. Maniakes was extremely pleased by their arrival, for he relied very much on their assistance. He set sail with a huge force and landed in Sicily. He first attacked Messina, since it lay very close to the shore where he had landed, and forced [the inhabitants] to negotiate its surrender ...[52]

51 Georges Maniakes (d. 1043) was a Byzantine general who in 1038–40 used Norman cavalry troops, recruited through Guaimar IV of Salerno, to reconquer Sicily for the Byzantine emperor.

52 Messina (prov. Messina).

72   Amatus of Montecassino, History of the Normans

Amatus, monk of Montecassino, wrote his History of the Normans *c.* 1080–82; the Latin text has not survived, but the contents are known from a later French translation.

Storia de' Normanni di Amato di Montecassino, ed. V. de Bartholomaeis (Rome, 1935), pp. 23–4, 27–8, 112–14, 182–5, 194; trsl. P. Llewellyn.

[Book I, c. 18] And when this great victory [the siege of Salerno in 1015–16] had been won by the valour of these forty Norman pilgrims, the prince [Guaimar III, 999–1027] and all the people of Salerno gave them great thanks; and they offered them presents and promised them great rewards, and begged them to remain to defend the Christians. But the Normans did not wish to take a money reward for what they had done for the love of God. And they made their excuses for not being able to remain. Then the prince took counsel to invite Normans to come and sent them off to encourage others in all good will to go to those parts, because of the wealth that was there. So they sent the message with these victorious Normans and sent lemons and almonds and preserved fruits; imperial cloths too and iron instruments decorated with gold.[53] And so they begged that they ought to go to this land flowing with milk and honey and all these fine things. And that everything was as they saw it, these victorious Normans themselves bore witness in Normandy.

[Book I, c. 19] At that time there was hatred and bad feeling between two leading men of Normandy, Gilbert and William.[54] Gilbert, who was also called Buatère, plucked up his determination and courage against William, who had challenged his honour, and threw him down from a very high place from which he died. At the time that he was killed he had the office of vicomte over the whole land. Robert, count of the land, was greatly angry at his death and threatened to kill whoever had committed this murder; for, if this crime were not punished it would seem that licence had been granted for anyone to kill a vicomte. Gilbert had four brothers, namely Rainulf, Asclettin, Osmund and Rudolf. And although these had no share of guilt in the death of William, they all went off with their brother in accordance with the message of the prince of Salerno. And they came armed, not as enemies

53 This is an interesting reference to the sort of goods the Norman mercenaries received in return for their services.

54 Possibly the same person as William Repostel mentioned by Orderic Vitalis in no. 74.

but as angels and were welcomed by the whole of Italy. Everything necessary, food and drink, was given them by their lords and good people of Italy. They passed the city of Rome and came to Capua; there they found a man from Apulia called Melus who had been chased out from there for rebellion against the emperor of Constantinople ...

[Book I, c. 21] These therefore went to the aid of Melus, crossing the borders of Apulia with him. They began to fight against the Greeks and saw that they were like women. From there, their Apulian camp at Arenula, they attacked their spiritless foes, and brought great grief through the many deaths they caused ... [lacuna] Again they set themselves to battle. And when they heard of the boldness of the knights who were attacking the land, he ordered the strongest men he could find against the Normans. And when these orders came, they ranged themselves for a second battle. But the Greeks lost and the Normans stood ever firm. And this was a great sorrow to the emperor. He ordered a great multitude of men and ranged them for a third battle, and a fourth and a fifth. And in every one the Normans were victorious. And so Melus through the Normans' strength won the seat of office ...

[Book II, c. 46] At this time that I am talking about, there came from Normandy one Robert, later called also Guiscard, who had come to help his brother.[55] And he requested also some land benefice. He did not only come to assist his brother but also to give him counsel. This Robert entered the entourage of his lord to whom he gave in good faith a warrior's service. But it saddened his heart when he saw that he was not the equal of those who had castles and various lands, but being a valiant brother to the count he followed his contingent. For a long time he persisted like this out of desire to hold land although constrained for poverty in the things of the land. But to God alone is the sole disposition of the various peoples ...

[Book IV, c. 3] When Robert became count on the death of his brother Count Humphrey, as I said, he determined to go to Calabria.[56] He sought out the camp and the hilltop that he had already acquired and within a short time had taken and conquered all the fortresses of that country except for Reggio; this would not yield to him voluntarily, so he had to take it by force. For this achievement Robert rose to such great state that he was no longer called count but duke. But he never

55 The brother was either Count William of Apulia (1042–46) or Count Drogo (1046–51).

56 Count Humphrey died in 1057.

lost the nickname Guiscard. When Robert Guiscard had conquered and overcome all the fortresses of Calabria and had become duke of Calabria he left it with all his armed men and went into Apulia. And he seized the whole plain of Apulia and besieged Troia and took it by force of arms ...

[Book IV, c. 17] Duke Robert had conquered Apulia and Calabria and daily his honour grew and in everything the hand of God gave him aid. But Duke Robert wept for the sins he had committed in the past, and kept himself from sins of the present and for the future. For this reason he began to show love towards God's church, and to hold the clergy in reverence. And now that he was grown rich, he made amends and satisfaction for all the deeds of his poverty. And he made Peter, whom we mentioned earlier and who had supported him in his poverty, richer than he had ever been.[57] And he gave the two daughters of this Peter to rich husbands ... So Robert thinking on these matters, found that Alberada, whom he held as wife, could not be his wife as they were related, and so he let her go. And he requested of Prince Gisulf of Salerno his sister whom he desired for the sake of her [lands] which she had received from Guaimar. And Gisulf gave him his sister with as large a dowry as he could.

73 Robert Guiscard, Pledge to Pope Nicholas II, 1059

A document of 1059 confirms the relationship of Robert Guiscard and Pope Nicholas II, in which Robert Guiscard pledges to pay tribute.

Le Liber Censuum de l'église romaine, ed. P. Fabre (Paris, 1905), i, pp. 421–2; trsl. G. A. Loud.

I Robert, by the grace of God and St Peter, duke of Apulia and Calabria and with the help of both in future of Sicily, in confirmation of the grant and in recognition of fealty, promise to pay annually from all the land which I hold personally under my rule, and which I have not up to the present time conceded to be held by any person from beyond the Alps, a tribute [*pensio*] from every yoke of oxen, namely twelve 'denarii' of Pavia, to be paid to you, my lord pope Nicholas, and to all your successors, or to you and your successors' representatives. This tribute shall be paid each year by the Sunday of the Holy Resurrection. I shall bind myself and my heirs or successors to this

57 Peter, son of Ami, the 'governor' of Bisignano in Calabria (Loud, 1991, 54–6).

obligation by paying tribute to you, my lord pope Nicholas, and to your successors. So help me God.

74 Orderic Vitalis, Deeds of the Dukes of the Normans

In *c.* 1109–13 Orderic Vitalis, monk at Saint-Evroult in Normandy, inserted into the Deeds of the Dukes of the Normans several chapters on the exploits of the Normans in southern Italy. His monastery had provided abbots and monks for several monasteries in Italy and Orderic was reasonably well informed. The legendary behaviour of Thurstan Scitel, however, has to be taken with a pinch of salt.

GND, ii. 155–9.

[Book VII, c. (30)] Then in the days of the Emperor Henry, son of Conrad, and Duke Robert of the Normans, Osmond Drengot, a courageous soldier, went to Apulia together with several other Normans.[58] This was because he had killed William named Repostel, a very well-known soldier, while hunting in the presence of Duke Robert.[59] Fearing the duke's anger and the fury of the noble family of the honourable soldier, he fled to Apulia. There out of regard for his great honesty the inhabitants of Benevento gave him an honourable welcome. Thereafter, from time to time, active Normans and Breton soldiers, inspired by Drengot's example, set out for Italy, where at first they bravely assisted the Lombards in their fight against the Saracens and the Greeks. By force of arms they often defeated the barbarians, and when all had experienced their strength they became much feared. The Lombards, however, having regained their security began to despise the Normans and withhold their pay from them. But when the Normans saw this they appointed one of their number as leader and took up arms against the Lombards. They captured the fortifications and valiantly subjugated the local inhabitants. The first leader of the Normans in Apulia, while they were still as newcomers mercenaries of Gaimar, duke of Salerno, was Thurstan called Scitel, a man skilled in many affairs.[60] Among other

58 Orderic conflates Henry II (1002–24) with Conrad II's son Henry III (1039–56); Osmond Drengot may be the same as Osmond, brother of Gilbert Buatère (above, no. **72**). According to Oderic (ii, 56) he fled first to Brittany and England.

59 William Repostel may be the same as Gilbert Buatère's companion William (above, no. **72**). Orderic (ii, 56) gives a more elaborate account in his Ecclesiastical History.

60 This Thurstan is sometimes identified with Trostayne/Torstainus Balbus, the leader of the Normans mentioned by the chroniclers at Montecassino.

examples of his courage, he once wrested a goat out of the mouth of a lion; the lion was furious that the goat should have been taken away from him, but Thurstan seized it with his bare hands and threw it over the walls of the duke's palace as if it were only some little dog. The Lombards with great envy wished him dead and led him to a certain spot where an enormous dragon dwelt, together with a vast multitude of snakes. Then seeing the dragon coming, they fled headlong. When Thurstan, ignorant of this trick, saw his comrades fly and in his amazement asked his armourbearer the reason for such a sudden flight, the flame-vomiting dragon suddenly came towards him and with his open mouth attacked the head of Thurstan's horse. Thurstan, his sword drawn, struck bravely and soon killed the wild beast, but infected by the dragon's poisonous breath he died two days later. Amazingly the flame erupted from the dragon's mouth had burnt his whole shield in an instant.

After the death of Thurstan the Normans chose Rainulf and Richard as their leaders, and under them avenged Thurstan's death by raising a serious rebellion against the Lombards.[61] Some time later Drogo of the Cotentin, son of Tancred of Hauteville, was chosen leader of the Normans in Apulia. He was praiseworthy in Christian religion and military prowess. Waszo, count of Naples, killed him at the altar of the church of St Laurence while he was invoking God and St Laurence during the eve of 10 August.[62] Thereafter his brother succeeded him in the principality and subjugated the whole of Apulia to the Normans. When Humphrey saw the end of his life approaching he entrusted his son Abelard together with the duchy to his brother Robert who was called Guiscard because of his cunning. This Robert surpassed his brothers, who were all dukes or counts, in courage, intellect and eminence, for he conquered Apulia, Calabria and Sicily and crossed the sea to invade a great part of Greece.[63] After inflicting a humiliating defeat on the Emperor Alexius, who had wickedly rebelled against his lord the Emperor Michael [VII Dukas, 1071–78], he forced him and his huge army to flee. He also performed many good deeds and restored many bishoprics and monasteries. As we mentioned above, he received Dom Robert, abbot of Saint-Evroult,

61 Rainulf, count of Aversa (c. 1029–45) is perhaps the same as Rainulf brother of Gilbert Buatère. Richard, son of Anquetil of Quarrel, is perhaps the son of Anquetil brother of Gilbert Buatère; he was count of Aversa from 1050 and prince of Capua from 1058 to 1078.

62 Count Drogo was killed in 1051.

63 See no. 77.

with kindness and gave him a little church situated on the coast of the
Calabrian sea, which was dedicated in honour of the virgin and
martyr St Eufemia.[64] In this magnanimous way he founded there a
great monastery and assembled a great number of monks to fight for
God. Bishops and nobles loved Father Robert, revering him and
supporting him with all their effort. Although he was indifferent to
the care of his own body, he sufficiently maintained those subject to
him with food and clothes and constrained and calmed their minds
with the discipline of the Rule. He was abbot of the same monastery
for almost seventeen years until on 13 December he happily passed to
the Lord.[65]

75   Orderic Vitalis, Ecclesiastical History

Orderic Vitalis (d. *c.* 1142) wrote his Ecclesiastical History from *c.* 1110 to *c.*
1142. In Book III, originally Book I, he gives a slightly different version
compared with his earlier work, no. 74.

Orderic, ii, 99–105.

After the death of Nicholas, Alexander [II, 1061–73] became pope; to
him came Abbot Robert with eleven monks of Saint-Evroult, and
gave a full and truthful account of the wrongs done to him and his
monks. The pope consoled them with paternal solicitude and gave
them the use of the church of St Paul the Apostle in the city of Rome,
so that they could live there according to their rule until he found a
dwelling suitable for them. Then Robert sought aid from his cousin
William of Montreuil, and found him more than willing to give help.[66]
This soldier, who was standard-bearer of the pope, had conquered
Campania by force of arms and forced the inhabitants, who were then
schismatics cut off from the Catholic Church, to accept the authority
of St Peter the Apostle. He gave his exiled kinsman and his monks
half an ancient city called Aquino. Afterwards Robert approached
Richard prince of Capua, son of Anquetil of Quarrel, who gave him
fair words, but never followed them up with deeds. When Robert
realised that he was being deceived by empty promises, he angrily
reminded the prince of his base parentage, of which he was well

64 Robert II of Grandmesnil, formerly abbot of Saint-Evroult, arrived in Calabria in
   1061.
65 He died after having taken part in the battle of Durazzo in December 1081.
66 William of Montreuil (d. between 1098 and 1114) was a son of Hugh of
   Grandmesnil and a nephew of his father's brother Abbot Robert.

ware; and shaking the dust off his feet he betook himself to Robert
Guiscard, duke of Calabria. The duke entertained him honourably as
is lord, and pressed him and his monks to settle permanently there.
His father Tancred of Hauteville was a native of the Cotentin, who
ad had twelve sons and several daughters by his two lawful wives.
He passed on his whole inheritance to his son Geoffrey, and advised
he others to seek their living by their strength and wits outside their
ative land.[67] They separately and at various times journeyed to
pulia, disguised as pilgrims with scrip and staff for fear of capture by
he Romans; all of them prospered in one way or another and became
ukes or counts in Apulia or Sicily: and their glorious and valiant
eeds have been described by the monk Geoffrey called Malaterra,
who recently wrote a distinguished book at the command of Roger,
ount of Sicily.[68] The greatest and most powerful of all was Robert
Guiscard, who held the principality of Apulia for many years after the
eath of his brothers Drogo and Humphrey. Next he won the duchy
f Calabria, by triumphing in battle over the Lombards and Greeks
who tried to defend their ancient rights and liberties behind the walls
f their great cities and towns. Crossing the Ionian sea with a small
ut formidable force of Normans and other northern people, he invaded
Macedonia, twice engaged Alexius the emperor of Constantinople in
attle and put him to flight with all his army after defeating him on
and and sea.[69]

The same warrior, as I was saying, welcomed Abbot Robert and his
monks with all honour and gave him the church of Sainte-Eufemia,
which stands on the shore of the Adriatic sea, where the ruins of an
ncient city called Brixia are still visible, telling him to build a
monastery there in honour of Mary the holy mother of God. The
reat duke and other Norman lords endowed the church with great
states, and commended themselves to the prayers of the faithful who
ere to fight for Christ then and in the years to come. Fresenda, wife
f Tancred of Hauteville, was buried there; and in return her son
Guiscard gave a large estate to the church. The same prince put the
monastery of the Holy Trinity at Venosa under the authority of
rother Robert.[70] He selected Berengar son of Arnold of Heugon,

---

7 Orderic is mistaken here. Not Geoffrey but Serlo stayed in Normandy, see no. **71**.
8 The author Geoffrey Malaterra dedicated his work to Roger I, count of Sicily
(1072–1101).
9 The battle of Durazzo took place in 1081.
0 Venosa was restored by Drogo of Hauteville between 1046–51. His only surviving
Italian charter is for Venosa (Ménager, no. 1).

monk of Saint-Evroul, to govern the monastery at Venosa, an
presented him to Pope Alexander. After his blessing he governed th
church of Venosa ably throughout the pontificates of Alexander [II
and Gregory [VII, 1073–85] and Desiderius [1086–87], until in th
time of Pope Urban [II 1088–99] he was elected by the people a
bishop of the city.[71] He was nobly born and had been brought up fror
childhood under Abbot Thierry at Saint-Evroult as a soldier of Chris
he excelled in reading and chanting and above all in calligraphy.
Following his abbot, as I have related, he received from him th
pastoral cure. The little flock of twenty monks entrusted to his car
was entirely given up to wordly vanities and neglectful of divir
worship; but by the grace of God he increased their number to
hundred and reformed their morals so thoroughly that they provide
several bishops and abbots to govern the holy church for the glory o
the true King and the salvation of souls. In addition the generou
duke gave a third monastery, built in the city of Mileto in honour o
St Michael, to Abbot Robert; and he appointed as its head Willian
son of Ingran, who had been born and ordained priest at Sain
Evroul, but took his monastic vows at Sainte-Eufemia. So in thes
three Italian monasteries the liturgy of Saint-Evroult is chanted an
the monastic rule has been observed to the present day, as far as th
customs of the region and the allegiance of the inhabitants allow.

Abbot Robert had two sisters, Judith and Emma, who had taken u
their abode in the chapel of Saint-Evroul at Ouche and were believe
to have renounced the world to take the veil and serve God alone i
purity of heart and body. But when they heard that their brothe
Robert was honoured by the secular power in Apulia, whilst they i
Normandy were despised and helpless, they took the road for Ital
and, putting off the sacred veil, threw themselves whole-heartedl
into a wordly life. Both married without telling their husbands tha
they were vowed to God. Roger, count of Sicily, took Judith to wif
and another count whose name I cannot recall married Emma.[73] S
both of them abandoned the veil, the token of holy religion, for love o
the world; and because they were faithless to their first vows bot
remained childless all their lives, and for a short period of earthl
happiness incurred the wrath of the heavenly bridegroom.[74]

71 For Abbot Berengar, see Ménager, nos 50, 58 and 60.

72 Thierry, abbot of Saint-Evroult (c. 1048–57).

73 Judith married Count Roger I of Sicily (d. 1101); Emma's husband is unidentifie

74 Judith had several children, including at least five daughters, three of whom ar
   known by name: Matilda, Adelisa and Emma (Houben, 1996, 108–9).

76 Robert of Torigni, Deeds of the Dukes of the Normans

Robert of Torigni, monk at Le Bec, wrote his interpolations in the Deeds of the Dukes of the Normans *c.* 1139.

GND, ii, 191–3.

[Book VII, c. (43)] At that time Robert Guiscard, Norman-born duke of Apulia, died. This man had been divorced on grounds of consanguinity from his first wife, by whom he had a son called Bohemond, and he had then married Sichelgaita, the eldest daughter of Gaimar, prince of Salerno, with the permission of her brother Gisulf, who had succeeded his father. A younger sister Gatteclima [Gaitelgrima] married Jordan, prince of Capua, son of Richard the elder and father of Richard the younger. Jordan's grandfather was Rainulf, who had been the first leader of the Normans in Apulia and who had also founded the town of Aversa. By Sichelgaita Robert Guiscard had three sons and five daughters, who were married off so highly that one of them even was betrothed to the emperor of Constantinople.[75] This Robert defeated two emperors in one year, Alexius of the Greeks in Greece and Henry of the Romans in Italy.[76] So complete was Henry's rout that, aware of the duke's fame and rightly trusting neither the Saxon nor the German forces, nor the walls of that city, which is the capital of the world, to protect him, he fled in haste. Because he had many possessions in Apulia, Bohemond finally succeeded in subduing the Saracens, who then held most of the cities in Romania, with the help of other Normans and Frenchmen. After this victory over the heathens, and those over the cities of Antioch and Jerusalem as well as many others, Bohemond was chosen prince of Antioch, as after him his heirs, namely his son Bohemond born of Constance daughter of Philip, king of the French, and after him Raymond son of William, count of Poitou, who had married Bohemond II's daughter.[77]

When Robert [Guiscard] died, Roger, nicknamed Borsa, who was his son by a second wife [Sichelgaita], succeeded him.[78] After Roger's death as well as that of his sons, his nephew Roger, son of Roger, count of Sicily and brother of Robert Guiscard, was sole ruler of both

75 See no. **77**.

76 Robert exaggerates this, for the battle of Durazzo took place in 1081 and the start of the siege of Rome in 1084.

77 Bohemond I, prince of Antioch (d. 1111); Bohemond II (d. 1130); his daughter Constance married in 1136 Raymond of Poitou.

78 Roger Borsa, duke of Apulia (1085–1111).

Apulia and Sicily.[79] Duke Roger II in due course became king, which was a bone of contention between two rival popes who were both ordained at Rome, namely Innocent II and Peter Leonis.[80] The latter had allowed Duke Roger to be crowned on the condition that the duke would support his case. This took place about the year of the Lord 1130, after which year both lived for almost eight more years.

Byzantium

77 Anna Comnena, Life of Alexius Comnenus (on Robert Guiscard)

The biography of Emperor Alexius Comnenus (1081–1118), known as the *Alexiad*, was written by his eldest daughter Anna Comnena between *c.* 1138 and her death in the mid-1150s, when she was an elderly widow living outside the court in exile. Anna herself was born on 1 December 1084. After a brief engagement to Constantine, son of Emperor Michael VII Dukas, she married the statesman and historian Nicephorus Bryennius (d. 1134). They had four children, two sons Alexius and John, and two daughters of whom one was called Irene. Anna's biography of her father is one of the few medieval chronicles written by a woman and the only one written by a daughter about her father. Her account of the Normans in Italy is highly biased in favour of Alexius and negative about Robert Guiscard and his sons Roger and Bohemond. Despite her bitterness towards the Normans she cannot conceal her admiration for Robert Guiscard. Her portrait of him is one of the most famous passages from her book. Anna never met Robert or his sons but she relied on her father's stories as well as other eyewitness accounts of those who had seen them in the flesh, above all her husband Nicephorus Bryennius who was one of the Byzantine commanders dealing with Bohemond in 1097 and 1107.[81]

The Alexiad of Anna Comnena, trsl. E. R. A. Sewter (Harmondsworth, 1969) pp. 53–5, 57, 58–61, 66, 69, 131–3, 139, 142–5.

[Book I, c. 10] ... Sometimes, though, it was Fate which introduced into it [the Roman state = Italy] from outside certain foreign pretenders – an evil hard to combat, an incurable disease. One such was that braggart Robert, notorious for his power-lust, born in Normandy, but

79 Roger's son William died in 1127. Roger II, count of Sicily (1105–30), king of Sicily (1130–54).

80 Innocent II (1130–43) and Anacletus II (Peter Leonis) (1130–38).

81 For commentaries on Anna's work, see Howard-Johnston, 1996, 260–302 and Loud, 1991, 41–57.

nursed and nourished by manifold Evil.[82] This was the man whose
enmity the Roman empire [Byzantium] drew upon itself when it gave
a pretext to our foes for the wars he waged – a marriage with a
foreigner and a barbarian, from our point of view quite inexpedient.
To be more accurate, one should blame the imprudence of the
emperor then reigning, who linked our family with that of the Ducas.
Now if I should find fault with any one of my own blood-relations (for
I too on my mother's side am related to the Ducas), let nobody be
angry. I have chosen to write the truth above all and as far as this
man is concerned I have toned down the universal condemnation of
him. This particular emperor, Michael Ducas, promised his own son
Constantine in marriage to the daughter of this barbarian Robert, and
from that sprang their hostile acts.[83] About Constantine, the terms of
his marriage contract and the foreign alliance in general, his handsome appearance and stature, his physical and moral qualities we
shall speak in due course, when I relate the sorry tale of my own misfortunes. Before that I will give an account of this proposed wedding,
the defeat of the whole barbarian force and the destruction of
these pretenders from Normandy – pretenders whom Michael in his
folly raised up against the Roman empire. But first I must carry my
story back somewhat to describe this man Robert, his lineage and
fortune; I must show to what heights of power the force of circumstances raised him, or rather, to speak more reverently, how far Providence allowed him to advance, indulging his ill-natured ambitions
and schemings.

This Robert was a Norman by birth, of obscure origin, with an
overbearing character and a thoroughly villainous mind; he was a
brave fighter, very cunning in his assaults on the wealth and power of
great men; in achieving his aims absolutely inexorable, diverting
criticism by incontrovertible argument. He was a man of immense
stature, surpassing even the biggest men; he had a ruddy complexion,
fair hair, broad shoulders, eyes that all but shot sparks of fire. In a
well-built man one looks for breadth here and slimness there; in him

32 Robert Guiscard, son of Tancred of Hauteville, came to Italy *c.* 1046, where he
became duke of Calabria and Apulia in 1059 and died in 1085. His wars against
Alexius Comnenus (1081–1118) in the Balkans lasted several years during the
early 1080s.

33 Michael VII Dukas (1071–78). His son Constantine was betrothed first to Robert
Guiscard's daughter Helena, also known as Olympias, in 1074. She went to Constantinople in 1076 but after the fall of Michael Dukas in 1078, according to
Orderic Vitalis, was eventually sent back to Italy (Von Valkenhausen, 1982, 56–
73). Constantine was then betrothed to Anna Comnena herself.

all was admirably well-proportioned and elegant. Thus from head to foot the man was graceful (I have often heard from many witnesses that this was so). Homer remarked of Achilles that when he shouted his hearers had the impression of a multitude in uproar, but Robert's bellow, so they say, put tens of thousands to flight. With such endowments of fortune and nature and soul, he was, as you would expect, no man's slave, owing obedience to nobody in all the world. Such are men of powerful character, people say, even if they are of humbler origin.

[Book I, c. 11] Robert then, being a man of such character, wholly incapable of being led, set out from Normandy with some knights; there were five of them and thirty foot-soldiers in all. After leaving his native land, he spent some time amid the mountain peaks and caves and hills of Lombardy, at the head of a band of pirates, attacking wayfarers. Sometimes he acquired horses, sometimes other possessions and arms. The start of his career was marked by bloodshed and many murders. While he loitered in the districts of Lombardy, he did not escape the notice of William Mascabeles who at that time happened to be the ruler of most of the territory adjacent to Lombardy.[84] From it he derived a rich income every year, and he also recruited adequate forces from the same area [where] he was a powerful magnate. Having learnt what kind of man Robert was, from a moral as well as a physical point of view, he unwisely attached the man to himself and betrothed one of his daughters to him. The marriage was celebrated and William admired his son-in-law for his strength and military prowess, but things did not prosper for him as he had hoped. He had already given him a city as something of a wedding present and had shown certain other signs of friendship. Robert, however, became obnoxious and plotted rebellion ...

[Then follows the story of William's defeat and imprisonment by Robert Guiscard]

In this way Robert put an end to their charge, and as for 'Mascabeles', he was at once led off as a prisoner-of-war in bonds to the very castle which he had given to Robert as a wedding present when he betrothed to him his daughter. So it came about that the city then had its own

---

84 Anna Comnena is mistaken about William Mascabeles. He was not the father-in-law of Robert Guiscard. Her mistake is founded in legends surrounding Robert Guiscard which reached her from southern Italy; it might be based on a corruption of the biblical epithet 'Maccabeus' carried by two members of the Buonalberge family, to whom Robert's first wife Alberada belonged, at the beginning of the twelfth century (Loud, 1991, 55–6).

1aster as a prisoner, and naturally was thereafter called 'Phrourion' 'garrisoned fort']. The details of Robert's cruelty are horrifying in the extreme, for when he had 'Mascabeles' completely in his power, he rst had all his teeth pulled out, demanding for each one of them an normous sum of money and asking him where he had hidden it. As e did not cease pulling out the teeth till all had gone, and as teeth nd money were exhausted at the same time, he then turned to William's eyes. Grudging him the power of sight, he blinded him.

Book I, c. 12] He was now master of all and from that time his ower increased day by day. As his ambitions grew he kept adding ity to city and piling up his wealth. To cut a long story short, he ttained high rank and was named 'Duke of all Lombardy', which rovoked the jealousy of everyone.[85] However, being a wary fellow, he nitigated the popular movements against himself, cajoling some of is adversaries and bribing others; by his cleverness he moderated the nvy of the nobles. Occasionally he had recourse to arms. By these neans he brought under his personal control the whole of Lombardy nd the surrounding areas. He was always thinking out some more mbitious project. He seized on the pretext of his connexion by mar- iage with the Emperor Michael [VII Dukas, 1071–78] and dreamed f ascending the throne himself. The war against the Romans Byzantines] was kindled anew. We have mentioned before that Michael, for some extraordinary reason, had agreed to unite his own on Constantine in marriage with Robert's daughter (the lady's name vas Helena) ... Robert who from a most undignified condition had ttained great distinction, having gathered about him powerful forces vas aiming to become Roman [Byzantine] emperor. Consequently he vas devising plausible excuses for his hatred and warlike attitude to he Romans [Byzantines].

At this point there are two different versions of the story. Accord- ng to one, which is widespread and first reached our ears, a monk alled Raiktor impersonated the Emperor Michael and fled to Robert, he father of his (supposed) daughter-in-law. He told him a pitiable ale of his own misfortunes. This Michael, you see, had seized the Roman sceptre after Diogenes and for a brief moment graced the hrone, but was deprived of power by the rebel Botaniates;[86] he submitted to the life of a monk and later wore the alb of a high priest

---

5 *Longobardia* (Lombardy) was the Greek name for the province of Apulia.

36 Romanus IV Diogenes, emperor 1068–71; Nicephorus III Botaniates, emperor 1078–81; John was the brother of Constantine X, emperor 1059–67.

and the mitre; you may even add the humeral. It was the Caesar John
his paternal uncle, who counselled him to do this, for he knew the
fickleness of the new emperor and feared that some more dreadful fate
might befall him. The aforementioned monk, Raiktor, pretended that
he was Michael, but maybe I had better call him Rektes, for he was
the most brazen-faced 'doer' of them all. Well, he approached Robert
because forsooth he was related to him by marriage, and he acted out
his tale of injustice, how he had been deprived of the imperial throne
and reduced to his present state, which Robert could see for himself.
Helena, the lovely young wife of his son, he said, had been left
defenceless, entirely cut off from her young bridegroom, for his son
Constantine and the Empress Maria, he proclaimed loudly, had been
forced against their will to join the party of Botaniates.[87] With these
words he stirred the anger of the barbarian and drove him to arms in
a war against the Romans [Byzantines]. Such is the story which came
to my ears and I do not find it surprising that some persons of
completely obscure origin impersonate others of noble birth and
glorious reputation. But my ears are also assailed by another version
of the affair and this is more convincing.

According to the second authority it was not a monk who impersonated Michael, nor was it any such action which prompted Robert
to make war on the Romans [Byzantines], but the barbarian himself
with great versatility willingly invented the whole story. The subsequent events apparently came about as follows. Robert, they say,
was a thoroughly unscrupulous rascal and working hard for a conflict
with the Romans [Byzantines]; he had for a long time been making
preparations for the war; but he was prevented by some of his more
reputable friends and by his own wife Gaita [Sichelgaita], on the
grounds that he would be starting an unjust war and one directed
against Christians.[88] Several times his attempts to begin such an
enterprise were put off. However, as he was determined to invent an
excuse for war that would be plausible, he sent some men to Corone
with certain instructions (having informed them first of his secret
designs). If they met any monk who was willing to cross from there to
Italy in order to worship at the shrine of the two great apostles, the
patron saints of Rome, and if his outward appearance did not manifest
too lowly an origin, they were to embrace him gladly, make a friend of
him, and bring him to Robert. When they discovered the afore-

---

87 Empress Maria had married both Michael VII and Nicephorus III Botaniates.

88 Robert Guiscard had first married Alberada, whom he divorced in 1058 or 1059
when he married Sichelgaita, daughter of Guaimar IV of Salerno.

mentioned Raiktor, who was a clever fellow, a criminal beyond compare, they sent a message to Robert in a letter (he was staying at Salerno at the time). It read: 'Your kinsman Michael, deposed from his throne, has arrived and asks for your assistance.' This was the secret code which Robert had asked them to use. With this letter in his hand Robert at once went to his wife and read it aloud to her privately. Then he gathered together all the counts and, again privately, showed them the letter. He thought no doubt that he had seized on a fine excuse and they would no longer oppose his schemes. Since they all supported his plan without hesitation, he brought Raiktor over and made his acquaintance. After that he dramatised the whole business, with the monk at the centre of the stage. It was said that he was the Emperor Michael; that he had been deprived of his throne; that his wife and son and all his possessions had been taken from him by the pretender Botaniates; that contrary to justice and all right dealing he had been invested not with the crown and emperor's headband, but with the garb of a monk. 'Now', said Robert, 'he has come as a suppliant to us.' These remarks were made public by Robert and he said it was of prime importance that he should be restored because of his kinship with himself. The monk was every day honoured by him as if he were indeed the Emperor Michael; he was allotted a better seat at the table, a more elevated throne and exceptional respect. Robert's public speeches were suited to the occasion: sometimes he spoke in self-pity, bewailing the fate of his daughter; at other times he would spare the feelings of his 'kinsman' by not referring to the troubles which had befallen on him; and then again he would rouse the barbarians about him and incite them to war by cleverly promising heaps of gold which he guaranteed to get for them from the Roman empire. Thus he led them all by the nose and when he set out he drew after him rich and poor alike – it might be more accurate to say that he drew away the whole of Lombardy when he occupied Salerno, the capital city of Amalfi. There he made excellent arrangements for his other daughters and then prepared for the campaign. Two of the daughters were with him;[89] the third, of course, who had been unfortunate from the day of her betrothal, was held in Constantinople. Her young betrothed, being still a young boy, shrank from the union from the outset, just as babies are scared by Mormo.[90] One daughter he had pledged to Raymond, son of the count Barcinon

---

89 For Robert's daughters, apart from Helena, see Chalandon, 1907, i, 283 and above, no. **70**.

90 A horrible monster used by nurses to frighten children.

[Barcelona];[91] the other he married off to Ebalus, who was himself a count of great distinction.[92] Nor did these alliances prove unprofitable for Robert; in fact, from all sources he had consolidated and amassed power for himself – from his family, from his rule, from his inheritance rights, from all manner of ways which another man would not even consider ...

[Book I, c. 14] [Robert prepares to cross the Adriatic Sea] ... He did, however, send an additional note to the pope, saying that he had instructed his son Roger (whom he had appointed ruler of all Apulia together with his brother Boritylas) to go with the utmost zeal to the aid of the pope, whenever he called for it; he was to attack King Henry [IV] with a strong force. His younger son Bohemond he sent with powerful forces to our country.[93] He was to descend on the districts round Avlona. Bohemond resembled his father in all respects, in daring, strength, aristocratic and indomitable spirit. In short, Bohemond was the exact replica and living image of his father. He at once attacked Canina, Hiericho and Avlona like a streaking thunderbolt, with threats and irrepressible fury. He seized them and fighting on took the surrounding areas bit by bit and destroyed them by fire. Bohemond was in fact like the acrid smoke which preceded the fire, the preliminary skirmish which comes before the great assault. Father and son you might liken to caterpillars and locusts, for what was left by Robert, his son fed on and devoured. But we must not get him across to Avlona yet. Let us examine what he did on the opposite mainland ...

[Book I, c. 15] Robert set out from Salerno and arrived at Otranto. There he stayed for a few days waiting for his wife Gaita [Sichelgaita] (she went on campaign with her husband and when she donned armour was indeed a formidable sight). She came and he embraced her; then both started with all the army again for Brindisi, the seaport with the finest harbour in the whole of Japygia.[94] He swooped down on the city and stopped there, watching anxiously for the assembling of all his forces and all his ships, transports and long ships and

---

91 Matilda married first Raymond-Berengar, count of Barcelona (d. 1082) and secondly Aimery, vicomte of Narbonne (Szabolcs de Vajay, 1971, 129–47).

92 Sibyl married Ebalus, count of Roucy (d. 1103).

93 Roger Borsa, son of Robert Guiscard and Sichelgaita, duke of Apulia (1085–1111); Bohemond, later prince of Antioch (1098–1111), was his son by Alberada; Boritylas is Robert Guiscard's nephew Count Robert I of Loritello, son of his brother Geoffrey.

94 *Japygia*, Roman name for 'heel' of Italy.

fighting vessels, because it was from Brindisi that he expected to sail to these shores ...

[Book I, c. 16] Robert concentrated his whole force at Brindisi, ships and men.[95] The ships numbered 150, and the soldiers, all told, came to 30,000 each ship carrying 200 men with armour and horses. The expedition was equipped thus because they would probably meet the enemy in full armour and mounted when they landed. He intended to disembark at the city of Epidamnos, which in accordance with modern tradition we will call Dyrrachium.[96] He had thought of crossing from Otranto to Nicopolis and of capturing Naupaktos and all the country and forts around it, but as the distance by sea between these two towns was far greater than the voyage from Brindisi to Dyrrachium, he chose the latter; it was not only the fastest route but he was looking to the comfort of his men, for it was the winter season and the sun being on its way to the southern hemisphere and approaching the Tropic of Capricorn the daylight hours were shortened. Rather than leave Otranto at daybreak and voyage by night with possible heavy weather, he preferred to cross from Brindisi under full sail. The Adriatic is not so wide at this point so the sea distance is correspondingly shorter. Robert altered his mind about his son Roger. Originally, when he appointed him count of Apulia he had intended to leave him behind, but for some unknown reason he included him in his retinue. On the voyage to Dyrrachium a side-expedition made him master of the strongly fortified town of Corfu and some other of our forts. He received hostages from Lombardy and Apulia, raised money and exacted tribute from the whole country and looked forward to a landing at Dyrrachium.

[Book III, c. 12] ... Meanwhile Robert arrived at Otranto, and after handing over all his own authority to his son Roger (including the government of Lombardy itself) he went from there to the harbour of Brindisi. In that city he learnt that Palaeologus had reached Dyrrachium.[97] Without delay wooden towers were constructed in the larger vessels and covered with leather hides; everything essential for a siege was hastily put on board the ships; horses and armed knights embarked on dromons; and when military supplies from all quarters had been made ready with extraordinary rapidity, Robert was anxious

95 For Robert Guiscard's naval tactics, see Bennett, 1992, 41–58.

96 Dyrrachium is now called Durazzo.

97 George Palaeologus was the Byzantine governor (*doux*) of Dyrrachium.

to make the crossing at once. His plan was to surround Dyrrachium the moment he got there with *helepoleis* by land and sea – for two reasons:[98] first, he would terrify the inhabitants; second, having isolated them completely, he would take the city at the first assault. News of these preparations filled the islanders with consternation; people living on the coast by Dyrrachium were equally dismayed. When he was satisfied that all was ready, the stern cables were loosed and the whole fleet of dromons, triremes and monoremes, drawn up in order of battle according to naval tradition, began the voyage in disciplined fashion. Robert had a favourable wind, made Avlona on the other side, and coasted along as far as Butrinto. There he was joined by his son Bohemond, who had crossed before him and had captured Avlona without difficulty. The whole army was now divided into two: one half, under Robert himself, was to make the sea passage to Dyrrachium (that was Robert's intention); the other, entrusted to Bohemond, was to march on the city by land. Robert had actually passed Corfu and altered course for Dyrrachium when, off a promontory called Glossa, he was suddenly struck by a tremendous storm. There was a heavy fall of snow and winds blowing furiously from the mountains lashed up the sea. There was a howling noise as the waves built up; oars snapped off as the rowers plunged them into the water, the sails were torn to shreds by the blasts, yard-arms were crushed and fell on the decks; and now ships were being swallowed up, crew and all. And yet it was summer season; the sun had already passed the Tropic of Cancer and was on its way to the Lion – the season when the Dog-star rises, so they say. Everybody was confused and dismayed, not knowing what to do, unable to resist such enemies. A terrible cry arose as they groaned and lamented, calling on God, imploring His aid and praying that they might see the mainland. But the tempest did not die down, as if God were venting His wrath on Robert for the unyielding, presumptuous arrogance of the man; as if He were showing by a sign at the very outset that the end would be disastrous. Anyway, some of the ships sank and their crews drowned with them, others were dashed against the headlands and broke up. The hides that covered the towers were slackened by the rain, so that the nails fell out and the hides naturally became heavier; their weight caused the wooden towers to collapse. They fell in ruins and sank the ships. Robert's own vessel, although half-shattered, barely made its way to safety, and some transport ships also escaped, unbelievably without

98 *Helepoleis* are siege engines.

losing their crews. Many corpses were thrown up by the waves, and not a few purses and other objects brought by the sailors of Robert's fleet were strewn on the sand. The survivors buried their dead with all due ceremony, but because it was no easy matter to inter so many they suffered horribly from the stench. They would soon have perished of hunger too, for all their supplies had been lost, if all the crops had not been ripe and fields and gardens bursting with fruits. What had happened was significant to all men of right judgement, but not to Robert. None of it frightened him or affected his iron nerve. If he did pray that his life might be spared, it was only, I suppose, for as long as he could wage war on his chosen enemies. The disaster by no means deterred him from the immediate aim and with the survivors (for a few had been rescued from danger by the invincible might of God) he stayed for a week in Glabinitza to recover his own strength and rest his shipwrecked mariners, but also to give time to the soldiers left behind in Brindisi, indeed to those whom he was expecting from another quarter to arrive by sea. He was also waiting for the heavily armed knights and infantry, together with light-armed forces, to cross by the overland route (they had started a little before himself). When all contingents, coming by land and sea, were united, he occupied the Illyrian plain in full force. The Latin who gave me this information was with him, an envoy, he said, from the bishop of Bari sent to Robert.[99] They set up huts inside the ruined walls of the city formerly called Epidamnos. It was in this place that Pyrrhus, king of Epirus, once lived. He joined with the men of Tarentum against the [classical] Romans and fought a fierce campaign in Apulia. As a result there was so much carnage that the whole population was put to the sword without exception and the city was left entirely without inhabitants. In later times, however, according to Greek tradition and indeed according to the evidence of carved inscriptions there, Amphion and Zethos restored it to its present condition and the name was immediately changed to Dyrrachium. So much then for my digression on this place; with it I end my third book. The fourth will relate what happened thereafter ...

[Book IV, c. 3] ... Robert's warlike instinct told him that the war must go on; he would have to fight hard. But there were difficulties: because of the winter he was unable to launch his ships; the Roman

---

99 Archbishop Ursus of Bari (1080–89) was one of Robert Guiscard's key ecclesiastical supporters (Loud, 1991, 46). This passage is a good example of Anna's use of eyewitness accounts.

and Venetian fleets, tirelessly patrolling the straits, prevented reinforcements crossing from Lombardy and the delivery of necessary supplies to him from that area was impeded. But when the spring came and the winter storms died down, the Venetians made the first move. They weighed anchor and took the offensive. Behind them came Maurice with the Roman fleet.[100] Very heavy fighting ensued and Robert's men were routed again. This convinced him that all his ships would have to be dragged up on land, whereupon the islanders, the inhabitants of the little palaces along the coast of the mainland, and all the others who were paying tribute to Robert, becoming courageous at his misfortunes and hearing about his defeat on the sea, were not so ready to meet the heavy obligations he laid on them. Obviously he would have to plan the war with greater care; a new campaign by sea and land was inevitable. He had ideas but it was impossible to carry them out: strong winds were blowing at that time and through dread of shipwreck he lingered for two months in the port of Hiericho. Nevertheless he was making ready and organising his forces for battle, intending to fight by sea and land. To the best of their ability the Venetians and Romans kept up their naval blockade and when there was a little improvement in the weather – enough to encourage would-be sailors – they thwarted all efforts at a crossing from the west. Robert's men, bivouacking by the River Glykys, meanwhile found it no easy matter to get supplies from the mainland, for when they left their entrenchments to forage or bring in other necessities there was interference from Dyrrachium. They began to starve. There was other trouble: the strangeness of the climate distressed them much, so that in the course of three months, it is said, up to 10,000 men perished. This disease attacked Robert's cavalry too and many died; in fact, of the knights as many as 500 counts and elite fighting men became victims of disease and famine, while in the lower ranks of the cavalry the number of dead was incalculable. His ships, as I have said, were drawn up on land by Glykys, but when after the winter and the coming of the spring the weather became hotter and rainless, the water-level dropped; there was not the normal flow from the mountain streams. Consequently he was in an awkward situation; the ships could not now be launched in the sea again. Despite his troubles, Robert, being a man of great intelligence and versatility, ordered piles to be driven in on either side of the river; these were then tightly bound together with osiers; very tall trees were felled at the roots and laid behind these piles; and sand was spread on them, in

100 Maurice, a Byzantine naval commander of outstanding skill and experience.

order to direct the flow into one course, concentrated so to speak into one canal formed by the stakes. Gradually pools formed and the water filled the whole of the artificial channel until it became deep enough to raise the ships, which had rested on the land and were now afloat. After that, when there was a good flow of water, the vessels were easily launched into the sea.

[Book IV, c. 4] [Palaeologus requests support from Constantinople, and Emperor Alexius, having decided to come himself, hears the latest news of Robert's preparation for the siege of Dyrrachium] ... On his arrival at Thessalonica, many informers confirmed the news about Robert, and in greater detail. When Robert was ready and when he had built up his soldiers' morale, he collected a great amount of wood on the plain of Dyrrachium and pitched camp about a bow-shot's length from the walls. There was news too of Palaeologus; from several sources the emperor heard about his careful preparations. He had already made up his mind to burn the wooden tower built by Robert and on the walls there were catapults, naphtha, pitch and small pieces of dry wood. He waited for the enemy's attack. As he expected it to take place on the next day, he set up a wooden tower of his own, inside the city and directly opposite the other. It was ready well in time; in fact, all through the night he experimented with a beam placed on top of it. The intention was to thrust forward this beam against the doors of Robert's tower when it was brought to the wall. He was testing it, to find out whether it could be moved without difficulty and falling right in the path of the enemy's doors stop them from being opened in the usual way. Being assured that the beam did thrust forward easily and could successfully perform its function, he had no more worries about the coming battle. On the next day, Robert ordered all his men to take up arms; some 500, infantry and fully equipped horsemen, were led into the tower and it was brought near to the wall. They hurried to open the door on the top, intending to use it as a draw-bridge to cross over into the citadel, but Palaeologus at that very moment thrust forward his own huge beam by means of the mechanical devices prepared in advance and with the help of many brave men. As the beam made it absolutely impossible to open the door, Robert's strategem was frustrated. Then a never-ending shower of arrows was directed at the Kelts on the summit and they, unable to bear it any longer, took cover.[101] He now gave orders to set the tower alight; before the last words were uttered the thing

101 For Kelts as one of the names for Normans, see Shepard, 1992, 277.

was on fire. The Kelts on top threw themselves over, those below
opened up the door at the bottom and fled. Seeing this Palaeologus
immediately led out some fully armed soldiers by the postern gate and
others with axes, to smash up the tower. Here too he was successful,
for with the top on fire and the lower parts broken up with stone-
cutters' tools, it was completely destroyed.

[Book IV, c. 5] According to the informant, Robert was hastening to
build a second tower, similar to the first, and was making ready
helepoleis against the city. Aware of the need for speedy help, Alexius
pressed on. When he arrived at Dyrrachium, he made an entrench-
ment for his army by the banks of the River Charzanes. Without
delay messengers were sent to ask Robert why he had come and what
he intended to do. Alexius meanwhile went off to the sanctuary
dedicated to Nicholas, the greatest of pontiffs, which was four stades
from the city. He reconnoitred the ground, hoping to pick the most
favourable site for a battle-line before Robert could do so. It was then
15 October. A neck of land extended from Dalmatia to the sea, ending
in a promontory which was almost surrounded by water; on this the
sanctuary was built. On the side facing Dyrrachium there was a gentle
slope down to the plain, with the sea on the left and a high, over-
hanging mountain on the right. At this point the Roman army was
concentrated and camp pitched. Then George Palaeologus was
summoned. But he, with long experience of such matters, refused to
come, making it clear to the emperor that he reckoned it unwise to
leave the city. Alexius again sent for him, more urgently this time, but
in vain. Palaeologus replied: 'To me it seems absolutely fatal to leave
the citadel under siege. Unless I see your majesty's seal-ring, I will
not come out.' The ring was sent and he at once joined the emperor
with some warships. Alexius asked him about Robert's actions and
when he had received a full and accurate account went on, 'Ought I to
risk a battle with him?' Palaeologus thought not, for the time being.
Certain others too who had many years of experience in war earnestly
opposed the idea and advised him to adopt a waiting policy; he should
try to reduce Robert by skirmishing and by preventing his men from
leaving camp to forage or plunder; the same plan should be forced on
Bodinus and the Dalmatians and the rest of the chieftains in the
neighbouring districts. They were sure that Robert could be easily
defeated if he took these measures. The majority of the young chieftains preferred to fight, especially Constantinus Porphyrogenitus,
Nicephorus Synadenus, Nampites the commander of the Varangians,

and even the sons of the former emperor Romanus Diogenes, Leo and Nicephorus.[102] While these arguments were going on the envoys returned from Robert and delivered his answer: 'I have not come to fight your majesty – that was not my intention at all – but rather to avenge the wrong done to my father-in-law. If you wish to make peace with me, I too welcome it, provided that you are ready to fulfil the conditions stated by my ambassadors to you.' He was demanding quite impossible terms, which were also harmful to the empire, although he did promise at the same time that, if he got what he wanted, he would regard Lombardy itself as his by permission of the emperor, and he would help us when need arose. It was merely a pretext: by demanding terms he would give the appearance of desiring peace himself; by proposing the impossible and failing to obtain it he would have an excuse to make war, and then hold the Roman emperor responsible for the fighting. Anyway his proposals were out of the question and he failed. So, having called together all the counts, he addressed them: 'You know the wrong done by the emperor Nicephorus Botaniates to my father-in-law, and the disgrace suffered by my daughter Helena when she was thrown out of the palace with him. Finding this intolerable we have left our country to avenge the insult and punish Botaniates. But he has been deprived of his throne and now we have to deal with a young emperor and a brave soldier, who has acquired an experience of the military art beyond his years; we must not take up his challenge in a light-hearted manner. Where there are many masters, there will be confusion, brought about by the diverse strategies of the many. In future therefore one man among us should command the rest; he should consult all, not adopting his own schemes in an autocratic way and according to his own caprice; the others will openly express to him their own opinions, but at the same time accept the counsel of the elected leader. Here is one man who is ready to obey your unanimously elected leader – I am the first to agree.' Everyone praised this plan and complimented Robert on his speech. There and then, without any dissension, they offered him the leadership. For a while he dissembled, like a girl acting coyly, and refused to accept, but they pressed him all the more and begged him. In the end he yielded, apparently in reply to their entreaties, although

102 Constantinus Dukas, son of Michael VII (born 1060), died at the battle of Durazzo in 1081 as did Nicephorus Synadenus. Nampites was a leader of the Anglo-Saxon Varangians and, thus, probably of English origin. The sons of Romanus IV Diogenes are also known from other sources. I am indebted to Jonathan Shepard for these details.

he had been plotting this in fact for a long time. After an involved series of arguments and a catalogue of reasons cleverly linked together, he made it appear, to those who did not understand his mentality, that he was coming involuntarily to what he really desired with all his heart. He ended his speech thus: 'Listen to my advice, you counts and the rest of the army. We have left our native lands and come here to fight against an emperor of great courage, one who has only recently seized the helmet of power, but has won many wars in the reigns of his predecessors and brought to them most powerful rebels as prisoners of war. All our energies therefore must be devoted to this struggle. If God grants us the victory, we shall no longer be in want of money. That is why we must burn all our baggage, hole our transport ships and send them to the bottom of the sea, and take up this challenge from him as if today is the supreme decider of life and death.' They all agreed with him.

78   Anna Comnena, Life of Alexius Comnenus (on Roussel of Bailleul)

Anna Comnena on Roussel of Bailleul (d. *c.* 1080), one of the Norman mercenaries in Byzantium.

The Alexiad of Anna Comnena, trsl. E. R. A. Sewter (Harmondsworth, 1969), pp. 31–2, 33, 36.

[Book I, c. 1] In the reign of Michael Ducas after the downfall of the Emperor Diogenes, the Roussel episode proved how valiant he was.[103] Roussel was a Kelt and had previously joined the Roman [= Byzantine] army. His good fortune made him conceited and he gathered an army of his own, a considerable force made up partly of his own countrymen and partly of other nationalities. He was a formidable rebel. His attack on the Roman empire was launched at a moment when his leadership had received many setbacks and the Turks had established their superiority. Roman prestige had fallen; the ground was giving way, as it were beneath their feet. Roussel was in any case an extremely ambitious man, but at this crisis, when the condition of the Empire was so desperate, he was even more tempted to rebel openly. He plundered almost all the eastern provinces. The operations against him were entrusted to many generals renowned for their

---

103 Roussel is identified as a Norman by Amatus and as coming from Bailleul by Geoffrey Malaterra.

bravery, men who had vast experience in battle as army commanders, but he was clearly master of these veterans ... As Roussel was descending on our people like a flood in full spate, he was captured and within a few days the affairs of the East were settled. Alexius was quick to see the opportune course of action, even quicker in carrying it out. As to the manner in which Roussel was caught, that is described by the Caesar in his second book, but I will here also give my account, as far as it concerns my own history ... He pretended to blind Roussel. The man was stretched out on the ground, the executioner brought the branding-iron near to his face, and Roussel howled and groaned; he was like a roaring lion. To all appearances he was being blinded. But in fact the apparent victim had been ordered to shout and bawl; the executioner who seemed to be gouging out his eyes was told to glare horribly at the prostrate Roussel and act like a raving madman – in other words, to simulate the punishment. So he was blinded, but not in reality, and the people clapped their hands and noisely spread the news all over the city that Roussel had lost his eyes. This bit of play-acting persuaded the whole mob, citizens and foreigners alike to give money to the fund. They were busy as bees. The whole point of my father's strategem was that those who were disinclined to contribute and were plotting to steal Roussel away from him might give up in despair when they were foiled; they might abandon their original plan for his and quickly become his allies. Thus the emperor's displeasure would be averted. With this in view he seized Roussel and kept him like a lion in a cage, still wearing bandages over his eyes as evidence of the supposed blinding. Despite the glory already won, he was far from satisfied; other tasks still remained to be done. Many other cities and strongholds were subdued; those areas which had fared badly under Roussel's government were incorporated in the Empire.

79 Michael Psellus, Fourteen Byzantine Rulers (on Robert Crispin)

Michael Psellus wrote his Fourteen Byzantine Rulers (*Chronographia*) before the end of the reign of Emperor Michael VII *c.* 1077–78. Robert Crispin belonged to the family of Crispin, castellans of Tillières and benefactors of Le Bec, who had taken service with the Byzantine emperor.

Michael Psellus, Fourteen Byzantine Rulers, trsl. E. R. A. Sewter (Harmondsworth, 1966), pp. 363–4.

[Book VII, c. 30] Facing Chatatoures with his army also arranged for battle was Andronicus.[104] Before the soldiers formed up in close order and the two armies came to grips, Crispinus the Frank – I am writing these words on the very day he died – was standing with Andronicus and they were encouraging one another.[105] This Crispinus had at first appeared as an enemy to the Romans, but later he changed his attitude, and his new loyalty was no less evident than his former hostility. Seeing Diogenes's men [Byzantines] now prepared for battle, Crispinus exhorted Andronicus to trust him, saying that he was going to charge the enemy cavalry. With that, he and his men rode at full gallop against the centre. He cut right through the ranks and, when he saw resistance was feeble, the rebels only withstanding his attack for a few moments and then running away, he pursued the fugitives with a handful of his knights. Thus he inflicted heavy losses and took still more prisoners.

Diogenes's army was broken and routed. Andronicus meanwhile returned in triumph with Crispinus to the tent which had been prepared for him. Later, one of the knights came up, bringing to the general an enemy captive. It was the Armenian Chatatoures. In the flight, he said, he had fallen from his horse at a ditch and had crept under a bush. One of the pursuers had spotted him and would have made short work of him, but, when he saw the Armenian's tears, he merely stripped him of his clothes and went away, leaving him naked under the bush. Then a second warrior, seeing him in his sorry plight rushed up to kill him, but Chatatoures told him that if he would spare him and take him away to a certain general (whom he mentioned by name) he would be most handsomely rewarded. Recognising who the man was, Andronicus felt doubly victorious. However, clothes and equipment were provided for him, and, though he was kept a prisoner, no constraint was put upon him, as befitted a brave leader.

104 Chatatoures was an Armenian military commander; Andronicus Dukas, son of John Dukas, was Greek.

105 Robert Crispin had arrived in Byzantium c. 1069. In 1071 he fought with Roussel on Alexius's side at Mantzikert. Robert died c. 1073 (Van Houts, 1985, 556 and Shepard, 1992, 277–8, 297–8).

80   Amatus of Montecassino, History of the Normans

Amatus, monk of Montecassino, wrote his History of the Normans *c.* 1080–82. He is an indirect source for our information about the Norman mercenaries in Byzantium. It is worth pointing out that Robert Crispin in 1066 had been at Montecassino before going to Byzantium.[106] Amatus's account of Roussel's actions is confused and unreliable.[107]

Storia de' Normanni di Amato di Montecassino, ed. V. de Bartholomaeis (Rome, 1935), pp. 15–20; trsl. P. Llewellyn.

[Book I , c. 8][108] Crespin, for shame, was unwilling to return to his own country, so he went to his countrymen who were in Italy where he remained for several years. Then he went to Constantinople, to campaign under the emperor; and there he had many triumphs and many victories, and then he died.

[Book I, c. 9] At the time of his death there were many coming from various parts of the world to take the emperor's pay. Among those from Normandy who came to take the emperor's pay was Roussel, a worthy warrior, true and faithful. Having conquered the country of Slavonia, he went to give aid to the emperor's people for whom he fought. The emperor saw that he was a fine warrior and a proven man; he ordered him against the Turks in support of his father, but by God's just judgement, the Turks had the victory; there was a great killing of Christians and the Augustus and Roussel were taken captive and with them all their soldiers, but they were honourably received by the Turks' duke.

[Book I, c. 10] The man I mentioned waited for help from the emperor; but the contrary happened, through the advice of his uncle, who was Caesar.[109] And hearing by trustworthy report that her mother had been imprisoned, the wife of the wise Caesar covered her head, beat her breast in mourning for her husband, and became a nun.[110] And Roussel's wife, a noble lady, they put in prison, but God's counsel does not afford help to those men whose malice seeks such destruction.

106 In June1066 he was at Montecassino where he witnessed a charter of Richard I of Capua (Loud, 1981c, 121–2, no. 13).

107 For the unreliability of information on Roussel, see Mathieu, 1950, 94–6 and Shepard, 1992, 299–302.

108 This follows straight on from no. **83**.

109 The 'emperor' is Michael VII, whose uncle was Caesar John Dukas.

110 She is unidentified.

[Book I, c. 11] The captive emperor then gave his son in marriage to the daughter of the king of the Turks, for she had been baptised and made a Christian. For this reason he and Roussel were freed and dismissed with honour; and no small part of the empire requested the aid of the Turks.

[Book I, c. 12] The Caesar, who had risen against the Augustus his father, was imprisoned and chained in the dungeon he had prepared for others; and he was imprisoned all this time not by the emperor but by others. But by great gifts of gold and silver he was freed from prison.

[Book I, c. 13] And from this affair there came great evil; for at the escape of his son-in-law the Caesar, the Caesar's father the emperor had his eyes put out on the orders of the other emperor, and died of the pain of it.

[Book I, c. 14] And Roussel, great-hearted man and fine warrior that he was, at that time conquered Armenia, which then paid tribute to him. And he came to Constantinople to free his wife; he laid siege to it and did such damage that he plundered and killed and burnt all that he found. And such was his anger against the Greeks that he forced the emperor, who had not wished to do so, to yield him his wife against his will.[111]

[Book I, c. 15] Now since the Greeks used many times to overcome their enemies by wicked arguments or subtle agreements, they wrote to the Turks. They made an agreement concerning Roussel, for they were betraying him. By gifts of much gold, they arranged for the Turks to imprison Roussel, and he was bound in chains.

Spain and the Holy Land

81 Dudo of Saint-Quentin, History of the Dukes of the Normans

Dudo of Saint-Quentin in his History of the Dukes of the Normans refers very briefly to a group of vikings/Normans who refused to convert to Christianity and c. 966 were expelled from Normandy by Duke Richard I. They went to Spain, where they raided the coast; see also no. 53.

---

111 The Greek sources do not mention a wife. For a reconstruction of Roussel's rebellion, see Shepard, 1992, 299–302.

Dudo, 287–8; *Dudo of St Quentin, History of the Normans*, trsl. E. Christiansen (Woodbridge, 1998), pp. 162–3.

[Book IV c. 124] … And those who desired to wander in the ways of paganism, he [Duke Richard I] had them guided to Spain by guides from Coutances.[112] And in the course of that voyage they captured eighteen cities, and won for themselves what they found in them. Raiding here and there, they attacked Spain and began afflicting it severely with burning and plundering. But at last the Spaniards put together an army of exasperated rustics and met the Northmen in battle. And in the rage of Mars the Spaniards turned their backs to the foreigners after there had been a terrible slaughter. And on the third day, the Northmen went back to the field of battle and when they were turning over the dead to rob them of their clothing, they found the parts of the bodies of the dusky ones and the Ethiopians lying next to the ground to be whiter than snow; but they noticed that the rest of the body had kept the original colour …

82 Adémar of Chabannes, Chronicle (on Roger of Tosny)

Adémar of Chabannes wrote his chronicle in Aquitaine before 1034. For Roger of Tosny, see also no. **63**.

Adémar de Chabannes, Chronique, ed. J. Chavanon (Paris, 1897), pp. 178–9.

[Book III, c. 55] … The Normans, however, under their leader Roger had set out to kill pagans in Spain and wiped out a vast number of Saracens and took their cities and fortifications away from them.[113] When he first arrived Roger captured the Saracens, cut one of them each day into halves and with the rest of them as onlookers boiled one half into hot water just like pork, and gave it to them to eat, the other half he pretended to eat at home with his men. Having thus dealt with all of them in this way, he permitted the most recent captives to escape from his custody, making it look like negligence, so that he would reveal this monstrous behaviour to the Saracens. This news struck them with fear and the Saracens from neighbouring Spain along with their king 'Musetus' sought peace with Ermensend, countess of Barcelona

---

112 An interesting reference to the people of Coutances with knowledge about Spain. For Coutances, see no. **8**.

113 Roger I of Tosny went to Spain and on his return founded the abbey of Saint-Pierre at Conches (see no. **63**). Orderic Vitalis knew him as Roger of Spain.

and promised to pay an annual tribute.[114] For Ermensend was a widow, who had joined her daughter in marriage to Roger.[115] When peace was established among them, Roger resolved to make war upon a further area of Spain [*ulteriore Hispania*] and one day with only forty Christians he ran into an ambush of 500 chosen Saracens lying in wait for him. Engaging with them he lost his brother-in-law, went into battle three times, and killed more than one hundred of the enemy and returned with his own men.[116] Nor did the Saracens dare to follow him as he fled.

83   Amatus of Montecassino, History of the Normans (on Robert Crispin)

Amatus, monk of Montecassino, wrote his History of the Normans *c.* 1080–82. What he knew about the Norman mercenaries in Spain and especially about Robert Crispin may ultimately derive from Robert's own story, told, perhaps, when he was at Montecassino in 1066, see no. **80**.

Storia de' Normanni di Amato di Montecassino, ed. V. de Bartholomaeis (Rome, 1935), pp. 13–15; trsl. P. Llewellyn.

[Book I, c. 5] ... There were also in attendance powerful Normans, and these undertook the duty of going to Spain that the military power of the Saracens there assembled might be seized and subjected to the Christians. And for this task was chosen a man named Robert Crispin;[117] when he was chosen he went off to make his preparations for the campaign he had been told to make ... [lacuna] And they called in God's help; and God was present to give aid to those who had asked for it. By their trust in God they had victory in battle, in which a great part of the Saracens were slain.[118] And they gave thanks to God for the victory He had given to his people.

[Book I, c. 6] Then the city called Barbastro was taken, well furnished with extensive lands full of great richness. And the whole host

114 'Musetus' has not been identified.

115 Ermensend (d. 1058) was the widow of Count Raymond Borrell of Barcelona (d. 1018). Their daughter Estephania married Roger of Tosny (Aurell i Cardona, 1993, 214–15).

116 The brother-in-law (Estephania's brother?) is unidentified.

117 Robert Crispin left Normandy sometime in the early 1060s (Van Houts, 1985, 555).

118 The battle of Argasto.

vowed that it should be assigned to Robert Crispin to guard until this army, or another greater, should return in two years, to take others of the cities of Spain.[119]

[Book I, c. 7] But the Devil, armed with his most subtle malice, out of envy of this good undertaking for the faith, took thought to spite it, and set the minds of God's warriors to thoughts of lust. In seeking to raise themselves, they lowered themselves, and for this reason Christ was angered, since the warriors gave themselves up to the love of fame. And so on account of their sins they lost that which they had gained and were pursued by the Saracens. They lost the city; some of them were killed, others were taken prisoner and yet others were saved by flight.

84 Orderic Vitalis, Ecclesiastical History (on Robert Bordet)

Orderic Vitalis on Robert Bordet (d. 1155), a Norman adventurer who was active in the Spanish *Reconquista* from 1114 onwards. Between 1129 and 1146 he was the leader of a short-lived crusader principality at Tarragona.

Orderic, vi, 402–5, 411.

At that time [*c.* 1124] a Norman knight, Robert Bordet of Cullei, decided to stay in Spain, and made his way to a town called Tarragona in ancient books.[120] This, as we may read, was a place where in the time of Emperor Gallienus, the holy martyr of Christ, Bishop Fructuosus and the deacons Augurius and Eulogius suffered ... There was a metropolitan see at Tarragona, and Oldegar, an old archbishop of great learning, flourished there and performed the duties enjoined on him in villages and towns of his diocese.[121] But oaks and beeches and other tall trees were already growing in the cathedral church, and had for a long time covered the ground inside the walls of the city, for the former inhabitants who had lived there had been slaughtered or driven out by the cruelty of the Saracens. At length Robert, prompted by the bishop, went to Pope Honorius [II, 1124–30], revealed his wishes to him, and was granted the county of Tarragona free from all secular exactions by the pope's gift. He returned and with the help of courageous companions whom he had gathered round himself, he has guarded the city up to the present time, fighting off the pagans.

119 The battle of Barbastro took place in 1064–65.

120 For Robert Bordet, see McCrank, 1981, 67–82.

121 St Oldegar, bishop of Barcelona (1116– after 1128) and archbishop of Tarragona (1118– after 1128).

During the time that he was travelling to Rome, and again when he returned to Normandy to raise companions-in-arms, his wife Sibyl, the daughter of William la Chèvre, took charge of Tarragona.[122] She was as brave as she was beautiful. During her husband's absence she kept sleepless watch; every night she put on a hauberk like a soldier and carrying a rod in her hand mounted on to the battlements, patrolled the circuit of the walls, kept the guards on the alert and encouraged everyone with good counsel to be on the alert for the enemy's strategems. How greatly the young countess deserves praise for serving her husband with such loyalty and unfaltering love, and watching dutifully over God's people with such sleepless care! ...

[The battle of Fraga in 1133 between King Alfonso I of Aragon (1104–34) and the Almoravides who came from Africa to help the Muslims]

Meanwhile Robert Bordet, count of Tarragona, and other vassals, who had received the news of the attack on the king, quickly armed themselves and, urging on their horses, galloped up at speed, shouting out battle cries in the name of Jesus. They charged the weary pagans in a sudden attack, shattered their ranks and drove them defeated from the field. They took many prisoners, but killed more; having won the day, they secured rich booty by stripping their enemies and gave joyful thanks to God, the victor.

85   Priest Raol, The Conquest of Lisbon

The Conquest of Lisbon is an account of the Christian conquest of Lisbon from the Moors in 1147 by a group of crusaders from England and the Low Countries. The Anglo-Norman contingent is consistently described as 'the Normans and the English', suggesting a very clear consciousness of ethnic coexistence. The text was written in Portugal in the winter of 1147–48 by the priest Raol and addressed to Osbert of Bawdsey.[123] Hervey of Glanville, the leader of the Anglo-Norman contingent, was the father of Ranulf of Glanville, chief justice of England.

De expugnatione Lyxbonensi: The Conquest of Lisbon, ed. and trsl. C. W. David (New York, 1936), pp. 105–6, 176–7.

[Speech of Hervey of Glanville in Lisbon to persuade the Normans and English contingent to stay][124]

---

122 Domesday Book lists William la Chèvre as a tenant-in-chief in Somerset in 1086.

123 The authorship was recently established by Livermore, 1990, 1–16.

124 For the Glanville family, see *Henry, Archdeacon of Huntingdon, Historia Anglorum*, ed. and trsl. D. Greenway (Oxford, 1996), pp. xxiii–xxv.

'... For the glorious deeds of the ancients kept in memory by posterity are the marks of both affection and honour. If you show yourself
worthy emulators of the ancients, honour and glory will be yours, but
if unworthy, then the disgraceful reproaches. Who does not know that
the race of the Normans declines no labor in the practice of continuous valour? – the Normans, that is to say, whose military spirit, ever
tempered by experience of the greatest hardships, is not quickly
subverted in adversity, and in prosperity, which is beset by so many
difficulties, cannot be overcome by slothful idleness; for it has learned
how with activity always to frustrate the vice of idleness. But because,
by I know not what manner of perverseness – as it were through lust
of honour and glory – envy has crept in among us as a handmaid,
while she cannot infect the men of alien race who are here with us, she
pours out the largest part of her poison among our very selves.
Brothers, take heed, and attend to the reform of your morals. Take an
example from your neighbours for your own confusion. The men of
Cologne are not at cross purposes with their fellows of Cologne, the
Flemings do not look askance at Flemings. Who indeed would deny
that the Scots are barbarians? Yet, among us in this enterprise they
have never overstepped bounds of due friendship. And what else can
be said except that something abnormal appears in you, since we are
all sons of one mother – as if the tongue should deny to the palate, or
the mouth to the stomach, or one foot to the other, or one hand to its
mate, to the office of mutual service? You wish to depart hence, and
well may it be with you. But we are certainly remaining here, as has
already been decided by common consent, with the exception only of
your smaller number, a thing which I am compelled to say without
sorrow. You do no injury to God by this conduct, but only to your-
selves. For, if you should remain here, God's power is not augmented
by your presence; if you should depart, it is not diminished. If this city
should be taken by us, what will you say to that? Even though I
remain silent concerning the sin of a violated association you will
become the objects of universal infamy and shame. Through fear of a
glorious death you have withdrawn your support from your
associates. The mere desire for booty yet to be acquired, you have
bought at the cost of eternal dishonour. The race of your innocent
colleagues will be held responsible for this your crime; and it is
certainly a shame that Normandy, the mother of our race, must bear,
and that undeservedly, in the eyes of so many peoples who are here
represented the everlasting opprobrium of your outrageous reaction.'

[The moral restraint displayed by the Normans and the English after the fall of Lisbon is contrasted with the greed and cruelty of the other nations; the cruelty committed to the pregnant horse of the Portuguese military leader is singled out as an act of Flemish atrocity]

... Thereupon the men of Cologne and the Flemings, when they saw so many temptations to greed in the city, observed not the bond of their oath or plighted faith. They rushed about hither and thither; they pillaged; they broke open doors; they tore open the innermost parts of every house; they drove out the citizens and treated them with insults, against right and justice; they scattered utensils and clothing; they secretly snatched away all those things which ought to have been made the common property of all the forces. They even slew the aged bishop of the city, against all right and decency, by cutting his throat. They seized the alcayde [mayor] himself and carried everything out of his house. And his mare, above mentioned, the count of Aerschot seized with his own hands, and at the demand of the king and of all our men that he give her up, he held on to her so obstinately that, because with an emission of blood she had lost her foal, the alcayde himself spoke out and branded the abominable action as disgusting. But the Normans and the English, for whom good faith and scruples of conscience were matters of the highest import, remained quietly at the posts to which they had been assigned, while they wondered what such an event might portend, preferring to keep their hands from all rapine rather than violate their engagements and the ordinances of the oath-bound association – an episode which covered the count of Aerschot and Christian and their principal followers with shame, since through the disregarding of their oath their unmixed greed now stood openly revealed to us.

The Holy Land

86   Orderic Vitalis, Ecclesiastical History

Orderic Vitalis incorporated excerpts from Baudri of Bourgueil's History of the Crusades into his Ecclesiastical History c. 1136. In addition he inserted otherwise unknown material concerning Norman participation in the First Crusade. The most remarkable story is that of Hugh Bunel who had fled from Normandy.

Orderic, v, 33–7, 157–9, 171–3.

[Book IX, c. 4] ... In September Robert, duke of the Normans committed Normandy to King William and after receiving ten thousand marks in silver from him, set out on crusade at the head of a formidable army of knights and foot-soldiers.[125] With him went his uncle Odo bishop of Bayeux, and Philip the clerk, Count Roger's son, Rotrou son of Geoffrey count of Mortagne, Walter count of Saint-Valéry, a great-grandson of Richard III duke of Normandy by his daughter Papia, also Gerard of Gournay, Ralph the Breton of Gael and Hugh of Saint-Pol, Ivo and Aubrey the sons of Hugh of Grand-mesnil and many other brave knights ... Robert the Norman and his brother-in-law Stephen of Blois with Hugh the Great and Robert of Flanders and many others crossed the Alps and entered Italy;[126] travelling through Rome in peace they wintered in Apulia and Calabria. Duke Roger Borsa welcomed the duke of Normandy with his companions as his natural lord and provided liberally for all his needs.[127] Mark Bohemond was besieging a fortress with his uncle Roger, count of Sicily, when he heard of the movements of leaders and many peoples.[128] He inquired immediately about the character of the different men and their emblems and after examining them closely commanded a very precious cloak to be brought to him. Cutting it into strips he handed a cross to each of his men, keeping one for himself. At once a great crowd of knights flocked round him and old Roger, left almost alone to carry on the siege, returned to Sicily with a handful of men, lamenting that he had lost his army. Bohemond provident and experienced as he was, soberly planned his route and prepared transport, crossed the sea with his magnates and large forces of armed men and finally after a calm crossing landed on the shores of Bulgaria. His chief companions were the following men: Tancred son of Odobonus the marquis, and the count of Roscignolo with his brothers, Richard of the principality [of Capua] and Ranulf his brother; Robert of Anzi and Robert of Sourdeval, Robert son of Thurstan, Herman of Canne and Humphrey son of Ralph, Richard son of count Ranulf and Bartholomew Boel of Chartres, Aubrey of Cagnano

---

125 In September 1096 Robert Curthose, duke of Normandy (1087–1106) mortgaged Normandy to his brother King William Rufus of England.

126 Stephen of Blois had married Robert Curthose's sister Adela. He died in 1102. Hugh the Great of Vermandois, brother of Louis VI of France; Robert II, count of Flanders (1093–1111).

127 Roger Borsa, duke of Apulia (1085–1111).

128 Bohemond I, later prince of Antioch (d. 1111); Roger I, count of Sicily (1072–1101).

and Humphrey of Montescaglioso. All these with their dependants followed Bohemond as one man, and swore that they would obey him faithfully and never leave him in the crusade.

[Book IX, c. 15] ... At that time Hugh Bunel, son of Robert of La Roche Mabille a most experienced soldier, came to the duke of Normandy and faithfully offered him his service as his natural lord;[129] being well received by the duke [Robert Curthose] he gave great assistance to the men besieging Jerusalem both by his counsel and in battle. Long before in Normandy this man had hacked off the head of the Countess Mabel, because she had taken away his paternal inheritance by force.[130] Because of the terrible crime he had committed, the knight Hugh fled with his brothers Ralph, Richard and Joscelin to Apulia and from there to Sicily; subsequently he withdrew to the Emperor Alexius [Comnenus, 1081–1118] in Greece, but he was never able to remain safely for long in any one place. For William the Bastard, king of England, and all Mabel's children sent out emissaries all over the world to seek him out, and promised rewards and gifts to any spies who could kill the exiled assassin in whatever land they might find him. So the brave Hugh, fearing the king's strong hand and long arm, left the Latin world and, distrusting the Christian peoples, lived long in exile among the Saracens. For twenty years he studied their customs and language. Therefore when he was received by the duke of Normandy he was able to do his countrymen great service, by explaining to them the habits of the pagans and their deceitful stratagems and the tricks that they practised against the faithful ...

The Armenians, Greeks and Syrians who had previously been ruled by the Turks in Jerusalem, had continued to practise the Christian rites as best they could, in great affliction. When they saw that the Christians had broken violently into the city, they all fled together to the church of the Holy Sepulchre; there, devoutly chanting 'Kyrie eleison' and other prayers suitable to the occasion, they awaited the outcome of events. Tancred who did not know the way came there with his forces by God's will and realised that these men were worshippers of Christ from their prayers and gestures. 'These men', he said, 'are Christians. None of you therefore should harm them in any way. We did not come here to harm the servants of Christ, but to free them from their cruel persecutors. They are our brothers and friends;

129 At Jerusalem in 1099.
130 In 1077 (Orderic, iii, 134–6).

faithful up to now through their many tribulations, they have been proved as gold in the furnace.' Then the noble champion left behind Ilger Bigod, the commander of the knights, with two hundred knights and appointed him guardian of the place so the infidels could not enter it again.[131] He himself with the rest of his forces went out to storm the fortifications and helped his comrades, who were scouring the city and were occupied with killing the Saracens.

Meanwhile the native Christians, who had remained in the church with Ilger, spoke secretly with him and wishing to secure his protection, obligingly guided him and his companions to the holy places, namely the Lord's sepulchre and other sacred places; they showed them also certain things that they and their ancestors had long kept hidden in secret places out of fear of the pagans. Ilger then found there among other relics in a marble capital which was hollowed out under the altar to serve as tabernacle for the host, a little ball of the hair of Mary, the holy Mother of God. This he afterwards took to France and shared out piously between the sanctuaries of the bishoprics and monasteries ... I have written this account into my book because Ilger Bigod gave two of the holy hairs to his kinsman, the monk Arnold at Chartres, and Arnold displayed them in the church of Maule, where many sick persons have been cured through them.

87   Eadmer of Canterbury, History of Recent Events

Eadmer of Canterbury wrote his History of Recent Events in England c. 1093–c. 1119. As secretary of Archbishop Anselm (1093–1109) he was an invaluable source of information for stories about Anselm's abbacy at Le Bec and his archiepiscopal office in England. Here he complements Orderic's account on Ilger Bigod.

Eadmeri Historia novorum in Anglia, ed. M. Rule (London, 1884), pp. 179–80; Eadmer's History of Recent Events in England: Historia Novorum in Anglia, trsl. G. Bosanquet (London 1964), pp. 192–4.

While Anselm was at Rouen there arrived there Bohemond [I d. 111], one of the most noted leaders of the Jerusalem campaign, who had in his company a cardinal of the church of Rome named Bruno. This cardinal had a master of the knights named Ilger an active man of no little repute among his fellows. He had been known to Anselm

---

131 This event took place in 1106. Ilger Bigod's relationship with Robert Bigod and Roger Bigod of Norfolk has never been established. He is undoubtedly the same person as Ilger, leader of Bohemond's soldiers, who features below, in no. **87**.

from his youth and had received many kindnesses from him. So, being on terms of friendship with Anselm, he entertained him with a great deal of agreeable talk of the wars he had been through, of cities captured, of the situation of the places and not a few other pieces of information which he had picked up on the Jerusalem campaign. He also disclosed to him the fact that he was in possession of many relics of saints and the way in which he had come by them. Among these and indeed above all those he possessed, he prided himself especially on some hairs of Mary, the blessed mother of God, of which he said that some had been given him by the patriarch of Antioch when he held there the post of master of the knights under Bohemond. He added: 'I should not, I confess, have dared to take these hairs, had I not been moved to do so by love of this my native land where I was born and brought up. I hoped some day to come safely back here and with these relics to glorify my country. So now, as under God's protection I have not been disappointed in that hope, I have determined to give two of them to this church [Rouen] which is the very centre of Christianity for the whole of Normandy, two to the abbey of St Peter and St Ouen [Rouen], two to the monastery of that same Virgin of Virgins [Le Bec] in which under your care I grew up to man's estate and two to yourself [Anselm]. The bishop of Antioch gave me twelve of them altogether, declaring that according to what as he asserted, he found written in the records of ancient writing which among them were held to be of great authority and were kept with the archives of the church over which he presided, these hairs had been torn out by that Lady herself when, standing beside the cross of her Son, a sword pierced through her soul.' That is what he said. Anselm, filled with joy over these relics, after making with the archbishop of Rouen [William, 1078–1110] and Bohemond and those back from Jerusalem the arrangements which seemed appropriate returned to Bec. But, as the hairs of which Ilger had spoken had been left at Chartres where Bohemond's retinue and most of his goods were awaiting his return, the archbishop of Rouen and the abbot of Bec [William, 1093–1124] sent some men of the monastic order to fetch them.

REFERENCES

Abulafia, 1984   D. Abulafia, 'The Norman kingdom of Africa and the Norman expeditions to Majorca and the Muslim Mediterranean', *ANS*, 7 (1984), 26–49

Adigard des Gautries, 1951   J. Adigard des Gautries, 'Les Noms de lieux de la Manche attestés entre 911–1066', *AN*, 1 (1951), 9–44

Adigard des Gautries, 1954   J. Adigard des Gautries, *Les Noms de personnes scandinaves en Normandie de 911 à 1066* (Lund, 1954)

Adigard des Gautries, 1956–59   J. Adigard des Gautries, 'Les Noms de lieux de la Seine-Maritime attestés entre 911 et 1066', *AN*, 6 (1956), 119–34, 223–44; 7 (1957), 135–58; 8 (1958), 299–322; 9 (1959), 151–67, 273–83

Arnoux, 1992   M. Arnoux, 'Classe agricole, pouvoir seigneurial et autorité ducale: L'Évolution de la Normandie féodale d'après le témoignage des chroniqueurs (Xe-XIIe siècles)', *Le Moyen Age*, 5th s., 6 (1992), 35–60

Aurell i Cardona, 1993   M. Aurell i Cardona, 'Les Avatars de la viduité princière: Ermessende (ca. 975–1058)', in *Veuves et veuvage dans la haut Moyen*, ed. M. Parisse (Paris, 1993), pp. 201–32

Barlow, 1970   F. Barlow, *Edward the Confessor* (London, 1970)

Barlow, 1979   F. Barlow, *The English Church 1000–1066*, 2nd edn (London, 1979)

Barthélemy, 1992   D. Barthélemy, 'Qu'est-ce que le servage, en France, au XIe siècle?', *Revue Historique*, no. 582 (1992), 233–84

Bartlett, 1993   R. Bartlett, *The Making of Europe* (London, 1993)

Bates, 1982   D. Bates, *Normandy before 1066* (London, 1982)

Bates, 1987   D. Bates, 'Lord Sudeley's ancestors: the family of the counts of Amiens, Valois and Vexin in France and England during the eleventh century', in *The Sudeleys – Lords of Toddington*, The Manorial Record Society of Great Britain (London, 1987), pp. 34–48

Baylé, 1982   M. Baylé, 'Interlace patterns in Norman Romanesque sculpture: regional groups and their historical background', *ANS*, 5 (1982), 1–20

Baylé, 1985   M. Baylé, 'Troarn (Calvados), tombeau du chevalier Hugues', Les siècles romans en Basse-Normandie, *Art de Basse-Normandie*, 92 (1985), 136–7

Baylé, 1990   M. Baylé, 'Réminiscenses anglo-scandinaves dans la sculpture de Normandie', *ANS*, 13 (1990), 35–48

Benediktsson, 1993   J. B. Benediktsson, 'Islendingabók', in *Medieval Scandinavia: An Encyclopedia*, ed. P. Pulsiano (New York, 1993), pp. 332–3

Bennett, 1992   M. Bennett, 'Norman naval activity in the Mediterranean, c. 1060–c. 1108', *ANS*, 15 (1992), 41–58

Beresford, 1981   G. Beresford, 'Goltho manor, Lincolnshire: the buildings and their surrounding defences c. 850–1150', *ANS*, 4 (1981), 13–36

Bliese, 1991   J. Bliese, 'The courage of the Normans - a comparative study of battle rhetoric', *Nottingham Medieval Studies*, 35 (1991), 1–26

Boehm, 1969   L. Boehm, 'Nomen gentis Normannorum: Der Aufstieg der Normannen im Spiegel der normannischen Historiographie', in *I Normanni...* (1969), 623–704

Bouet, 1994   P. Bouet, 'Les Normands, le nouveau peuple élu', in *Les Normands en Méditerranée*, ed. P. Bouet and F. Neveux (Caen, 1994), pp. 239–52

Bouvris, 1985   J. M. Bouvris, 'Contribution à une étude de l'institution vicomtale en Normandie au XIe siècle ...', in *Autour du pouvoir ducal normand (XIe–XIIe siècles)*, ed. L. Musset, J. M. Bouvris and J. M. Maillefer (Caen, 1985), pp. 149–74

Bréhier, 1912   L. Bréhier, 'Les Aventures d'un chef normand en Orient au XIe siècle', *Revue des cours et des conférences*, 20 (1912), 172–88

Brown, 1984   R. A. Brown, *The Norman Conquest*, Documents of Medieval History, 5 (London, 1984)

Brown, 1985   R. A. Brown, *The Normans and the Norman Conquest*, 2nd edn (Woodbridge, 1985)

Bulst, 1973   N. Bulst, *Untersuchungen zu den Klosterreformen Wilhelms von Dijon, 962–1031* (Bonn, 1973)

Chalandon, 1907   F. Chalandon, *Histoire de la domination normande en Italie et en Sicile*, 2 vols (Paris, 1907)

Chibnall, 1982   M. Chibnall, 'Military service in Normandy before 1066', *ANS*, 4 (1982), 65–77

Chibnall, 1989   M. Chibnall, 'Anglo-French relations in the work of Orderic Vitalis', in *Documenting the Past: Essays in Medieval History Presented to George Peddy Cuttino*, ed. J. S. Hamilton and P. J. Bradley (Woodbridge, 1989), pp. 5–19

Chibnall, 1991   M. Chibnall, *The Empress Matilda, Queen Consort, Queen Mother and Lady of the English* (Oxford, 1991)

Chibnall, 1995   M. Chibnall, 'La Carrière de Geoffroi de Montbray', in *Les évêques normands du XIe siècle*, ed. P. Bouet and F. Neveux (Caen, 1995), pp. 279–93

Chibnall, 1999   M. Chibnall, *The Debate on the Norman Conquest* (Manchester, 1999)

Clark, 1978   C. Clark, 'Women's names in post-conquest England: observations and speculations', *Speculum*, 53 (1978), 223–51

Coupland, 1998   S. Coupland, 'From poachers to gamekeepers: Scandinavian warlords and Carolingian kings', *Early Medieval Europe*, 7 (1998), 85–114

Crawford, 1987   B. E. Crawford, *Scandinavian Scotland* (Leicester, 1987)

David, 1920   C. W. David, *Robert Curthose, Duke of Normandy* (Cambridge, Mass., 1920)

Davis, 1976   R. H. C. Davis, *The Normans and their Myth* (London, 1976)

Davis, 1978   R. H. C. Davis, 'The Carmen de Hastingae Proelio', *EHR*, 93 (1978), 241–61

Defourneaux, 1949   M. Defourneaux, *Les Français en Espagne aux XIe et XIIe siècles* (Paris, 1949)

Dolley and Yvon, 1971   M. Dolley and J. Yvon, 'A group of tenth-century coins found at Mont-Saint-Michel', *British Numismatical Journal*, 40 (1971), 1–16

Douglas, 1946   D. C. Douglas, 'The earliest Norman counts', *EHR*, 61 (1946), 129–56

Douglas, 1977   D. C. Douglas, *Time and the Hour: Some Collected Papers of David Douglas* (London, 1977)

Dumas, 1979   F. Dumas, 'Les Monnaies normandes (Xe–XIIe siècles) avec répertoire des trouvailles', *Revue Numismatique*, 6th s., 21 (1979), 84–140

Eames, 1952   E. Eames, 'Mariage et concubinage légal en Norvège à l'époque des vikings', *AN*, 2 (1952), 195–208

Fawtier, 1923   R. Fawtier, 'Les Reliques rouennaises de sainte Catherine d'Alexandrie', *Analecta Bollandiana*, 41 (1923), 357–68

Fellows-Jensen, 1990   G. Fellows-Jensen, 'Scandinavian personal names in foreign fields', in *Recueil d'études en hommage à Lucien Musset* (Caen, 1990), pp. 149–59

Fleming, 1998   R. Fleming, *Domesday Book and the Law: Society and the Legal Custom in Early Medieval England* (Cambridge, 1998)

France, 1991   J. France, 'The occasion of the coming of the Normans to southern Italy', *Journal of Medieval History*, 17 (1991), 185–205

Garnett, 1986   G. Garnett, 'Coronation and propaganda: some implications of the Norman claim to the throne of England in 1066', *Transactions of the Royal Historical Society*, 5th s., 36 (1986), 91–116

Garnett, 1994   G. Garnett, '"Ducal" succession in early Normandy', in *Law and Government in Medieval England and Normandy: Essays in Honour of Sir James Holt*, ed. G. Garnett and J. Hudson (Cambridge, 1994), pp. 80–110

Gauthiez, 1991   B. Gauthiez, 'Hypothèses sur la fortification de Rouen au onzième siècle: Le Donjon, la tour de Richard II et l'enceinte de Guillaume', *ANS*, 14 (1991), 61–76

Gibson, 1978   M. Gibson, *Lanfranc of Bec* (Oxford, 1978)

Gillingham, 1981   J. Gillingham, 'The introduction of knight service into England', *ANS*, 4 (1981), 53–64

Gransden, 1995   A. Gransden, 'The composition and authorship of the "De miraculis sancti Eadmundi" attributed to "Hermann the archdeacon"', *Journal of Medieval Latin*, 5 (1995), 1–52

Green, 1982   J. Green 'The sheriffs of William the Conqueror', *ANS*, 5 (1982), 129–45

Green, 1984   J. Green, 'Lords of the Norman Vexin', in *War and Government in the Middle Ages: Essays in Honour of J. O. Prestwich*, ed. J. Gillingham and J. Holt (Woodbridge, 1984), pp. 47–61

Green, 1986   J. Green, *The Government of England under Henry I* (Cambridge, 1986)

Guillot, 1981   O. Guillot, 'La Conversion des Normands peu après 911', *Cahiers de Civilisation Médiévale*, 24 (1981), 101–16 and 181–219

Hanawalt, 1995   E. A. Hanawalt, 'Scandinavians in Byzantium and Normandy', in *Peace and War in Byzantium: Essays in Honor of George T. Dennis*, ed. S. J. Miller and J. Nesbitt (Washington, 1995), pp. 114–22

Harper-Bill, 1978   C. Harper-Bill, 'Herluin, abbot of Bec and his biographer', *Studies in Church History*, 15 (1978), 15–25

Hart, 1996   C. Hart, 'William Malet and his family', *ANS*, 19 (1996), 123–66

Haskins, 1915   C. H. Haskins, *The Normans in European History* (New York, 1915)

Haskins, 1918   C. H. Haskins, *Norman Institutions* (New York, 1918)

Hermans, 1979   J. Hermans, 'The Byzantine view of the Normans', *ANS*, 2 (1979), 78–92

Hoffmann, 1969   H. Hoffmann, 'Die Anfänge der Normannen in Süditalien', *Quellen und Forschungen aus italienischen Archiven und Bibliotheken*, 49 (1969), 95–144

Hollister, 1986   C. W. Hollister, *Monarchy, Magnates and Institutions in the Anglo-Norman World* (London, 1986)

Hollister, 1987   C. W. Hollister, 'The greater Domesday tenants-in-chief', in *Domesday Studies*, ed. J. C. Holt (Woodbridge, 1987), pp. 219–48

Holt, 1983   J. C. Holt, 'The introduction of knight service in England', *ANS*, 6 (1983), 89–106

Hooper, 1985   N. Hooper, 'Edgar the aetheling: Anglo-Saxon prince, rebel and crusader', *Anglo-Saxon England*, 14 (1985), 197–214

Houben, 1996   H. Houben, 'Adelaide "del Vasto" nella storia del regno normanno di Sicilia', in *Mezzogiorno normanno-svevo: Monasteri e castelli, ebrei e muselmani*, ed. H. Houben (Naples, 1996), pp. 81–113

Howard-Johnston, 1996   J. Howard-Johnston, 'Anna Comnena and the Alexiad', in *Alexios I Komnenos*, ed. M. Mullett and D. Smythe, Belfast Byzantine Texts and Translations, 4.1 (Belfast, 1996), pp. 260–302

I Normanni, 1969   *I Normanni e la loro espansione in Europa nell'alto medioevo 18–24 Aprile 1968*, Settimane di studio del centro italiano di studi sull'alto medioevo, 16 (Spoleto, 1969)

Jahn, 1989   W. Jahn, *Untersuchungen zur normannischen Herrschaft in Süditalien (1040–1100)*, Europäischen Hochschulschriften, Reihe 3, Bd. 401 (Frankfurt am Main, 1989)

Jesch, 1991   J. Jesch, *Women in the Viking Age* (Woodbridge, 1991)

Jesch, 1996   J. Jesch, 'Norse historical traditions and the "Historia Gruffudd vab Kenan": Magnús berfoettr and Haraldr hárfagri', in *Gruffudd ap Cynan: A Collaborative Biography*, ed. K. L. Maund (Woodbridge, 1996), pp. 117–47

Joranson, 1948   E. Joranson, 'The inception of the career of the Normans in Italy: legend and history', *Speculum*, 23 (1948), 353–96

Keats-Rohan, 1990   K. S. B. Keats-Rohan, 'William I and the Breton contingent in the non-Norman conquest 1060–1087', *ANS*, 13 (1990), 157–72.

Keats-Rohan, 1993a   K. S. B. Keats-Rohan, 'Aspects of Robert of Torigny's genealogies revisited', *Nottingham Medieval Studies*, 37 (1993), 21–7

Keats-Rohan, 1993b   K. S. B. Keats-Rohan, 'The prosopography of post-conquest England; four case studies', *Medieval Prosopography*, 14, 1 (1993), 1–51

Keats-Rohan, 1997a   K. S. B. Keats-Rohan, 'Poppa "of Bayeux" and her family', *The American Genealogist*, 72 (1997), 187–204

Keats-Rohan, 1997b   K. S. B. Keats-Rohan, 'Domesday Book and the Malets: Patrimony and the Private Histories of Public Lives', *Nottingham Medieval Studies*, 41 (1997), 13–55

Keynes, 1990   S. Keynes, 'The aethelings in Normandy', *ANS*, 13 (1990), 173–206

Keynes, 1991   S. Keynes, 'The historical context of the battle of Maldon', in *The Battle of Maldon AD 991*, ed. D. G. Scragg (Oxford, 1991), pp. 81–113

Keynes 1996   S. Keynes, 'Giso, bishop of Wells (1061–88)', *ANS*, 19 (1996), 204–71

Le Maho, 1976   J. Le Maho, 'L'Apparition des seigneuries châtelaines dans le Grand-Caux à l'époque ducale', *Archéologie Médiévale*, 6 (1976), 5–148.

Le Maho, 1994   J. Le Maho, 'Les Fouilles de la cathédrale de Rouen 1985–93', *Archéologie Médiévale*, 24 (1994), 1–51

Lewis, 1992   A. W. Lewis, 'Observations sur la frontière franco-normande', in *Le Roi de France et son royaume autour de l'an mil*, ed. M. Parisse and X. Barral i Altet (Paris, 1992), pp. 147–56

Lewis, 1990   C. P. Lewis, 'The early earls of Norman England', *ANS*, 13 (1990), 207–24

Lewis, 1994   C. P. Lewis, 'The French in England before the Norman Conquest', *ANS*, 17 (1994), 123–44

Lewis, 1996   C. P. Lewis, 'Gruffudd ap Cynan and the Normans', in *Gruffudd ap Cynan: A Collaborative Biography*, ed. K. L. Maund (Woodbridge, 1996), pp. 61–77

Lifshitz, 1995   F. Lifshitz, *The Norman Conquest of Pious Neustria: Historiographic Discourse and Saintly Relics 684–1090*, Studies and Texts, 122 (Toronto, 1995)

Livermore, 1990 H. Livermore, 'The "Conquest of Lisbon" and its author', *Portuguese Studies*, 6 (1990), 1–16

Lot, 1908 F. Lot, 'La Grande Invasion normande de 856–862', *Bibliothèque de l'École des Chartes*, 69 (1908), 5–62

Loud, 1981a G. A. Loud, 'How "Norman" was the Norman conquest of southern Italy?', *Nottingham Medieval Studies*, 25 (1981), 13–34

Loud, 1981b G. A. Loud, 'The Gens Normannorum - myth or reality?', *ANS*, 4 (1981), 104–16

Loud, 1981c G. A. Loud, 'A calender of the diplomas of the Norman princes of Capua', *Papers of the British School at Rome*, 49 (1981), 99–143

Loud, 1985 G. A. Loud, *Church and Society in the Norman Principality of Capua, 1058–1197* (Oxford, 1985)

Loud, 1991 G. A. Loud, 'Anna Komnena and her sources for the Normans of southern Italy', in *Church and Chronicle in the Middle Ages: Essays Presented to John Taylor*, ed. I. Wood and G. A. Loud (London, 1991), pp. 41–57

Loud, 1996 G. A. Loud, 'Continuity and change in Norman Italy: the Campania during the eleventh and twelfth centuries', *Journal of Medieval History*, 22 (1996), 313–43.

Loud, 1998 G. A. Loud, 'Betrachtungen über die normannische Eroberung Süditaliens', in *Forschungen zur Reichs-, Papst- und Landesgeschichte. Peter Herde zum 65. Geburtstag von Freunde, Schülern und Kollegen dargebracht*, ed. K. Borchardt and E. Bünz (Stuttgart, 1998), pp. 115–31

McCrank, 1981 L. J. McCrank, 'Norman crusaders in the Catalan reconquest: Robert Burdet and the principality of Tarragona, 1129–55', *Journal of Medieval History*, 7 (1981), 67–82

Mason, 1990 E. Mason, *St Wulfstan of Worcester* (Oxford, 1990)

Mathieu, 1950 M. Mathieu, 'Une Source negligée de la bataille de Mantzikert: Les "Gesta Roberti Wiscardi" de Guillaume d'Apulie', *Byzantion*, 20 (1950), 89–103

Matthew, 1992 D. Matthew, *The Norman Kingdom of Sicily* (Cambridge, 1992)

Ménager, 1981 L. R. Ménager, *Hommes et institutions de l'Italie normande*, Variorum Collected Studies Series (London, 1981)

Morris, 1985 C. Morris, 'Viking Orkney: a survey', in *The Prehistory of Orkney*, ed. C. Renfrew (Edinburgh, 1985), pp. 210–42

Musset, 1959 L. Musset, 'A-t-il existé en Normandie une aristocratie d'argent?', *AN*, 9 (1959), 285–99

Musset, 1962 L. Musset, 'Recherches sur les pèlerins et les pèlerinages en Normandie jusqu'à la première croisade', *AN*, 12 (1962), 127–50

Musset, 1967 *Les Actes de Guillaume le Conquérant et de la reine Mathilde pour les abbayes caennaises*, ed. L. Musset (Caen, 1967)

Musset, 1970 L. Musset, 'Naissance de la Normandie (Ve - XIe siècles)', in *Histoire de la Normandie*, ed. M. de Bouard (Toulouse, 1970), pp. 96–129

Musset, 1971 L. Musset, *Les Invasions: Le Second Assaut contre l'Europe chrétienne (VIIe–XIe siècles)*, (Paris, 1971)

Musset, 1977 L. Musset, 'Aux origines d'une classe dirigéante: Les Tosny, grands barons Normands du Xe au XIIIe siècle', *Francia*, 5 (1977), 45–80

Musset, 1985 L. Musset, 'Autour des modalités juridiques de l'expansion normande au XIe siècle: le droit d'exil', in *Autour du pouvoir ducal normand, Xe–XIIe siècles*, ed. L. Musset et al. (Caen, 1985), pp. 45–59

Musset, 1988   L. Musset, 'Réflections autour du problème de l'esclavage et du servage en Normandie ducale (Xe–XIIe siècles), in *Aspects de la société et de l'économie dans la Normandie médiévale (Xe–XIIIe siècles)*, ed. L. Musset, J.-M. Bouvris and V. Gazeau (Caen, 1988), pp. 5–24

Musset and Chanteux, 1973   L. Musset and H. Chanteux, 'Essai sur les invasions bretonnes et normandes dans le Maine aux IXe et Xe siècles', *Bulletin de la Commission Historique et Archéologique de la Mayenne*, n.s. 29 (1972–73), 37–59

Nelson, 1992   J. L. Nelson, *Charles the Bald* (London, 1992)

Nelson, 1997   J. L. Nelson, 'The Frankish Empire', in *The Oxford Illustrated History of the Vikings*, ed. P. Sawyer (Oxford, 1997), pp. 19–47

Neveux, 1994   F. Neveux, 'Quelques aspects de l'impérialisme normand au XIe siècle en Italie et en Angleterre', in *Les Normands en Méditerranée*, ed. P. Bouet and F. Neveux (Caen, 1994), pp. 51–62

Nip, 1998   R. Nip, 'The political relations between England and Flanders (1066–1128)', *ANS*, 21 (1998), 145–67

Norwich, 1967   J. J. Norwich, *The Normans in the South, 1016–1130* (London, 1967)

Orlandi, 1996   G. Orlandi, 'Some afterthoughts on the Carmen de Hastingae Proelio', in *Media Latinitas: A Collection of Essays to Mark the Occasion of the Retirement of L. J. Engels*, ed. R. I. A. Nip, H. van Dijk, E. M. C. van Houts *et al.* (Turnhout, 1996), pp. 117–27

Le Patourel, 1944   J. Le Patourel, 'Geoffrey de Montbray, bishop of Coutances, 1049–1093', *EHR*, 59 (1944), 129–61

Perin, 1990   P. Perin, 'Les Objets vikings du Musée des Antiquités de la Seine-Maritime, à Rouen', in *Recueil d'études en hommage à Lucien Musset* (Caen, 1990), pp. 161–88

Platelle, 1967   H. Platelle, 'Les relations entre l'abbaye Saint-Amand de Rouen e l'abbaye Saint-Amand d'Elnone', *La Normandie bénédictine au temps de Guillaume l Conquérant (XIe siècle)* (Lille, 1967), pp. 83–106

Porée, 1901   A. Porée, *Histoire de l'abbaye du Bec*, 2 vols (Evreux, 1901)

Potts, 1989   C. Potts, 'Normandy or Brittany? A conflict of interests at Mont-Saint Michel', *ANS*, 12 (1989), 135–56

Potts, 1992   C. Potts, 'The earliest Norman counts revisited: the lords of Mortain *The Haskins Society Journal*, 4 (1992), 25–35

Potts, 1995   C. Potts, 'Atque unum ex diversis gentibus populum effecit: historica tradition and the Norman identity', *ANS*, 18 (1995), 139–52

Potts, 1997   C. Potts, *Monastic Revival and Regional Identity in Early Norman* (Woodbridge, 1997)

Pounds, 1990   N. J. G. Pounds, *The Medieval Castle in England and Wales* (Cambridg 1990)

Power, 1994   D. Power, 'What did the frontier of Angevin Normandy comprise? *ANS*, 17 (1994), 181–202

Sawyer and Sawyer, 1993   B. and P. Sawyer, *Medieval Scandinavia: From Conversion Reformation circa 800–1500* (Minneapolis-London, 1993)

Schlumberger, 1881   G. Schlumberger, 'Deux chefs normands des armées byzantin au XIe siècle', *Revue Historique*, 6 (1881), 289–303

Searle, 1980   E. Searle, 'Women and the legitimization of succession at the Norma Conquest', *ANS*, 3 (1980), 159–70

Searle, 1985   E. Searle, 'Frankish rivalries and Norse warriors', *ANS*, 8 (1985), 198–2

Searle, 1988   E. Searle, *Predatory Kinship and the Creation of Norman Power, 840–1066* (Berkeley, 1988)

Shepard, 1992   J. Shepard, 'The uses of the Franks in eleventh-century Byzantium', *ANS*, 15 (1992), 275–305

Shopkow, 1989   L. Shopkow, 'The Carolingian world of Dudo of Saint-Quentin', *Journal of Medieval History*, 15 (1989), 19–37

Shopkow, 1997   L. Shopkow, *History and Community: Norman Historical Writing in the Eleventh and Twelfth Centuries* (Washington, 1997)

Short, 1995   I. Short, 'Tam Angli quam Franci: self-definition in Anglo-Norman England', *ANS*, 18 (1995), 153–76

Smith, 1992   J. M. H. Smith, *Province and Empire: Brittany and the Carolingians* (Cambridge, 1992)

Sot, 1993   M. Sot, *Un historien et son église: Flodoard de Reims* (Paris, 1993)

Stafford, 1994   P. Stafford, 'Women and the Norman Conquest', *Transactions of the Royal Historical Society*, 6th s., 4 (1994), 221–49

Stafford, 1997   P. Stafford, *Queen Emma and Queen Edith: Queenship and Women's Power in Eleventh-Century England* (Oxford, 1997)

Stasser, 1990   T. Stasser, '"Mathilde, fille du comte Richard", essai d'identification', *AN*, 40 (1990), 49–64

Strickland, 1996   M. Strickland, 'Military technology and conquest: the anomaly of Anglo-Saxon England', *ANS*, 19 (1996), 353–82

Szabolcs de Vajay, 1971   Szabolcs de Vajay, 'Mahaut de Pouille, comtesse de Barcelone et vicomtesse de Narbonne dans le contexte social de son temps', in *Béziers et le Biterrois: Fédération historique du Languedoc méditerranéen et du Roussillon, XLIIIe congrès (Béziers, 30–31 mai 1970)*, (Montpellier, 1971), 129–47

Tabuteau, 1988   E. Z. Tabuteau, *Transfers of Property in Eleventh-Century Norman Law* (Chapel Hill-London, 1988)

Taviani-Carozzi, 1991   H. Taviani-Carozzi, *La Principauté Lombarde de Salerne, IXe - XIe siècle*, 2 vols (Rome, 1991)

Thompson, 1995   K. Thompson, 'The lords of Laigle: ambition and insecurity on the borders of Normandy', *ANS*, 18 (1995), 177–99

Van Houts, 1983   E. M. C. van Houts, 'Scandinavian influence in Norman literature of the eleventh century', *ANS*, 6 (1983), 107–21

Van Houts, 1985   E. M. C. van Houts, 'Normandy and Byzantium', *Byzantion*, 55 (1985), 544–59

Van Houts, 1987   E. M. C. van Houts, 'The Ship List of William the Conqueror', *ANS*, 10 (1987), 159–184

Van Houts, 1989a   E. M. C. van Houts, 'Latin poetry and the Anglo-Norman court', *Journal of Medieval History*, 15 (1989), 39–62

Van Houts, 1989b   E. M. C. van Houts, 'Historiography and hagiography at Saint-Wandrille: the Inventio et miracula sancti Vulfranni', *ANS*, 12 (1989), 233–51

Van Houts, 1995   E. van Houts, 'The Norman Conquest through European eyes', *EHR*, 110 (1995), 832–53

Van Houts, 1996a   E. van Houts, 'The memory of 1066 in written and oral tradition', *ANS*, 19 (1996), 167–80

Van Houts, 1996b   E. van Houts, 'The trauma of 1066', *History Today*, 46 (1996), 9–15

Van Houts, 1998a   E. van Houts, review of Warner of Rouen, *Moriuht*, ed. and trsl. C. McDonough (Toronto, 1995), *Speculum*, 73 (1998), 621–3

Van Houts, 1998b   E. van Houts, 'The Anglo-Flemish treaty of 1101', *ANS*, 21 (1998), 169–74.

Van Houts, 1999   E. van Houts, *Memory and Gender in Medieval Europe, 900–1200* (London, 1999)

Vercauteren, 1963   F. Vercauteren, 'Une parentèle dans la France du nord aux XIe et XIIe siècles', *Le Moyen Age*, 69 (1963), 223–45

Von Valkenhausen, 1977   V. von Valkenhausen, 'I ceti dirigenti prenormanni al tempo della costituzioni degli stati normanni nell'Italia meridionale e in Sicilia', in *Forme di potere e struttura sociale in Italia nel Medioevo*, ed. G. Rossetti (Bologna, 1977), pp. 321–77

Von Valkenhausen, 1982   V. von Valkenhausen, 'Olympias, eine normannische Prinzessin in Konstantinopel', in *Bisanzio e l'Italia: Raccolta di studi in memoria di A. Pertusi* (Milan, 1982), pp. 56–73

Werner, 1976   K. F. Werner, 'Quelques observations au sujet des débuts du "duché" de Normandie', in *Droit privé et institutions régionales: Etudes historiques offertes à Jean Yver*, ed. R. Aubreton *et al.* (Paris, 1976), pp. 691–709

Williams, 1995   A. Williams, *The English and the Norman Conquest* (Woodbridge, 1995)

Wolf, 1995   K. B. Wolf, *Making History: The Normans and their Historians in Eleventh-Century Italy* (Philadelphia, 1995)

Yver, 1955   J. Yver, 'Les Châteaux forts en Normandie jusqu'au milieu du XIIe siècle', *Bulletin de la Société des Antiquaires de Normandie*, 53 (1955), 28–115

Yver, 1969   J. Yver, 'Les Premières Institutions du duché de Normandie', *I Normanni* … (Spoleto, 1969), pp. 299–366

FURTHER READING

What follows is only a small selection of the vast growing literature on the Normans in general and their history in Normandy, England and southern Italy. From 1978 specialist papers on all aspects of the history of the Normans have appeared in *Anglo-Norman Studies: The Proceedings of the Battle Conference*, while a comprehensive annual bibliography is published in the *Annales de Normandie*.

Useful surveys of the history of the Normans in general are C. H. Haskins, *The Normans in European History* (New York, 1915), D. C. Douglas, *The Norman Achievement* (London, 1969) and *The Norman Fate* (London, 1976), and R. H. C. Davis, *The Normans and Their Myth* (London, 1976). An important collection of conference papers was published by the Italian centre of early medieval studies at Spoleto: *I Normanni e la loro espansione in Europa nell'alto medioevo*, Settimane di studio del centro italiano di studi sull'alto medioevo, 16 (Spoleto, 1969). A splendid catalogue of a recent exhibition on the Normans organised in Rome, *I Normanni: popolo d'Europa 1030–1200*, ed. M. d'Onofrio (Venice, 1994), provides ample illustrative material for the history of the Normans in Europe.

Chapters I and II 'From vikings to Normans' and 'The Normans in Normandy'

The essential studies are D. Bates, *Normandy before 1066* (London, 1982) and C. Searle, *Predatory Kinship and the Creation of Norman Power, 840–1066* (Berkeley, 1988). These are now complemented by C. Potts, *Monastic Revival and Regional Identity in Early Normandy* (Woodbridge, 1997), who concentrates on the history of the Church. For the administrative and institutional history of Normandy, C. H. Haskins, *Norman Institutions* (New York, 1918) is a classic study but should be complemented by others, like J. Yver, 'Les premières Institutions du duché de Normandie', *I Normanni e la loro espansione in Europa nell'alto medioevo 18–24 aprile 1968*, Settimane di studio del centro italiano di studi sull'alto medioevo, 16 (Spoleto, 1969), 299–366, K. F. Werner, 'Quelques observations au sujet des débuts du "duché" de Normandie', in *Droit privé et institutions régionales: Études historiques offertes à Jean Yver*, ed. R. Aubreton (Paris, 1976), pp. 691–709 and the vast oeuvre of Lucien Musset. For a selection of his papers, see *Autour du pouvoir ducal normand, Xe–XIIe siècles*, ed. L. Musset *et al.*, Cahier des Annales de Normandie, 17 (Caen, 1985) and *Aspects de la société et de l'économie dans la Normandie médiévale (Xe–XIIIe siècles)*, Cahier des Annales de Normandie, 22 (Caen, 1988). For legal history, E. Z. Tabuteau, *Transfers of Property in*

Eleventh-Century Norman Law (Chapel Hill-London, 1988) is essential.

The Norman ducal charters can be found in *Recueil des actes des ducs de Normandie de 911 à 1066*, ed. M. Fauroux (Caen, 1961) and for the period 1066–87 in *Regesta regum Anglo-Normannorum: The Acta of William I (1066–1087)*, ed. D. Bates (Oxford, 1998). For the chroniclers, see the introductions of the following works: *Dudo of St Quentin, History of the Normans*, trsl. E. Christiansen (Woodbridge, 1998), viii–xxxvii, *The Gesta Normannorum Ducum of William of Jumièges, Orderic Vitalis and Robert of Torigni*, ed. and trsl. E. M. C. van Houts, 2 vols (Oxford, 1992–95), i, pp. xix–cxxxiii and *The Gesta Guillelmi of William of Poitiers*, ed. and trsl. R. H. C. Davis and M. Chibnall (Oxford, 1998), pp. xv–xlvii and *The Ecclesiastical History of Orderic Vitalis*, ed. and trsl. M. Chibnall, 6 vols (Oxford, 1969–80) as well as M. Chibnall, *The World of Orderic Vitalis* (Oxford, 1984). A modern study of Norman historiography can be found in L. Shopkow, *History and Community: Norman Historical Writing in the Eleventh and Twelfth Centuries* (Washington, 1997).

A beautifully illustrated catalogue of an important exhibition *Tresors des abbayes normandes* was published by the Musée des Antiquités at Rouen in 1979. The monumental survey of Norman architecture edited by Maylis Baylé (*L'Architecture normande au Moyen Age*, ed. M. Baylé, 2 vols (Caen, 1997)) gives a comprehensive survey of the latest research on monastic, military and domestic architecture in the province.

Chapter III 'The Normans and Britain: the Norman Conquest'

The literature on this topic is vast. A regularly up-dated bibliography is S. Keynes, *Anglo-Saxon History: A Select Bibliography*, Old English Newsletter subsidia, 13 (Michigan, 1998, 3rd rev. edn). An electronic version is on the Internet at the following address: http://www.wmich.edu/medieval/rawl/keynes1/index.html. An excellent recent guide to the debates on the Norman Conquest and its various effects is M. Chibnall, *The Debate on the Norman Conquest* (Manchester, 1999), whose chapters on feudalism and lordship, pp. 79–96, law and the family, pp. 97–114, empire and colonisation, pp. 115–24, peoples and frontiers, pp. 125–38 and the Church and economy, pp. 139–54, provide a comprehensive modern bibliography.

The Blackwell Encyclopaedia of Anglo-Saxon England, ed. M. Lapidge, J. Blair, S. Keynes and D. Scragg (Oxford, 1998), contains many entries which cover the Anglo-Norman period as well.

The classic but now outdated study of the Norman Conquest is by E. A Freeman, *History of the Norman Conquest*, 6 vols (Oxford, 1867–79; 2nd edn of vols 1–4, 1870–76; 3rd edn of vols 1–2, 1877). D. C. Douglas, *William th Conqueror* (London, 1964) is the standard biography of William the Conqueror for a different perspective see D. Bates, *William the Conqueror* (London, 1989) Useful narratives of the main events of the Conquest are R. A. Brown, *Th Normans and the Norman Conquest* (Woodbridge, 1985, 2nd rev. edn) and A Williams, *The English and the Norman Conquest* (Woodbridge, 1995). For th English historiographical sources, see the excellent general survey by A

Gransden, *Historical Writing in England c. 550 to c. 1307* (London, 1974) and for the Norman ones, see the above section on Normandy. The non-English and non-Norman views of the Conquest come under scrutiny in E. van Houts, 'The Norman Conquest through European eyes', *EHR*, 110 (1995), 832–53.

The post-conquest charters of William the Conqueror can now be consulted in the *Regesta regum Anglo-Normannorum: The Acta of William I (1066–1087)*, ed. D. Bates (Oxford, 1998) and the introduction provides a good guide to the continuity of English practices after 1066 and to a comparison between diplomatic styles in Normandy and England. The change of land ownership and the ensuing litigation is a fruitful area of research into the effects of the Conquest. This is made easier by having a modern English translation of all judicial cases in Domesday Book provided by R. Fleming, *Domesday Book and the Law* (Cambridge, 1998).

Prosopographical studies have illuminated the origins of the continental landowners in post-conquest England, see K. S. B. Keats-Rohan, *Domesday People: A Prosopography of Persons Occurring in English Documents, 1066–1166. I: Domesday Book* (Woodbridge, 1999).

For Anglo-Saxon culture, its survival and the influence of continental Romanesque art, see the two catalogues of exhibitions for *The Golden Age of Anglo-Saxon Art, 966–1066*, ed. J. Backhouse, D. H. Turner and L. Webster (British Museum, London, 1984) and *English Romanesque Art, 1066–1200*, ed. G. Zarnecki, J. Holt and T. Holland (Hayward Gallery, London, 1984).

Chapter IV 'The Normans and their neighbours'

A general introduction (up to 1066) is provided by D. Bates, *Normandy before 1066* (London, 1982), pp. 46–93, and for the period 1066 to 1204, his 'The rise and fall of Normandy, *c.* 911–1204', in *England and Normandy in the Middle Ages*, ed. D. Bates and A. Curry (London, 1994), pp. 19–36. A wider French context is given by J. Martindale, 'Succession and politics in the romance-speaking world, *c.* 1000–1140', in *England and her Neighbours 1066–1453: Essays in Honour of Pierre Chaplais*, ed. M. Jones and M. Vale (London, 1989), pp. 19–41. For the relationship between Normandy and France, see C. W. Hollister, 'Normandy, France and the Anglo-Norman "Regnum"', in his *Monarchy, Magnates and Institutions in the Anglo-Norman World* (London, 1986), pp. 17–58, but see the comments of D. Bates, 'Normandy and England after 1066', *EHR*, 104 (1989), 851–80. Also important for the debate is M. Chibnall, 'Anglo-French relations in the work of Orderic Vitalis', in *Documenting the Past: Essays in Medieval History Presented to George Peddy Cuttino*, ed. J. S. Hamilton and P. J. Bradley (Woodbridge, 1989), pp. 5–19. The problem of the Vexin as a border area is discussed by J. Green, 'Lords of the Norman Vexin', in *War and Government in the Middle Ages*, ed. J. Gillingham and J. C. Holt (Woodbridge, 1984), pp. 47–61. Otherwise the reader needs to consult the regional histories of the principalities surrounding Normandy for scattered references to the relationships between their inhabitants and the Normans. Martindale (see above) provides an excellent starting point.

Chapter V 'The Normans in the Mediterranean'

The classic study of the Norman expansion into the Mediterranean is F. Chalandon, *Histoire de la domination normande en Italie et en Sicile*, 2 vols (Paris, 1907). More recent is J. J. Norwich, *The Normans in the South, 1016–1130* (London, 1967). The main chroniclers of the Norman period in Italy are the subject of K. B. Wolf, *Making History: The Normans and their Historians in Eleventh-Century Italy* (Philadelphia, 1995). For the different historiographical traditions on the arrival of the Normans in Italy, see E. Joranson, 'The inception of the career of the Normans in Italy: legend and history', *Speculum*, 23 (1948), 353–96 and J. France, 'The occasion of the coming of the Normans to southern Italy', *Journal of Medieval History*, 17 (1991), 185–205.

For the Norman origin of the conquerors, see L. R. Ménager, *Hommes et institutions de l'Italie normande*, Variorum Collected Studies Series (London, 1981), no. IV, pp. 189–214 and G. A. Loud, 'How "Norman" was the Norman conquest of southern Italy?', *Nottingham Medieval Studies*, 25 (1981), 13–34.

For the conquest of southern Italy important studies are H. Hoffmann, 'Die Anfänge der Normannen in Süditalien', *Quellen und Forschungen aus italienischen Archiven und Bibliotheken*, 49 (1969), 95–144. Graham Loud's case study of Campania provides a stimulating study on 'Continuity and change in Norman Italy: the Campania during the eleventh and twelfth centuries', *Journal of Medieval History*, 22 (1996), 313–43. For the Church, see G. A. Loud, *Church and Society in the Norman Principality of Capua, 1058–1197* (Oxford, 1985). Studies on the effects of the Norman Conquest on government and administration are V. von Valkenhausen, 'I ceti dirigenti prenormanni al tempo della costituzione degli stati normanni nell'Italia meridionale e in Sicilia', in *Forme di potere e struttura sociale in Italia nel Medioevo*, ed. G. Rossetti (Bologna, 1977), pp. 321–77 and W. Jahn, *Untersuchungen zur normannischen Herrschaft in Süditalien (1040–1100)*, Europäischen Hochschulschriften, Reihe 3, Bd. 401 (Frankfurt am Main, 1989). The charters of the early Norman dukes can be consulted in *Recueil des actes des ducs normands d'Italie (1046–1127)*, vol. 1: *Les Premiers Ducs (1046–1087)*, ed. L. R. Ménager, Società di storia patria per la Puglia: Documenti e monografie, 45 (Bari, 1980).

A French collection of articles on southern Italy *Les Normands en Méditerranée*, ed. P. Bouet and F. Neveux, Colloque de Cerisy-la-Salle (24–27 septembre 1992), (Caen, 1994) is particularly good for several studies on Norman military architecture and fortification, for example, H. Bresc (pp. 63–76), A.-M. Héricher-Flambard (pp. 89–110) and G. Coppola (pp. 203–21).

For the conquest of Sicily, see D. Matthew, *The Norman Kingdom of Sicily* (Cambridge, 1992) and J. J. Norwich, *The Kingdom in the Sun* (London, 1970). For government and administration, see H. Takayama, *The Administration of the Norman Kingdom of Sicily* (Leiden, 1993).

The fundamental studies for the Normans in Byzantium are J. Shepard, 'The uses of the Franks in eleventh-century Byzantium', *ANS*, 15 (1992), 275–305 and E. M. C. van Houts, 'Normandy and Byzantium', *Byzantion*, 55 (1985), 544–59.

The early arrival of the Normans in Spain is discussed by M. Defourneaux, *Les Français en Espagne aux XIe et XIIe siècles* (Paris, 1949), pp. 132–9 and for the later settlement at Tarragona, see L. J. McCrank, 'Norman crusaders in the Catalan reconquest: Robert Burdet and the principality of Tarragona, 1129–55', *Journal of Medieval History*, 7 (1981), 67–82.

The Norman and Norman Italian origin of the crusaders is the subject of A. V. Murray's, 'How Norman was the principality of Antioch? Prolegomena to a study of the origins of the nobility of a crusader state', in *Family Trees and the Roots of Politics: The Prosopography of Britain and France from the Tenth to the Twelfth Century*, ed. K. S. B. Keats-Rohan (Woodbridge, 1997), pp. 349–60. An excellent, but dated, survey of Robert Curthose and his Norman followers on the First Crusade is C. W. David, *Robert Curthose, Duke of Normandy* (Cambridge, Mass., 1920), pp. 89–119 and 190–204.

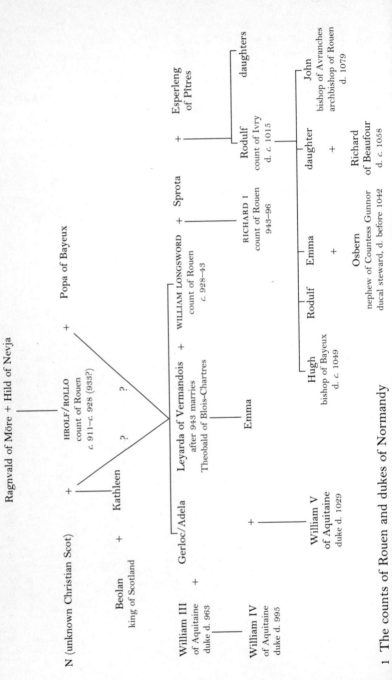

1 The counts of Rouen and dukes of Normandy

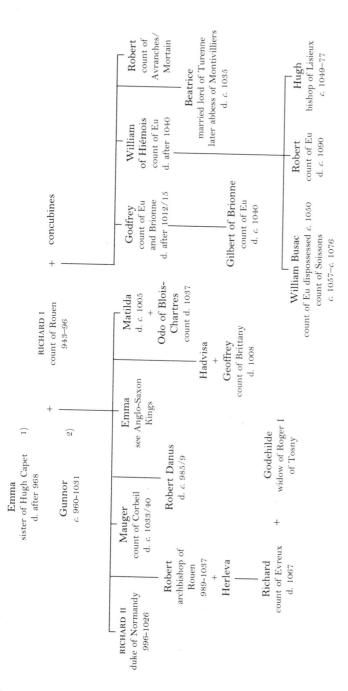

2 The counts of Rouen and dukes of Normandy

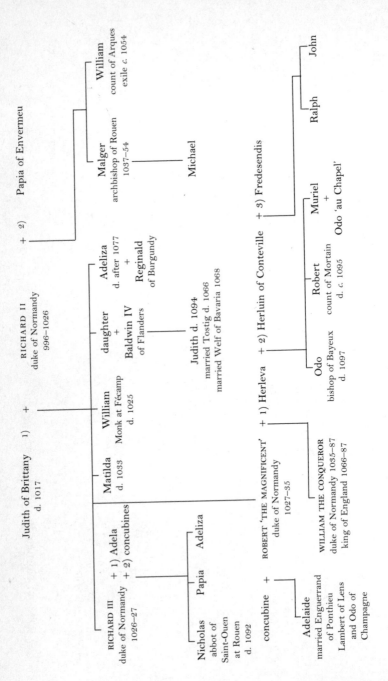

3 The dukes of Normandy

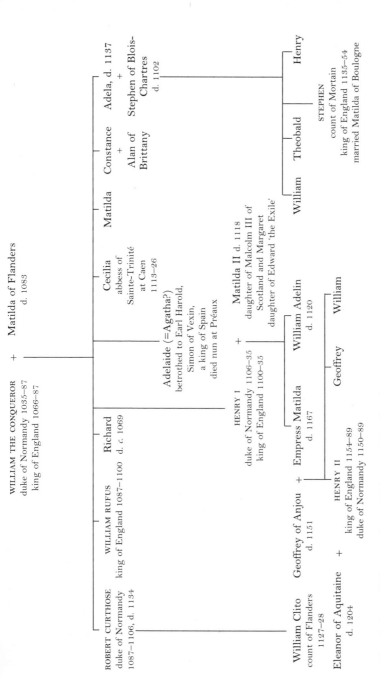

4 The dukes of Normandy and kings of England

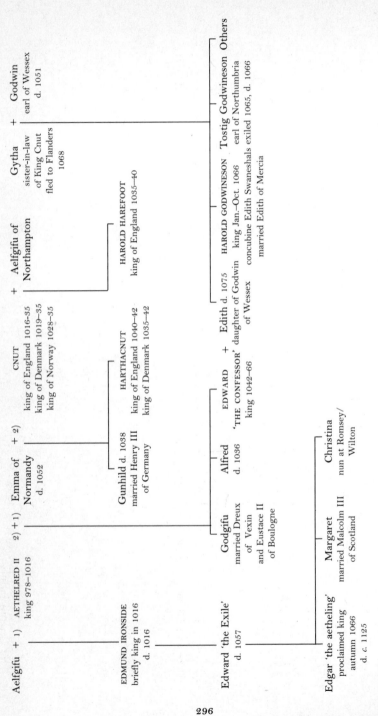

5 The Anglo-Saxon kings

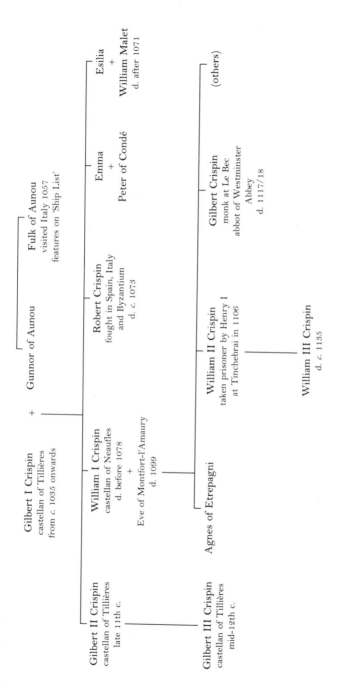

6 The Crispin family

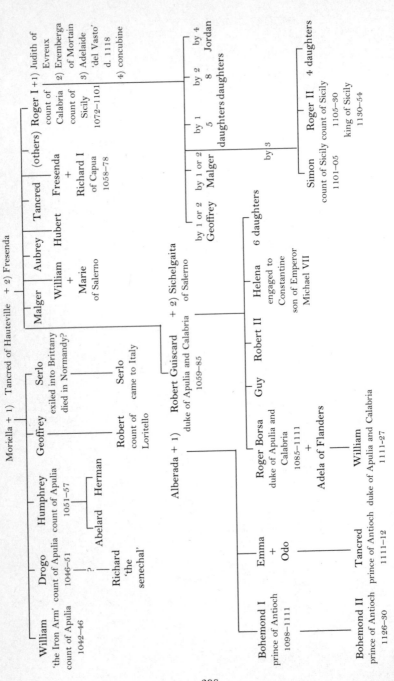

7 The Hauteville family

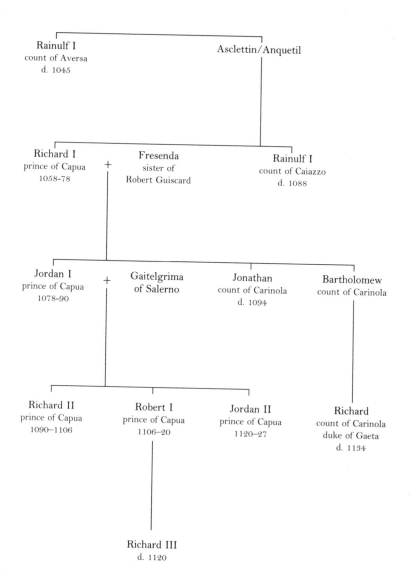

8 The Norman princes of Capua

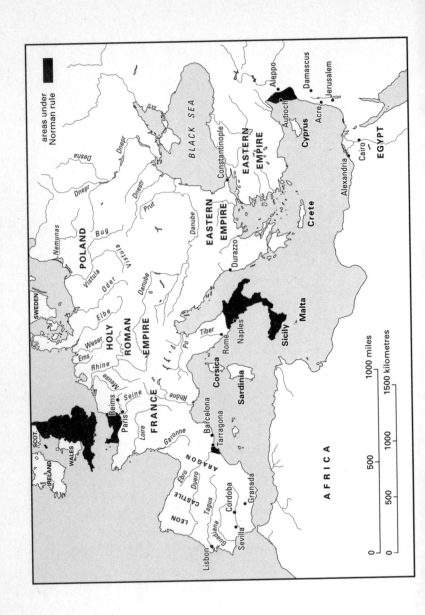

areas under
Norman rule

SWEDEN

POLAND

Nemunas

Desna

Dnepr

Dnepr

Dnestr

Prut

BLACK SEA

Constantinople

EASTERN EMPIRE

Aleppo

Damascus

Jerusalem

Antioch

Acre

Cyprus

EGYPT

Cairo

Alexandria

Crete

Malta

Durazzo

EASTERN EMPIRE

Vistula

Bug

Oder

Danube

Vistula

Elbe

Weser

Ems

Rhine

Meuse

Seine

Reims

Paris

HOLY ROMAN EMPIRE

Danube

Loire

Po

Tiber

Rome

Naples

Sicily

Corsica

Sardinia

FRANCE

Rhône

Garonne

Loire

SCOT.

IRELAND

WALES

ARAGON

Barcelona

Tarragona

Ebro

Duero

CASTILE

LEÓN

Tagus

Guadiana

Cordoba

Sevilla

Granada

Lisbon

AFRICA

0   500   1000 miles

0   500   1000   1500 kilometres

300

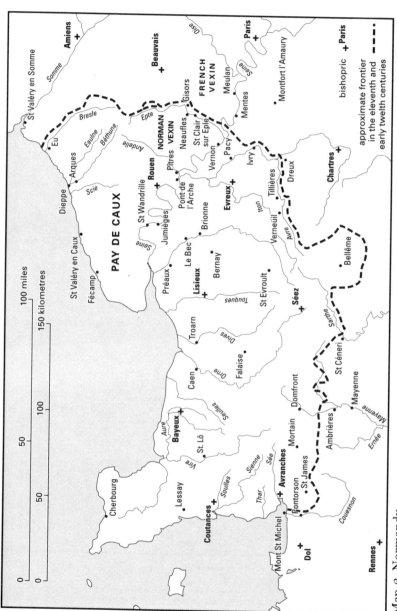

Map 2 Normandy

Map 3 Britain

Map 4 Southern Italy

INDEX